The contributors

D. N. Ashton

*Department of Sociology,
University of Leicester*

R. K. Brown

*Department of Sociology and Social
Administration, University of Durham*

P. Duncan

*Department of Engineering,
University of Cambridge*

Eric Dunning

*Department of Sociology,
University of Leicester*

S. W. F. Holloway

*Department of Sociology,
University of Leicester*

Geoffrey Hurd

*Department of Sociology,
University of Leicester*

Terence J. Johnson

*Department of Sociology,
University of Leicester*

Mary McIntosh

*Nuffield College,
Oxford*

Sami Zubaida

*Department of Politics and Sociology,
Birkbeck College, University of London*

Human Societies
An introduction to sociology

Geoffrey Hurd

Senior Lecturer in Sociology
Dean of the Faculty of the Social Sciences
University of Leicester

with

D. N. Ashton   R. K. Brown
P. Duncan   Eric Dunning
S. W. F. Holloway   Terence J. Johnson
Mary McIntosh   Sami Zubaida

Routledge & Kegan Paul
London and Boston

First published in 1973
by Routledge & Kegan Paul Ltd
Broadway House, 68–74 Carter Lane,
London, EC4V 5EL and
9 Park Street,
Boston, Mass. 02108, USA
Printed in Great Britain by
Cox & Wyman Ltd, London, Reading and Fakenham
© Routledge & Kegan Paul Ltd, 1973

ISBN 0 7100 7611 8 (C)
0 7100 7612 6 (P)

Library of Congress Catalog Card Number 73 – 77041

Contents

Preface

This book has been written for those who are coming to sociology for the first time. No prior knowledge of the subject is assumed but we hope that, in addition to providing an introductory textbook, we have managed to say something of significance about various aspects of the developing structures of human societies. Human societies are full of complexities and we have tried to confront some of these while retaining the clarity needed in a book of this kind. At the end of each chapter we have provided two brief lists of books. Some of these take up in more detail problems raised in the text; others deal with matter which, for the sake of brevity, had to be omitted; others provide a point of view different from that of the authors. Under the heading 'Reading' the majority of the books are clearly written, informative and often comprehensive. The books under the heading 'Further reading' are mostly either more difficult or more detailed studies.

As it is unusual for nine writers to be involved in the production of a unitary book, a word about how it was written may be of interest. For many years there has been an interest at the University of Leicester in the challenges and problems of teaching sociology to newcomers to the field. This interest has been pursued at various times by a number of the authors of this volume and one of them has undertaken research in this area. While collaboration seemed the best way to take advantage of this common interest and of the different specialist interests within the Department of Sociology here, we felt that a book such as this should have a unity of approach and style which would be lacking in a mere collection of essays. The authors therefore agreed to submit their contributions to the ultimate control of the editor, whose task was to ensure the unity of the whole volume and to carry out such revisions and re-writing as this made necessary. Perhaps it would not be out of place for me to express my gratitude for the forbearance of those whose contributions I thought it necessary to alter, and my even deeper gratitude to those whose contributions appear virtually unchanged. Authors of the chapters are as follows:

D. N. Ashton, 'Political aspects of social development'

R. K. Brown, 'Industrial relations'

P. Duncan, 'Socialization'

Eric Dunning, 'Race relations'

S. W. F. Holloway, 'Population'

Geoffrey Hurd, 'Sociology—a way of looking at societies, 'Economic aspects of social development', 'Education', 'Social stratification', 'Religion'

Terence J. Johnson, 'The professions'

Mary McIntosh, 'Urbanization', 'Crime'

Sami Zubaida, 'The family'.

All the authors are, or have been, members of the Department of Sociology at the University of Leicester, and this book tries to reflect something of the comparative and developmental approach to sociology which has developed there under the leadership of Professor Ilya Neustadt. Only those who know the Leicester Department will fully appreciate the huge debt we have all incurred to Professor Neustadt. As long as he remains Head of the Department, to teach sociology at Leicester will continue to be an education of the best and most exciting kind. That so many of the contributors to this book agree about so much is largely due to his influence. The pattern of the book has also been considerably influenced by Professor Norbert Elias, whose introductory course in Sociology inspired his fellow teachers as well as his students.

In the preparation of this book I have incurred many debts, some of which I have forgotten but which are none the less significant for that. Others will forgive me if I single out Audrey Craig and Doreen Butler who typed the various drafts and helped in a number of other ways.

Geoffrey Hurd
University of Leicester

1 Sociology—a way of looking at societies

This is not a book *about* sociology; it is a book about human societies. It is, however, written by sociologists and presents a sociological way of looking at societies. We believe that sociology offers a perspective from which we can gain some understanding of the world in which we live, and of the variety of situations and problems in which men find themselves. There is, however, a great deal of misunderstanding about what sociology is so we have prefaced this book about human societies with a chapter about sociology—what it is, how sociologists go about their work, what kind of assumptions they make, and so on.

The most common short answer to the question 'what is sociology?' is that it is the study of human society. This fails to take us very far: history, too, is the study of human society; so, in their different ways, are many other academic disciplines—especially those we call the social sciences. It is more helpful to say that sociology is a particular way of studying human society; or, better still, a particular way of studying human *societies*. There is little that is distinctive in *what* sociologists study. The most important distinguishing feature of sociology lies rather in the viewpoint from which societies are studied. The distinguishing mark of the sociologist is the *way* he thinks about societies.

Sociology is generally regarded as being a branch of the social sciences and, as its name implies, this group of subjects attempts to bring a scientific attitude to bear upon various aspects of social life. This is not the way most people (even if they are physical or biological scientists) view society. The political revolutionary wants to overthrow society; the reformer wants to change it; the evangelist wants to save it. Everybody looks at society from their own viewpoint. The viewpoint of the sociologist is basically one of curiosity: he wants to find out what a particular society (or some part of it) is like.

A number of points are relevant to this sociological view of societies. The first is that science is morally neutral. It is not the task of a sociologist to say whether a pattern of behaviour or an organization is right or wrong, good or bad. It is his task to find out what the behaviour or organization consists of, to explain how it came about and to demonstrate its consequences. This non-evaluative approach to society is perhaps the characteristic which sets sociology apart from popular views of society more than any other. Second, in industrial societies it is usual to think of society in terms of *individual* people. The sociologist, by contrast, places the emphasis on social relationships and these are by no means exhausted by relationships between individual people. Indeed, sociology is more concerned with the relationships between the major parts of a society, and these can be viewed independently of any one individual in them. Sociology, then, focuses on the interaction between the parts of societies. Third, it is an assumption of sociology (an assumption based on countless observations) that relationships between people, groups of people and social institutions do not occur randomly; that there are regularities in the social life of mankind. The search for these regularities, and their description and explanation is one of the major tasks of the sociologist. Fourth, the way in which sociologists go about their tasks is, in one respect, very similar to the activities of physical scientists. In both fields there is a combination of observation and the formulation of theory. In another way, however, the methods are very different from most (but not all) physical and biological sciences. Because of the nature of his subject matter the sociologist cannot test his theories by experiment. In a laboratory it is possible to control the variables in a situation. Thus water can be turned into ice by lowering the temperature and/or by increasing the pressure, or into steam by raising the temperature and/or reducing the pressure. The variables of temperature and pressure can be altered experimentally and manipulated in such a way as to demonstrate how the substance performs at different temperatures and pressures. Because of the high level of control, theories can be tested experimentally. Such experimentation is not possible in the social sciences; the various aspects of a social situation cannot be isolated experimentally in this way. One cannot experiment to see what England would be like with a Communist government or if Hinduism were the dominant religion. The sociologist has to find other ways of 'controlling' the phenomenon he is investigating and, in particular, he attempts to approximate to a controlled situation through the use of comparison between different societies or between different parts of the same society.

These are the most important ways in which sociologists differ from most other people in their view of society. They form the core of the sociological perspective. Let us now look at them in a little more detail, for to understand them is to go a long way towards understanding what sociologists are trying to do.

The non-evaluative character of sociology

Many of the aspects of a society that are studied by sociologists concern things that ordinary people often have very strong views about—birth control and bureaucracy; revolution and religion; politics and professions; strikes and schooling. Most people have opinions on how human affairs in these matters could (and in their opinion should) be re-arranged so as to make life in some way better and more worth while. Sociology, however. is the study of social situations *as they are*, not as they 'ought' to be. It is not the task of the sociologist to comment on the value or otherwise of what he studies. He is not interested in whether a custom is good or bad, whether a belief is right or wrong. He is concerned with trying to understand it. For example, when we study the class structure of Britain we are not called upon *as*

sociologists to say whether we think the system is immoral and should be changed or whether we think it is good and valuable and should be preserved. Rather, we have to discover the character of the relationships between the groups we call classes and how they are changing, to explain how the present system came about, and to find out what its consequences are in other areas of social life. Or again, when we study religion we are not concerned whether the beliefs of any particular religion are true or false, beneficial or otherwise. It is an important social fact that people subscribe to a particular set of beliefs and belong to a certain type of religious organization, a fact which affects both the behaviour of the people concerned and the nature of the whole society.

One of the clearest expressions of this duty of the sociologist to maintain a 'value free' approach to society was that by the great German sociologist Max Weber. Referring, in this instance, to politics, Weber wrote:[1]

> To take a practical political stand is one thing, and to analyze political structures and party positions is another. When speaking in a political meeting about democracy, one does not hide one's personal standpoint; indeed to come out clearly and take one's stand is one's damned duty. The words one uses in such a meeting are not means of scientific analysis but means of canvassing votes and winning over others. They are not ploughshares to loosen the soil of contemplative thought; they are swords against the enemies: such words are weapons. It would be an outrage, however, to use words in this fashion in a lecture or in the lecture room. If, for instance, 'democracy' is under discussion, one considers its various forms, analyzes them in the way they function, determines what results for the conditions of life the one form has as compared with the other . . . But the true teacher will beware of imposing from the platform any political position upon the student, whether it is expressed or suggested.

It is these matters of fact and interpretation we are interested in as sociologists, but sociologists are also people! As individuals and as citizens, sociologists do hold opinions about the beliefs they study and the class structure or political party they observe (and these opinions are, often enough, influenced by their work as sociologists). This is one of the central dilemmas of a sociologist. He has to try to make an impartial analysis of problems about which people (including himself) feel very strongly. He has, to this extent, to try to separate his own opinions about a problem from his investigation of it. Unless he can detach himself from his prior values and beliefs in this way, his values will cause him to misinterpret or distort the very things he is trying to clarify. It is hardly surprising that sociologists are not always entirely successful in this. It is, however, the ideal for which they must strive.

All this, however, is itself something of an evaluation. It assumes that science—in this case sociology—is something worthwhile, something of value; that understanding how societies work is an activity worth spending time, money and energy on. At the level of particular research investigations, every research project involves a similar evaluation of the topic to be investigated. It may be that the researcher's high evaluation of science leads him to choose the type of research that is likely to result in the greatest advance of the discipline of sociology itself. On the other hand—and this is where his other personal values are likely to intrude—he may choose his area of research on the grounds of political or other social values he holds. Thus he may choose to study problems of economic development because of a humanitarian concern for the plight of peoples of the underdeveloped world; or he may study the relationship between social class and educational opportunity because of a feeling that the distribution of educational opportunity is unjust; or he may study race relations because of his disquiet at the exploitation of one group, or his desire to maintain the dominance of another. This is all very well if the non-scientific values of the investigator are not allowed to influence the way in which the research is carried out. To the extent that this is allowed to happen the result will be bad sociology, that is, descriptions and explanations which mislead or distort. (One important check on such distortion is the fact that others are likely to be working in the same field. So colleagues, who may not share the investigator's personal values, can check up on his work.)

There is one other question with regard to values that needs to be raised. One of the more common misconceptions about sociology is that it is concerned with promoting reform. On the contrary, sociology is not concerned with promoting anything except our understanding of human societies. It is not concerned with the making of policy or the advocacy of changes or reforms, with the maintenance of democracy, or with the development of any particular sort of society. But this is not to say that sociology has no practical applications. In the first place, it is possible to use sociological knowledge in the promotion of social reform or, indeed, in the promotion of almost anything. There are many fields of practical decision-making which might draw on sociology for the more efficient implementation of policies, and an increasing number of organizations employ sociologists with this in mind. Sociological insights with regard to the causes of crime may be utilized in the treatment of prisoners; clarification of the social consequences of certain types of urban situations may be used by town planners to avoid what they consider to be undesirable situations; knowledge of the nature of the socialization of children may be used in the execution of educational policy. Individual firms and organizations may also be able to use sociologists or their findings in carrying out the policy of the organization.

At the same time, the growth of sociological knowledge may *influence* the policy decisions that are taken by governments and firms—that is to say, it may influence the *objectives* of the policy makers. Thus the objectives of prisons, town plans, education and the like may be defined differently because of the discoveries of sociological research. In other words, the work of the sociologist (or the nuclear physicist, or the astronomer) may have implications for the values that are held by the public at large or at least by significant sections of the public. Changes in scientific knowledge have, in the past, frequently challenged the dominant values of a society in this way. This requires, however, the assimilation of such knowledge by the leaders of public opinion and (in Britain anyway) sociology has, until recently, been unfashionable. Nevertheless, values underlying the creation of new policy have not been unaffected by the findings of sociologists since the second world war.

So sociological knowledge can be of use to policy makers in a variety of fields and may even influence the formulation of policy. The actual determination of policy, however, lies outside the sphere of sociology. The *aims* of applied sociology cannot be determined within the field of sociology, although professional sociologists, since they are also citizens, may be found in the ranks of policy makers.

A study of inter-relationships

'No man is an iland, intire of it selfe; every man is a peece of the continent, a part of the maine....' The well-known words of John Donne serve to illustrate one of the tasks of sociology—namely to show the way in which man is essentially a social animal. Along with the sister discipline of social psychology, sociology has shown how a variety of social factors are involved in the development of an individual person. We have come to see that the life of an individual cannot be understood in isolation from the socio-historical situation in which he finds himself. These disciplines further show something of the way in which individuals interact within a group situation. Thus one of the aspects of a sociological study of the family is the study of the *relationships* between members of the family—the way in which they behave towards each other, who 'wears the trousers', what degree of independence the children have, and so on. Moreover, it is not only at the level of the analysis of small groups like the family that the sociologist places the emphasis on social relationships. What is specifically 'sociological' in the study of a particular feature of a society is the attempt to relate that feature to the rest of the society. The family, for example, is no more 'an island' than are its individual members. The sort of relationships which exist between family members in a given society is closely related to the class structure, the nature of education, the prevailing economic activity and other features of the wider society. Sometimes this interaction helps to maintain the *status quo*. In traditional India, for example, the Hindu doctrine of re-incarnation reinforced the caste system by discouraging social mobility, since only by accepting one's position in this life could one hope for any improvement in the next. Sometimes, however, the interaction between the institutions of a society (or, indeed, interaction between societies) brings about changes. Thus the English educational system owes its present form, and in some ways even its existence, partly to nineteenth-century industrial development, partly to the class system which prevailed throughout its growth, partly to the influence of the churches, partly to changes in the political system. It cannot be understood in purely educational terms, in isolation from the rest of the society. At the same time, the educational developments in England have affected religion, the class structure, the distribution of political power and subsequent industrial developments. And so one could continue for any feature of any society. *Social* changes consist of changes in the relationships between the parts of a society—changes in the *structure* of the society—and the parts influence each other reciprocally. It is far more important to understand this than to ask the often unanswerable question of which changed first.

Many changes occur unintentionally. Others occur as a direct result of human planning, but even such intentional changes invariably have unintended consequences. When, for example, British colonial officials in West Africa at the beginning of the twentieth century used the traditional chiefs to pass on and enforce their demands, the *intention* was to make the administration of the colonies efficient and cheap. Very frequently, however, the unintended consequence was that the performance of this task changed the nature of the relationship between chief and people so that the chiefs were identified with the colonial power and lost much of their influence over their people. Practically every human activity or social organization has unintended consequences of this kind in addition to those which are planned, and it may even be that the intended consequences do not occur. Because of the inter-relatedness of the various institutions of a society, planned changes in one sphere may also have unintended effects on others and on the relationship between the institutions. Thus the implementation of a re-housing policy may alter fundamentally the relationships between family members, or changes in the pattern of recruitment of industrial managers may alter the emphasis on school or college examinations. The fact that such changes are unintended and often unrecognized (and may even be unwanted) does not make them any less significant.

In short, it is the sociologist's way to look for the inter-relationships between social institutions and social processes. Such inter-relationships are perhaps the major element of a society that is brought into focus by the sociological approach.

The search for regularities

This inter-relationship between institutions and processes is systematic: or to put it in other terms, there are regularities in the occurrence of clusters of factors. Textbooks in the physical sciences often speak of physical or chemical laws, by which they mean to imply an invariable relationship between events in a given situation. In the nineteenth century the early sociologists tended to write of social laws in much the same way, but today the term 'regularities' seems preferable since it does not have quite the same ring of inevitability.

Of course, there are many people who would deny that there are *any* regularities in social life, just as there were those in the sixteenth and seventeenth centuries who refused to believe that the earth was not the centre of the universe, and those in the nineteenth century who would not accept the doctrine of evolution. Those of us who have been brought up to believe that the earth revolves around the sun have no difficulty in accepting it, but the idea that there are regularities in social life is one that many are still unfamiliar with. The problem is especially acute where people are brought up to value individualism very highly (as they are in most 'Western' countries). Any suggestion of regularities seems (at first sight anyway) to limit the freedom of the individual and is consequently rejected out of hand. Yet such regularities are demonstrated again and again in the chapters that follow. The number of births and deaths per thousand inhabitants remains constant for a given country *year after year*: some industries *consistently* have more strikes than others; some social groups *regularly* commit more crime than others. Regularities can also be shown in non-statistical terms. Relationships between husband and wife or between doctors and their patients, for example, vary *systematically* in relation to economic factors.

In the past such regularities have rarely been recognized. In Western industrial societies the ethic of individualism has led to a concentration on the position and activities of the individual and to individualistic explanations. People have not seen the regularities in patterns of social behaviour but only the individual differences. In other words, in this respect as well as in the other points we have considered, a sociological way of thinking is not the normal way of thinking in our society. On the contrary most people think individualistically. The tendency is to emphasize the individual's responsibility for his actions, and this is so even in the case of children (in Britain, for example, the age of criminal responsibility is ten). So most people explain crime in terms of individual wickedness or lack of self control; strikes in terms of the personality characteristics of trade union leaders; religious revivals in terms of the personal magnetism of the evangelist. But such explanations, although they may have some relevance to an individual case, cannot explain the amount of crime in a society; why some industries have more strikes than others; what makes a revivalist successful at one time and place but not another. We have suggested that to seek out and explain social regularities is one of the main tasks of sociology; and it is one of the main claims of sociology that these social phenomena cannot be *explained* in individualistic terms.

How the sociologist finds out

(a) Fact and theory

Human societies are extremely complex. There is an almost infinite number of phenomena present to be noticed and no one person, no one investigation, can possibly describe any social situation exhaustively. The result is that all observers, whether social scientists, journalists, politicians or lay participants, select some things from the total situation as being worthy of note and, explicitly or implicitly, reject others. We notice what we want to notice, or what we have been trained to notice, or what we consider to be important for the problem we are interested in. We therefore develop a frame of reference which points our attention to certain aspects of the total situation. The sociological perspective itself draws attention to certain things that are usually neglected. Many of the regularities referred to in the last section are not noticed by a non-sociologist simply because he does not have an orientation which enables him to notice them. So our general observations of society are guided not only by what is there, but also by the sort of questions we ask ourselves. What seems clear and obvious to a person with one set of questions in mind is obscure to those whose focus is on a different set of problems. Part of the training of a sociologist is to learn to ask questions about the regularities of social phenomena and their inter-relatedness. Within this general sociological orientation, however, we select some areas of society to investigate; and in any given area the questions we ask determine to a considerable extent what we observe.

What one selects depends upon what one is trying to do. A politician in a parliamentary debate is likely to select evidence that supports his case. This may be through a conscious rejection of contrary evidence but is more likely to be because he has only been looking for evidence to support his case. This tendency is much more crudely in evidence in everyday arguments, where most of us, at one time or another, 'weight' the evidence we produce in order to make our case more strongly. To the sociologist, however, the point is not to put forward a particular line of argument, not to advocate a particular policy, but to explain the nature and development of social structures. The questions he asks must be subservient to what he observes in the following way. The explanations put forward in the social sciences—especially in the early stages of an investigation—are tentative, hypothetical. A hypothesis may or may not be 'correct', but it focuses attention on those aspects of the situation that are particularly related to that explanation. In other words, a hypothesis sharpens observations of certain aspects of the problem. Where there is a lack of agreement between the hypothesis and the observations, the hypothesis is refined or altered to accommodate the new observations. The new hypothesis may enable yet more elements in the situation to be noticed; elements which may in turn require a further modification of the hypothesis. So the process continues until a hypothesis is formulated which, for the time being at any rate, is adequate to explain the observations. It may be that a particular hypothesis is held to be an adequate explanation of a set of phenomena for many years before it is found wanting and a more adequate explanation is offered. What needs emphasizing is that there are no *final* answers; there is always the possibility of further discoveries that may upset the present position.

Thus one of the essential differences between the procedure of social scientists and that of laymen is that, while the layman is generally trying to 'prove' his point of view, the task of the sociologist is to try to *falsify* his hypothesis. Only when he has tried his hardest to do this and failed can he suggest that his hypothesis is an adequate one in the present state of knowledge. Of course, sociologists, like other people, are rarely saints and sometimes fall short of this ideal. A favourite hypothesis may be clung to grimly in the face of mounting contrary evidence. In the long run, however, science is a product of all its practitioners so even where the individual fails to test his hypothesis adequately someone else will do so.

(b) The uses of comparison

Comparison is the essence of sociology. The comparison may be historical—a comparison between the same society at different points in time; it may be inter-societal—a comparison between societies; or it may be intra-societal—a comparison between parts of the same society. To a sociologist comparison is important even if he is primarily interested in one specific society. It may be possible to describe social relationships in a given situation by concentrating on that situation alone. If, however, one wants to explain *why* they take one form rather than another, one needs to know under what conditions such relationships prevail elsewhere, and under what conditions the relationships are different.

Thus a man may be interested in, say, what happened in the French Revolution, and he may explain the occurrence of the Revolution in terms of the particular pattern of events in France. This is quite legitimate, but it is unlikely to be sociology. The sociologist may also be interested in the French Revolution, but he is likely to be equally interested in the phenomenon of revolutions. So he may make a comparative study of the French, Russian, Cuban and other revolutions in order to find out what they have in common and how they differ. His interest in any one revolution is primarily the contribution it can make to his understanding of revolutions in general; but at the same time he is interested in the nature of revolutions partly because this general study provides him with intellectual tools with which he can analyse and further understand specific revolutionary movements. In other words, the sociologist is interested both in specific events and in general phenomena; he is interested in the specific for what it tells him about the general, and he is interested in the general for what it tells him about the specific.

In the illustration of the study of revolutions we are comparing phenomena in which we perceive considerable likeness (although what are conventionally labelled revolutions may turn out to be very different social phenomena—for example, the American and the Russian 'revolutions'). It may also be useful to compare unlike phenomena. Thus an understanding of industrial societies is often heightened by comparing them with non-industrial societies; understanding the middle classes is more easily achieved by comparing them with the working classes; an understanding of town life is increased by comparison with rural life. Nor is it possible to assess the consequences for a society of a particular institution unless we make comparison with societies where that institution is different or absent. For example, the effects of colonialism can best be seen by comparing colonies or ex-colonies with societies that are broadly similar except for the absence of a formal colonial relationship. Such a comparison—say, between Sierra Leone and Liberia or Malaysia and Thailand—will enable us better to understand the institution of colonialism and so better to understand countries which have been colonies.

Above all, the proper use of comparison saves us from sweeping statements about 'human nature', by bringing to our notice the infinite variety of arrangements by which human beings conduct their affairs. The Chinese peasant; the international diplomat; the Australian stockman; the Pygmy hunter; the Latin American revolutionary; the French dock labourer; all these and thousands more must be taken into account before we can adequately comment on 'human nature'. Most comments on 'human nature' refer to patterns of behaviour that have been learned in a specific social context and represent only the viewpoint of one small group. One of the salutary experiences of studying sociology is the realization that the customs, habits and patterns of relationships which exist in our own society and which we regard as 'normal' are by no means common to all societies. It is the task of sociology to encompass the variety of the societies of mankind, thereby gaining knowledge which can be used in the analysis of specific societies.

Note

1 Max Weber, 'Science as a Vocation', in H. H. Gerth and C. W. Mills, *From Max Weber: Essays* *in Sociology*, London: Routledge & Kegan Paul and New York: Galaxy, 1958, p. 145.

Reading

Aron, R., *Eighteen Lectures on Industrial Society*, London: Weidenfeld & Nicolson, 1967, chapter 1. An introductory lecture by a French sociologist.

Berger, P., *Invitation to Sociology*, Harmondsworth: Penguin, 1966. A stylish and often witty commentary upon sociology; what it is and what it is not. Written for those with no previous knowledge of the subject.

Chinoy, E., *The Sociological Perspective*, New York: Random House, 1968. A short and clearly written survey of the field of sociology by an American sociologist.

Neustadt, I., *Teaching Sociology*, Leicester University Press, 1964. A sociologist's view of his subject and how to approach it. Originally delivered as an inaugural lecture.

Further reading

Durkheim, E., *The Rules of Sociological Methods*, Chicago: Free Press, 1950. The characteristics of the sociological approach, viewed by one of the most influential sociologists of all time.

Elias, N., 'Some problems of involvement and detachment', *British Journal of Sociology*, 7, 1956. A discussion of the problems of the sociologist's involvement with his subject matter.

Merton, R. K., *Social Theory and Social Structure*, Chicago: Free Press, 1949, chapters 2 and 3. A plea for a close relationship between the theoretical and empirical aspects of sociological analysis.

Mills, C. Wright, *The Sociological Imagination*, Harmondsworth: Penguin, 1970. An American sociologist's attack upon 'grand theory' and 'abstracted empiricism'; two trends in American sociology which he sees as a threat to the (more fruitful) classical sociology.

Tiryakian, E. A. (ed.), *The Phenomenon of Sociology*, New York: Appleton-Century-Crofts, 1971. A collection of articles and excerpts about sociology—its nature and its growth.

Pre-industrial economic development

One of the most striking things about human societies is their immense variety. There are large societies and small societies; urban societies and rural societies; rich societies and poor societies; industrial societies and agricultural societies. But perhaps an even more significant variation is in the degree of homogeneity within a society. Many societies contain both rich *and* poor; towns *and* villages; industry *and* agriculture; while a few contemporary and many past societies lack such differentiation.

In the simplest societies we know about, life revolves around hunting or some other form of food-getting such as gathering wild fruits. Typically, the men engage in hunting and women in the collection of wild fruits and berries. There are few, if any, comforts or luxuries. Houses are of rudimentary construction and require little labour to build and maintain them; there are virtually no clothes to be made; there are few tools to make or repair. So food-getting is virtually the only economic activity. Only a sparse population can be sustained by 'living on the land' in this way and the roving bands that comprise hunting societies are necessarily small, rarely exceeding thirty or forty members. These bands are made up entirely of kinsmen and their wives and children. Everybody takes part in all the activities of daily life and these are conducted within the context of the whole community. There are no specialist economic tasks and the band is not subdivided in any way. This is what we mean when we refer to such societies as simple societies.

Nowadays, the only surviving band societies are to be found in inhospitable desert or forest areas or on isolated islands (and even these are now changing as a result of their increasing contact with other societies). The pygmy peoples of the Congo and Malaya; the Bushmen of the Kalahari desert; the Aborigines of central Australia; and the inhabitants of the Andaman Islands in the Indian Ocean are the best-known contemporary (or nearly contemporary) examples.

The following description of the Bushmen gives some idea of life in such a society:[1]

The Bushmen are one of the most primitive peoples living on earth. They dig roots and pick berries because they have no crops. The desert is too dry for anything but desert plants to grow naturally, and the Bushmen, who quickly consume all the wild food available in one place, cannot stay anywhere long enough to tend crops or wait for them to grow. There is not enough water to water livestock, and for this reason Bushmen have no domestic animals. Instead of herding, Bushmen hunt wild antelope with tiny arrows poisoned with a terrible poison extracted from a certain grub. Most of the meat is dried to preserve it, causing it to last at least a few weeks, but sooner or later every last bit of it is eaten, even the mucous lining of the nostrils and the gristle inside the ears. They sometimes eat the hide, sometimes work it into leather to use for clothing, and if the antelope bones are not all cracked for the marrow, pieces are worked into arrow points to shoot another antelope.

In order to live as they do, Bushmen must travel through the veld, changing their abode every few days in search of food. Because of their way of life, they do not need villages to live in, so they rarely bother to build strong scherms, making small domes of grass for themselves instead, just a little shade for their heads. Sometimes they do not even bother with this, but push little sticks into the ground to mark their places. . . .

The immediate family, a man, his wife, or wives, and children, is the only solid social unit; otherwise the small bands are always breaking up and recombining with other small bands as the structures of single families change, through marriages, divorces, deaths, or as the family decides to pay a prolonged visit to a different group of relatives. Any Bushman will be related by blood or marriage or will be acquainted with all the other Bushmen in his area but this is as far as Bushmen go in their affinities. They do not recognize as their own people strange Bushmen who speak the same language; in fact they suspect and fear them as they do any stranger.

The first human societies to develop were probably very similar to the simplest societies of today. Moreover, the greater part of man's time on earth has been dominated by such societies. With the gradual development of cultivation and the domestication of animals, however, new forms of social organization become possible. These developments represent an important step in man's control over nature. He is no longer passively dependent upon nature's bounty but takes active steps to alter and direct it. The greater productivity per acre allows a greater density of population, and greater productivity per capita releases some people from full-time food production to engage, for part of the time at least, in other tasks. Handicrafts develop, at first as part-time occupations and later, under suitable conditions, as full-time occupations. Religious specialists emerge in the same way. The members of such societies no longer carry out identical tasks.

Such specialization raises trade to the level of an economic necessity. It may take the form of barter—a direct exchange of commodities between the producers, or it may involve the use of money of one sort or another. Usually it involves specialization within the village community, as in medieval Europe where a single village would be likely to contain a blacksmith, herdsmen, and perhaps a miller, a priest, and some weavers, as well as those whose primary task was growing crops. Similarly, in India the majority of villages contain many people who neither own nor work on the land. They engage in a variety of occupations: sweepers; leather-workers; potters; carpenters; washermen; water carriers; merchants; and many more. These specialists are frequently attached to specific households of cultivators for whom they perform their service in exchange for a stipulated amount of grain each year. In addition they engage in reciprocal exchange of services with other specialists—again at stipulated rates of exchange. Such a system is common in all peasant societies. The distinctive feature of the Indian system is that each person is, from birth, tied to his specialized occupation by membership of a particular caste. He is not free to engage in another occupation even if the village has greater need of the alternative service.

More rarely specialization occurs between villages. In these cases each village normally engages in cultivation as well as in one particular craft. A few communities may specialize almost entirely on their craft product. Periodically, the people from the various villages meet at a market-place to exchange their goods and produce. Many areas of rural central America and in the Andes; most of West Africa; and parts of Indonesia (Java for example) are characterized by this kind of specialization and trade. Among the Tiv—a tribe of central Nigeria—markets are held every five days in special market-places and are attended by anything from fifty to over ten thousand people. Essentially, however, market trading is supplementary to the subsistence agriculture of the area —only special foods, luxury items such as clothes, and a few other craft goods are exchanged solely through the market. In addition to supplementing the food a man grows and the goods he makes for family consumption, these regular markets provide places where the leaders of the community discuss their problems and decide the appropriate course of action; where disputes of a legal nature are judged and settled; and where dancing, beer-drinking and other forms of recreation take place. The Tiv market illustrates well the lack of distinction between economic, political and recreational activities and institutions in simpler societies.

The further specialization develops, however, and the more economic productivity increases, the greater is the likelihood that the non-agriculturalists—the craftsmen, the religious specialists, the politicians—may gather together in residential groups, and in this way towns are formed. The process of urbanization is thus closely related to such economic developments.

This *differentiation* of occupations creates a situation in which inequality becomes a possibility. Whereas the simplest societies are egalitarian, as soon as differentiation occurs, wealth, power and prestige are distributed unequally. Some people manage to gain control of crucial resources and so are able to retain for themselves and their families a larger share of goods and services than is available to the rest of the population. In the earliest states of which we have records—the city states of Mesopotamia and Egypt—those who mediated the favours of the gods also controlled the distribution of wealth and commanded general obedience. But in those early state societies, the agricultural surplus was only sufficient to support a tiny minority in non-agricultural activities. This was also the case for the much larger and more complex empires of the ancient world—even for the two largest, Rome in the west and China in the east. With their greater agricultural efficiency, however, and, in the case of Rome, with the military strength to exact tribute in grain from its provinces, these societies were able to support large cities within which very considerable occupational specialization was possible. The relatively high level of complexity of the Roman Empire is reflected in the considerable differentiation of occupations. Rome itself—in the second century A.D. a city of more than one million inhabitants—achieved the highest level of development. Even the task of feeding the inhabitants of the capital depended upon a highly complex system of distribution. Grain—the staple food—came mainly as tribute from Egypt and north Africa and was trans-shipped at Ostia (the port of ancient Rome) into barges for transportation up the river Tiber. The size of the task was immense, as is indicated by the fact that the barge-*owners'* guild at Ostia had a membership of 258. The inscriptions at Ostia indicate, in addition, the presence of thousands of labourers working as measurers, stevedores, bargemen, warehousemen, and record-keepers. Retail distribution was equally complicated. 'Salesmen carried their wares from house to house, peddlers of sulphur matches, retailers of sausages, warm puddings, or pies thronged the streets of Rome, and bakers' boys sold their wares on street corners.'[2] We have no accurate records of how many people were employed in these and similar activities but it must have been a considerable

number. Similarly, a large labour force would have been required to maintain buildings and waterworks in effective operation. At one time there were more than seven hundred slaves employed in the Imperial Water Bureau making and laying lead pipes for the distribution of water to baths, palaces, gardens and public fountains. In addition to the slaves there were water gangs divided into several categories of free workmen: overseers, reservoir-keepers, inspectors, pavers, plasterers and other workmen. Rome was also a centre of arts and crafts and numbered among its inhabitants woodcarvers, glassblowers, weavers, carpenters, shoemakers, brickmakers, goldsmiths and many more craftsmen. Within many crafts there was further specialization. In the process of making copper, for example, the metal was melted, mixed with tin or zinc, cast in special moulds that could only be produced by skilled craftsmen, and then finally sent to trained artisans to be polished, carved and forged. Each of these stages was carried out by different groups of workers, each specializing in their task. The whole process implied a far-reaching division of labour within the craft. In addition there were the activities of teachers, doctors, architects and accountants (most of which were carried out by slaves); of commerce and administration; and the upper stratum pastimes of politics and law.

Such a diversified (and in terms of food, unproductive) metropolitan society relied, for its very existence, upon military supremacy. Nothing like a balance of trade was ever achieved, or indeed attempted; the imported food was exacted from conquered or subject territories. As Cicero once remarked of republican Rome: 'if they restored all that belonged to others they would have to return to hovels and lie down in misery and want.'[3] And in the Empire as a whole, of course, the vast majority of the population *was* engaged in agriculture. It was not for more than a thousand years after the fall of the Roman Empire that the technological developments occurred which made it possible for a minority of a population to supply the food for a whole society.

Levels of economic development in the twentieth century

The greater variety of human activities is reflected in the greater complexity of societies. The increasingly specialized activities come to be carried out more and more in specialized institutions; separate organizations of government, trade, religion, family life and education become differentiated. But these specialized institutions do not exist in isolation. They are related to, and in large measure dependent upon, one another. The more there are of them, the more complicated these relationships become; or in other words, the more complex the society becomes. The gradual process of social change from a simpler to a more complex structure of society is known as the process of social development.

On the whole there is a close correlation between the level of social development and the wealth of a society (although, as we shall see later, crude figures of societal wealth can sometimes be misleading). Just as the relative complexity and affluence of ancient Rome is evidenced in the diversity of occupations, so the General Register Office's *Classification of Occupations* for 1960 lists somewhere in the region of 31,000 occupations in contemporary Britain—a far more complex and wealthy society. Related to the multiplication of specialist occupations, however, there occurs a redistribution of the labour force between various types of economic activity. In its early stages, social development invariably involves the movement of labour from agriculture into non-agricultural activities. This movement has continued (with some setbacks) throughout the

process of development so far and so the proportion of the population in non-agricultural activities provides a rough and ready guide to a society's level of development. The extent of this movement of labour in selected countries during the last hundred years can be seen in Table 2.1. By the time reasonably accurate figures became available, some three-quarters of the working population of Britain was already engaged in non-agricultural activities—a factor which is related to Britain's early establishment as an industrial and trading country. The greater part of the change had occurred in the previous hundred and fifty years, for in 1688 Gregory King estimated that three-quarters of the working population was wholly or partly engaged in agriculture. The exodus from agriculture in other European countries and in the USA, however, is clearly shown in the table. In these cases, as well as in Britain, the greater part of the redistribution of labour has been associated with the growth of factory production. The proportion of the population employed in non-agricultural activities, however, is not, in itself, a very accurate guide to the degree of industrialization in a country. As the example of metropolitan Rome demonstrates, a non-agricultural population may have other bases than manufacturing industry.

Table 2.1 Percentage of the working population of selected countries engaged in agriculture

	1840	1850	1860	1870	1880	1890	1900	1910	1920	1930	1940	1950	1960	1970
Great Britain	22·3	21·9	18·8	15·3	13·3	10·7	9·1	8·8	7·1	6·0	—	5·1	3·6	1·5
USA	—	64·0	59·4	50·2	50·1	42·8	37·6	31·6	27·4	22·0	15·6	11·9	6·5	4·4
Belgium	—	50·9	46·8	44·4	39·5	32·2	27·1	23·3	21·1	17·3	—	12·5	7·4	5·2
New Zealand	—	—	—	—	—	—	32·9	26·1	29·7	25·7	27·2	17·4*	14·4	13·3
Denmark	—	49·4	48·6	47·8	50·4	44·8	46·6	41·7	34·9	35·3	28·5	25·1	17·5	—
France	—	51·8*	—	—	—	46·0*	41·8	41·0	41·5	35·6	36·0*	31·0*	20·0	15·8
South Africa	—	—	—	—	—	—	—	58·8	69·5	—	48·3	32·8	29·8	—
Japan	—	—	—	84·9	82·3	76·1	70·0	63·0	53·5	49·4	44·0	48·3	32·6	17·4
USSR	—	—	—	—	—	58·6	—	—	—	86·1†	—	—	44·3	24·5
Poland	—	—	—	—	—	—	—	—	75·9	65·0	—	57·2	47·7	—
Brazil	—	—	—	—	—	—	—	—	70·5	—	67·4	60·6	51·6	44·2
Mexico	—	—	—	—	—	—	—	63·7	63·0	67·8	65·4	58·3	54·2	—
Greece	—	—	—	—	—	—	—	—	—	49·6	53·7	—	48·2	55·3
UAR	—	—	—	—	—	—	—	69·1	69·2	60·3	70·7	63·7	58·0	49·2
India	—	—	—	—	—	—	67·1	71·9	72·5	67·2	—	73·6	72·9	—

*Interpolated —figures unavailable
†This figure is much higher than most estimates. The more widely supported figure of about 70 per cent is more likely.

Sources: *International Historical Statistics*, vol. 1 (P. Bairoch, director), *The Working Population and its Structure*, Brussels: Editions de l'Institut de Sociologie de l'Université Libre de Bruxelles, 1968; *Yearbook of Labour Statistics 1971*, Geneva: International Labour Office; *British Labour Statistics, Yearbook 1970*, London: HMSO, 1972.

Table 2.2   Occupational distribution of the employed population in selected countries, 1 (per cent)

	Great Britain 1970	USA 1970	Japan 1970	Chile 1970	Vene-zuela 1970	USSR 1970	Brazil 1970	UAR 1969	Ghana 1960	Pakis-tan 1968	Thai-land 1960	Niger 1960
Agriculture, etc.	1·5	4·4	17·4	21·2	21·8	24·5	44·2	49·2	61·7	69·1	82·3	96·9
Mining	1·7	0·8	0·4	1·8	2·0	2·0	} 17·8	} 11·1	1·9	—	0·2	—
Manufacturing	34·8	24·7	27·0	22·9	17·6	25·4			9·2	9·5	3·4	} 0·6
Construction	5·3	4·2	7·7	8·0	6·2	8·4		4·2	3·5	2·1	0·5	
Electricity, gas and water services	1·5	5·7	6·9	0·7	1·7	0·6	*	0·7	0·5	0·2	0·1	—
Commerce, banking, etc.	15·1	21·7	22·4	13·2	17·2	5·6	8·9	9·9	14·5	7·8	5·7	0·8
Transport and communications	6·3	5·3	*	8·3	6·1	8·7	4·3	4·1	2·7	3·6	1·2	0·2
Services and administration	24·8	27·4	17·9	23·1	26·0	21·8	19·7	20·8	6·0	6·4	4·8	0·9
Activities not adequately described	9·0	5·8	0·3	0·8	1·4	3·0	5·1	—	—	1·3	1·8	0·6
All occupations	100·0	100·0	100·0	100·0	100·0	100·0	100·0	100·0	100·0	100·0	100·0	100·0

*Included elsewhere

Sources: *International Historical Statistics*, vol. 1 (P. Bairoch, director), *The Working Population and its Structure*, Brussels: Editions de l'Institut de Sociologie de l'Université Libre de Bruxelles, 1968; *Yearbook of Labour Statistics 1971*, Geneva: International Labour Office, Tables 2A and 3; *Annual Abstract of Statistics 1971*, London: HMSO.

The more detailed information on the activities of the labour force shown for contemporary societies in Table 2.2 gives us a more accurate (but also more complicated) guide to industrialization and other economic development, and thus to the nature of social relationships. In Table 2.2 the size of the manufacturing sector, of the commercial sector, and of the 'service' sector (the professions, administration, social services, entertainment, transport and the like) is taken into account. These figures provide some indication of the enormous differences between societies of the contemporary world, from societies like Niger and Thailand to those like Britain and the USA. Differences in the proportion of the labour force engaged in agriculture are striking, but they are of less significance as indices of industrialization than the proportion in manufacturing (although the two are clearly related). Even this, however, can be misleading. The manufacturing sector of the employed population of the USA, for example, is proportionately smaller than that of Britain not because industry is less dominant in America, nor even because agriculture is more important, but rather because the greater productivity of American industry (based upon a higher level of technology, greater specialization and an earlier and more whole-hearted use of mass production and automation) releases labour *from* manufacturing. Thus, a larger proportion of the population is engaged in administration, commerce, and in professional services than is the case in Britain. Moreover, Table 2.2 conceals important differ-

ences within its broad categories. The nature of the occupations within the manufacturing sector is rather different in Britain and America. In America, because of the higher level of automation, a greater proportion of the *industrial* labour force is engaged in what are usually called 'non-manual' activities. This greater 'modernity' of American industry is not reflected in these figures. Similarly in Table 2.2 the proportion of the Ghanaian labour force in 'commerce, banking and insurance' is almost as high as for Britain. The more detailed national information from which international statistics are derived, however, shows that the majority of those in 'commerce' in Ghana are engaged in very small-scale retail trade —hawking bread, plantains, yams and nuts with a turnover that does not always even ensure subsistence. In fact nearly 80 per cent are women, and their economic activities are essentially supplementary to those of their menfolk. To compare them with the bankworkers, salesmen, insurance clerks and traders of industrial societies is scarcely realistic. Such are the hazards and limitations of international statistical comparisons.

Nevertheless, simplifications of this sort do show up some general differences between societies in the distribution of their labour force. In Table 2.3 we have presented the figures for these same countries in even more simplified form in order to highlight the differences between industrial and non-industrial countries. To the right of the table are those societies where agriculture predominates; in these societies there is little or no industrial

Table 2.3 Occupational distribution of the employed population in selected countries, 2 (per cent)

	Great Britain 1970	USA 1970	Japan 1970	Chile 1970	Venezuela 1970	USSR 1970	Brazil 1970	UAR 1969	Ghana 1960	Pakistan 1968	Thailand 1960	Niger 1960
Agriculture	1·5	4·4	17·4	21·2	21·8	24·5	44·2	49·2	61·7	69·1	82·3	96·9
Industry	41·8	29·7	35·1	32·7	25·8	35·8	17·8	15·3	14·6	11·6	4·1	0·6
Commerce, administration	47·7	60·1	47·2	45·3	51·0	36·7	32·9	35·5	23·7	18·0	11·8	1·9
Activities not adequately described	9·0	5·8	0·3	0·8	1·4	3·0	5·1	—	—	1·3	1·8	0·6
All occupations	100·0	100·0	100·0	100·0	100·0	100·0	100·0	100·0	100·0	100·0	100·0	100·0

Sources: *International Historical Statistics*, vol. 1 (P. Bairoch, director), *The Working Population and its Structure*, Brussels: Editions de l'Institut de Sociologie de l'Université Libre de Bruxelles, 1968; *Yearbook of Labour Statistics 1971*, Geneva: International Labour Office, Tables 2A and 3; *Annual Abstract of Statistics 1971*, London: HMSO.

development. To the left of the table are those societies whose labour force is heavily concentrated in services, commerce and industry; these are the societies where industrialization has long been established. Between these extremes are societies with substantial industrial development; with highly articulated commerce and services; and at the same time, with a large proportion of the population in agriculture. These overall and somewhat crude, differences between various types of societies should be borne in mind in the discussions that follow.

The significance of these differences and changes becomes clearer when we consider the nature of industrialization more closely. In many ways the emergence of industry has been the most significant economic development since the domestication of crops. One of the most noticeable changes it has involved has been massive economic growth; wherever there has been industrialization there has also been a sharp increase in income per head—a tendency which, with only a few temporary setbacks, has been a continuous characteristic of successfully industrializing societies. But this is only one of the important factors; industrialization involves not only economic growth but economic *development* as well. It is a new type of economic activity carried out in a new set of economic institutions—factories—under the dominance of machine power. These new activities and institutions co-exist with the older agriculture and handicrafts. It is in this sense that industrialization was 'revolutionary'. It was a fundamental change in the nature of the production process which led to rapid changes in the structure of society—that is to say, to changes in the *relationships* between the different groupings of people and between the various parts of the society concerned.

There were many towns and rural areas in eighteenth-century England in which production was expanding and which were experiencing economic growth. But in most of them—in Birmingham for instance—production continued to be by craftsmen working in small workshops. For the most part they were to remain isolated pockets of manufacturing until they adopted factory production. In many places technical and organizational changes were vehemently resisted by the craftsmen's guilds. The new cotton town of Manchester which emerged during the second half of the eighteenth century was quite different. In place of the domestic textile production of an earlier generation the new textile industry was fairly and squarely based upon factory production and steam power. It thus provides us with the first historical example of industrialization. And far from being a local phenomenon its effects were felt throughout England and, indeed, throughout the world. The changes in social relationships between employer and operative in the textile industry were important enough, but they pale into relative insignificance beside the impact of industry upon the structure of the total society. New organizations emerged; often enough wealth passed increasingly into the hands of people who owed their position to little but their own talent and good fortune; new groups were drawn into the political process. With these changes in the location of power, relationships between social strata changed; new towns sprang up; age-old customs and practices were abandoned or altered beyond recognition. The whole character of the society was transformed.

This has been the fate of all societies which have successfully undergone industrialization and in this, as much as in any quantitative changes in national income or income per capita, lies the importance of industrialization. This can be seen more clearly, and some of the necessary qualifications can be made, if we look in more detail at the economic changes in some specific situations.

The first industrialization process

The early industrialization of Britain was, in many ways, unique. All subsequent industrializers were able to utilize British know-how and copy British industrial technology: Britain had to pioneer such developments. All later comers could make use of capital already accumulated by the British industrialists who were willing and often eager to add overseas investments to those they made at home: Britain's industrialization was based on no such giant capital accumulation. All other countries attempting to industrialize were faced with competition from an established industrial power which could undersell them in markets at home and abroad. The British industrialists' only competition was from craft manufacturers—the handloom weavers of Lancashire and Bengal—who were priced out of the market. In other words, Britain's industrialization was unique because it represented mankind's first excursion into the realm of factory production and the use of inanimate power on a large scale.

In other ways, too, the case of Britain has been atypical. Compared with most other industrializing countries, eighteenth-century Britain was a highly differentiated society. Commerce and trade had grown apace throughout the previous century; considerable urbanization had occurred; and, in general, economic specialization was well advanced. In the nature of landownership (and consequently in agricultural relations), in the importance of trade, in the extensiveness of a money economy, and in her international political position, early eighteenth-century Britain was unusual. Here, perhaps, lies part of the explanation for the development of manufacturing industry. The high degree of concentration of landownership (in 1750, 75 per cent of the land was in the hands of a couple of thousand landlords) not only provided a foundation for the huge surplus food production presupposed by industrialization, but also fashioned in the rural areas, a wage labour force that was potentially mobile. The destruction of the peasantry, as it is sometimes called, created a class of persons who were free of ties to the land and could migrate to the towns in search of the higher levels of industrial wages. Indeed, the rural population growth of the period forced rural workers into the towns. In addition, concentration of landownership, and with it the concentration

of profit in the hands of a few landowners, made possible the accumulation of capital for industrial investment. Yet much of the important industrial development took place from small beginnings. The early entrepreneurs were more often artisans or craftsmen than landed gentlemen. The early decades of industrial development saw a good many 'self-made men' achieve positions of wealth. This was possible because of the relatively modest demands made on capital by early manufacturing industry. Cotton manufacture, for example, grew strong on the basis of piecemeal development and relatively cheap machines—the spinning jenny, the water frame, and power looms.

The highly developed system of trade provided another source of wealth for the establishment of the first factories. Most of Britain was already involved in a money market, and British merchants had, with government support, engaged in trade with most parts of the world. The early stages of industrialization were closely tied to overseas trade and so implicated the merchants from the start. Britain had emerged victorious in the struggle for the markets of the world. Her political and naval supremacy in Europe had eliminated effective competition for the trade of the non-European world. And by a policy of vigorous protection of British trading interests local competition outside Europe was crushed. Thus war and colonialism were at the heart of the early British industrialization experience. And economic interests in their turn were to play a part in the development of the British style of colonialism. For, as Macaulay argued before parliament in 1833 when supporting the education of Indians:[4]

> It would be far better for us that the people of India were ruled by their own kings, but wearing our broadcloth, and working with our cutlery, than that they were performing their salaams to English collectors and English magistrates, but were too ignorant to value, or too poor to buy, English manufactures. To trade with civilized men is infinitely more profitable than to govern savages.

Home politics played an important part in Britain's industrialization too. Gradually, throughout the eighteenth century, the commerce lobby was defeated by the manufacturing lobby so that government support was assured.

The cotton industry—the 'leading sector' of British industry for the first few decades—

illustrates these points well: compared with later industrial development it required no expensive capital equipment, no complex skills, and, although oriented towards world trade, its survival depended, in the first instance, upon the political influence of manufacturers in their conflict with the merchants. (Wool manufacturers had managed in the teeth of merchant opposition, to erect tariff barriers against Indian textiles—a factor which allowed Lancashire cotton manufacturers to dominate the home market, ultimately, ironically enough, to the virtual extinction of wool manufacture.) Most important of all, the Lancashire cotton industry stood at the hub of world trade. The importation of raw cotton from the West Indies and the southern part of North America; the export of textiles to many parts of the world but especially (initially) to India; to say nothing of the earlier shipping of slaves from Africa to man the plantations of the New World: all these had their trading centre in Liverpool. The creation and maintenance of British markets in India and the Far East had much to do with the evolution of Britain as the world's major colonial power and was carried out at the expense of the domestic production of textiles in India itself. The Indian handloom weavers were denied the tariff protection which enabled the Lancashire cotton manufacturers to grow strong. Once its strength was achieved, Lancashire could therefore undersell local products in India. To this extent social development in Britain was at the expense of the domestic textile producers of India. A similar fate (and one which is much more widely known) awaited the handloom weavers of Britain. At the other end of the production line, a satisfactory supply of raw cotton was provided by the slave economy of the American south. Thus, the fortunes of vast communities as far apart as the Mississippi and the Ganges were determined by British industrialists. And to a very considerable extent the fortunes of British industry were closely related to particular patterns of social relations in North America and India. When one adds to this the more widely known social conditions in early English factories it is apparent that the early industrial era was marked by (and dependent on) gross inequalities of power and wealth throughout the world.

The control exercised by early industrial Britain over a large part of the world's trade and production has never subsequently been approached by a single country. The wealth it generated and the stirrings of industrialization elsewhere—especially in the USA—provided the basis for the diversification of British industry. The growing population of the industrial towns and the major sea-ports provided a rapidly expanding initial market for coal; the industrialization of the USA and Western Europe demanded iron and steel which, at first, could only be produced in Britain; and, above all, the railways which covered Britain from 1837 (and rapidly spread to other industrializing societies) had a seemingly inexhaustible appetite for iron, steel and coal. On this basis the capital goods industries thrived. By 1850 there were 200,000 miners in Britain; by 1880, half a million; and by 1914 well over one million. The development of the iron ship and the application of steam power to sea transport provided a further stimulus to the basic industries as well as a growth in shipbuilding and heavy engineering.

These developments in the economy had implications that were far wider than their importance for Britain's continued economic growth—significant though that was. It was among miners, dockers, shipbuilders and other workers in heavy industry that working-class politics grew into an organized movement. It was these workers, rather than the earlier organizers of 'craft' unions, who were destined to play an important part in the development of the trade union movement and the formation and growth of the Labour party. The nature of British politics ever since has been affected by the incorporation of these groups into the political process.

Many of the factors we have so far referred to help us to understand the changing position of British industry during the last decades of the nineteenth century. These years brought a new phase in the world economic situation. Britain no longer stood alone. The USA and Germany both surpassed Britain in steel production and, for the first time for over a hundred years, Britain had serious economic competitors. For some time the markets of these competitor-nations had been protected against British goods, but in most of the rest of the world Britain's economic and political hegemony had its reward in a monopoly of trade. Much of the world could sell its products nowhere but in Britain and was allowed no other source of supply for manufactured articles. Even in the markets of the under-developed world, however, there was increasing competition, a fact witnessed by the Treaty of Berlin (1870) at which the as yet little explored continent of Africa was divided into colonies and shared out between the major European powers. No longer was Britain the undisputed leader. Still, the Empire was sufficiently large to provide a satisfactory market for her industrial goods and, when competition from other industrial countries threatened some of her traditional markets, imperial preference provided a cushion which was to last a further half a century. Rather than meeting the challenge of competition with further diversification and with the adoption of new technologies, British industrialists continued to make traditional articles for which they sought new markets. The innovating economic developments of the twentieth century have taken place elsewhere—particularly in the USA.

Dominant among the new industries both in America and elsewhere have been a whole range of electrical industries, the motor industry, a variety of chemical industries, and, more recently, the electronics industry. Mid-twentieth-century industry is not dominated, as was mid-nineteenth-century industry, by coal, iron and steel, and textiles. But it is not only that the products of industry have changed and diversified; but techniques of production are also very different. It is in this field that the Americans have been the pioneers, first in the introduction of mass production and more recently in automation, and it is upon these new technologies, as well as upon her great natural resources, that the economy of the richest nation in the world is based. However, there have been other important consequences than the increased standard of living— changes which are mirrored in other industrial societies in so far as they adopt a similar pattern of industrial organization and technology. In quantitative terms, manual workers have declined as a proportion of the employed population. Moreover, within the working classes the miners, steel workers and dockers—so crucial a part of the occupational structure of all industrial societies at the outbreak of the first world war—are no longer such a dominant occupational group. They are far outnumbered by semi-skilled factory workers producing car components, valves for television sets, machinery parts, and the like. Lacking numbers their power in the labour movement, and thus in society more generally, has also declined relative to other groups of manual workers.

By contrast, in all highly industrial societies 'white collar' occupations have been expanding rapidly, both in absolute terms and as a proportion of the working population. The number of clerks and typists, for example, grew rapidly throughout the first half of the twentieth century and numeri-

cally these occupations seem to be surviving the automation of some of their former tasks. Other non-manual occupational groups are growing still faster. This is partly because the growth industries of the twentieth century increasingly demand considerable scientific and technical skills, partly because of the complexity of the product itself, and partly because of the complexity of automated production processes. In the American aircraft industry, for example, technical personnel account for a quarter of the labour force; managerial staff for 10 per cent; lower-grade white collar workers for 23 per cent; and production workers for only 40 per cent. The general pattern of an expansion of 'white collar' staff at the expense of 'blue collar' staff is a common one. In addition, a wide variety of service occupations, from taxi drivers to shop assistants, are still on the increase despite the growth of car ownership and self-service stores. At the more skilled and more remunerative level a plethora of professional occupations grows as the affluence of modern industrial societies and the problems of life they generate produce clients for domestic architects, income tax consultants and heart surgeons.

These changes in the proportions between various occupational groups and the growth of new occupations are merely indicative of the important changes in patterns of life in modern industrial societies, changes which affect all members of society. Levels of consumption rise; leisure-time increases; the average period of education is extended. Changing patterns of employment give new significance and power to some groups, notably women and young people. These are just some of the changing relationships to which we shall return in later chapters.

Industrialization and the state

Britain's industrialization took place in the context of a non-industrial world, and the existence of an industrial Britain fundamentally altered the course of economic development all over the world. Throughout the nineteenth century all economic development occurred under the influence of Britain. The industrialization of Western Europe, of the USA, of Imperial Russia and the USSR, and of Japan followed different courses largely because of the example of Britain and the availability of external sources of investment and technology. The other major difference between the industrialization of Britain and that of most other nations lay in the part played by governments who, aware of the results of industrialization sought to imitate Britain. In this, however, there was more variation. In Britain the part of the government had been restricted to the creation, through diplomacy and military action, of world trading conditions favourable to her own sons. Important as this was it does not compare with more direct government action elsewhere: the government subsidies to industry in Japan; the government-guaranteed railways of Prussia; and the government ownership of mines and factories in both Imperial and Soviet Russia.

The early industrialization of Japan and Russia illustrates the point well. In both cases the initial stimulus to industrialize came from outside, industrialization being seen as a means of achieving political ends as much as economic ones, and being actively promoted by the central government. The defeat of the Russians in the Crimean war and the humiliation of the Japanese in 1853 by American gunboats under Commander Perry both demonstrated the military superiority of industrial powers. The lesson was not lost and important changes followed quickly. The abolition of serfdom in Russia in 1861 was the first, and most important, of the changes which laid the foundation for the rapid industrialization of the 1890s, for prior to this only those who owned serfs were assured of industrial labour. This was one reason for the stagnation of mining and textile manufacture after their establishment by Peter the Great. (Even so it is not always realized that mining and textiles together employed nearly a million workers by the mid-1860s.) The main reason for the great industrial spurt of the 1890s, however, was the fact that the development of industry became the major plank of the Tsar's policy. In particular, the decision to develop railway transport at the government's expense created a demand for iron and steel which first gave Russian industry the concentration on heavy industry which has characterized it ever since. Moreover, the iron and steel industry which was established in the last decade of the nineteenth century was one of the most modern in the world. The technology adopted was that of the efficient German industry rather than the outmoded British; the plants were the largest in the world; and the output per unit of the blast furnaces was second only to that in the USA.

Japan, before 1853, existed virtually in isolation from the rest of the world for no foreigners were allowed there. As in Russia there were legal restrictions on the movement of peasants from the land and there were additional restrictions on travel, trade, and upon changing one's occupation. Under the Treaties of 1858 and 1866 Japan was obliged to allow American and European traders to carry out their business and was forbidden to erect tariffs of more than 5 per cent. This forcible opening up of Japan to world trade under semi-colonial terms caused considerable internal problems. In particular, handicraft production of cotton goods, sugar and paper was virtually extinguished by the foreign industrial competition. These were the conditions in which the Meiji regime undertook its drastic reformation of Japanese society. Most important from the economic point of view, freedom of movement and freedom of trade were restored, and people were allowed to choose their occupation. In addition, primary education with a Western-style curriculum was made compulsory. The government, unable to help infant industries in the usual way through tariff protection, became directly involved in the process of industrialization. Railways, banks, insurance companies and factories often began life as state enterprises. Some of them were later passed over to private owners as going concerns, and many private firms were subsidized— government subsidies to the Mitsibishi Shipping Company, for example, were partly responsible for the important position Japan had achieved in international shipping by the first world war. It was largely by such energetic and direct government support for industry, particularly heavy industry, that Japan achieved the distinction of being the only nation so far to industrialize without significant tariff protection. Subsequently, as her industrial and military strength increased, Japan was able to renounce the unfavourable trade agreements with the Western world and to establish colonies of her own in Korea (1910) and extensions of territory, notably in Manchuria, which provided markets for consumer goods. In addition, however, she captured the markets of established industrial countries. To give a single example: in 1913 Britain supplied 97.1 per cent of India's cotton imports; Japan supplied 0.3 per cent. Twenty years later the Indian market was shared equally between the two industrial nations.

By far the most dramatic instance of industrialization under state control, however, is that of the USSR. The chaos created by the first world war, and by the civil war which followed the Bolshevik seizure of power in 1917, meant that the first task of Soviet economic policy after 1921 was to rebuild the farms and factories which had been destroyed. Because the industrial countries of the world were unwilling to give loans or make investments in the new regime, and often refused to trade as well, reconstruction had to be carried out entirely from internal resources. The pre-war (1913) level of output in both industry and agriculture was reached in 1925–6. Only then could new industrial growth seriously be considered. The distinctiveness (at that time) of the Soviet process of industrialization was that it was not only state controlled but entirely state sponsored. It was the 14th Party Congress, in 1925, that resolved:

That the Soviet Union be converted from a country which imports machines to a country which produces machines, in order that by this means the Soviet Union, in the midst of capitalist encirclement, should not become an economic appendage of the capitalist world economy but an independent economic unit which is building Socialism.

The influence of political considerations upon economic policy is clear enough. Add to this the fact that it was a primarily political body which was taking the decisions, and the fusion of the political and the economic becomes stronger than anything to be experienced in the 'capitalist' world until after 1945.

The other major distinctive feature of Soviet economic development after 1928 was the establishment of the five year plans. The basic decision was to increase the rate of industrialization, and the keynote of the first five year plans was the high rate of investment. This amounted to between one-quarter and one-third of the national income, and three-quarters of this investment was to be in heavy industry. There was an attempt to plan the development of the whole society. Resources were allocated to areas of shortage and to priority concerns. In the first plans (and in practice) priority was given to heavy industry rather than to consumer industries, and to agricultural developments to feed the growing towns. This was partly because of the need to manufacture their own machinery and industrial plant consequent upon a decision to industrialize quickly; and partly, throughout the 1930s, because of the needs of rearmament created by the expansionist policies of Germany in the west and Japan in the east. In agriculture, what was planned as a gradual spread of farming co-operatives aroused the hostility of a large section of the peasantry (chiefly the richer peasants (Kulaks)

and the middle-level peasants). The government reacted to this opposition by wholesale collectivization of farms and widespread deportation of Kulaks so that the Kulaks as an economic group (and a potential political force) were destroyed. The economic cost of collectivization was to be felt for a decade, however, since the chief form of peasant protest was the widespread slaughter of livestock. In 1933 the numbers of livestock were still less than half those in 1928, and the 1928 level was not fully regained until 1953. The other major agricultural change was the establishment of state farms, usually on virgin soil, as a crash programme for providing the food without which the proposed rapid industrialization could not proceed. By 1932, state and collective farms produced 84 per cent of the grain marketed in the Soviet Union and 83 per cent of the cotton.

The years 1928-37—the years of the first and second five year plans—witnessed a major change in the structure of the Soviet economy. In the space of ten years there was a colossal movement of labour out of agriculture—the proportion of the labour force engaged in agriculture declined from about 71 per cent to 54 per cent—and at the same time a substantial increase in agricultural output, which was made possible by increased mechanization. In the same decade industrial output rose from 52 per cent to 69 per cent of the gross national product. All this, moreover, took place in the context of the rapid overall economic growth which was one of the most striking features of the Soviet economy of the period. Between 1928 and 1938 output of iron and steel increased by 400 per cent; coal by 350 per cent; oil by 300 per cent; and electricity by 700 per cent. At the same time many new industries were established, including heavy chemicals (for example, plastics and synthetic rubber), aluminium, nickel and copper. The USSR had become the world's leading producer of tractors (an increase of 600 per cent in the period 1928-32 alone) and railway engines—indicative of two of the priorities of the government planners.

The growth of consumption was much more modest. The world depression (which affected the Soviet Union because it lowered the value of her exports) and armament needs necessitated the revision of the plans from time to time, and in this period it was always the consumption industries which were kept in short supply. The overall estimates of Western economists are that during this decade food consumption rose by about 10 per cent and the output of other consumable goods rose by somewhere between 40 per cent and 50 per cent.

The other area in which there was heavy investment during the 1930s was education. Education, like everything else, was part of the overall plan and its development was related to the economic needs of the country. A major literacy drive had, by 1939, eliminated illiteracy in the population aged under fifty. By 1953 there were nearly two million people who had received higher education compared with a mere 136,000 in 1913. More than two and a half million had, by 1953, been trained as skilled workers in middle-level technical institutes. In 1913 there had been only 54,000. It is this emphasis on technical education that characterizes Soviet education in comparison with that of the Western industrial world. Although enrolment in higher education is much lower than in the USA (about 16 per 1,000 compared with 44 per 1,000) more than half of the Soviet graduates, and less than a quarter of the American graduates, are scientists and engineers. The result is that the number of science and engineering graduates per head of population is strikingly similar (9 per 1,000 in the USSR and 10 per 1,000 in the USA).

The USSR provides us with the most extreme case of state ownership and domination of industry. Yet in all highly industrial societies the state is more and more in evidence in economic affairs. Even in the USA, which, of all industrial societies, at one time came closest to the freedom from state intervention which characterized early industrial England, and which still retains an ideology of non-intervention in economic affairs, the state has become increasingly important.

There are three main reasons for this increasing pervasion of the state in non-socialist industrial countries. The first is that the state has become the largest single employer. Tax-collectors, transport workers, secretaries, policemen, administrators, refuse-collectors and teachers are, more often than not, in direct government employment. In the USA—the closest to a free enterprise economy in the contemporary world—there were in 1969 more than twelve million people directly employed by federal and state governments in addition to the three million men in the armed forces.

Second, the state itself has become the largest single customer of industry. In some fields—armaments and military defence are the obvious examples—it is the only significant customer. The government therefore controls the fortunes of large sectors of industry by its military decisions and by the placement of its contracts. More than 90 per cent of the business of the American aircraft industry is supplied by government defence contracts. The General Dynamics Corporation of the USA is a spectacular example of a company which owes its prosperity entirely to defence contracts, 80 per cent of its work being in this field. It had recorded losses over the preceding years when, in 1962, it was given the contract for the hugely expensive F-111 all-purpose military aircraft. In 1967-8 the Corporation received more arms contracts than any other American company—to the value of two thousand million dollars. In such deals the government maintains close control over all aspects of the industry, including the level of profit or loss. Some indication of the importance of the United States government as a customer of industry can be gauged from the total bill for defence spending, which during the 1960s was running at more than 10 per cent of the gross national product. Government decisions on military matters, then, clearly have considerable impact in the industrial world; re-armament or disarmament are economic as well as political issues. The same is true for government enterprises which are not directly (or solely) military. The decision of the Kennedy administration to send men to the moon before 1970, for example, was an important *economic* decision in that it resulted in important economic changes in American industry and in American life more generally.

Third, the general economic activities of government have expanded, particularly in the years since the second world war. Governments have always been involved in economic matters through the necessity of raising taxes. Even in this field, however, a change has occurred as direct taxation has become increasingly a tool of social as well as economic policy—a means of redistributing part of a nation's income. In other ways, too, governments in Western Europe and North America have attempted to prevent or ameliorate some of the consequences of economic changes. This, of course, has a long history, stretching back to the Factory Acts of early nineteenth-century England. Since the great depression of the early 1930s, however, government intervention has been economic as well as legal, and has been especially important in the attempt to maintain full employment. Today, in all the major industrial nations of the world, governments attempt to *direct* economic changes. Thus, British governments of the 1960s offered inducements to industrial firms to move to 'development areas'; they attempted to reverse the movement of the labour force into tertiary occupations by operating a selective employment tax which was levied on all employers of labour other than manufacturers; they subsidized the aircraft industry in order that it could keep abreast of the rapidly changing aero-technology; and they subsidized airlines so that they could buy the latest products of the aircraft industry. The list could be extended, or could be duplicated for other Western nations. Finally, in most industrial societies—for example, in Sweden, Australia and Italy as well as in the USA and Britain—the State has power to arbitrate, or otherwise intervene, in industrial disputes.

One of the most significant features of this increased state involvement in the economies of non-socialist countries is that it is most intense in the newly-developed industries. In the USA it is marked in the space and missile industries with their reliance on electronics, partly because of the importance of these industries in the defence programme (80 per cent of the spending on armaments goes on aircraft, missiles and electronics). Elsewhere, it is sometimes only the state that has the resources needed to develop these new fields. Whatever the reason, this concentration of government economic activities suggests that the increase in state involvement will continue. Clearly, state involvement in the economy is no longer dependent upon a socialist political ideology. Yet equally clearly there still remains a difference between state ownership, as practised in the USSR, and the United States government's policy of giving contracts to private industry. Both the degree and nature of the involvement differ, although this has less effect upon the strictly economic relations than might at first be expected.

Contemporary modernizing[5] societies

Just as the existence of an industrial Britain affected the course of subsequent economic development in Germany, the USA and elsewhere, so the existence of the industrial world affects the development of the non-industrial world today. The knowledge, techniques and machines of advanced industrial societies can be diffused to the 'under-developed' world enabling 'short cuts' to be taken in the establishment of efficient communications networks and sometimes of factory production. This can, in some instances, enable considerable economic growth to take place; less often, but sometimes, it results in

industrialization. Yet it may be that the most advanced industrial technology is not that which is best suited to the resources of a given non-industrial society. The expensive labour-saving devices of modern American industry, for example, were developed in response to a situation of labour scarcity. When applied in India they may use an unnecessary amount of the scarce capital of that country and ignore the abundant supply of labour. The 'modern' also has an attraction of its own that is hard to resist.

However, in the diffusion of technology, as in other things, the relationship between industrial and non-industrial countries is not one between equals. It is one between the economically (and politically) powerful and the relatively powerless. Very often in the last hundred years or more it has taken the form of colonialism (although this has not always been the case and the formality of imperialism is less important than the fact of its existence). We have already noticed something of the effect of colonialism on the economic development of Britain. Its effects upon the colonized were no less dramatic. Sometimes the imposition of colonialism was initially associated with rapid economic growth and development. The exploitation of copper mines in the then Northern Rhodesia and Belgian Congo; the introduction of cocoa to West Africa; the commercial mining of tin and the planting of rubber in Malaya; and the spread of coffee plantations in the south and east of non-colonial Brazil: all this represented major diversification in what had previously been relatively simple economies. Similarly, in each case there was an immediate increase in the gross national product of the countries concerned. The capital accumulation which had occurred in Western industrial countries had been so great that investment in non-industrial countries could proceed without in any way bringing a shortage of capital at home. Furthermore, the requirements of the industrial world for raw materials, and the increasingly urban character of European societies which meant that they were unable to provide their own food, provided a ready market which made such investment very attractive. Thus, the initial impulse for economic diversification came from the already industrializing countries, and capital and skills were diffused from Europe and the USA to Africa, Asia and Latin America.

There were two consequences of this, however, which were crucial to the subsequent structure of modernizing societies. The first of these was that a large part of the profit from these economic

Table 2.4 Major importers of the produce of selected modernizing societies, 1966 (per cent)

	Brazil	Chile	Congo	Ghana	India	Nigeria	Senegal	Zambia
Belgium	2·2	3·0	54·4	3·6	1·5	2·6	0·9	1·4
Canada	1·3	0·1	0·1	2·7	2·7	3·5	—	—
France	3·4	4·4	6·9	0·7	1·6	9·3	73·8	8·6
Italy	6·3	5·2	10·5	3·6	1·3	4·9	3·9	8·8
Japan	2·4	10·4	—	5·5	9·2	1·5	1·3	14·1
Netherlands	5·1	13·2	2·7	7·6	1·0	9·4	0·7	0·1
UK	4·3	15·0	8·3	16·9	17·3	37·8	1·1	32·5
USA	33·4	24·9	4·2	16·2	18·8	8·0	0·1	—
West Germany	7·7	9·5	4·3	8·3	2·2	10·0	2·2	14·1
Other countries	33·9	14·3	8·6	34·9	44·4	13·0	16·9	20·4
	100·0	100·0	100·0	100·0	100·0	100·0	100·0	100·0

Source: *International Trade Statistics 1966*, New York: United Nations, 1968.

enterprises went (and still goes) overseas to the investors in the industrial countries. Thus, whereas in the early stages of European industrialization such profits were available for ploughing back into further development, this is less the case in today's modernizing societies. This is a problem that was hardly tackled in Africa until the 'independence decade' of the 1960s. Most independent African states have now attempted to come to terms with this particular problem by limiting the proportion of the profit which may be taken out of the country. Yet, important as political independence may be, it is not the only factor. One estimate of the relations between the USA and the 'developing' world suggests that between 1950 and 1965 the USA (which has never been a significant colonial power) invested some $9.0 billion while there was $25.6 billion profit on investments in the 'under-developed' world.[6] While such figures should not be taken to mean that there is no benefit to modernizing societies—such investment usually stimulates employment and provision of supporting services of one kind or another and may be the necessary first step in further development—they do suggest that aid to, and investment in, the Third World is by no means as altruistic an enterprise as it is sometimes made out to be.

The second consequence of the external source of economic development has been that such development has taken place as part of the much wider process of what is sometimes called the international division of labour. The development which has taken place has been overwhelmingly in primary production; that is, either in agriculture or in mining. Typically, exports consist of

raw materials—cotton (Egypt); sugar (the West Indies); coffee (Brazil); bananas (Ecuador); cocoa (Ghana); copper (Zambia and Chile); tin (Malaysia); oil (Libya, Iraq and Venezuela). Occasionally the raw materials are exported after the first stage of processing has been carried out. This pattern of development has resulted in economies which are tied, by international trade, to the economies of industrial societies, sometimes to those of only one or two industrial societies. Thus, in 1966, Belgium provided the market for more than half the exports of the Congo; the United Kingdom bought 40 per cent of Nigeria's exports and a third of Zambia's; a third of the exports of Brazil and a quarter of those of Chile went to the USA (see Table 2.4). This reliance on a restricted market (and if one groups together the two or three major importers the concentration is even more marked) further reduces the freedom of action of modernizing societies. Both investment and sales are controlled from abroad.

Colonialism, or other forms of domination by industrial countries, then, tends to result in initial economic development which usually proceeds no further than the emergence of primary production for the world market. Typically, the colonial economy was frozen at this level of primary production. The economic development of Ghana shows this common pattern (although compared with many modernizing societies Ghana is well endowed and relatively rich and prosperous). Before its formal colonization in 1874 the economy of the Gold Coast had made few responses to the centuries of sporadic contact with Europeans. There was some exporting of forest products—

particularly palm products, rubber and timber, which together accounted for more than three-quarters of the total exports. Earlier, in the eighteenth century, the area had been an important source of supply for the slave trade, exporting about 10,000 slaves per year. In addition to these exports there were, by 1891, some 1,500 persons employed directly by the colonial government; and a little over 2,000 persons employed in the gold mines, where the first attempts at commercial exploitation had been made in the late 1870s. Other than these groups and those employed in construction there was little economic activity except for farming—usually at subsistence level.

In the next twenty years the economy was transformed, principally by diversification in two directions. Firstly, the Gold Coast became a not insignificant producer of gold. In particular, the formation in 1897 of the Ashanti Goldfields Corporation, which has remained an important influence ever since, was associated with important discoveries of gold deposits and their commercial exploitation. By 1901, employment in the mines, and in the construction of a railway to serve them, was over 16,000. Second, and perhaps more important, farmers in the eastern part of the colony had begun to invest in a new crop—cocoa. By 1911 more than 600,000 acres were given over to cocoa production, compared with a mere 500 acres in 1891. The scale on which this new crop, based upon a new rural technology, was taken up is staggering. One estimate[7] puts the labour force involved in cocoa production in 1911 at 185,000 (out of a *total* population for the Gold Coast colony and Ashanti of some one and a half million). The whole economy became dependent upon these two products; together they accounted for 74 per cent of the goods exported from the Gold Coast. The mobilization of these resources, then, implied diversification and resulted in considerable economic growth. But the only other developments in the economy were those which were closely tied to this exportation of primary produce—the construction of roads, railways, harbours and the like. There was little attempt to develop manufacturing industry and one can only find isolated examples of the processing of forest products (for example, sawmills) or the provision of light construction materials (such as brickworks). Even the cocoa was processed in Europe or North America and the Gold Coast remained dependent upon Britain for manufactured consumer goods, machinery and capital goods. It was not until the granting of independence in 1957 that serious

efforts were made to introduce manufacturing industry. Indeed, the export figures for 1960 show that gold and cocoa still accounted for 77 per cent of all exports. Real per capita income approximately doubled in the last half-century of colonial rule, but the *structure* of the economy remained essentially the same.

The arresting of economic development at the level of primary production has usually been achieved by indirect processes rather than by legal restrictions upon the development of manufacturing industry. The mechanisms, however, were none the less effective for their informality. The refusal of European governments to allow tariffs barriers against their products—a policy which was often justified by an ideological appeal to the notion of free trade—stultified any growth of manufacturing industries. Other things being equal, embryo industries can rarely compete with established ones. It is very largely for this reason that political independence can be so important in the economic development of modernizing societies. Political independence allows the possibility of tariff protection for infant industries faced with competition from foreign established giants, and so makes further economic development a possibility. Under these conditions, or in time of war when international trade is dislocated, there is an opportunity to substitute home produced goods for those made in the industrial world.

It would, however, be unwise to claim too much in this direction for political independence, for the influence of industrial nations over non-industrial nations does not end with the death of colonialism. The economy frequently remains closely linked to (and sometimes controlled by) the economy of the former colonial power (see Table 2.4). The mechanisms of this economic link are no different in their essentials from those linking colony to colonizer; the most important are the factors of market dependency and foreign ownership that we have already discussed.

It is this *economic* dependence, outlasting the formal political dependence, that is termed neo-colonialism, and it shows that political independence is not always the clean break it is sometimes thought to be. Indeed, one of the most influential of the industrial nations has hardly been a colonial power in the formal sense at all. Yet American influence in the Third World, and especially in Latin America, is very considerable, and even extends to political influence. (The same, of course, could be said of the USSR and her relations with the relatively more industrial nations of Eastern Europe.) Similarly, the most important international relationships of most Latin American countries in the last 150 years have not been with Spain and Portugal, the former colonial powers, but with Britain and the USA.

Take, for example, the case of Brazil: the very process of independence in 1822 was hastened by the British in response to restrictive Portuguese trade policies which hampered the operations of British traders. The all important development of the coffee plantations was dependent upon the world (mostly American) market, and subsequent expansion was closely related to the building of railways—often British-owned or financed by British loans and built with British machinery by British engineers and technicians. For good or ill the economic development of Brazil in the second half of the nineteenth century was inextricably tied to the industrial world. As the Brazilian minister in London noted, somewhat bitterly, in 1854:[8]

> The commerce between the two countries is carried on with English capital, on English ships, by English companies. The profits, the interest on the capital, the payments for insurance, the commissions, and the dividends for the business, everything goes in to the pockets of Englishmen.

It is therefore not surprising that merchants and businessmen favoured the international division of labour. Any reduction of this specialization through diversification of the Brazilian economy was clearly seen to be against the interests of those who profited from trade, commerce and insurance. Yet, at the same time, profits were also being made by Brazilians. In particular, foreigners never controlled the production of the coffee in the way they controlled its transportation. And it was upon the basis of profits made by Brazilian planters (and behind the shield provided by world war) that initial industrial developments were later to proceed. Brazilian-British relations, however, effectively demonstrate that even political intervention does not depend upon a formal colonial relationship. On the question of the abolition of slavery in Brazil in the 1870s and 1880s, nobody (in Britain anyway) seems to have questioned the appropriateness of British intervention. Thus, the British navy not only cut off the supply of slaves by naval blockade (a Bill was introduced in the *British* parliament and entered the statute book in 1845 as the Aberdeen Act,

giving the Admiralty the right to treat all *Brazilian* slave ships as pirates), but in 1850 British ships entered Brazilian ports and rivers and seized any ships they found fitted out for the slave trade.

For the last hundred years, then, all economic development in the modernizing world has taken place in the context of world trade and international relations. It is equally clear that, while some aspects of this global situation promote economic growth and development in modernizing societies, other aspects hinder these processes. It is on the basis of such an analysis of the economic aspects of social development that we suggest that any *assumption* of industrialization, or even of substantial and continued economic growth, in modernizing societies in the short run (say the next hundred years) is by no means incontestable. In the last hundred years some countries which were little industrialized have managed to achieve self-sustaining growth and continuing differentiation through industrialization. Japan and the USSR are the most striking examples. They have joined the ranks of industrial societies with all that this implies for the standard of living, the nature of work, the process of government, and so on. It is probable that some of the contemporary modernizing societies will also become increasingly industrial. Countries like Brazil, India and Ghana show some signs of doing so. Others, such as the oil-producing countries, are undergoing substantial economic growth but with less change in the fundamental nature of the society. In all these societies there are enclaves of industrial development, of modern urban life, of bureaucracy, in the midst of a more slowly moving rural society. These are societies of great contrasts— greater, perhaps, than any society has known for a couple of centuries. In many ways the widely used term 'dual societies' is not inappropriate. Still other societies seem unlikely to undergo further significant development in the foreseeable future (unless, that is, they are incorporated into other, more developed, societies by diplomacy or conquest). Their absolute level of poverty is often extreme; high rates of population growth eat up any growth in the total output of the economy; competition from existing industrial nations makes industrial development difficult if not impossible; the interests of powerful nations demand their retention as primary producers . . . . The list is almost endless. Yet one further factor needs to be emphasized. The climate of world opinion today has been forged largely in the presently industrial societies. Standards of health, education, security and comfort have been reached in these rich societies of which the whole world is aware, for modern communications make such standards common knowledge, In this sense, too, the world is now one world. The thirst for education, the desire to live long healthy lives, and the wherewithal to achieve these ambitions have been among the more successful of the exports of the industrial world. Politicians in modernizing societies, often from the noblest of motives, frequently attempt to provide services for their people which the country simply cannot afford, and which may be detrimental to the overall economy. It is this that underlies the basic differences between the occupational differentiation of industrializing societies in the nineteenth century and the contemporary

differentiation of modernizing societies. As we noted earlier, substantial development of tertiary (service) occupations in the industrial west is a relatively recent phenomenon. It occurred *after* the huge growth of secondary (manufacturing) occupations and consequently only after high levels of societal wealth had been achieved. The development of the occupational structures of modernizing societies, with their characteristic of movement from primary occupations directly into tertiary occupations, is therefore symptomatic of the dilemma of these societies. It may well be that in this, as in other matters, the example of the development of the industrial world is as much an encumbrance to economic development as it is a help.

Notes

1 E. M. Thomas, *The Harmless People*, Harmondsworth: Penguin, 1969, pp. 20–2.
2 T. Frank, *An Economic Survey of Ancient Rome*, Baltimore: Johns Hopkins Press, 1940, volume V, p. 280.
3 Quoted in F. R. Cowell, *Cicero and the Roman Republic*, Harmondsworth: Penguin, 1956, p. 43.
4 Quoted in Taya Zinkin, *India*, London: Thames & Hudson, 1965, p. 45.
5 This term is chosen, with considerable misgivings, to refer to what are variously called 'developing countries'; 'under-developed countries'; 'countries of the Third World'; 'new nations'; or even 'industrializing countries'. It is open to most of the criticisms one might address to these alternatives and we do not use it with the usual connotation (which is a nuisance but an unavoidable one). In particular we do not argue that 'modernizing societies' are necessarily becoming more like

industrial societies. Rather, we use the term 'modernization' to refer to processes of development in predominantly non-industrial societies which are occurring *under the influence of societies which are already industrial*. Thus, in our usage, 'modernization' may involve industrialization or it may not. In short, it does not necessarily mean 'becoming more modern' if, by that, we mean 'becoming like Britain' or 'becoming like the USA'.
6 See Harry Magdoff, 'Economic aspects of US imperialism', *Monthly Review*, 18, 6 November 1966, p. 39.
7 See R. Szereszewski, *Structural Changes in the Economy of Ghana*, London: Weidenfeld & Nicolson, 1965, p. 57.
8 Quoted in Richard Graham, *Britain and the Onset of Modernization in Brazil, 1850–1914*, Cambridge University Press, 1968, p. 73.

Reading

Childe, V. G., *Man Makes Himself*, London: Collins/Fontana, 1966. A deservedly famous study of the emergence of man's earliest civilizations. Based upon archaeological evidence.
Hobsbawm, E. J., *Industry and Empire*, Harmondsworth: Penguin, 1969. A study of Britain's economic development from 1750 to mid-twentieth century. The early part of the book is especially valuable for demonstrating the international character of England's industrialization.
Maddison, A., *Economic Growth in Japan and the USSR*, London: Allen & Unwin, 1969. A short historical summary of the industrialization of two

important 'late-comers'.
Mead, M. (ed.), *Cultural Patterns and Technical Change*, New York: Mentor, 1955, ch. 2 (pp. 23–176). Consists of studies of the impact of technical change on post-second-world-war Greece, Burma, Tiv (Nigeria), Palau, and the Spanish Americans of New Mexico.
Thomas, E. M., *The Harmless People*, Harmondsworth: Penguin, 1969. A vivid description, by an anthropologist/traveller, of an expedition to the 'kung Bushmen of the Kalahari desert. Gives an insight into many aspects of Bushman life.

Further reading

Cowell, F. R., *Cicero and the Roman Republic*, Harmondsworth: Penguin, 1956. A social, political and economic history of republican Rome. Lively and readable.

Dobb, M., *An Economic History of Russia since 1917: Soviet Economic Development since 1917*, London: Routledge & Kegan Paul, 1966. A standard, but still highly readable interpretation of Soviet economic development.

Gibbs, P. (ed.), *Peoples of Africa*, New York: Holt, Rinehart & Winston, 1965. Contains short descriptions of the social institutions and way of life of fifteen traditional African societies. Useful for political, religious and family background as well as for economic background.

Kerr, C. *et al.*, *Industrialism and Industrial Man*, London: Heinemann, 1962. Suggests that the 'logic of industrialism' is making industrial societies more alike.

Postan, M. M. (ed.), *The Cambridge Economic History of Europe*, vol. VI, Cambridge University Press, 1966. Provides an authoritative and detailed account of the economic development of Europe.

Robson, P. and Lury, D. A. (eds), *The Economies of Africa*, London: Allen & Unwin, 1968. Brief and informative studies of seven African countries. Each section is written by an economist with personal knowledge of the society.

Wolf, E., *Sons of the Shaking Earth*, London: University of Chicago Press, 1959. A stylish and scholarly account of Middle American Society, tracing the emergence and growth of the Maya and Aztec civilizations and the transformation under the Spanish conquest.

3 Political aspects of social development

Parliaments; dictatorships; presidents; diplomacy; political parties; international assemblies: these are some of the more common pictures aroused in most of us by the term politics. Yet even with their considerable diversity they scarcely begin to cover the very considerable variety of social situation within which the art of politics is practised. They do, however, comprise some of the more important institutions through which law and order are maintained in and between the industrial nations of the twentieth century. And, because industrial nation states dominate the contemporary world, their politics forms the greater part of our subject matter. In industrial nations the majority of the population participates in politics in one way or another. The decisions of political leaders affect everybody in the society. They are discussed, with more or less frankness, in newspapers, on the radio and on television, and are consequently exposed to public scrutiny. In terms of human history, however, all this is very new. Only two hundred years ago 'the people' were not involved in state politics at all. Affairs of state were, in most pre-industrial societies, matters for the king or emperor and for selected members of his court. In earlier and still simpler societies, political organization was even more different from that of industrial societies. And in the simplest, a specialized political organization could not be distinguished from social organization more generally. It is with such societies we must start if we are to reach an understanding of politics.

Politics in simple societies

In the simplest societies of which we have records there are no differentiated political institutions nor persons who specialize in political activities. Take, for example, the Bushmen of the Kalahari desert:[1]

> The social structure of Bushmen is not complicated. They have no chiefs or Kings, only headmen who in function are virtually indistinguishable from the people they lead, and sometimes a band will not even have a headman. A leader is not really necessary, however, because the Bushmen roam about together in small family bands rarely numbering more than twenty people. A band may consist of an old man and his wife, their daughters, their daughters' husbands, perhaps an unmarried son or two, and their daughters' children.

Yet the absence of kings, chiefs, armies, courts, police forces and administrators does not mean that political life is chaotic. On the contrary, political life is the concern of the whole society; political authority is dispersed throughout the society.

In societies where the dominant economic activity is hunting wild animals and gathering wild fruits, the sheer struggle for survival is often such as to reduce physical violence and armed conflict between groups to a mininum. The scarcity of food (at any rate in most *surviving* societies of this type) means that the size of the group is rarely more than a few dozen and even this group often splits up for relatively long periods. This small size also facilitates harmony. Perhaps the most important factor, however, is the uncertainty that is attendant upon a hand-to-mouth existence of this kind. Where food is so hard to come by, the very survival of the group may be dependent upon a hunter's willingness to share his catch. Often, too, success in hunting is dependent upon co-operation between the hunters. These simplest societies, then, far from Hobbes' 'war of every man against every man', provide what is probably the most peaceful and co-operative type of society the world has ever known. Social relationships in such societies are governed by informal group controls and they apply pressures which are none the less effective for their informality. A hunter refusing to share his kill, for example, would probably be excluded from all social contact (although so heinous an offence is all but unthinkable). A punishment like this is virtually a death sentence.

In some societies only a little more complex than the hunting band, however, the potentialities for the outbreak of violence are much greater. There are well-defined customs, rights and obligations which lay down the occasions and conditions justifying the use of force, but no general limitation as to who may use it. Which person or group is empowered to administer a punishment depends very much on the nature of the offence. Kinship ties are particularly important. Often, as for example among the Nuer of the southern Sudan or the Tonga of Zambia, kinship is organized on the basis of lineages. These may be reckoned either through the male line (Nuer), in which case sons and daughters are members of their father's lineage; or through the female line (Tonga), in which case they are members of the mother's lineage. In either case there are solemn obligations to one's lineage—including the duty to protect the property and honour of the lineage. These help to maintain the peace, for the threat of revenge by aggrieved kinsmen is usually a sufficient guarantee of conformity to the customs of the society. Apart from fear of personal injury, it is universally recognized in these small-scale societies that open conflict is too inconvenient to be tolerated. In addition, lineages are invariably exogamous—that is to say, marriage within the lineage is forbidden. There are consequently numerous marriage ties between the lineages; and men think twice about attacking a rival lineage if their daughters are married into the rival group. Thus inter-lineage marriage mitigates conflict between lineages.

Kinship ties, however, are by no means the only obligations of a member of a simple society. There are other important characteristics of 'stateless' societies that intensify the inconvenience of con-flict and so militate against it. These provide further ties which bind members of one kinship group to another. Frequently the lineage does not live together in a territorial block but is dispersed among a number of villages. So conflict with a neighbouring village involves conflict with members of one's own lineage; conflict with another lineage is likely to involve conflict with one's neighbours. Among both Nuer and Tonga, lineage and residence are the most important of the 'cross-cutting ties' that reduce the likelihood of resort to violence, for if a dispute does occur there are influential social pressures for a peaceful settlement.

In a number of East African tribes, the Turkana, the Karimojong and the Kikuyu for instance, the most important of these 'cross-cutting ties' is the existence of age grades. All those initiated into adulthood at any one time (or in any one period) are members of the same age grade and are bound together by vows of mutual obligation. Yet the age grade is scattered geographically throughout the society and consequently a dispute with, say, a neighbouring village will involve conflict with one's age mates. Such divided allegiances provide added pressures to resolve disputes peacefully.

In addition there is, in all simple societies, a variety of common features which bind members of the society to one another. A common language; common customs; a common religion; all provide some attachment to the group, however vague. Religion is often the most effective of these. Great rituals and religious festivals have an important unifying effect. This can clearly be seen among the Tallensi—a tribe of northern Ghana. Quarrels, fighting and even warfare were common between the various clans of the Tallensi but all had to come together in peace for the great religious ceremonies. In the words of the foremost student of this society:[2]

> The Great Festivals . . . are periods of ritually sanctioned truce, when all conflicts and disputes must be abandoned for the sake of ceremonial co-operation . . . . In this festival cycle, therefore, the widest Tale community emerges . . . . It means the dominance, for a period, of the forces of integration ever present in the social structure—in kinship, clanship, chiefship and tendaanaship (priesthood)—but generally submerged by the sectional interest, springing from these same institutions, that divide Tale society into a multitude of independent corporate units.

As well as this ritual unification, there are super-natural sanctions to command obedience to custom. Thus, among the Turkana, murder is virtually unknown since it is believed to prevent rain; and to a pastoralist people in semi-desert country there can be no greater threat.

These are some of the most important mechanisms that serve to integrate societies which have no centralized political authority. But such societies provide (even in their twentieth-century examples) an almost endless variety. The one thing they have in common is an absence of the specialized political institutions that we call the state (or the government). With the emergence of the state the nature of politics (and of society) changes drastically.

The development of the state

The most important characteristic of the state which distinguishes it from the simpler societies we have so far considered is that it is able to exert power; if necessary it can *force* its members to carry out certain tasks. More accurately one should say that those in control of the state apparatus are able to force others to do their will. Those who control the state monopolize the rightful use of physical force. They use it to maintain order; to protect the state against other states; to enforce the laws of the state (which reinforce the less formal custom): and they forbid its use by private individuals or groups. Violence becomes the prerogative of the officers of the state. In order that this may be achieved, armies, police forces and the like are developed which owe their loyalty to the central authority; courts develop to decide the fate of those who break the law; and kings to whom these organizations are responsible stand at the head of the hierarchy. All this is expensive: so states invariably develop some sort of tax system to centralize resources. This may involve a monetary system of taxation; it may involve gifts in kind to the central authority; it may involve some form of labour tax, either voluntary or forced labour, which at its extreme may resemble slavery. Whatever the details, state formation is characterized by the gradual establishment, within a given territory, of twin monopolies: over the use of physical force, and over taxation. The other major aspect of the process of state formation is a gradual growth in the size of territory. This results from the incessant competition between states and the absorption or conquest of the weaker states by the stronger ones.

We know relatively little about the very early stages of this process as it occurred in Mesopotamia, in Egypt, in the new world Maya and Inca societies, and in the ancient Chinese civilization which centred on the Yellow River. The initial growth of the specialized political institutions of the state in such societies, however, is probably closely linked to the emergence of social stratification. Some groups manage to organize military, administrative and religious affairs in a way which acts to their advantage. The establishment of further state offices of law and taxation furthers this process. Thus (especially in less developed states) the law tends to protect the interests of the ruling group; taxes are paid *by* peasants *to* priests or kings; the army is commanded by the strong at the expense of the weak. The emergence of the political state, then, is one manifestation of the growth in wealth and power of one small section of the population. It presupposes the establishment of surplus production which in turn must (except in an exceptionally favourable area) be based upon the domestication of crops or animals. Yet the emergence of the state is by no means inevitable. We know of many simple agricultural societies which have existed for hundreds of years without developing a state form of organization.

Under certain conditions this administrative complexity, and even the central authority itself, breaks down. With the decay of the administrative system, the king or emperor has less control over his territory and becomes increasingly reliant upon provincial lords for the administration of the land and the provision of revenue. The revenue of the state declines so that the central authority can no longer pay armies, and the decreased power of the ruler often means that he cannot conscript soldiers. He becomes increasingly dependent upon the lords for the military power of the state. Sometimes, as most spectacularly in China, again and again one of the provincial lords rises to pre-eminence and, claiming the mandate of heaven, reinstitutes a new dynasty. Thus, the Chinese Empire lasted for some two thousand years but with many different dynasties.

As the size of the state increases, as the demand for taxes arises, as military and administrative problems multiply, and as the king delegates some of his authority, so the organs of administration expand and become more bureaucratic. The development of literacy is crucial since it makes possible the impersonal promulgation of rules. The establishment of a centralized political authority is but the beginning of the process; it is followed by continual differentiation within the political realm. Some of the authority which initially pertains to the *person* of the king is given to officers of the state. Generals fight wars; judges enforce the law; administrators collect taxes; all in the name of the ruler. This delegation of authority creates a recognizable machinery of state. And the further the specialization of state tasks is taken, the more bureaucratic the administration becomes. So in modern industrial states or the imperial states of China or Rome the administrative machinery becomes very complex. But the process of state formation is not irreversible. Or, to put it another way, political changes are not always in the direction of larger, more highly centralized, more complex units. Sometimes the exercise of power becomes fragmented and decentralized. In the place of the once powerful state there emerges a whole series of smaller units in competition with each other for relatively small territories. From this base, the process of state formation starts again.

It was a process of this kind which followed the decline of the Roman Empire in Europe. In what later came to be called England, a series of invasions by Germanic tribes subjugated the local population with more or less success, and a multiplicity of small kingdoms was established. The rulers of these kingdoms were engaged in a perpetual struggle with the Britons and with each other. In the course of these struggles the warriors formed alliances for the purposes of conquest or defence, and frequently enough, these developed into stable political units. Wessex, for example, is thought to have its origins in a confederation formed to drive the Britons out of the South Midlands. By the seventh century this competition between the Angle and Saxon kingdoms had led to the emergence of the three giants—Northumbria, Mercia, and Wessex—each with a variable group of satellites. For the next three hundred years, the rulers of these three major kingdoms were engaged in a struggle to consolidate their power and to establish control over the whole of England. Fortunes fluctuated. First Northumbria, then Mercia, and finally Wessex established dominance. The smaller kingdoms, such as Essex, Kent, and Sussex were increasingly subordinated to their larger neighbours. But while the units of political organization were growing larger, the techniques of warfare and the methods of raising and organizing an army had remained essentially the same. In Mercia and Northumbria in the ninth century, they proved inadequate in the face of Danish invasions. Faced with the same problem Alfred developed something approaching a standing army, introduced new military tactics based upon the use of fortresses, and established a fleet of sailing ships. These military reforms provided an important part of the basis upon which his descendants were able to consolidate their control over a united Kingdom of England. A similar process of the enlargement and consolidation that is so important a part of state formation was evident in other parts of Europe and, indeed, the process is still continuing. The current tentative and hesitating steps towards the creation of some kind of European union are illustrative.

The early English societies also provide a series of instructive cases in the establishment of the monopolies over the use of force and the raising of revenue. The authority that Alfred's descendants were able to exert over the greater part of England was relatively weak because the development of these monopolies was in its early stages. The kings had no centralized administration through which to rule. They were consequently dependent upon the loyalty of ealdormen—the local lords through whom they ruled. It was the ealdorman who collected the local taxes, dispensed justice, and raised and led the forces of his district in war. The king was unable effectively to monopolize the use of force because of his military dependence on the ealdormen; and he only received a proportion of the taxes which the ealdormen collected. This dispersal of power to the local level constituted a threat to the stability of the kingdom—especially at times when the succession was in dispute. The king's weakness and dependence on his ealdormen severely circumscribed his action, for he could not afford to antagonize them as a group. It was not until a later stage of state formation, when effective monopolies over force and taxation had been established, that the king's authority was increased.

A number of the Kingdoms of East Africa were undergoing a similar process of state formation in the nineteenth century when colonization by the more powerful states of Europe upset the process. (Of course, colonization is itself part of the development of larger political units.) The myths of origin of several of these states—Buganda, Ankole, Nyoro, Toro and Ruanda—suggest that conquest and competition was crucial. The conquering groups were nomadic tribes from the north who, probably because they were nomadic, proved to be militarily superior to the settled agriculturalists. After conquest the defeated agriculturalists were made to provide food for the far smaller numbers of victorious pastoralists. This economic exploitation proceeded in step with political domination. The normal course was for the 'inferior' agriculturalists to be forbidden any form of military service so that military power was monopolized by the upper stratum.

These states were only loosely integrated, with the aristocratic pastoralists paying allegiance to the king and rendering him military service in return for the spoils of war. The king and his court provided a central authority but there was little in the way of a central administration. The authority of the king was mediated through a series of chiefs, each administering a local territory. In their territories, the chiefs controlled the militia, collected the revenue, and administered justice. Their loyalty to the king was dependent upon his continued effective protection. In addition there was continual conflict between states. The stronger states, like Buganda, were expanding at the expense of the smaller and weaker ones, many of which were only able to retain a measure of autonomy by the payment of tribute. So the situation was constantly changing.

One aspect of the further development of the state is the emergence of a specialized central administration and a more specialized (and eventually full-time) army, both directly responsible to the ruler. Inca society, for example, had a military organization that was dependent on the ruler and paid by him. The central administration was staffed by specialists whose sole task was to carry out the ruler's commands. Since they, too, were paid by the ruler and had no other sources of livelihood, they proved relatively easy to control. The existence of a standing army and a permanent administration enables a much more efficient appropriation of surplus wealth through taxation to be effected. As these institutions of state develop, the balance of power between the ruler and his lieutenants is tilted in the ruler's favour, and the inequalities of income and wealth increase. Such inequalities require justification, for no state relies *solely* upon force to command the obedience of its members. There is always an ideology that it is right that the ruling group should rule; that the government is legitimate. Sometimes this is based upon a notion of the 'fitness' of the king or aristocracy to rule; upon the idea that they are natural rulers. Most often in the less developed states, however, the government gained its legiti-

macy from the dominant religion of the society. Thus, the pharaohs of Egypt were themselves considered to be divine (and divine kingship was common among the simpler states of pre-twentieth-century Africa). In ancient China the emperor ruled with the mandate of heaven; in Mesopotamia the king was also the priest who interpreted the will of God; and in many more recent states the ruler has been viewed as the representative of the god or gods. The ruling group also tends to have a monopoly of knowledge (whether religious or secular) and so is able to control the flow of information to the rest of the population. This helps to secure legitimacy for the state and its major function of concentrating power and so supporting the social, political and economic superiority of some groups at the expense of others.

The huge inequalities in wealth and power meant that politics, which in this type of society centred on the struggle for the establishment and control of the apparatus of state, became the sole preserve of the ruler and his court. It was out of societies of this type that the contemporary industrial nation states developed, so it is to a more detailed consideration of the European manifestation of this type of state that we now turn.

Politics in the dynastic states of Europe

In the sixteenth and seventeenth centuries, European politics were the exclusive preserve of the monarch, his court, and members of the aristocracy. Together they made all the major decisions concerning the maintenance of law and order, and they were the only persons concerned with 'foreign affairs'. The majority of the population had no part in the political process and the hereditary nature of kingship meant that succession to the most powerful office in the land was not contestable. Politics consequently tended to be restricted to preserving the interests of king and aristocracy. This involved two things: the continued subjugation of the mass of the population; and increasing the wealth, power and territory of the kingdom at the expense of other kingdoms.

The exclusion of the mass of the population from participation in the political affairs of the state reflected the huge gap that existed between the wealth and power of rulers and ruled. The monarch invariably owned a large part of the territory he ruled (in one estimate for eighteenth-century Prussia, for example, the royal estates comprised at least a third of the total arable area);

he controlled the administration of justice; he was empowered to collect taxes; and he commanded the obedience of the army. With such a concentration of political and economic power the vast majority of the population had no political significance. In Russia, in the middle of the nineteenth century, the 27 million men and women who were state peasants were regarded as the property of the Tsar and could be moved around like pawns in a giant game of chess. Earlier, between 1762 and 1801, Catherine the Great and her son Paul gave away 1,400,000 of them without seriously depleting the resources of the House of Romanov. Differences in wealth and power between rulers and ruled were reinforced by differences of language, education and style of life.

In such a society the control of the monarch and aristocracy over the peasants was highly effective. The peasants were usually economically dependent upon their social superiors, and they were invariably tied to one locality. This fostered a parochial outlook in which the affairs of state were seen as being of little relevance (apart from the unpleasant necessity to pay 'taxes'). More importantly, however, the peasant is typically isolated from other peasants and this isolation prevents the growth of any permanent political organization based upon their common interests. When, in spite of these factors, conditions were so bad as to prompt some sort of rebellion, the protest either took the form of an appeal (sometimes violent, sometimes peaceful) that the monarch himself should rectify the situation or, alternatively, an appeal to God that he should intervene. In this latter case the protest took on a religious flavour, usually with strong millenarian overtones. In either case, however, the clash of interests was always resolved in favour of the rulers since, in the last analysis, the pitchforks of peasants are scarcely a match for the military might and discipline of professional soldiers. Invariably rebellions that were temporarily successful occurred in remote, mountainous regions where the local knowledge and the nature of the terrain made the struggle more equal.

However, the monarch was not all-powerful. He was dependent upon the support of the aristocracy, very largely because they were the other important landowners. Their power lay primarily in the fact that their wealth and property provided a potential source of independence from and opposition to the king. Furthermore, it was from this group that the king had to recruit trustworthy staff to man his household and administration. Thus, as long as agriculture was the major source of wealth, ownership and control of land were the most important requirements for entry into the ruling group.

Even at this time, however, land was not the only source of wealth. Increasingly, the dynastic states of Europe were affected by commerce. The buying, selling and transport of goods and services increased throughout this period with the spread of a money economy and with the growth of markets. Towns and cities, in which this type of activity was centred, flourished, and the merchants, who controlled trade, grew more wealthy and more powerful. One of the ways in which merchants translated their wealth into political power was by underwriting the expenses of the monarch. Financing day-to-day administration and court life, to say nothing of keeping up with the increasing cost of warfare, was a continual problem, and by turning to the merchants for support many kings were able to avoid excessive reliance on the aristocracy. Thus, the aristocracy as a group, gradually lost some of their power to the new merchant classes. Or to put it another way: political participation extended to include the wealthy merchants.

The struggle for power between these three groups—monarchy, aristocracy and merchants—dominates the political life of this type of society. Its consequences, however, were not identical in all European states. The English aristocracy had the greatest success in curtailing the centralization of power in the hands of the king. One of the reasons for this was that, with the development of the warship, the Tudor monarchs devoted a large part of their resources to the establishment of a strong navy to the neglect of the army. The English kings were thus unable to call upon a large army in their disputes with the aristocracy, and navies, however effective for external defence, are severely limited as a means of maintaining internal control. The aristocracy, through their control of parliament, were gradually able to restrict the power of the king. When a standing army did develop in England, it did so under the financial control of parliament, which, in turn, was dominated by the aristocracy.

By contrast the other European monarchs relied for the defence of their countries on large standing armies, and therefore placed the control and financing of the army high on their list of priorities. Their tighter control over the army gave them a greater power over the aristocracy than the English kings had. Louis XIV of France, for example, was successful in establishing a powerful army and making it responsible solely to himself. It was because of this that he was able to insist on the attendance of the French aristocracy at his court; they were not powerful enough to risk disobedience. Moreover, he was able to reduce aristocratic power still further by appointing a number of non-aristocrats to important positions in his administration.

In both France and England, however, effective internal control was achieved, and this made possible the collection of the relatively large tax income which was necessary to support the armed forces and administration. For the peaceful administration of states the size of seventeenth-century England the eighteenth-century France required a relatively complex and bureaucratic administration. Members of the royal household began to be paid for their service with salaries— the beginnings of modern civil services. While this initially enhanced the power of the king at the expense of the aristocracy, in the long run it brought new forces into the political arena. For officials emerged with some form of specialized training and/or skills and they became more and more indispensable to the central government. They thus abrogated some power to themselves, although in the early days this was strictly limited. At the lower levels of administration there was a similar growth of officials paid by the crown in order to assist in the execution of royal policy. In England the justices of the peace developed in this manner, being appointed by and responsible to the crown and so reducing the king's dependence on the aristocracy who had previously performed these tasks.

In terms of naked power, then, the monarch played one group off against another and, with varying degrees of success, managed to control those groups that threatened his position. Yet since no government relies solely on coercion to ensure the obedience of its subjects, all rulers attempt to establish the legitimacy of their rule. In the dynastic states the right to rule was hereditary; the throne was monopolized by a single family for several generations. Thus in England the Tudors and then the Stuarts were dominant; in France the Bourbons ruled. The 'rightness' of the succession was supported by the dominant religion, a support that was symbolized by the religious nature of the coronation itself. Moreover, not only the succession but the rule itself received ecclesiastical approval and so was made more generally acceptable. At its height this was formalized in the doctrine of the divine right of kings, in which the king was seen to rule on behalf of God and therefore could do no wrong. The close relationship between church and state was further reinforced by the frequent practice whereby the monarch appointed church leaders to positions of secular power. In short, the church and the monarchy were mutually supportive.

The development of the industrial state

The monarchs in the dynastic states were successful in establishing the twin monopolies of physical force and taxation and the beginning of a permanent administrative system. In the industrial state, the problem is no longer how the machinery of state will be established, but in whose interests it will be used. This change is reflected in the gradual development of a more effective administration, in the bureaucratization of the state, and an extension in the tasks it performs. Originally state administrations consist of servants and domestics recruited by the king on the basis of their personal loyalty to him, or often their family connections with him. In industrial states they consist of relatively autonomous bureaucratic organizations which recruit their employees from a wide variety of sections of the population according to impersonal criteria like the educational qualifications they hold.

Already in the European dynastic states many specialized offices of state had developed. In England, for example, the Lord Chamberlain was originally responsible for looking after the king's chamber, a task which included responsibility for the money which the king habitually kept there. By the time of Henry VIII his tasks had been narrowed down until his sole charge was the administration of finance. In this way the king's staff grew large and more specialized—partly because of the increase in size of the territories, which necessitated a larger and more efficient administration. Later the development of colonialism continued this expansion and led to the growth of new aspects of government administration. Other factors, however, were rather more important in the continued and increased expansion of government in nineteenth- and twentieth-century Europe. One particularly important factor is the increasing division of labour in the society as a whole. Old tasks are more and more subdivided and new specialized tasks emerge in the course of technological innovations. As a result of this, more people are required to co-ordinate these specialized tasks. So the growth of government administration reflects the increasing specialization in the society as a whole.

Moreover, with the increase in political participation the activities of the state expand to include the provision of education, health and social security in addition to the maintenance of law and order and external defence. Increasingly, too, the governments of contemporary industrial societies are becoming more directly involved in the field of economic affairs. The governments of some industrial societies have, of course, been directly involved with the management of the economy from the start. This is especially the case in socialist countries, but the Japanese government has shown a similar, though less extreme, concern. Since the great depression of the 1930s, the governments of capitalist countries, too, have taken more action in the direction of the economy, especially with regard to the control of unemployment and the rate of economic growth. The dominance of government contracts (especially military contracts) in many industries brings further government involvement. This expansion of the activities of the state, then, helps us to understand the massive growth in size of government bureaucracies.

There have also been important changes in the nature of state administrations. The personal loyalty to the rulers of the dynastic states was often achieved by appointing relatives or friends to influential positions. But frequently the king did not have the monetary resources to pay all his servants and officials a regular income. (Often his wealth was tied up in immobile assets like land.) There were a number of ways in which this problem was solved. A common solution was to allow officers of state to extract an income from their job: thus the Lord Chief Justice in England was allowed to keep a proportion of the fines he imposed. The subtle distinction between the public income of the office and the private income of the individual had not yet developed. Because many official positions were highly lucrative and could be used as a means of amassing fortunes it was possible to sell them to help fill the exchequer. In this way Louis XIV sold state positions in France to merchants. In England, too, this solution was common. Henry Bishop, the inventor of the post mark, paid £21,500 for the position of Postmaster General—a lucrative post which later cost more than £40,000.

The considerable capital outlay on such an 'investment' severely restricted recruitment to government service which became a highly desirable career for the sons of the aristocracy and landed gentry. The lack of differentiation between 'politician' and 'administrator' allowed gentlemen to combine the opportunity to exercise their 'natural' political leadership with the chance to amass a fortune. The financial gains of office, however, did not only come from taxpayers and offenders against the law. The government itself was a constant source of remuneration—in kind if not always in cash. To take one example, once in office in the England of George III, further offices were often given as an encouragement to vote for the government. Often enough, though, the cash pay-off was substantial: it is said that in a single morning George III paid £25,000 to members of parliament who supported him on the Treaty of Utrecht.

During the nineteenth century the revenue available to the governments of European societies gradually increased, and states were able to pay regular salaries to their personnel. With this development a strict separation was more and more enforced between the salary of the administrator and the wealth he administered in his work. With the nineteenth-century competition between European states it also became evident that competence and ability were crucial to effective administration: and the rise of the middle classes made it increasingly clear that these virtues were not the monopoly of the aristocracy. The second half of the nineteenth century is characterized by a number of important changes. In England these were formalized in a variety of legislative reforms: Haldane's army reforms, Gladstone's reform of the civil service, and a variety of local government reforms. The effect of these was to abolish patronage and the sale of government office, and to make appointment to government service more or less dependent upon success in competitive examinations. This did not radically alter patterns of recruitment into government service, for only the aristocracy and the *nouveaux riches* could afford the education necessary for examination success. Nevertheless, it did mean that the civil service became a full-time career with the possibility of appointment and promotion on merit, rather than a way to get rich quick from the legislative and executive offices of parliament. Being full-time employees largely dependent upon their salary for a livelihood, the behaviour of the 'new' civil servant was more easily controlled by his superiors. He was dependent upon his employment and consequently vulnerable to threats of dismissal or loss of promotion.

These changes in the organization of the civil service also laid the basis for a new and different code of public morality. It became 'wrong' for civil servants (and, by extension, employees of large public or private companies) to use the money they handled at work for their personal gain. It became 'wrong' for a public servant to use his influence to get friends and relatives government jobs. It became 'wrong' for a civil servant to accept bribes for providing a more efficient service or for steering a government contract into certain hands. (Although, of course, all these things do go on in industrial societies, albeit illegally and to a limited extent.) These changes in public morality have only become possible with the distinction between office and office holder.

Class formation and the balance of power

Wherever industrialization has occurred it has been associated with important changes in the relationship between rulers and ruled. In particular, in non-socialist societies at any rate, it has been related to the emergence of social classes and the changing distribution of power between them. The development of commerce had resulted in an increase in the power of the merchants. The growth of manufacturing industry led to the growth of a new middle class whose position was based upon manufacture rather than trade, and who controlled an ever-increasing proportion of the wealth of the country. Although their wealth came from a different source, the political position of the industrialist and the merchant was similar. The rulers were increasingly dependent upon them to finance the international wars of expansion and defence upon which the relative standing of the states of Europe was based. In spite of their increasing wealth, however, the industrialists and businessmen were effectively excluded from important political positions. The disregard of their interests by the ruling élite led to an intense political struggle. The ruling group—particularly the aristocracy—tried to maintain their privileges and their domination of the peasants. The manufacturers and businessmen demanded the abolition of such privilege: the introduction of a rational and 'equitable' tax system; an efficient system of administration; and, more generally, social conditions in which free enterprise could flourish.

In France, where the aristocracy persistently resisted these demands, middle-class political frustration coincided with mounting peasant unrest to produce a violent overthrow of the dynastic state. The French Revolution with its expulsion of the aristocracy and the establishment of some sort of 'peoples' government' (albeit on a very restricted franchise) demonstrated the fragility of the political framework of the dynastic states and the possibility of a sudden extension of political participation. Political power was transferred from the king and aristocracy to the middle classes, although the working classes and the peasantry were excluded from the political community until after 1848.

In England, where as a result of the civil war power had already passed from the king to the aristocracy in parliament, the conflict was eventually resolved through the opening of parliament to members of the middle classes. The extension of political participation, in the form of the franchise, to the middle classes in the reforms of 1832 thus marked the conclusion of a long struggle with the aristocracy. The aristocrats' hereditary right to rule was no longer unquestioned; there were now pressures to allow those who had been economically successful a full share in government. Aristocratic monopoly of political power was broken, and for the rest of the nineteenth century the middle classes gradually increased their representation in parliament (and even in the cabinet) at the expense of aristocratic families. After 1832 the main battleground for the struggle between the landed aristocracy and the manufacturers was parliament itself, and the continued intensity of the conflict can be seen from controversies such as that surrounding the corn laws. Here the conflict of interest between the two groups is clear—the landowners trying to protect their prices through the maintenance of taxes on imported corn, and the industrialists attempting to keep the cost of food (and therefore labour) down by abolishing such protection. That the abolitionists were ultimately successful shows how far the balance of power had already changed by the middle of the nineteenth century.

In addition to increasing the wealth and power of the middle classes, the growth of manufacturing industry created new conditions of work for the mass of the population. The agricultural wage labourers who migrated to the industrial towns found themselves in a very different situation. They were concentrated in large numbers near the factories in which they worked and their increased awareness of their common situation, coupled with the greater ease of communicating with each other, made them more capable of sustained political action. Moreover, the growth of collective action enabled them to halt industrial production and this gave them a powerful weapon in their fight with the enfranchised classes. In short the conditions of an urban, industrial society transformed them into a new class of industrial workers.

By the middle of the nineteenth century the working classes in England already had a history of political protest. Initially they had lent their support to the middle classes in the struggle with the aristocracy but the failure of the 1832 Reform Act to concede anything to the working classes contributed to the growth of the Chartist movement. The Chartists had some success in mobilizing support among the urban population and the movement was significant partly because it illustrated the power potential of the workers. Thereafter, and especially with the emergence of trade unions, working-class organization for political and industrial activities became more efficient and more effective. The formal reflection of this was the succession of Acts of Parliament which gradually extended the franchise to include working-class men. As the franchise was extended to include all adult men in the society (and later women too) so the basis of recruitment into parliament widened. The miners Keir Hardie and Ernest Bevin, the ironworker Arthur Henderson and the insurance clerk Philip Snowden joined the aristocrats, industrialists and businessmen at Westminster.

It was not until after the first world war, however, that the representatives of the working classes were able to achieve any position of real power *within* parliament. Even today professional politicians are, on the whole, drawn disproportionately from some social groups rather than others although there have, of course, been considerable changes in the last hundred years. Government may now claim to be very largely *for* the people; to what extent is it directly *by* the people? Such a question clearly would not have occurred in the dynastic states, ruled as they were by a small élite. But even much later, when wider groups were involved in politics and *influenced* political decisions, those who *took* the decisions were still highly unrepresentative even of the electorate. In mid-nineteenth-century Britain, for example, the landowning classes still provided the majority of members of the cabinet. In the period from 1830 to 1868 there were 103 cabinet members. Fifty-six

of them were large territorial Lords or the sons of such Lords; twelve were country gentlemen; twenty-one were from the mercantile and administrative upper class; and fourteen were *hommes nouveaux* of 'no family' (most of them were lawyers).[3] By the middle of the twentieth century the proportion of aristocrats had declined but the cabinet was still somewhat socially exclusive. Thus nearly one half of the cabinet members between 1935 and 1955 were either aristocrats and landowners or had attended one of the seven 'top' public schools. The broadening of the social background of members of the cabinet since that time has been reflected in the declining representation of aristocrats (never, of course, conspicuous in Labour ranks). A large proportion of cabinet members, however, have been ex-public schoolboys (about 40 per cent of Labour members and 90 per cent of Conservative members). Thus, the extension of political participation has resulted in some broadening of the social groups from which political leaders are recruited, although cabinets are by no means representative (in terms of social background) of the population as a whole.

The political scene today then is very different from that in the dynastic states of Europe. In contemporary industrial societies politics is no longer the exclusive province of the king and the aristocracy; rulers of industrial societies do not regard the state as their own property. *All* groups and *all* strata in the society are involved with the affairs of state. Major political decisions—say the provision of more schools or the regulation of the economy—are therefore made not only in terms of the interests of the rulers but also have to take account of the interests of other sections of the population. And even in less important matters governments have to take account of the views of any well-organized groups that will be affected.

In the contemporary situation of international competition and rivalry, the power of each state depends upon economic productivity as well as upon the size and capacity of its armed forces. It is because of this that threats, from any section of the population, to disrupt the economy have such political importance. The ruling group has become dependent upon the performance of the whole population. Thus, the government of General de Gaulle was seriously threatened by the general strike of 1967 and was only able to save itself (and then only temporarily) by meeting some of the demands of the workers. In highly complex societies the refusal (or inability) of any specialized group, be they dockers, doctors, diplomats or dustmen, to continue with their activities can disrupt the working of the whole society.

One of the results of this twin process—the extension of political participation and the growing interdependence of sections of industrial societies—is that governments have had to become more and more concerned with the provision of social welfare. The nineteenth-century involvement of the government with elementary education in England and Wales derived partly from both of these sources. The Reform Acts of 1832 and 1867 were crucial to this involvement as were the increasing requirements of industry for workers with some rudimentary education. The growth of government health services had similar stimuli. Perhaps the nineteenth-century public health measures were primarily based upon what, to the upper classes, must have been a distressing lack of class discrimination on behalf of epidemic diseases as they ravaged the densely populated towns. Public health was consequently in their interests as much as anyone's. The twentieth-century spread of medical care, however, derived chiefly from other changes in the nature of the society. In industry and in warfare, in particular, it became impossible to maximize efficiency because of the poor health of the population. Yet the nature of both modern industry and twentieth-century warfare was such that maximum efficiency from *everybody* was required for success. Thus increased dependence upon the ordinary worker and soldier was important.

So all sections of modern society have become indispensable to the government. Directly, governments are often (but not always) dependent upon votes to remain in office. Economically and militarily they are dependent upon the services of the population. This dependence has been instrumental in the extension of the role of government (which, in turn, makes each individual more dependent upon the state).

Political parties

The gradual widening of the scope of politics has occurred in all industrial societies, but it has taken place within different forms of political organization. In Western Europe the context has been that of multi-party states; in the Soviet Union a similar process has occurred within the framework of a one-party state. In the case of the Soviet Union many of the processes we have already discussed

for England have been evident in the years since the second world war. The Soviet government has increasingly had to take into account the interest of the mass of the population, and this has resulted in the provision of better housing, health facilities and pensions, greater security of employment, and, more recently, the decision to devote more of the country's resources to the production of consumer goods. This reorientation from the harsher days of more 'absolute' rule is reflected in the following extract from an anti-China speech made by Nikita Kruschev in 1964:[4]

> There are people in the world who call themselves Marxist-Leninists and at the same time say there is no need to strive for a better life. According to them only one thing is important—revolution. *Communism will achieve little if it cannot give the people what they want.* The important thing is that we should have more to eat, schools, housing, and ballet.

This view, however, is a recent one and the outcome of relative affluence. The earlier development of the Communist party of the Soviet Union (as it later came to be known) similarly reflects the condition of the society as a whole. Originally, the party was only one of forty competing factions that comprised the revolutionary movement in late nineteenth-century Russia. Political power in Russia at this time (as in other dynastic states) was concentrated in the office of the emperor; the mass of the population, including the small but growing industrial middle and working classes, was excluded from positions of power. The collapse of the Russian Empire, and especially the destruction of the army in 1917, provided these revolutionary groups with the chance to seize power. They had enough mass support and were sufficiently well organized to carry out and consolidate the revolution.

Once they had established a monopoly of the use of physical force, the leaders of the Communist party were faced with the task of stabilizing the new state. Territorial integrity had to be preserved against other states, and the various sections of the old Russian state had to be made to live together in peace. The ideology of Marxism fitted well with these requirements, for the further and rapid development of industry would help to provide a technologically more efficient army, and the party provided a means whereby the population could be controlled. The monolithic nature of the party, however, emerged only slowly. The decision that industrialization should be totally controlled by the state was a gradual one and centralization was not fully effected until the late 1920s. In the event, the Communist party became *the* vehicle of transformation, and gradually all spheres of social and economic life were brought under the direct control of the party. This included not only government, industry and commerce, but also agriculture, the trade unions, education, literature and the arts.

Thus, monopoly of political power and a refusal to tolerate any independent organization which might develop as a centre of opposition characterizes the single-party state. Through their control of the mass media the party leaders are able to determine which issues shall come up for public discussion, and this affects the expression of public opinion through the party. The party is also the mechanism through which political leaders are selected and demands are made to the political leaders. Finally, the party organization provides a country-wide framework of supervision, ensuring that the party's policy is correctly interpreted and followed.

The demands for ideological commitment and strict obedience to the leadership result in a party organization which is exclusive and selective in its membership policy. Even in the early 1960s only 7 per cent of the total population was in party membership. So, with their monopoly of political power, the party leaders determine the extent and nature of political participation. In practice, at various times in the history of the Soviet Union some groups—intellectuals for example—have been denied party membership. But the extension of political participation has now resulted in a situation where representatives of all groups are to be found in membership. As in all industrial societies there has been a tendency for persons from professional and other non-manual occupations to be more actively involved in politics than manual workers. In the Soviet Union, however, this has been counteracted to some extent by periodic party recruitment drives among the industrial and agricultural manual workers. The limited effectiveness of these campaigns can be seen in Table 3.1 which shows such groups still to be under-represented in the party.

Elections, although they do not provide the population as a whole with any control over the political leaders, are designed to give all adults a sense of involvement in the political process. They also enable the party to legitimate its position and proclaim its achievements. There are also oppor-

Table 3.1 Occupational distribution of employed population of the USSR and of members of the Communist party of the Soviet Union (1961) (per cent)

Occupational group	Distribution of employed population	Distribution of C.P.S.U. members
Workers	47·3	34·5
Peasants	32·0	17·5
Mental workers and intelligentsia	20·7	48·0
Total	100·0 (107,600,000)	100·0 (10,000,000)

Source: Adapted from Z. Brzezinski and S. P. Huntington, *Political Power: USA/USSR*, New York: Viking, 1965, p. 100.

tunities for participation in the administration of the state, especially at the local level. The twenty million people who are said to participate in the work of the national, regional and local Soviets include many who are not members of the Communist party. Such activity heightens identification with the state, thereby consolidating the legitimacy of the government.

The lack of opposition parties does not necessarily mean the suppression of all opposition to the government or that political conflict is not present. Where there is a single party, then the struggle for power occurs within the party. This means that the struggle for power is restricted to a relatively small circle of interest groups. State industries, police, army, and the various levels of party officials struggle for control of the party, and changes in party policy are the outcome of the changing balance of power between these groups. So the decision of Kruschev to decentralize authority to a local level and to reduce the supervisory functions of the party represented a triumph of these local interests. It led to an alliance between the regional party secretaries, members of the central party organization and members of the state administration, all of whom saw their position threatened by the reforms. In the event, this alliance proved to be powerful enough not only to reverse the reforms but to secure the dismissal of Kruschev himself.

Multi-party states have developed almost exclusively in societies where industrialization has been led by independent entrepreneurs. The growth of the modern party system in England, for example, dates from the extension of political participation, which we have already traced to the broad process of industrialization. Before this, the politicians (that is to say, the aristocracy) were split into two factions, the Whigs and the Tories. As new groups and classes entered the political arena the nature of these factions changed. In order to survive they had to appeal for support to a larger (and still growing) proportion of the population. In order to secure support in elections they were obliged to develop national organizations and more explicit political programmes. In other words, the old aristocratic factions evolved into modern political parties. The Liberal party under Gladstone was the first to develop this new type of organization and was rapidly followed by Disraeli's Conservative party. Equally important, these new political parties represented the interests of the major classes rather than, as formerly, differences of interest within the aristocracy. Initially the Conservative party was largely the representative of the landed classes, but with the decline of the landed interest it has come to represent primarily the industrial and commercial middle and upper classes. In this sense it has taken over the mantle of the nineteenth-century Liberal party. The other major party in contemporary Britain—the Labour party—was founded on the growth of the working classes as a conscious group and so has been from the start, a class-based party. (Throughout Europe socialist parties have emerged in this way from groups whose interests were inadequately served by existing parties.) The major interests represented by the two major political parties in contemporary Britain can be seen quite clearly from the way the parties are financed. Thus industry and commerce is the major source of funds for the Conservative party while the Labour party is largely financed by the trade unions. The class basis of British party politics is also reflected in the way various sections of the population vote. The large Labour majorities exist in the working-class industrial areas such as the Rhondda Valley and the Exchange division of Liverpool, while the Conservatives get their biggest majorities in middle-class suburbs like Solihull in Birmingham and in the country districts of southern England. However, party allegiance is not determined directly by class membership. If this were the case the greater numbers of the working classes would ensure the perpetual return to office of a Labour government. In fact, at most elections between one quarter and one half of the working classes vote Conservative. Ever since Disraeli first won substantial working-class support for the Conservative party, electoral success has de-

pended upon at least some working-class support.

In the United States of America, there is also a tendency for modern party support to follow class lines but the situation is much less clear cut than in Britain. It is broadly true that the Republican party derives its greatest support from the more wealthy middle and upper classes, and the Democratic party relies mainly on electoral support from lower classes. In 1948, for example, nearly 80 per cent of the manual workers voted Democrat. In America, however, religious, ethnic and regional factors are also of considerable importance. America's modern political parties emerged from the Civil War: the Republican party as a refurbishment of the 'Grand Old Party' of the north; the Democratic party as the party of the south. The Republican party therefore represented the northern establishment, and any Democratic success in New England in the nineteenth and first part of the twentieth century was dependent upon an appeal to the newly arrived and relatively underprivileged immigrants. Thus began the association of the Democratic party with the Irish in particular and, through them, with Roman Catholicism. In the southern states, however, the situation developed very differently. After the Civil War the southern establishment remained antagonistic to the victorious north and thus to the Republican party. So, while the Democratic party developed in the north as the party of the underdog, the faction of the 'Southern Democrats' represented the wealthy (and often right-wing) southerners. Historically, then, those black Americans who were involved in politics at all tended to give their support to the Republican party with its image as 'the party of Lincoln'. Since the Democratic president Roosevelt introduced the 'New Deal' with its appeal to underprivileged Americans, however, black Americans have been wooed away from their traditional Republican allegiance. For the Democratic party, as well as being the more attractive proposition for the economically underprivileged, has been the party more favourable to the extension of civil rights to black Americans as, indeed, it had been earlier to non-property-holders and immigrants. (In Britain, too, there are examples of parties that are not simply class-based. The growth of Scottish and Welsh nationalist parties is a response to geographically uneven economic growth and perceived regional disparities. The party structure of Northern Ireland is as much based upon religion as class.)

Such is the political control of the establishment

in some American states that the party of the establishment is the only party in existence. In several southern states there are Democratic candidates returned to Congress unopposed and in some northern states the same is true for Republicans. In this way some states have some of the characteristics of a one-party state whilst in others, and at the Federal level, a two-party system operates—a combination uniquely American.

American political parties are much less centralized and less disciplined than British parties. In Britain the fact that the prime minister and cabinet can only remain in office so long as they command a majority in the House of Commons requires strict and effective party discipline if the the system is to work. By contrast, in America the president is elected separately from the legislature and is free to choose his own administration. He thus has far greater autonomy than the British prime minister and often, indeed, represents a different party from that which dominates the legislature. In this situation, party discipline can be much less rigid and a nationally organized party structure is only in evidence at the time of a presidential election.

In complex multi-party states, then, politics has become a struggle between mass-based parties. But in order to govern effectively, and sometimes even in order to get elected, governments and parties have to deal with a wide range of organizations representing the specific interests of various sections of the population. Some of these may be economically based—the Trade Union Congress or the Confederation of British Industries for example. Others have a very different basis—the Lord's Day Observance Society, the League of Empire Loyalists, a variety of Civil Rights movements, Oxfam and so on. The more powerful of these are often consulted before major government decisions are taken. Thus the TUC and the CBI are powerful enough to force any government to consult them. Yet they are allied chiefly to the Labour and Conservative parties respectively, and they are influential in the formulation of party programmes, particularly at election time. Others are only able to exert pressure when legislation is proposed which threatens the interests of their members. Many of them also number members of parliament among their members who can act in their interests behind the scenes.

The growth of nations

We have reserved the term nation-state for a limited number of contemporary states, for only in the twentieth century have states emerged in which all adult members have been able to take some part in politics. But the concept of nation suggests more than this. It implies that the majority of the population *identify* with the nation; they consider themselves a part of the nation; they are willing to subordinate their own interests to interests of the nation. Loyalty to the nation overrides loyalty to family, class, religion and region.

It is this identification with and loyalty to the idea of nationhood, as distinct from, say, the person of a monarch or president that is new. In the nineteenth century, Prussian or Polish nobles no more identified with the peasants they controlled than with the horses they owned. German and French aristocrats identified themselves more with each other than with the peasants in their own country. The enormous power differentials between aristocracy and peasantry, and the concomitant social barriers, militated against the development of any emotional ties which might lead the two groups to identify with each other. Such patriotism as existed was expressed in personal loyalty to the king and in concern for the furtherance of *his* interests. But while a subject might support his king in a dispute with a rival monarch, this in no way affected any relationships he might have with subjects of the rival king. Thus, while monarchs and their armies waged war their subjects would continue to trade with each other. *They* were not at war.

The mutual identification of all groups in the society initially emerged out of the struggle of the middle classes to gain access to positions of political power. Intellectuals began to distinguish between the monarch, the ruling class and the nation; and the embodiment of the nation, they argued, was not to be found in the person of the king but in 'the people' (by which they meant the property-owning middle class, i.e. themselves). So the concept of nation came to refer to 'the people'; the qualities of the nation to the qualities of 'the people'. It was not until the late nineteenth and early twentieth centuries, however, that the definition of the groups forming the nation was extended to include the working classes. In other words, it was only as the power of the working classes increased and the social barriers segregating them from their 'superiors' began to break down that identification of members of the working class with others as Englishmen, Frenchmen, Germans and so on took precedence over other loyalties. Patriotic loyalty was gradually transferred from the person of the king to the nation—the collective that was formed by all members of the society. The gradual nature of the change, however, can be seen from the mood of England during the first world war when men still fought and died 'for *king* and country'.

As the twentieth century has worn on, it has increasingly been the nationalist sentiment that has evoked a response from all members of the society. In each of the major European states men have regarded their own nation as the greatest and best. Englishmen have sought to spread Anglo-Saxon institutions throughout the world; Frenchmen have believed in the civilizing mission of France; Germans have extolled the supremacy of their *Kultur*. Symbols of nationhood such as national flags and national anthems have become vested with emotional qualities and represent national values and qualities. Nor has this process been confined to Western Europe. In Soviet Russia a similar (although more violent) process of change has destroyed the social barriers which existed between social groups under Tsarist rule, and has provided the basis for a common identification of all members of the society. In the USA the process was considerably helped by the retreat from isolationism, since the idea of a nation always implies the existence and competition of other nations. In these two 'supernations' of the mid-twentieth century the space race is the most recent symbol of national identity, pride and competition.

Nationalism, then, unites the members of one society in opposition to members of other societies and thus tends to intensify conflict between societies. It also feeds upon international conflict and is at its most intense in times of war or international crisis. Inter*national* relations are different from those between other states. Warfare, to cite the most dramatic example, involves and disrupts all sectors of the society. This is partly because of technological changes which have increased the scale of war, but war also involves the subordination of individual needs to the needs of the nation. Nationalistic sentiment becomes one of the most important means by which the whole population is mobilized for the war effort.

Politics and modernization

It is precisely this nationalistic sentiment that is appealed to by many of the leaders of the 'new' states of Africa and Asia. Thus we can find several examples of speeches from these leaders which parallel anything said by a Churchill or a Hitler. In many of these societies, however, the level of development reached so far is lower than that of the industrial states and identification with the state is relatively low. There are interesting comparisons to be made with the earlier development of the industrial nations, but the different context within which they are developing—and in particular the political subjugation of most of them under colonialism during an important period of their development—has led to important differences as well.

In Africa the differences are particularly sharp. Because of the relative simplicity of most African societies in the late nineteenth century the very boundaries between contemporary African states are more the outcome of competition between European nations than between African states themselves. In some areas the monopolization of the use of force and the establishment of a centralized system of administration first occurred under colonialism. The situation was very varied, however. A country like Nigeria was formed out of a large number of very different societies ranging from those with no differentiated political system at all (such as the Tiv) to the highly centralized and hierarchical Hausa-Fulani Emirates in the north. So the imposition of colonialism throughout tropical Africa resulted in unification of many areas as well as the more widely publicized 'partition' of Africa. One consequence of this has been that the process of political development in Ghana, Guinea, Tanzania, Nigeria and the rest of the societies of tropical Africa has been far more rapid than the process of state formation in Europe. Yet these states do not always command the identification of their subjects. More accurately, they are as yet states rather than nations, and the major political task in the decades after independence is the creation of this sense of nationhood.

In most of Latin America, however, the colonial era ended a century and a half ago, yet identification with the political order is, in most cases, still weak. A more complex level of social development has been reached than in tropical Africa, including, in Argentina and Brazil particularly, some industrialization. Yet the political struggle is still for the most part between industrialists and landowners, with the mass of the population being used as pawns to support the position of one or other. This gives them some influence but little power. In modernizing societies until recently then, the monopoly of the use of force which characterizes the state was held either by a small indigenous minority group or by an alien power. As always, administration was based upon the beliefs and values of the rulers and not those of the mass of the population.

The most clear-cut and dramatic of these situations has been that of formal colonialism. Although colonialism was imposed upon a wide variety of societies it always had important implications for the distribution of power. Sometimes the colonial administrators attempted to govern direct from the European capital. The most powerful colonizer—Britain—however, encouraged a good deal of local autonomy (partly because it was cheaper) and attempted to incorporate traditional rulers into the colonial administration. Even in this case the distribution of power and the nature and basis of authority was radically changed. Where the traditional society was relatively complex (as in most of southern Asia and parts of Africa such as northern Nigeria and Buganda) and had firmly established political institutions and rulers, colonialism undermined the traditional rule. The new administration invariably restricted the traditional rulers' use of the physical force upon which their power had rested and it became increasingly clear that the 'power behind the throne' was the colonial administration (and if necessary the colonial army). By transforming traditional rulers into mere administrators for an alien conqueror their authority, which had rested upon a traditional—often hereditary—right to *rule*, was undermined. In those (predominantly African) societies where there were no separate political institutions as such and where there were no 'rulers', this type of indirect rule created even more disruption. For the colonists' incomprehension of such societies led them to mistake elders and family heads for political leaders and to invest them with a power they had never previously possessed. The legitimacy of this power was rarely conceded by the rest of the society—a factor which resulted in considerable unrest whenever unpopular decisions had to be put into effect. (For example, the lack of ability of the Kikuyu 'chiefs' to control their 'subjects' to the satisfaction of the British during the Mau Mau rebellions in Kenya during the 1950s stemmed largely from this situation.) And on top of this, real power—the effective use of force—always lay with the colonial administration.

So whatever the form of the traditional political system, the impact of colonialism makes radical changes in the distribution of power and in the nature of authority. These changes were enhanced by the non-political accompaniments of colonialism. Christianity; the growth of wage labour and a money economy; urbanization; the gradual extension of Western education: together these changed the conditions under which men lived. Furthermore, they exposed people to new values and beliefs which, in turn, led to a questioning of the old ways of life. These forces of change impinged especially on those who went to the Western style schools and colleges. Frequently, in spite of their educational qualifications, this group was excluded from the most important and best paid positions in the administration. These posts were reserved for colonial officials. The social distance between colonizer and colonized was heightened by its association with race. It was seen to be because of his colour that the African or the Indian was allocated an inferior position; for in settler colonies there was no such discrimination against the white population. It was this educated group, taught to believe in the importance of ability and the irrelevance of race and nationality, and yet in their own country denied the positions for which they were qualified, who first built up modern forms of party organization to aid them in their struggle against both the colonial and traditional rulers.

These educated leaders of the twentieth-century independence movements of Asia and Africa achieved their success by mobilizing the urban population and the more modern of the farmers. Thus, the overthrow of colonialism involved the participation of a substantial proportion, and sometimes a majority, of the total population. It is in this period of the struggle for independence that the modernizing societies of Asia and Africa come closest to nationhood. For the colonial power provides a focus against which all the varied ethnic groups, regional sections and strata can unite in the common objective of independence. Yet the mood is more one of antipathy towards the colonial power than of positive identification with and emotional attachment to the new nation. The highly developed occupational specialization and interdependence, upon which the collective identification of industrial societies is largely dependent simply does not exist.

Only in one sense, then, was independence a triumph of nationalism. The leaders of independence movements owed much of their position to their ability to unite the country to this end. As well as the ideology of nationalism, however, these leaders (especially but not only in Africa) derived much of their support from a *personal* magnetism and a faith in their *personal* ability. Men like Nkrumah of Ghana, Gandhi of India, Banda of Malawi, Sekou Touré of Guinea and Kenyatta of Kenya were followed because they could deliver the goods—the goods in question being independence and the establishment of a more equitable social order. The achievement of independence and the durability of inequality has created enormous problems for the continued unity of many modernizing societies. With the removal of the crisis situation of colonialism, the nationalistic identification with the country as a whole sometimes disintegrates in the face of sectionalism of various kinds. Small farmers, who form the majority of the population, tend to spend the whole of their lives in one locality and, under normal circumstances, are likely to identify with this locality or tribe rather than with the state. Indeed, it was those groups who were most involved in a country-wide (or even world-wide) economy—the traders, businessmen, wage earners and cash croppers—who were most easily recruited to the cause of independence.

This sort of sectionalism may provide the basis for the development of a multi-party system somewhat after the lines of those of Western Europe. The basis for the parties, however, may well be different. Whereas in Europe mass-based political parties had a class basis in Asia or Africa political parties are more likely to have their basis in ethnic or regional differences. Thus, in Nigeria before the military coup of 1966 and the civil war which followed it, the three major political parties represented the three regions dominated respectively by Hausa, Yoruba and Ibo majorities. In other circumstances the political parties represent factions within the ruling élite (not altogether dissimilar to the Whigs and Tories of nineteenth-century England) and are not mass-based at all. This was the situation in Vietnam shortly after independence and a similar position has arisen in Bolivia.

Where a substantial degree of industrialization has occurred, however, and with it some class formation, parties may exist on a basis similar to that in the industrial world. The Communist party of India has, in the last decade, made some headway in the towns as a party of the urban working classes and the unemployed. In Argentina by the time of the military coup of 1943, there were more workers employed in industry than in agriculture and cattle raising. It was, therefore

possible for Colonel Juan Perón, who as head of the Secretariat of Labour encouraged the development of trade unions, to rise to power very largely on working-class votes and with the support of the trade unions. In most modernizing societies, however, class formation is in an embryonic state and therefore does not provide a basis for political parties.

The nature of political parties in modernizing societies often reflects a long struggle between the local population and a colonial administration. This sometimes results in fairly permanent unification of the various influential sections of the society. To some extent the success of an independence movement depends upon its ability to unify all the political elements in the colony. At independence, therefore, there is sometimes only one party with anything like a national organization and the capability of ruling. So one-party systems characterize many modernizing societies. While in Western Europe the development of multi-party states reflected the struggle of successive groups to achieve political participation, most of the 'new countries' are created with universal suffrage from the start. The factor which stimulated the growth of several parties in nineteenth-century Europe is consequently absent. Universal suffrage, however, does not give political *power* to groups unless they are politically organized, and, with the majority of the population dispersed through the country as small-scale farmers, this political organization is not present. To this extent the rulers are not (in spite of universal enfranchisement) dependent upon the active co-operation of the mass of the population. In such a social situation a mass-based political party may function less as a means whereby sectional interests can influence a government, and more as a means of controlling the population and mobilizing their support *for* the government. Elections thus become a time at which the legitimacy of the government is re-asserted.

The problem of enforcement of law and order is particularly complex. The rapid urbanization; the lessened ability of rural traditional authorities to control social behaviour; and the changing codes of conduct all combine to make the task a difficult one. Some of the newest states are still engaged in the process of establishing a monopoly of the legitimate use of violence. So the very right to administer the territory of the state is sometimes in dispute; the legitimacy of the state is in question. This complicates what may already be a relatively unstable situation.

These three factors, then —divisive sectional interests, the concentration of power in a small élite controlling a single party, and the special problems of law enforcement in modernizing societies—all affect the legitimacy of the government. Separately or together they may be enough to upset political stability. If a charismatic party leader *fails* to deliver the promised goods; if an ethnic group feels (rightly or wrongly) that it is being discriminated against; if a region thinks it is being neglected in the allocation of development funds; and if the civilian forces of law and order cannot control the subsequent protest: then the government may be overthrown. For, whereas in the 'old' nations the right of the state to ensure law and order and administer its territory is well established and is no longer seriously questioned, in many modernizing societies the problem is still to establish the legitimacy of the state and the enforcement of its authority.

It is in this political context that military intervention has become such a common feature of political life. First in Latin America, then in Asia and Africa, military coups (sometimes with police support) have become a normal occurrence, either to maintain in power a leader whose legitimacy has been questioned, or to restore law and order, or sometimes to support their own sectional interest. The entry of the military into politics is facilitated by the lack of active participation by the mass of the population. If there arc few sources of opposition to the government there are also few sources of opposition to the military. Indeed, where opposition parties are banned, the military may be the only possible source of opposition to the government.

The influence of industrial societies upon modernizing societies (often in the form of colonialism) has also influenced the growth of the civil service. We have seen that European civil services were founded on the highly differentiated occupational structures of European societies. There is, as yet, little such differentiation in modernizing societies. The civil services are modelled on those of Western societies, but, because of the differences in social context, they often operate in a very different way. Indeed, although the organization of government service is similar to that in contemporary industrial societies, its operation is often more akin to that of the European dynastic states. Where kinship ties are strong there are pressures to utilize one's office to the advantage of kinsmen; thus, in Aba—an eastern Nigerian town—local politicians habitually used their power on the local council to ensure that those of their relatives who were traders got the best pitches in the market. The distinction between public and private income is often obscure; so one member of Nkrumah's government in Ghana was, in a popular and semi-serious joke, reputed to be the wealthiest man in the country because he had held the most ministerial posts! And where junior service salaries are very low, officials may, as a means of supplementing their salaries, demand payment before providing a service. The point is not that such non-bureaucratic behaviour—'corruption' as it is usually called—is absent in industrial societies, for, of course, it is not. But in industrial societies it is universally disapproved and consequently much less common. In modernizing societies the rules are, as yet, far less clear cut and there are conflicting pressures on the civil servant. The 'Western' type of public morality which we discussed earlier has been transferred to the modernizing societies but has not yet been universally accepted. Until such bureaucratic rules are generally viewed as 'right' they will continue to be broken.

Notes

1 E. M. Thomas, *The Harmless People*, Harmondsworth: Penguin, 1969, p. 22.
2 M. Fortes, 'The Political system of the Tallensi', in M. Fortes and E. E. Evans-Pritchard, *African Political Systems*, London: Oxford University Press, 1940, pp. 263–4.
3 The information on the social background of members of the cabinet is taken from W. L. Guttsman, *The British Political Elite*, London: MacGibbon & Kee, 1963.
4 A. F. K. Organski, *The Stages of Political Development*, New York: Alfred Knopf, 1965, p. 178, our italics.

Reading

Black, C. E., *The Dynamics of Modernization*, New York: Harper & Row, 1967. A survey of political and social development which compares processes in a wide variety of societies—European, Asian and African.
Blondel, J., *Voters, Parties and Leaders*, Harmonds-

worth: Penguin, 1963. A summary of research on various aspects of contemporary British politics.

Carr, E. H., *Nationalism and After*, London: Macmillan, 1945. Part 1 of this two-part essay consists of an analysis of nationalism in Europe.

Coleman, J. S., 'Nationalism in tropical Africa', *American Political Science Review*, 48, 1954. One of the earliest systematic discussions of the growth of African 'nationalism'.

Hobsbawm, E. J., *The Age of Revolution*, London: Weidenfeld & Nicolson, 1962. Chapters 3, 6, and 7 contain an analysis of the French Revolution and, in general, of the social changes associated with the development of the modern nation States of Western Europe.

Krader, L., *The Development of the State*, Englewood Cliffs, N.J.: Prentice-Hall, 1968. A critical discussion of theories of state formation drawing upon examples from Africa, China, North America and Russia.

Mair, L., *Primitive Government*, Harmondsworth: Penguin, 1962. A survey of political processes in stateless societies and in simple kingdoms with examples from traditional societies of East Africa.

Further Reading

Apter, D., *Ghana in Transition*, New York: Atheneum, 1963. A case study of the overthrow of colonialism and the first years of an independent African state.

Bendix, R., *Nation-Building and Citizenship*, New York: Doubleday, 1969. A comparative analysis of nation-building in the Western and non-Western world, focusing on the transformation of authority relationships.

Butler, D. and Stokes, D., *Political Change in Britain*, Harmondsworth: Penguin, 1971. A detailed analysis of the various forces shaping electoral choice in Britain.

Finer, S. E., *The Man on Horseback*, London: Pall Mall, 1962. An attempt to explain why the military intervenes in politics.

Fortes, M. and Evans-Pritchard, E. E. (eds), *African Political Systems*, London: Oxford University Press, 1940. Anthropological monographs on the political systems of eight African traditional societies, together with an important introduction distinguishing between 'state societies' and 'stateless societies'.

Guttsman, W. L., *The British Political Elite*, London: MacGibbon & Kee, 1963. Discusses changes in the social composition of the British political elite, in the form of political organization, and in the distribution of power since 1832.

Moore, Barrington, Jnr, *The Social Origins of Dictatorship and Democracy*, Harmondsworth: Penguin, 1970. An attempt to explain the parts played by the landed upper classes and the peasantry in the development of one-party and multi-party states.

Smith, A. D., *Theories of Nationalism*, London: Duckworth, 1971. An analysis of different theories of nationalism and of the variety of forms that nationalism takes.

4 Urbanization

The city as we know it in the Western world today is essentially a product of industrialization. Without industry, the cities of the twentieth century would be very different in character and they would not exist on the scale they do. In this chapter we shall show how, in pre-industrial as well as industrial times, there has always been a close and complex relationship between technological development and the growth and growing importance of cities. Sociologists commonly measure the degree of urbanization in a country by the proportion of its population living in cities. (A city is usually defined as a place with more than so many inhabitants, the number depending upon what figures are available from the various census returns of different countries, commonly 100,000 20,000 or 2,500. This variability is a nuisance, but not as bad as it seems because countries with a high proportion living in places of 2,500 or more inhabitants also tend to have a high proportion living in places of 20,000 or more inhabitants, and so on. Thus although one cannot compare between the different measures of urbanization any one of the measures will do equally well for making comparisons over time.) The rate of urbanization is the rate at which this proportion increases over time. So an increase in population can produce an increase in the size of cities without altering their size relative to the whole population and therefore without urbanization. To clarify the relationship between technological level and urbanization it is convenient to divide urbanization as it has occurred in the world as a whole into three stages.

The first stage of urbanization—and historically by far the longest—was that from the first emergence of cities until the eighteenth century, when they were to be found in almost all parts of the world. In this stage the cities never reached a very great size (few had more than 100,000 people), and never housed a large proportion of the population; but where they existed they were of considerable importance and influence in the surrounding area. The actual rate of urbanization during the first stage, then, was slight, but by the end of the period the growth of cities was significant.

The second stage of urbanization was brief but of great importance; it was the stage of the very rapid growth of cities that accompanied early industrialization. There was, of course, an enormous increase in population during this period, so that cities would have grown in size even without urbanization. But to this growth must be added the fact that as industrialization progressed an ever-increasing proportion of the people were living in towns.

In more mature industrial societies, the rate of urbanization began to slow down and the second stage was overtaken by the third stage: that of metropolitanization. Metropolitanization is the process of urban centralization that accompanies the centralization of industry and the economy. The larger cities take on an increasing importance, both in terms of their population and in terms of the functions they serve in the society as a whole. The small town does not grow so fast and tends to become drawn into the orbit of a larger one and become a satellite to it. In this stage the towns and cities continue to gain a large number of people every year but this represents only a small *proportionate* growth because the urban population is so large already. Thus the rate of urbanization is low but the absolute increase in the number of those people living in towns is very considerable.

All the countries that are currently highly industrialized can be said to have passed through these three stages of urbanization. But in the countries that are currently modernizing, urbanization is following a somewhat different path and in many of them rapid urbanization is occurring without substantial industrialization. We shall discuss in detail each of the stages of urbanization as it has occurred in the Western world and then focus on urbanization in modernizing countries as an example of an alternative line of development which it is now possible for urbanization to take. But first we must consider what distinguishes the urban from the non-urban.

The urban way of life

What are the important differences between life in a city and life in the country? In what ways are the social relationships of townsmen different from those of countrymen? These are questions that have puzzled and fascinated men through the ages and in recent decades sociologists, too, have tried to answer them. They have suggested that there are three important characteristics of the city which help us to understand the distinctive nature of urban social life. The city is a relatively large, densely populated place, housing a variety of people: or, put more briefly, it is distinguished by its size, density and heterogeneity.

Size and density create problems of supply, co-ordination and control, the solution of which involves fairly elaborate forms of social organization. The people must be housed, fed and kept healthy; it must be possible for them to come and go safely and in an orderly manner. There must, therefore, be an effective system of production, an efficient system of distribution, and some form of government. This is just as true of the pre-industrial as of the industrial city, though the problems and their solutions will take somewhat different forms. We shall see later how the industrial city developed new techniques and new forms of organization in response to these specific problems. But size and density in themselves open up new and wider possibilities than can exist in rural areas; they open up the possibility of heterogeneity, of wide variations among people in status, occupation, style of life, opinions and attitudes. In the countryside one family or village is rather like the next. In towns there are extremes of wealth and poverty; there are people who spend their days making gloves, others who spend their days

keeping financial accounts, and others who live by stealing; some listen to Bach, some to Bartok, some to Billy Holiday and some to The Hollies; some believe in syndicalism and others in spiritualism. At the basis of this variety lies the division of labour that is possible in the city. The very existence of the city represents a division of labour; between the agriculture of rural areas and the manufacturing, commercial, religious, educational and governmental activities of the city. But within the city, too, there is an elaborate division of labour. For when a large number of people are gathered together, it becomes possible for some to specialize in one activity and to exchange their produce or services with others who specialize in complementary activities. In a similar way it sometimes happens that in a class of schoolboys one will specialize in doing the maths homework, another in the French and so on. The happy result is that the homework gets done quicker because each is doing his best subject, and the form's homework marks are better for the same reason. Unfortunately, the system is not thought to be very good educationally because it is felt that schoolboys should be well-rounded and not specialized. And so it is with the division of labour in society: the work gets done quicker and better but some would argue that modern man is over-specialized and incomplete as a result.

The division of labour also transforms people's relationships with one another. In the bustling urban life, they have fleeting contacts with hundreds of other people each day. They meet not as relatives or neighbours, but as people exchanging some goods or services. Look at the day of a shopkeeper, for instance: the bus conductress sells him a ticket, the shop assistant works for him in exchange for wages, the commercial traveller brings him news of new goods and tries to sell them to him, the customer buys his goods if they are a bargain, the landlord rents him his premises or the bank lends him money to buy them, the shopkeeper next door competes with him, the policeman enforces legal closing hours to control this competition and also protects his shop from burglary. Each of these relationships, and there are a hundred more, is very superficial, very specialized. The bus conductress is not expected to inquire or to care about his home, his business or his political views, nor he hers. Each deals with only one minor facet of the other's personality, and their relationship is relatively impersonal and rational. They each talk to the other primarily for a purpose of their own: she uses passengers to earn her living, he uses buses to get to work.

Of course, there are also personal, intimate relationships in urban life, among neighbours, friends, family, workmates and so on. But urban life opens up the possibility, which does not exist in rural communities, of a myriad of impersonal, fragmentary relationships, so that ties of kinship become much less important. As this happens groups based on specific interests and activities play a greater part. Political parties and movements, trades unions and professional associations, Christmas clubs and Masonic Lodges, churches and sects and a whole host of other voluntary societies, interested in anything from judo to jam-making, flourish in the urban environment.

We have been describing the way of life of the industrial city, but in essence it is a way of life that can arise in any city. In the cities of medieval Europe, the old, personal, feudal ties were broken and new, impersonal, calculative, relationships developed. People met, as it were, in the market-place, in the world of economic relationships. Thus it was in the cities of Europe that the first stirrings of capitalism were felt. In many pre-industrial cities, however, relationships of this kind did not predominate. Outside Europe, on the whole, kinship and tribal ties among people remained more important and co-existed with the new less personal relationships. People would not trade exploitatively with their kin, so that although there might be a considerable division of labour it did not go to the lengths of the capitalist system.

Nowadays, those of us who have been brought up in a highly urbanized and industrialized society may feel that this sharp distinction between urban and rural life has been exaggerated. In our experience, rural people often have highly specialized occupations, impersonal relations with others, weak ties with their relatives and strong ties with an angling club or the Women's Institute, with Christian Science or with the British Medical Association. In fact many of the things that have been identified as features of towns and cities are more properly described as features of all parts of industrial societies. But even more important is the fact that in countries like Britain there no longer exist many truly rural areas. The countryside may not have a very dense population (though it is much more dense than in most other countries), but tremendous improvements in transportation and communications have effectively compensated for the more sparse population. People can now move about and get in touch with many others almost as readily in the country as in the towns. And the towns have spread their tentacles of influence, establishing an elaborate division of labour both among themselves and with the intervening countryside. In brief then, many of the social relationships which we describe as typically urban apply to British society as a whole because in a very real sense Britain is an urban society.

Pre-industrial cities

As far as we know, the first cities in the world evolved from villages in Lower Mesopotamia, in the valleys of the Tigris and the Euphrates, around 3500 BC. The city of Ur is probably the best known, though not the earliest of these. They differed from villages not only in size—Ur is variously estimated to have held 10,000 to 34,000 people—but also in the variety of activities they embraced. Whereas in villages at that period everyone was engaged in agriculture, in the cities most worked only part-time as farmers and others were full-time craftsmen, merchants, priests and officials. In physical terms, cities were distinguished by their public buildings, such as temples, palaces and market-places. These characteristics serve to explain why cities emerged so comparatively late in man's history; for cities depend upon being able to extract an agricultural surplus from the surrounding countryside to support a population not engaged in food production. The earliest cities therefore appeared in the most fertile areas: in the valleys of the Tigris and Euphrates, of the Nile, of the Indus, and of the Yellow River in China. In Middle America shortly before the time of Christ, the cities of Maya were supported not by fertile land but by the use of maize, a crop which was peculiarly successful in a poor environment. In all these areas the technology was relatively advanced. The people had moved beyond hunting and gathering to settled agriculture using the plough and animal power. They were making efficient use of their land and their methods were not greatly to be improved upon until the mechanization of agriculture and the use of artificial fertilizers which came with industrialization.

The support of the city depended not only upon the existence of an agricultural surplus, but also upon the availability of means of conveying it to the city. The size and influence of the city was therefore limited by the difficulties of communication and transportation. Many of the earliest cities arose on natural transportation routes, such as rivers; but the later growth and spread of cities owed much to advances in writing (like the development from hieroglyphs on papyrus to alphabetic printing on paper), and to developments in transport (like the improvements in wheeled vehicles and in sailing ships).

In all these places, too, social relations were such that the cities had power over the surrounding rural areas, and they could ensure that the agricultural surplus would flow regularly into the cities. In the simplest societies, all men work at the same tasks and are more or less equal. Cities can only arise when some men become more powerful and are able to exert control over the lives of others.

Historians have disputed, however, as to what was the basis of this control. Some have said that the earliest cities were religious centres: as the sacred authority of religious leaders grew, shrine-villages in Mesopotamia became temple-cities. Others have suggested that they were originally fortresses or garrisons where powerful lords secured themselves against attack and mustered forces to dominate surrounding lands. The acropolis, the castle, the Anglo-Saxon 'burgh' are found as the basis of many early cities and testify to such military origins. Yet other writers, particularly those who have studied the Mediterranean trading cities of Tyre, Sidon and Phoenicia or the European cities of Genoa, Venice, Bruges or the Hanseatic League, have argued that the market is a central feature of the early city and trading one of its prime functions.

Yet none of these three forms of specialization (and the power relations associated with them) can be said to be *the* origin of the city. There have been cities such as Timbuctoo, that were trading cities long before they were graced by mosques and that were never fortified; there have been fortress cities, such as those of ancient Sumer, that survived for centuries before a market-place was added to their other facilities. Most cities have combined the three functions, as religious, military-political and economic centres and taken on other functions, as centres of more peaceable political administration and of education, as well. But every city has needed religious power or political power or economic power, or some combination of these, to enable it to extract the agricultural surplus from the surrounding areas, far or near.

The importance of this factor of social power can be seen very clearly when we come to examine the spread and proliferation of cities after these early beginnings in the most favourable places. In general the fortunes of cities depend upon these power relations: they rise and fall as their power rises and falls. The rulers of ancient cities, for example, depended very heavily on military power; military because they lived in a world where international law was unknown and were surrounded by peoples whose culture was alien and whose level of development was much lower. They could at any time be threatened by these barbarians around them and many of their cities were in the end destroyed by invading hordes.

The city-states of Greece and later of medieval Europe were themselves quite small in area, but each controlled a scattered 'empire' which gave it a wider economic base. Usually this did not involve direct rule over a wide area, but rather control of trade. The Italian city-states of Genoa, Pisa, and Venice, for instance, had small territories and trading depots in the eastern Mediterranean which enabled them to dominate trade between Europe and the Near East. In more recent times, urbanization in Europe has been supported in part by international trade and colonialism which permitted the townsmen of Europe to live off the agricultural surplus of the primary producing countries of the rest of the world. The early empires, too, favoured the spread of cities as well as their growth in size. For the mother-city, or metropolis, controlled its empire through the establishment of colonial cities. Many of the cities of modern Europe were founded in this way, particularly during the period of the Roman Empire; many names of English cities can be traced to Latin roots.

Thus, in the first and longest stage of urbanization, cities spread through much of the world and grew in importance as a social form. They depended for their growth upon the power of some of their inhabitants and in turn they helped increase this power. For in cities there were people with the leisure and literacy to make new inventions; merchants were interested in expanding their trade, rulers and soldiers in extending their dominion, religious leaders in spreading their faith.

Although there are striking similarities among pre-industrial cities there are also notable differences. The German sociologist Max Weber distinguished between what he called the Occidental (Western) city and the Oriental city. It was only in medieval Europe that townsmen—'burghers'—emerged as a separate estate, able to govern themselves independent (to some extent at least) of outside interference and with their own courts and their own partially autonomous law. In Europe there was an association or 'community' of citizens to which a man who came to the city might become affiliated. His status as citizen would then supersede any previous status. Thus a serf who left his manor would, after a certain period of town residence—commonly a year—cease to be a serf. It was said: 'City air makes man free.'

But outside Europe there was no concept of 'burgher' that contradicted that of countryman. To quote Weber:[1]

> The Chinese urban dweller legally belonged to his family and native village in which the temple of his ancestors stood and to which he conscientiously maintained affiliation . . . The Indian urban dweller remained a member of the caste.

Similarly, in Timbuctoo today, the members of different tribes are separate and distinct in their cultural traditions. Often people from the same tribal background live together in the same quarter of the city and, because they have little occasion to meet strangers, their way of life is little different from what it would have been in the country.

In pre-industrial Europe, on the other hand, the townsman was freed from these bonds of tradition and tied in a new way to a new type of community based upon trade and commercial relationships. The European city was thus the seed-bed for new developments that eventually brought about its own destruction. For, in the end, this kind of city community gave rise to industrialization which, in its maturity, made the city too small to survive as the most important unit of social life and gave the larger nation-state primacy.

Urbanization and industrialization

With industrialization comes the second stage of urbanization: a very rapid increase in the proportion of people living in towns. If we compare crude measures of industrialization (e.g. the proportion of the labour force in manufacturing occupations) with the degree of urbanization, we find that as countries become more industrialized they become more urbanized (Table 4.1) and that in general the countries that are most highly

Table 4.1 Urbanization and occupational distribution during industrialization in Belgium and the United States (per cent).

Country	Year	Population living in towns with over 2,500 inhabitants	Distribution of Labour force by sector		
			Agriculture	Manufacturing	Services
Belgium	1880	33	25	39	36
	1900	52	17	44	39
	1930	61	14	49	37
	1947	63	11	50	39
USA	1800	6	82	18	
	1860	20	60	20	20
	1900	40	38	28	34
	1930	56	22	32	46
	1950	61	12	35	53

Source: Simon Kuznets, 'Industrial distribution of national product and labour force', *Economic Development and Cultural Change*, V: 4, Supplement, 1957.

industrialized are also most highly urbanized (Table 4.2) The details of the urbanization process, however, have varied from one society to another.

The countries that began to industrialize early—Western European countries and especially England—did so more slowly and urbanized more slowly, whereas Japan and the USSR underwent rapid urbanization in association with rapid planned industrialization and with the fact that they were influenced by the prior urbanization and industrialization of other countries.

Overriding these differences there is a basic interdependence between urbanization and industrialization and the reasons for this are fairly obvious. Industrialization usually involves large-scale production, and particularly the use of the factory system of production which brings a labour force together to work in one place. In addition, anyone who wants to set up a factory is likely to site it near to existing factories so that they can draw upon a common pool of labour and share essential services such as power and transportation and the professional services of bankers, lawyers and the like.

Britain was the first country to become industrial and the first to become highly urbanized; and, as Table 4.2 shows, it is still the most urbanized and by some measures the most industrialized country in the world. In the late eighteenth and early nineteenth century British industry depended heavily upon sources of power which were difficult to move—on coal and on water power. Factories therefore tended to cluster near the coal

Table 4.2   Urbanization and industrialization
(25 selected countries—1950 and nearby years)

Country	Percentage of population living in cities of 20,000 or more	Percentage of total active labour force working in manufacturing
Haiti	5·4	2·0
Pakistan	7·8	1·3
Costa Rica	10·8	8·2
India	12·0	3·4
Philippines	12·7	4·9
Bolivia	14·0	3·8
Malaya	17·0	4·6
Mexico	24·0	8·4
Finland	24·0	18·4
Puerto Rico	27·1	16·2
Egypt	29·1	5·5
Venezuela	31·0	7·1
Switzerland	31·2	33·4
France	31·5	18·9
Sweden	34·5	28·7
Canada	35·1	24·6
Chile	39·5	13·6
Austria	39·8	21·5
Belgium	42·2	33·1
U.S.A.	42·8	26·3
West Germany	45·3	27·6
Argentina	48·3	17·3
Netherlands	56·4	21·1
Australia	56·8	25·2
United Kingdom	67·7	38·6

Source: *Report on the World Social Situation*, New York: United Nations, 1957, chapter VII, table 11, p. 127.

mines. The industry was usually labour-intensive so that each factory needed a large work-force to man it. This was the period of industrialization that produced the rapid growth of the northern cities in England. Blake's 'dark satanic mills'; the 'black country' in the West Midlands; such are the products of this period. Later parallel stages of industrialization brought the Ruhr in Germany and Pittsburgh in the USA.

Socially and physically, these cities were very different from the earlier pre-industrial towns. Instead of small individual workshops, they had great factories and mills powered by steam engines; instead of craftsmen organized into guilds they had an homogeneous and, until the rise of the trade unions, unorganized mass of 'hands'. These were men, women and sometimes children who had left the over-populated countryside to sell their labour in the towns. Charles Dickens gives a vivid picture of such places in his novel, *Hard Times*, written in 1854:[2]

[Coketown] was a town of red brick, or of brick that would have been red if the smoke and ashes had allowed it; but as matters stood it was a town of unnatural red and black like the painted face of a savage. It was a town of machinery and tall chimneys, out of which interminable serpents of smoke trailed themselves for ever and ever, and never got uncoiled. It had a black canal in it, and a river that ran purple with ill-smelling dye, and vast piles of buildings full of windows where there was a rattling and a trembling all day long, and where the piston of the steam engine worked monotonously up and down like the head of an elephant in a state of melancholy madness. It contained several large streets all very like one another, and many small streets still more like one another, inhabited by people equally like one another, who all went in and out at the same hours, with the same sound upon the same pavements, to do the same work, and to whom every day was the same as yesterday and tomorrow, and every year the counterpart of the last and the next.

These attributes of Coketown were in the main inseparable from the work by which it was sustained; against them were to be set off comforts of life which found their way all over the world. . . .

Paradoxically, as the economy and society in general became more complex, the cities became simpler and more specialized. Many of them grew very rapidly from almost nothing and this meant that they consisted almost entirely of the essentials of the industrial system: vast factories, railways and canals, and row upon row of cramped hastily-built houses for the workers.

It was this concentration on what appeared to be essentials that lay at the root of the frequently condemned features of towns during the period of rapid urbanization. The houses were close to the fumes, filth and noise of the factories in order that the workers could walk quickly to work. There were often no sewers nor any system for disposing of rubbish, so waste accumulated in the streets or was carried away in open drains, spreading disease and polluting the inadequate water supplies. The 1845 *Report on the State of*

Large Towns and Populous Districts paints a grim picture of sanitary conditions in urban areas and tells us, among other things, that 'in one part of Manchester in 1843–4 the wants of upward of 700 inhabitants were supplied by thirty-three necessaries only'—that is, one toilet to every 21.1 people. The houses themselves, as in Birmingham and Bradford, were frequently built back-to-back so that half the rooms had no daylight or ventilation. In the Scottish cities tall tenements were built and they were overcrowded, with many people sleeping in one room; and in Liverpool one-sixth of the population lived in 'underground cellars'. In such conditions, disease-bearing pests —rats, lice and flies—could flourish unchecked. There was no planning and little space was left for 'inessentials' such as public parks or children's playgrounds.

Thus the cities of the Industrial Revolution provided an even poorer environment than the rural slums of a decaying agricultural system. Disease, particularly infectious disease, debilitated the people and produced death-rates among both adults and babies that were higher than those in rural areas. Because of this the urban population could not reproduce itself, yet more and more people streamed in from the countryside to work in the factories and swell the ranks of the town dwellers.

It was in this setting that the early attempts at urban planning were made. There was pressure for some kind of control of the individual manufacturer's and builder's activities in the public interest. But although there was often concern about these problems, there was usually no authority in existence with adequate powers to exercise this control. The first attempts consciously to change the urban environment were therefore piecemeal in nature. Private societies, like the Peabody Trust, built better and more healthy artisans' dwellings during the period after 1840. Throughout the nineteenth and early twentieth century various 'model' villages and towns, designed to avoid the evils of ordinary towns, were established. The congestion in the centres of cities was to some extent relieved by the rapid development of suburbs on their peripheries. Cheaper tram and rail transportation, which appeared at the beginning of the twentieth century, made this possible: in London rows of new houses could be built for middle-class people in places like Clapham and Streatham, and artisans moved into what had before been middle-class areas, like Fulham, Hammersmith and Paddington.

Urban planning by public bodies, however, emerged only gradually. The duties of various local authorities were not well defined, so that it was not always clear, for instance, which body was responsible for the water supply or the enforcement of building regulations in an area. It was not until the last quarter of the nineteenth century that local government was reformed and rationalized, taking on the form that we know today with one authority responsible for many different aspects of life in one unified area: for health, housing, education, recreation facilities, roads, sewage, planning, welfare and so on. Even then, the local government had no powers actually to direct what should be built where. The Town Planning Acts of the twentieth century were to give them these powers, but by the time that this happened the third stage of urbanization had been reached.

Metropolitanization

When we look at modern industrial countries we are dealing with the third stage of urbanization when the rate of urbanization has slowed down considerably or even stopped altogether. In Britain the period of most rapid urbanization occurred between 1811 and 1851; for the next half-century it was very slightly slower; after 1900 it tailed off and by now seems to have stopped entirely. Of course, as the population increases the absolute number of people living in towns increases too, but in the recent period the proportion of the population living in towns has stayed more or less the same. Similar changes in the rate of urbanization are occurring in other industrial countries (see, for example, Table 4.1), though none of them is quite as far along the path as Britain. We shall therefore base our discussion on Britain, though much of what we shall say applies also elsewhere. On the basis of this experience, it seems that urbanization is a once-for-all phenomenon and there seems to be an urban saturation point. In the United Kingdom this was reached when about 70 per cent of the population lived in places of over 20,000 inhabitants, but it is likely that it will be at a lower point in many other countries since few will be able to contribute as little as Britain does to the world's agricultural production.

In the third stage of urbanization, then, the rate of urbanization slows down or even stops. Instead there is a reorganization of the urban population so that larger cities and urbanized areas gain in importance at the expense of smaller ones. This process has sometimes been labelled 'metropolitanization'. We have shown how the second stage of urbanization was closely linked to the development of manufacturing industry, with its rapid growth in the so-called 'secondary' sector of occupations; correspondingly, the third stage is linked to the later growth of the 'tertiary' or service sector of occupations.

During the nineteenth century, and especially during the second half, there developed a new kind of technology, based largely upon new inventions in transport, power, communications and office techniques. The motor car, electric power, cheap postage, the telephone and radio, all came into use for the first time; and office machines for typing, duplicating and calculating were invented. All of these heralded a new phase of industrialism. They made possible the growth of larger and more decentralized industrial organizations. Instead of the unitary firm with its office and factory on the same site, there could now be a complex firm consisting of a number of factories making different things or handling different stages of a process and a central 'home' office to administer the whole firm. This reorganization represents a greater division of labour within the firm, with the bureaucratic headquarters taking over many specialized functions like financing, decision-making and marketing. Another feature of this new industrialism is the emergence of new specialisms, particularly in the field of the service occupations. Activities like accounting, advertising and market research are increasingly separated from production and carried on by specialized firms.

These industrial changes are mirrored in an urban change: where once they were relatively discrete entities, cities became more and more involved in complex relationships with each other. For the cities within an area compete with each other as locations for the new co-ordinating headquarters. In the end one of them will predominate over the others, for it is advantageous for the headquarters of a number of firms to be close together so that they can share ancillary services. Then the other towns in the area take on specialized subordinate roles in relation to the central city. Some may specialize in manufacturing, housing the branch factories that are often run from the centre; others, the 'dormitory towns', specialize in residence; others may specialize to some extent in education (Cambridge), tourism (Stratford-on-Avon), retirement (Bournemouth) or holidays (Blackpool). A whole area becomes dependent upon, and supportive of, its central city or metropolis (which need not necessarily be its seat of government). Each place becomes more specialized in relation to the others. This is often reflected in complaints about the decline of local life in country towns or villages: the village chain store or city department store takes over from the local shop, the city hospital from the cottage hospital, the television from the pub sing-song, the 'Men from the Ministry' from the local council, the big construction consortium from the little local builder and so on. The metropolis comes to monopolize many specialist professions, crafts and retail trades and, outside the big cities, the services, supplies and entertainments are mainly mass produced. This big new city, then, has a high proportion of 'black coated workers', the new middle class who man its offices and services.

Physically, too, the metropolis merges confusingly into the surrounding suburbs, country and satellite towns so that it is difficult to identify meaningful boundaries. In Britain new entities, which cannot quite be called cities, have had a name coined for them in census reports. They are called 'conurbations' and are defined as 'continuously urbanized areas surrounding large population centres'. There are seven of them: Clydeside, Tyneside, West Yorkshire (Leeds and Bradford), Merseyside, the Manchester area, the West Midlands, and Greater London. Each of these great urban complexes dominates the surrounding area, but London dominates the whole country to a greater extent than any of the others. Between them, they contain about 40 per cent of the population and they are growing quite fast, in spite of the fact we have already mentioned that rates of population growth and urbanization in general are quite low.

A brief glance at regional studies such as *The South East Study*, published by the Ministry of Housing and Local Government in 1964, serves to reveal how, with metropolitanization, the region rather than the city alone becomes the important unit of study. In particular there has been concern at the rapid growth rate of the population of the London region. The study estimated that the south-east could expect to receive one million immigrants from the rest of the country and abroad in the period 1961–81. The natural increase in the area would add a further 2.4 millions. If no counter-measures were taken, most of this growth would take place in the areas immediately surrounding London. The population of the zone within about fifteen miles of the centre would not increase very much. In fact this type of zone tends to lose population as offices and shops take over from residential buildings and cramped housing is replaced. It is the belt between fifteen and forty miles from the centre that would bear the brunt of the expansion. For London, as the metropolis of the region and of the country, monopolizes many of the facilities that are so attractive to individuals and to firms.

The planners, however, have felt that this uncontrolled growth at the periphery of the city is a dangerous thing. They have feared that the inexorable spread of suburbs housing more and more office workers will mean the disappearance of any countryside accessible to Londoners; and that the increasing number of people travelling into central London for work would eventually paralyse the traffic system. They therefore put forward plans to decentralize growth in the area by founding three completely new cities to act as counter-magnets for population and by the drastic expansion of existing towns beyond the forty-mile radius.

The interest of this to the sociologist is that it illustrates how new meaningful social units are formed as the organization of production changes. It takes time before these new units are reflected in local government boundaries, but moves are slowly taking place in that direction. Among the signs of this is the formation of the Greater London Council.

We have shown how the modern metropolis comes into being, but what are its main characteristics? Its most striking features relate to its distinctive pattern of residence. The early industrial city could be divided, very crudely, into three areas. In the centre was the factory and business district; surrounding that were the homes of the working people; and further out, almost in the country, were the houses of the few middle-class people, the factory owners and managers, the clerks, the shopkeepers and the professional men. (This, incidentally, is the reverse of the pattern in the pre-industrial city where the wealthy people have their big houses in the centre and the poor live near the edge or even outside the walls.) As the industrial city grows into the metropolis, three things happen; some of the factories move out of the centre into new industrial zones; the business and shopping district spreads, invading the neighbouring residential zone; and most conspicuously, the city grows at the edges, spawning layer after layer of suburb.

The nature of these changes is such as to create an old stock of obsolete housing at the centre of the new metropolis. This problem is particularly acute in the area immediately around the business district, the area sometimes called the 'twilight zone'. The old houses in this zone frequently become slums. They are owned by landlords who do not find it worth their while to keep them in good repair and they are rented, often in single rooms, to people who cannot, for one reason or another, find anywhere 'better' to live. Such people are often the new arrivals in the city, who have come from other parts of the country or from abroad to find work; or they are the so-called 'problem families', especially those without a wage-earner, and the down-and-outs who are no longer struggling to find more comfortable surroundings, or they are the older people who were there when the neighbourhood 'saw better days' and now cannot afford to move away. In this zone, then, there is a concentration of unsettled people with a high proportion of males and of younger people.

A group of sociologists in the 1920s and 30s who have become known as the 'Chicago school' found that many of the problems of society were particularly acute in the twilight zone. They found, for example, that delinquency-rates, divorce-rates, illegitimacy-rates, suicide-rates, illiteracy-rates, and many others were highest in the twilight zone and gradually decreased as one moved out from the centre of the city. Attempts to solve the physical and social problems of the twilight zone, such as the rather draconian measure of pulling down large areas of old housing and replacing them with large new blocks of publicly owned flats have not always been successful. The root cause of the social problems, however, is not the state of the houses but the transience of the population and the consequent weakness of neighbourhood ties; and though the physical environment may be improved by urban renewal at the same time such minimal local community life as existed may be destroyed. Whereas the slum had some kind of loose and informal neighbourhood network, within which people found friendship and help if they needed it, the new housing project brings together people from many different places who have no ties with each other, who are isolated and free from either the interference or the support of their neighbours. In the light of this some people have suggested that it would be more valuable to encourage the development of the rudimentary informal social organization than to break it up completely by changing the physical surroundings. In some cities, and this is particularly so in America, community projects have been launched to stimulate self-help and local responsibility in these areas. These, however, are only successful to the extent that the areas become residentially stable. For the basic reason for the weakness of the local community is the fact that the twilight zone is the receiving area for newcomers to the city. Only when the city stops growing will this kind of transitional social problem disappear completely.

The twilight zone is only one of many distinct areas in the metropolis. In the small city different kinds of people are bound to live in fairly close proximity to one another whereas in the metropolis they tend to become much more segregated. Not only do middle-class and working-class people live in separate areas, but each of a variety of smaller groups within each class tends to cluster together, somewhat apart from other groups. Thus there may be an artists' quarter, a Jewish neighbourhood, a lower-middle-class suburb, an upper-crust district, and so on. The name of each locality conjures up an image of its typical inhabitant: think of the Gorbals, Mayfair, Sparkbrook or Woodford Green. This clustering means that although the population of the city itself is heterogeneous, the population of each neighbourhood tends to be homogeneous. People tend therefore to live among and mix with others who are rather similar to themselves. Usually people seem to prefer this; they would feel 'uncomfortable' and 'out of place' among people who were different. This kind of segregation is one of the factors in the preservation of differences between social class. The wealthy seldom see how the poor live in the slums, so they need not trouble to do anything about it; the poor do not see how extravagantly the rich live, so they do not feel resentful. The result is that people learn to see the world from the point of view of the group they live in.

One of the most conspicuous and extreme developments of this kind is the emergence of the 'ghetto'. The original ghettos were Jewish areas within European towns. Now, in industrial societies, we frequently find 'ghettos' of coloured people. In countries like South Africa this residential segregation is enforced by law. In countries with a predominantly white population it often comes about less formally, simply as a result of the relative poverty and powerlessness of the coloured people and the discriminating practices of house-agents and landlords. In England there are no complete 'ghettos' in the sense of areas that are entirely coloured. But coloured people do tend to be clustered in certain areas—in particular in the twilight zones of cities and in the poorer inner suburbs. The chances for neighbourly contact, for children going to school together and making friends between the races are thus very much restricted. Also, because these neighbourhoods in which coloured people find it easiest to get accommodation are the poorest ones, with the oldest schools, 'worst' accents, highest delinquency-rates and poorest job-opportunities, coloured people are less likely to be able to rise in the social scale. Thus, the way in which the residential pattern of big cities is organized may turn out to be a very important factor in turning the coloured group in Britain from a newly arrived immigrant group just finding its feet into a permanent sub-lower class, cut off from the rest of the community.

In addition to these new specialized areas near the centre of the city, the third stage of urbanization brings another kind of new area that has attracted much attention: the suburb. In terms of the space they occupy and the novel way of life they seem to embody, suburbs are probably the most striking feature of the metropolitan society. In Britain they began to grow during the nineteenth century with the advent of trains and trams to carry residents to their work cheaply. But the heyday of suburban expansion was in the inter-war period. A whole belt of land from five to fifteen miles around London was built up during this period. The housing density, at about 12–14 houses per acre, was much lower than in the central areas and the design of the houses and layout of the streets often more varied and informal in style. The result was that although the population of Greater London increased by 1.2 million (about 17 per cent) during the period from 1921 to 1938, the built-up area increased more than three-fold. The same kind of development has occurred around almost all the metropolitan centres in highly urbanized countries. Some observers deplore it, calling it 'suburban sprawl', predicting that it will engulf the entire countryside and characterizing its way of life as dull, standardized and in-growing. Others—and with them a large number of suburbanites—herald it as a move towards a pleasant, open environment for a life free at once from the inconvenience of the country and the stress and congestion of the city.

There is a popular stereotype of suburbia which is reflected not only in the work of novelists, but also in that of some sociologists. The 'suburban way of life' is described as a life where there is more contact with neighbours, more participation in neighbourhood activities, more concern about what the neighbours think, and more focus on family and domestic activities, on doing things together and on improving the home. But closer consideration casts doubt on whether these things are a characteristic of suburban life *as such* or whether they are not rather characteristic of middle-class life anywhere. Most people's image of the suburb is of middle-class suburbia; daily life in working-class suburbs is more similar to working-class life in the inner city.

The pattern of life in new suburbs, too, is very different from that in old-established ones. For new suburbs tend to have houses of similar size and price, so they are inhabited by families of similar income and at a similar stage in their family cycle. There may be mile after mile of lower-middle-class families with two or three young children. But as the suburb ages, some of these will stay and grow older, others will sell out to younger families. In the early stages the suburb is homogeneous, and common interests, together with the fact that the residents have all broken away from old ties, mean that there may be much neighbourly mixing. In the later stages the population of the suburb becomes more mixed and consequently there are greater opportunities for varied ways of life within it.

Urbanization and modernization

In modernizing societies the situation is rather different from what it was in the industrial nations that we have described so far. They are developing in interaction with more developed societies and, to some extent, after their example. One result is that they can see ahead what the fruits of economic growth will be and their people desire the higher standard of living that they know is available elsewhere. This has been described as 'the revolution of rising expectations' and one of its features is a dissatisfaction with primitive rural life, a dissatisfaction which makes many people move to the towns in search of 'better' things. People in modernizing societies also become aware of the independence and individualism of life in industrial societies. They can see American films in which young people live in their own homes and choose for themselves whom to marry, instead of

living under the parental roof and submitting to an arranged marriage. So young people, chafing at the traditional restrictions that surround them in their home village, go to the town partly to escape these bonds.

Contact with industrial societies also introduces a money economy into rural areas, so that even a farmer who grows crops for his own consumption may need cash to pay for some of his supplies and implements and to pay his taxes. Yet employment rewarded in cash may not be available to him in the country, so he, or one of his family, must take an urban job at least occasionally.

In many of these countries the population is increasing very rapidly so there is serious overpopulation of rural areas. People are forced off the land because the land can no longer support them and this too produces a flow of people to the cities. Thus in Africa, Asia and Latin America the proportion of people living in towns is much lower than in the industrial regions of the world but relative to their own level and type of economic development, it is very high.

Table 4.3 illustrates an important difference in this respect between urbanization in industrial societies and urbanization in modernizing societies. In many modernizing countries there have been large movements to the cities without any increase in the proportion of workers in industry. Indeed, in the cases cited in Table 4.3 the proportion of the labour force in industry has actually decreased

Table 4.3 Changes in urbanization and the distribution of the labour force in selected countries (per cent)

Country	Year	Population in localities of 20,000 or more	Labour force in Agriculture	Industry	Services
Chile	1920	28	39	30	31
	1952	40 (1950)	31	30	39
India	1911	4	74	13	13
	1951	12	74	10	16
Mexico	1910	11	70	22	8
	1950	24	61	17	22
Australia	1911	43	25	34	41
	1947	57	17	38	45
France	1906	25	43	30	27
	1954	33	28	37	35
USSR	1928	12 (1926)	80	8	12
	1955	32	43	31	26

Source: *Report on the World Social Situation*, New York: United Nations, 1957, chapter VII, table 10, p. 125.

in India and Mexico and remained constant in Chile while in each case the proportion of the population living in urban areas increased dramatically. In each of the industrial societies cited, however, the urbanization process has been accompanied by an increase in the proportion of industrial workers. In so far as we can take the proportion of industrial workers as an index of a society's level of economic growth we may suggest that in these modernizing societies the distribution of population between town and country does not contribute to economic growth and sometimes even inhibits it.

The figures in Table 4.3, however, probably exaggerate the situation because there is usually a shift from small-scale, craft manufacturing to large-scale, factory production, so that although the same proportion of workers may be involved, their productivity is higher. The increase in the 'service' category with urbanization in modernizing societies is particularly interesting. For these service occupations are not predominantly those connected with education, administration and the professions, as they are in industrial societies, but are the result of a lack of mechanization and rationalization. Porters, messengers and servants do work that in industrial countries is commonly mechanized; thousands of small traders, hawkers and market women do work that would be unnecessary in a rationalized retail system. Many of these people are grossly underemployed, picking up work or trade only occasionally. So these urban occupations contribute very little to the general economy.

Furthermore, because the migrants to the cities are usually driven off the land rather than attracted by job opportunities in the cities, there is a tendency for one or two very large cities in each country to grow disproportionately at the expense of the smaller ones. Such migrants are more likely to have heard about the big cities and are more likely to have relatives there; it is easier to travel to them and when they arrive they find it easier to find some way to earn a living, if only because there are already more people to whom they can offer their services. The result is that although the countries of Africa, Asia and Latin America are mostly not highly urbanized but on the contrary largely rural in character, in 1960 half of the twenty biggest 'urban agglomerations' in the world (with populations of over three million people each) were found in these areas.

These large cities tend to monopolize people and resources, so that the growth of medium-sized cities, which might be better suited to industrial development, is hindered. The absolute growth-rate of the cities is even faster than the urbanization rates would indicate because of the high rates of population increase in these countries. The result is that, in addition to hindering economic growth, such places experience all the social difficulties and health hazards of any rapidly expanding city. Indeed, they occur on an especially large scale because of the low level of per capita income and because of the vast size of the cities. There are fourteen cities in the modernizing, and mainly rural, countries that are larger than either Manchester or Birmingham today: cities like Shanghai, Calcutta, Bombay, Peking, Cairo and Rio de Janeiro. Their rapid growth is entirely unco-ordinated; their people huddle in shanty-towns and slums; and, unlike the cities of earlier industrializing countries at a similar stage, because of their huge size they suffer from acute transportation problems. A description of Calcutta serves to illustrate these tendencies:[3]

The shanties made of castaway materials that crowd the road from the airport at Dum-Dum and the stench of uncovered drains introduce the visitor to the condition of life of the vast majority of the city's inhabitants. More than three-fourths of the population of the city of Calcutta proper live in overcrowded tenement and bustee (slum) quarters. According to an official estimate 'two-thirds of the people live in kutcha (unbaked brick) buildings. More than 57 per cent of multimember families have one room to live in. For more than half the families cramped into one-room quarters there is only 30 square feet or less per family member.' One study showed that the indigent in the bustees share a single water tap among 25·6 to 30·1 persons and a single latrine among 21·1 to 23. . . . 8·6 per cent of the rooms in bustees are either partly or wholly places of work (as well as dwellings) . . . . Even in the midst of the central commercial and banking districts of the city, the traffic situation is appalling. On an average day 500,000 pedestrians and 30,000 vehicles will cross the Howrah bridge, and the traffic jams at both ends are constant. There are never enough taxis or buses. The progress these vehicles make through the streets is slowed by the rickshaws, which are patronized generously by the citizens of Calcutta, and by the numerous carts drawn by oxen, water buffaloes or men.

Thus the rate and form of urbanization in many modernizing countries is directly inimical to economic growth. Yet, indirectly, the movement to the towns can stimulate economic development by contributing to other aspects of modernization. For the town represents modern civilization: within it modern institutions develop and through its influence modern ways of life spread to rural areas.

Traditional social structure and forms of relationship may no longer be entirely appropriate in the city. A striking illustration of this can be seen in the way that caste definitions and rituals tend to weaken in Indian cities. The rules of caste define the activities that different people may engage in and the ways in which they may relate to other castes. Yet in the city a man must make his own living as best he can and he lives and works alongside strangers whose caste he does not know. At the local level, too, sub-castes are, to some extent, self-regulating associations. Yet when a man moves to the city he removes himself from the observation and control of his caste group. Caste is fundamentally a local phenomenon: not all castes can be found in any one area. So any geographical mobility puts men outside the local caste rules that they have learned and consequently disrupts the caste system. Finally, caste is a system of stratification in which, on the whole, those born into the higher castes are the richer and more powerful members of society. Yet if he moves to the city, a member of a low caste or even an untouchable may gain wealth or influence through success in trade or in a profession. Such a man is of high status in a new urban class structure where social mobility is possible and a man's status depends on his own achievements in life as well as on his caste origin.

In similar ways, many other traditional patterns of behaviour break down in an urban setting. An African townsman need no longer submit himself to tribal or village authority. The kinship network, such an important institution in all simpler societies, becomes weaker. The urban economy in which incomes are the reward of individual rather than collective effort, encourages self-reliance and self-sufficiency. So the townsman's sense of obligation towards his kin and the extent to which he is able to rely on them when in need diminish.

In the cities of West Africa there is a large number and variety of associations, membership of which is voluntary. These help to adapt migrants to their new situation in various ways. Some of them, in particular the tribal associations, enable the migrant to keep in touch with his own language and culture. But they differ from traditional tribalism in that the urban tribal association is not a corporate group; clear-cut traditional kinship rights and obligations are replaced by a vaguer sense of mutual obligation and of metaphysical brotherhood. Voluntary associations have their rules and regulations and often exercise great authority over their members. Thus they serve as a substitute for traditional agencies of social control. The Mende Dancing Compins of Freetown in Sierra Leone, for instance, fine members for street fighting, provide chaperons for the younger members, expel members convicted of a felony and help to patch up family quarrels. In youth associations, the young control their own behaviour instead of submitting to the authority of their elders. Voluntary associations in the cities also provide social security where traditional forms cannot operate effectively and where the state makes no provision. A common form of this in Ghana and Nigeria is a rota fund, which enables people to save regularly against times when they need money.

As well as providing substitutes for traditional institutions, however, voluntary associations play a part in social change. A peculiar characteristic of West African voluntary associations is the large proportion of their members who hold official positions within the association. Holding office, and, indeed, even ordinary membership in a highly organized association, helps to socialize the new townsman into the ways of urban life: he learns to engage in impersonal relationships revolving round specific tasks; he learns a new concept of time and punctuality; he learns to obey and create formal rules, rather than follow tradition. Such experience can be useful preparation for political action as well as for general participation in town life. Partly because of this and partly because political parties were often banned during the colonial period, voluntary associations were important in the growth of independence movements. An important example of this was the Egba Women's Union in Nigeria, a savings club which took an active part in the formation and support of the National Council of Nigeria and the Cameroons, the leading political party in the Eastern Region at the time of independence.

In the town the migrant also plays new roles which bring him into new relationships with other people. In particular, he is more likely to be employed for a wage, which involves him in a new kind of authority relationship with an employer. He finds that instead of owing deference to village and family elders he now owes it to those who are above him in the occupational structure, whatever their age. Furthermore, if he is employed in industry or commerce, he is likely to work alongside a large number of people, differing in tribal background and status, who are now considered his equals and with whom he has common interests. Thus industrial workers in modernizing countries begin to form trade unions that cut across the old barriers and represent a newly emerging social category, a category analogous to the working class in industrial societies.

The towns are also centres for other activities important in a modernizing society. The main educational and administrative institutions are located in towns. Thus the towns become symbols of modernity and those who live in them either participate in, or at least are affected by, modern literacy and rational bureaucratic control. Most of the people who are engaged in white collar

activities—a rapidly expanding group—are gathered together in the towns. They meet in their leisure time as well as in their work and develop a sense that they belong together and have common interests. In embryo they too represent the emergence of a new and distinct social group.

Many of those who go to the towns to work, however, do not settle there permanently. They may retire to their home village at the end of their working life or they may go as migrant workers, taking a town job at times when there is little work to be done on the farm. Such people may not become fully assimilated into modern life, but they do carry certain town ways back with them to the rural areas and they help to spread a money economy and a taste for manufactured consumer goods.

We may conclude that even in the places where urbanization occurs without concomitant industrialization, the towns themselves have an important part to play in the process of modernization. They epitomize a new way of life and their influence is felt throughout the whole society.

Notes

1 Max Weber, *The City*, Chicago: Free Press, 1958, pp. 81–2.
2 Charles Dickens, *Hard Times*, London: Dent, 1907, p. 19.
3 Nirmal Kumar Bose, 'Calcutta: a premature metropolis', in *Cities*, a *Scientific American* book, Harmondsworth: Penguin, 1968.

Reading

Cities, a *Scientific American* book, Harmondsworth: Penguin, 1968. A collection of articles that appeared in the magazine *Scientific American* in 1965. The articles by Davis and Sjoberg give a useful survey of urbanization from earliest times; and others describe varying urban situations in greater detail.

Breeze, Gerald, *Urbanization in Newly Developing Countries*, Englewood Cliffs, N. J.: Prentice-Hall, 1966. An introductory survey of urbanization in relation to the process of modernization.

Jacobs, Jane, *The Death and Life of Great American Cities*, Harmondsworth: Penguin, 1965. A lively attack, by an architectural journalist, on contemporary town planning. A fascinating and highly polemical analysis, rich with examples, leads her to the conclusion that the unplanned patterns of growth which represent the organizational complexity of the city, may be preferable to the simplistic ones imposed by planners.

Nottridge, Harold E., *The Sociology of Urban Living*, London: Routledge & Kegan Paul, 1972. A brief introduction to the study of the city, covering a wide range of research and theories.

Pahl, R. E., *Patterns of Urban Life*, London: Longmans, 1970. An introduction to the sociology of the city, with special reference to Britain. The first two chapters, on pre-industrial urbanism and the emergence of industrial urbanism in Britain, are of especial relevance to the theme of this chapter.

Pahl, R. E. (ed.), *Readings in Urban Sociology*, Oxford: Pergamon, 1968. An interesting collection of articles dealing mainly with non-American material, with a helpful introduction by the editor.

Further reading

Dobriner, W. M. (ed.), *The Suburban Community*, New York: Putnams, 1958. A collection of 24 papers which explore varied aspects of the distinctive nature of suburban life.

Hatt, P. K. and Reiss, A. J. (eds), *Cities & Society: The Revised Reader in Urban Sociology*, Chicago: Free Press, 1957. A large and varied collection of articles covering a wide range. Includes classic contributions by Simmel, Wirth, Davies and Golden, Sjoberg, McKenzie and Miner; but mainly deals with American cities.

McKenzie, R. D., *The Metropolitan Community*, New York: McGraw-Hill, 1933. A pioneering work on the changing nature of cities as urbanization proceeds. Gives special emphasis to ecological factors.

Miner, Horace (ed.), *The City in Modern Africa*, London: Pall Mall, 1967. An interesting collection of recent articles.

Reissman, Leonard, *The Urban Process*, New York: Free Press, 1964. Aims to find 'a theory explaining the industrial city and its development', using a comparative typology more elaborate than the series of stages we have used in this chapter. Includes a valuable critical survey of earlier schools of thought.

Weber, Max, *The City*, Chicago: Free Press, 1958. Weber's classic work on the development of the urban 'community' in the occident, with particular emphasis on urban political structures. Don Martindale's introduction to this edition gives a useful survey of American urban sociology.

5 Population

World population growth

Man or very close kin to man has been in existence for perhaps a million years. Although it is not known precisely when *homo sapiens* first appeared, there is clear evidence of his activities in Europe something like 25,000 to 30,000 years ago. For half a million years or more the human species grew in number very slowly, expanding temporarily in some areas, declining in others, but remaining sparse everywhere. Sustenance was obtained by hunting, fishing, and gathering, which required huge areas for few people. Although the domestication of animals and plants ultimately gave rise to some areas of far greater density of settlement than hitherto, it came so gradually that the rate of population growth was hardly raised at all. The emergence of settled pastoral and agrarian societies did, however, lead to a long-term increase in population from about five million in 8000 BC to eighty-six million in 4000 BC. By the beginning of the Christian era world population probably numbered between 200 and 300 million. By 1750 the population of the world had reached about 790 million. Today it is over 3,500 million. A simple analysis of these numbers reveals that an enormous increase in the rate of world population growth has occurred, especially during the past three centuries. As Philip M. Hauser has pointed out, it took most of the millennia of man's habitation of the earth to produce a population as large as one thousand million people simultaneously alive. This population was not achieved until about 1850. To produce a population of two thousand million required only an additional seventy-five years, for this was the world population by 1925. To reach a population of three thousand million required an additional thirty-seven years, for this was achieved by 1962.

Why has the rate of world population growth increased so greatly? The answer may be found by analysing the rates of population growth in different types of society and examining the reasons for these differences. Although the data are subject to error there are a number of conclusions which may legitimately be drawn.

One of the salient facts is that today population is growing faster in the underdeveloped countries than in the highly developed ones.[1] But this is a recent trend, dating from about 1920. Before the first world war the most rapid gains occurred in the more industrialized societies—in those developing economically and raising their levels of living. After 1920 it has been the non-industrial countries that have shown the more rapid growth.

Why is world population as a whole increasing at an accelerating pace? Why has the fastest growth shifted from the richer to the poorer countries? The major demographic cause of the great acceleration of population growth, first evident in Europe and in areas of European settlement, was the decline in the death-rate, not a rise in the birth-rate. Sharp declines in mortality were experienced while fertility remained at relatively high levels. The case of England and Wales can be taken as an illustration of a pattern experienced by all the now highly industrialized countries. In 1750 the birth-rate in England was about 35 live births per 1,000 persons per year. The death-rate stood at a level of about 32 deaths per 1,000 persons per year. Natural increase, the excess of births over deaths, approximated three persons

Figure 5.1 Demographic characteristics of societies at different levels of economic and social development

Level of social and economic development	Major demographic characteristics	Examples
Societies with low national income per capita. High percentage of labour force in agriculture. Low levels of urbanization.	HIGH birth-rates. HIGH death-rates. HIGH infant mortality-rates. LOW expectation of life at birth. LOW rate of natural increase. HIGH percentage of children. LOW percentage of old people. LOW percentage of persons 15–64.	All societies before 1700. Contemporary modernizing societies (e.g. India, Egypt, tropical Africa, most of Latin America and Asia before 1950).
Societies undergoing the early stages of industrialization. National income per capita increasing. Percentage of labour force in agriculture declining. Rising levels of urbanization.	HIGH birth-rates at first, gradual decline in later stages. DECLINING death-rates. DECLINING infant mortality-rates. RISING expectation of life at birth. VERY HIGH rate of natural increase at first, gradual decline as birth-rates fall in later stages. VERY HIGH percentage of children at first, declining later.	Britain, 1780–1880 USA, 1870–1910 W. Europe, 1830–1900 USSR, 1910–40 Japan, 1920–50
Societies with high national income per capita. Low percentage of labour force in agriculture. High levels of urbanization.	LOW birth-rates. LOW death-rates. LOW infant mortality-rates. HIGH expectation of life at birth. LOW rate of natural increase. LOW percentage of children. HIGH percentage of old people. HIGH percentage of persons 15–64.	Contemporary Britain, W. Europe, USA, USSR, Japan, Australia, New Zealand, Canada.

per 1,000 per year. A century later the death-rate had declined to a level of 23, while the birth-rate remained at the earlier high level. The natural increase was therefore twelve per thousand producing a rate of population increase nearly four times what it had been a century earlier (see Figure 5.2). As in the case of England and Wales, mortality in Western Europe began its relatively rapid decline at the end of the eighteenth century. It was only after a considerable time-lag that the birth-rate began to fall and, therefore, to dampen rates of population growth.

The decline in the death-rate was at first limited to those countries undergoing industrialization. The improvements in agriculture, transport, and commerce during the eighteenth and nineteenth centuries made better diets possible; the advances in manufacturing made improved clothing, housing, and other amenities more widely available. Technological gains and increased productivity made possible a general rise in levels of living. Moreover, the rise in real income facilitated the growth of public health measures and the development of medical science. During the nineteenth century great strides were made in purifying food

and water and in improving personal hygiene, which contributed materially to the elimination of parasitic and infectious diseases. But it was not until the present century and the advent of chemotherapy that medical science had much effect on the death-rate. Economic growth, not medicine, led to the decline in the death-rate in Western Europe, North America and Australasia.

Since 1920, however, the less developed countries have experienced much faster declines in death-rates than European countries ever experienced, and these declines have occurred without a comparable rate of economic growth—in many cases without any noticeable gain in *per capita* income at all. Death-rates have been brought down with amazing speed in the economically backward regions of the world because the latest medical discoveries, produced and financed in the highly industrialized countries, can be applied everywhere. In Europe the advances in medical science were the product of a very gradual process of development; today the underdeveloped nations are suddenly getting the benefit of the accumulated heritage of centuries as well as such new discoveries as are made each year. Death-rates in the Third

World are declining seemingly miraculously, but in reality such declines would be impossible without the previous social development of the now highly industrialized societies.

The most important causes of death being eliminated in Africa, Asia, and Latin America are infectious and contagious diseases. The transfer of medical skills, techniques, personnel and funds from the West, especially under the auspices of international agencies like WHO, UNESCO, UNICEF, FAO, etc., has made possible the conquest of such diseases. Insecticides like DDT, antibiotics like penicillin, vaccines like BCG, drugs like sulfanilamide, and systematic public health campaigns, made it feasible to control widespread diseases like malaria, yellow fever, syphilis, cholera, typhoid, smallpox, tuberculosis and dysentery at very low cost. The case of Ceylon (as it was then known) can be used as an illustration. For centuries the major cause of death and illness in Ceylon was malaria. Endemic malaria prevailed in two-thirds of the island and periodic epidemics occurred at regular intervals. The spread of the disease was favoured and magnified by the gross undernourishment of the population. The crude death-rate averaged 26·9 per 1,000 during 1920–29 and 24·5 during 1930–39. In 1946 it was still as

high as 20·3, but in that year the spraying with DDT of sites from which the adult mosquito attacked humans was begun. In one year the death-rate fell by 43 per cent (from 20·3 to 14·3) and by 1950 it was as low as 12·6. The malaria mortality-rate was decreased by 82·5 per cent between 1946 and 1949: this was accompanied by a marked reduction in infant and maternal mortality and in several of the other major causes of death. The costs were very low and even these were partly met from WHO funds. The DDT was imported and the experts involved either originated or were trained outside Ceylon. The Cingalese were not required to change their institutions, to acquire any knowledge of malaria and its control, nor to take any initiative. The spectacular decline in the death-rate was not the consequence of any basic economic or social development in Ceylon.

Similar trends are noticeable elsewhere. The death-rate of the Moslem population of Algeria in 1946–47 was higher than that of Sweden in 1771–80. By 1955 the fall in the death-rate in Algeria was greater in eight years than that experienced in Sweden during the century from 1775 to 1875. Between 1940 and 1960 Mexico, Costa Rica, Venezuela and Malaya were among the societies in which the death-rate decreased by

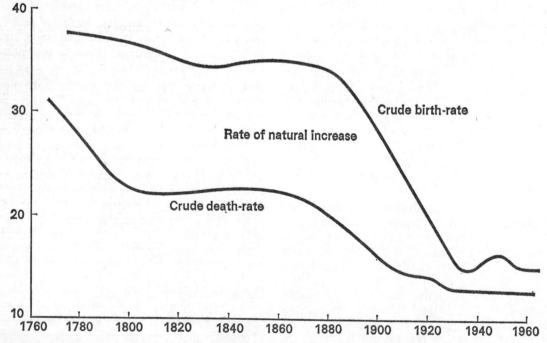

Figure 5.2 Birth-rates and death-rates, England and Wales, 1760–1960

Source: Phyllis Deane & W. A. Cole, *British Economic Growth 1688–1959*, Cambridge University Press, 1962, p. 127; D. V. Glass & E. Grebenik, 'World population 1800–1950', in H. J. Habakkuk & M. Postan (eds), *The Cambridge Economic History of Europe*, vol. VI, part 1, 1965, pp. 68–9.

more than 50 per cent. In 18 under-developed countries the average decline in the death-rate from 1945–9 to 1950–4 was 20 per cent.

Without question this spectacular decline in the death-rates of non-industrial countries has been the most important population phenomenon of the twentieth century. The rate of population growth in these societies today is much higher than that experienced by the economically advanced nations during the period of their rapid population growth. In the history of the highly industrialized societies the decline in mortality was spread out over nearly three centuries during the latter part of which (over periods ranging from fifty years to one and a half centuries) the birth-rate also began to decline. But in present-day non-industrial countries birth-rates remain high. While death-rates have fallen to levels between ten and twenty per thousand per year, birth-rates tend to average forty or more, a level little lower, if any, than it was centuries ago. This difference between the death-rate and the birth-rate gives a natural increase of between twenty and thirty—a population growth-rate of two to three per cent per annum. Moreover, whereas the present industrialized countries experienced falling birth-rates before their sharpest declines in mortality, the under-developed countries of today will do so, if at all, long after their death-rates have reached low levels. It is, as Kingsley Davis has pointed out, this dual fact—the unprecedented conquest of mortality by bringing mid-twentieth-century public health to the Third World, and the continuance of high birth-rates in these backward areas—that explains the extraordinary population growth in the non-industrialized three-quarters of the world. It also explains, along with the rise in birth-rates since the 1940s and continued lowering of mortality in the highly developed nations, the accelerating trend of the total world population.

Mortality

Mortality conditions in all societies once resembled those in the least developed countries of today. As we have seen, since the latter part of the eighteenth century there has been a very impressive reduction of mortality in the now highly industrialized societies. Precise information is not available but in all probability the expectation of life at birth in Egypt, Greece, and Rome around the beginning of the Christian era was not above thirty years. During the period 1650 to 1700 life expectation at birth in Western Europe was about thirty-three years and probably had not changed much during the preceding three or four centuries. By 1900 death-rates had declined to a point where expectation of life in Western Europe and North America had reached a level of forty-five to fifty years. By 1960 life expectation in all highly industrialized societies was about seventy years.

By far the greater part of this increase in expectation of life at birth has been brought about by a decline in infant mortality. The decline in mortality of other age groups is far less impressive. Mortality during the first year of life is extremely sensitive to changes in social conditions. The infant is entirely dependent upon the care of its parents, and that care is itself dependent upon the parents' standard of living (income, housing, level of education and access to medical care). In all societies the infant mortality-rate varies inversely with parents' income. It is highest in the lower income group and lowest in the wealthiest sector of society. Similarly the poorer countries of the world have the highest infant mortality-rates: in Pakistan and India the infant mortality-rate is over 200, in Sweden it is as low as 18. The great decline in mortality brought about by the social changes associated with the process of industrialization can by illustrated by taking the case of France. In the eighteenth century, of every 1,000 infants born, 233 had died before reaching the age of one, 498 had died before twenty, and 786 died before sixty. In contrast, of 1,000 infants born in present-day France only 40 die before reaching the age of one, only 60 before twenty, and only 246 before sixty. In eighteenth-century France of the original 1,000 infants only 214 survived to age sixty: in contemporary France 754 of the original 1,000 are still alive at sixty.

Before the development of modern transportation and industry hunger, malnutrition, and famine were recurrent features of human life. It has been estimated that in Britain between AD 10 and 1846 there were over 2,000 famines. China and India have recorded massive famines even in recent times, with enormous loss of life from hunger and from the disease and violence that hunger often begets. In China between 1876 and 1879 as many as 13 million people may have died from starvation, disease, and violence following a prolonged drought. Before man had developed the necessary techniques to minimize the effects of natural disasters, floods and drought frequently led to famines. Wars that have devastated the land or disrupted the normal routines of cultivation and exchange have also been the cause of famine. The

Thirty Years' War in Germany in the seventeenth century and more recently the internal strife following the breakdown of central government in the Congo and Nigeria led to famine and disease. But more important than the drastic but occasional occurrence of outright starvation in explaining the high mortality of non-industrial societies are the effects of malnutrition and the exigencies of poverty. In the modern world the likelihood of famine has, in any case, sharply diminished. Except in geographically isolated areas or those set apart for political reasons, the threat of famine is now likely to bring quick relief from other regions with agricultural surpluses. But low standards of living still prevail in many parts of the world, and the impact of poverty and low productivity on death-rates can be seen in the great differences still to be found between 'underdeveloped' countries and highly industrialized ones.

The long-term decline in the death-rate in Western Europe was preceded by the achievement of relatively long periods of peace and security as a result of the emergence of powerful and stable central government. This in itself was an essential prerequisite for the rapid expansion of productivity which not only lessened the frequent shortages of basic necessities but also brought with it technological and later medical advances that made possible the prevention and cure of disease. Improved sanitation, purification of water supplies and control of contagious diseases have all contributed greatly to lengthening the normal life span.

Patterns of disease

The recording of sickness and the registration of deaths and their causes present in themselves a significant contrast between societies at different levels of development. Industrial societies have comprehensive systems of registration of vital statistics and produce census data at regular intervals. 'Underdeveloped' societies do not have the administrative resources for collecting the statistics necessary for exact comparison with industrial societies so the data from these countries are based on special surveys and sample areas. But the differences between industrial and non-industrial societies are so great as to leave no doubts about the major contrasts. In highly industrialized societies many deaths are due to diseases whose causes are unknown and which cannot yet be prevented or cured. In less developed societies most deaths are due to diseases which can be controlled by medical science: the fact that they flourish in the face of this knowledge is one facet of the low level of development of these societies.

'Mass diseases' is the term used to describe those diseases which are so widespread and affect so high a proportion of the population that they mask other diseases to the point of making them medically or clinically irrelevant. The mass diseases may be regarded as the undergrowth of disease which has to be cleared before other forms of ill-health even reveal themselves. Mass diseases include: (a) infectious and contagious diseases like malaria, yaws, hookworm, tuberculosis, trachoma, syphilis, gastro-intestinal diseases, pneumonia, leprosy and sleeping sickness; (b) nutritional diseases like kwashiorkor, beri-beri, pellagra, and rickets; (c) pestilential diseases like cholera, small-pox, bubonic plague, typhus, typhoid, and yellow fever.

The term 'degenerative diseases' will be used to refer to those diseases which are associated with the older age groups—diseases of the heart and circulation (like arterio-sclerosis and thrombosis), brain-haemorrhages, organic and glandular disorders (like diabetes, some forms of rheumatism), 'stress' diseases (like gastric and duodenal ulcers), and cancers.

In the 'underdeveloped' countries the great health problem is the problem of mass diseases: this jungle undergrowth of disease has to be cleared before other forms of ill-health reveal themselves. In industrial societies mass diseases have, to a very large extent, been eliminated and the health problem is one of the control of degenerative diseases. Diseases of the heart and circulatory system and cancers and tumours alone now account for over fifty per cent of all deaths in the eight countries with the highest per capita national incomes and the percentage of deaths from these diseases is currently increasing. But it is only when mass diseases have been cleared away that the social and medical significance of degenerative diseases becomes apparent: only when a country has developed so far as to gain effective control of infectious and contagious diseases, when impure water and contaminated food are eliminated, when rodent and insect disease vectors (rats, flies, mosquitoes, etc.) are controlled, only when society reaches a certain stage of social development do degenerative diseases assume significant proportions.

There is a popular tendency to assume that since mass diseases are disproportionately high in the tropical countries, climate is the deciding factor in a society's state of health. But the state of health of a society depends more on the degree of social development than on the degree of latitude. This can be shown in three ways: first, by examining the changes in disease patterns which occur over time as a society industrializes; second, by examining the health conditions of different social groups living in the same area—groups that live side by side but have different standards and levels of living, differing health services, etc.; and third, by correlating indices of health and levels of indus-trialization *between* societies.

Societies which are now highly developed were once covered by a mantle of mass diseases. The patterns of mortality and morbidity of the now highly industrial societies were once like those current in today's non-industrial societies. We have already observed that the death-rates and more especially the infant mortality-rates of all industrial societies have fallen drastically over the past hundred and fifty years. Before the mid-nineteenth century, plague, cholera, typhus, and smallpox were common causes of death in Europe. Nutritional diseases like rickets and diseases such as tuberculosis, dysentery and syphilis were widespread.

A survey of the changing causes of death in England and Wales during the past hundred years, based on the published mortality statistics of the General Register Office, gives a good picture of the way the disease pattern of a society changes as economic development takes place. After allowance has been made for the changing age structure of the population, the male death-rate at all ages in 1947 was 42 per cent of the rate in 1846–50 and the female rate 35 per cent. Maximum improvement was among girls aged 5–9 years whose death-rate in 1947 was 9 per cent of the rate a hundred years before. The death-rate for boys aged 5–9 in 1947 was 11 per cent of the rate in 1846–50. The reduction in total mortality was such that whereas there were 515,591 civilian deaths registered in England and Wales in 1947, the total would have been over a million had the death-rates of 1848–73 still prevailed. In other words, if there had been no improvement in health conditions over half a million more people would have died.

Table 5.1 summarizes the changes that have taken place in the absolute death-rates from the main groups of diseases over the past hundred years. The figures shown in the table are the rates in 1947 expressed as percentages of the correspon-

Table 5.1 Death-rates in 1947 (people of all ages) as percentages of corresponding rates in 1848–72

	Males	Females
All causes	58	53
Infectious diseases	13	9
Tuberculosis (all forms)	20	12
Diseases of the nervous system and sense organs	34	46
Diseases of the respiratory system	36	27
Diseases of the digestive system	32	23
Non-venereal diseases of the genito-urinary system	186	231
Diseases of the circulatory system	418	328
Cancer	920	377

Source: W. P. D. Logan, 'Mortality in England and Wales from 1848 to 1947', *Population Studies*, IV, 2, 1950.

ding rates in 1848–72. The tremendous decline in mortality from 'mass diseases' is made clear in this table: the death-rate from infectious diseases for women in 1947 being only 9 per cent of what it had been a hundred years before, and that from tuberculosis being only 12 per cent. At the same time there has been a large absolute increase in the number of deaths attributed to 'degenerative diseases': since 1848–72 there has been a ninefold increase in the number of men dying from cancer and a fourfold increase in the number dying from circulatory diseases.

Up to now we have considered only the death-rates per thousand of the *total* population, which we have called absolute death-rates: now we wish to look at the death-rates per thousand *deaths* from all causes, which we will call the proportion-ate death-rates. If we concentrate upon these proportionate death-rates and the relative impor-tance of the various causes of death the same pattern emerges. Table 5.2 shows clearly that in 1848–72 about a third of the total number of deaths at all ages were due to infectious diseases: these were followed by diseases of the respiratory system, of the nervous system and of the digestive system. In 1947, on the other hand, diseases of the circulatory system came first with rather more than one-third of the total and these were followed by cancer.

In 1848–72, then, one death in every three in England and Wales was attributed to infectious disease: by 1947 infectious disease caused one male death in fourteen and one female death in seventeen. Within the group of infectious diseases in 1848–72 the highest individual cause of death

Table 5.2 The leading groups of causes of death in England and Wales in 1848–72 and in 1947 (proportionate rates per 1,000 deaths from all causes)

| | 1848–72 | | 1947 | |
	Males	Females	Males	Females
1 Infectious diseases	321	338	71	58
2 Respiratory diseases	148	134	91	68
3 Nervous diseases	129	117	76	101
4 Digestive diseases	83	85	45	36
5 Circulatory diseases	53	63	386	394
6 Cancer	9	22	149	161
All causes	1,000	1,000	1,000	1,000

1 Including typhoid, typhus, smallpox, measles, scarlet fever, whooping cough, diphtheria, influenza, cholera, dysentery, tuberculosis, syphilis.
2 Including bronchitis and all forms of pneumonia.
3 Including cerebral haemorrhage, apoplexy, etc.
4 Including ulcer of the stomach and duodenum, diarrhoea and enteritis, appendicitis, and cirrhosis of the liver.
5 Including heart diseases, diseases of the coronary arteries, and angina pectoris.

Source: W. P. D. Logan, 'Mortality in England and Wales from 1848 to 1947', *Population Studies*, IV, 2, 1950.

was respiratory tuberculosis. Scarlet fever and diphtheria came next, followed, in descending order of importance, by typhus, other forms of tuberculosis, smallpox, whooping cough, measles and cholera. By 1947 there had been a striking decline in the proportionate death-rate from infectious disease. Cholera and typhus had disappeared and smallpox and typhoid had, to all intents and purposes, been eliminated as causes of death. The reduction in mortality from scarlet fever was enormous: in 1848–72 it caused one death in twenty-five, in 1947 less than one in every ten thousand.

As the mass diseases were brought under control so the importance of degenerative diseases became clear. In 1848–72 less than one male death in a hundred was attributed to cancer: in 1947 one in seven was due to that disease. The female rates were one in forty-five in 1848–72 and one in six in 1947. Comparable in magnitude with the increase in cancer has been the rise in mortality from diseases of the circulatory system: in 1947 about one male death in ten and one female death in twenty was attributed to one of the diseases in this group, disease of the coronary arteries, a disease practically unknown as a cause of death at the beginning of this century.

The populations of industrial societies have not always had their present characteristics nor always experienced their current patterns of health and disease. When the present-day advanced economies were less complex the societies had demographic and health patterns, very like those current in contemporary modernizing countries. In nineteenth-century Britain the age structure, birth- and death-rates, and the causes of death, all resembled those now recorded in parts of Africa and other non-industrial countries. The British patterns have changed as the society has developed.

In Britain health and disease patterns characteristic of less developed and highly developed societies were separated in time during which the society became increasingly industrial. However, both patterns may be found existing side by side in those societies where a complex economy has been superimposed and as a result industrial and agrarian sectors co-exist. The Republic of South Africa is one country in which the two distinct patterns of disease can be observed co-existing. White South Africans in the cities enjoy the amenities and the health of an affluent industrial society, while in the tribal areas black South Africans retain the living standards and diseases of a non-industrial society. In Johannesburg the birth-, death- and morbidity-rates of the white population resident in the suburbs are similar to those of the population of a middle-class residential area in England. One such prosperous white suburb in Johannesburg is separated by only a main street from the Alexandra location, entirely populated by black South Africans. A study published in 1954 revealed that in the Alexandra location 10 per cent of the infant population died each summer from gastro-enteritis: tuberculosis was rampant and syphilis widespread. The black South Africans in Alexandra live in extreme poverty in overcrowed slums: in 1953 the average family of five members shared one room and lived on an income of about £3 a week.

This contrasting pattern of disease in adjacent neighbourhoods clearly has nothing to do with climate: it can only be explained in terms of the social development of South Africa. The rapid expansion of industry has greatly elevated the living standards of the politically and economically dominant white people. They form less than one-fifth of the total population but retain the ownership and control of industry and monopolize the better paid and more highly desired occupations. About one-tenth of the cultivable land of South Africa is in the hands of the black people who form four-fifths of the total population. Their reserves are overcrowded and impoverished and at any one time 50 to 70 per cent of the adult men are absent working in the mines and factories of the towns or on the farms owned by whites. This large body of unskilled migrants is the main labour force on which the continued expansion of South African industry depends.

This example illustrates the simple and direct relationship between standards of living and health conditions. Another way of demonstrating the same relationship is shown in Table 5.3. Instead of using data from only one society, we have here taken statistics from seventy-four countries in order to build up a broad comparative picture. The seventy-four countries have first been arranged into six groups by level of per capita national income (column A) and the group averages are given for one other rough indicator of economic development (percentage of male labour force in agriculture, column B) and for five indicators of health conditions. Columns C and D indicate the mortality levels in these societies. Column E gives some indication of the availability of health services. Although the lack of medical services in modernizing countries is underlined by these data, the figures none the less tend to exaggerate the general availability of physicians in the poorer countries. Physicians in these societies tend to concentrate in cities and to be more readily available to the rich than to the poor. Columns F and G are indicators of the levels of nutrition in the societies. Calorie intake is a measure of the quantity of the diet. For the maintenance of physical efficiency the daily calorie intake must be between 2,300 and 2,700. The actual level depends upon age and sex, type of activity, environmental temperature, and body weight. The average calorie supplies fall short of basic requirements in all regions of the world except Europe, North America, Australia, New Zealand, and Japan, that is the industrial societies. The calorie deficit in India may be as much as a quarter of the basic requirement. Column G gives an indication of the quality of the diet. Quality of diet depends on the presence in satisfactory amounts and proportions of vitamins and minerals. Animal protein level is probably the best indicator of quality because foods of animal origin are also good sources of protein and in turn of vitamins and minerals. Where the food supply is sufficient in calories it has usually a high protein content as well, whereas where there is a deficiency in calories the total amount of protein is usually small. Where the proportion of total calorie supply furnished by starchy staples exceeds 60 per cent it affords clear evidence that food supplies are nutritionally unbalanced. Such unbalanced diets (deficient in meat, milk, eggs, fish) have serious effects on health.

We have examined here some of the relationships between economic development and health. We have shown how patterns of disease change in one society over time; we have looked at co-existing but contrasting patterns of health within the same

Table 5.3 Health conditions and social development

	A	B	C	D	E	F	G
	National income per capita (1956–8) (average) US $	*Male labour force in agriculture (mid-1956) (est.) per cent*	*Expectation of life at birth in years (1955–8) (average)*	*Infant mortality-rate (1955–8) (average)*	*Inhabitants per physician*	*Calorie consumption per capita per day*	*Starchy staples as proportion of total calories consumed per cent*
Group 1	1,000+	17	70·6	24·9	885	3,153	45
Group 2	575–999	21	67·7	41·9	944	2,944	53
Group 3	350–574	35	65·4	56·9	1,724	2,920	60
Group 4	200–349	53	57·4	97·2	3,132	2,510	74
Group 5	100–199	64	50·0	131·1	5,185	2,240	76
Group 6	Under 100	74	41·7	180·0	13,450	2,070	77

Source: *Report on the World Social Situation*, New York: United Nations, 1961, p. 41.

country; and, finally, we have seen how, in the world at large, there is a correlation between certain indices of economic development and of mortality, health services and nutrition.

Fertility

Fertility in non-industrial societies[2]

A striking feature of agrarian societies is that all of them have much higher levels of fertility than industrial societies. Practically all of the world's 'underdeveloped' countries today, embracing three-quarters of the world's population, still have high birth-rates, that is, more than 30 live births per 1,000 inhabitants per year and more than four births per woman during her reproductive life (usually reckoned as 14–44). The key to the understanding of this well-documented fact is found, oddly enough, in the death-rate. Until recently, death-rates, especially infant mortality-rates, were extremely high in these areas. Agrarian societies therefore would not have survived had their high mortality not been matched by high fertility levels. This is not to say that parents plan to have children *in order to* maintain the total population, but rather that the *unintended* effect of having large families is to counter the large number of deaths. Probably many societies in the past failed to survive, their members dying faster than they could be replaced. Between 1900 and 1950, for example, it is estimated that nearly a hundred tribes became extinct in Brazil. The Kaingang from the State of São Paulo numbered 1,200 in 1912 but today have dwindled to 80; the Munduruku were 20,000 in 1925—in 1950 they numbered 1,200; the Kayapo of the river Araguaya were 2,500 in 1902 and 10 in 1950. The fate of the North American Indian is well known. The societies we know about today are necessarily the ones that did survive. They did so because they evolved (without any deliberation or planning) a social structure with a built-in system of incentives strong enough to induce their people to reproduce abundantly. If death-rates are very high a society which does not develop such an institutional structure may face extinction.

In analysing the institutional factors responsible for high fertility one must begin with the family, for the family in all human societies performs the functions of bearing, rearing, nourishing, and socializing children. In our society, as in all urban-industrial societies, the typical family consists of parents and their young or unmarried children. We shall call such a structure a 'conjugal' family. Such a family comes into existence with the birth of a first child in marriage; it continues to grow by the birth of other children; it undergoes partial dissolution as the children leave it, perhaps to set up households elsewhere, and comes to an end with the death of the parents. Sometimes, however, parents and children live in the same household or dwelling with other related people. A not uncommon arrangement in our society, particularly in stable working-class areas, is for grandparents to live with a married daughter and her children. In some respects this is paralleled among the Bemba of Zambia where a domestic group consisting of a man and his wife with their daughters and the husbands and children of the latter is found. The group breaks up, and new groups of the same kind are formed, when a man obtains permission to leave his parents-in-law, taking his wife and children with him. Far more prevalent in primitive and agrarian societies is what is sometimes called a patrilocal extended family: this is formed when sons remain in their father's family group bringing their wives to live with them so that their children also belong to the group. The household in all these instances consists of a kinship group larger than the conjugal family. We shall call such a grouping of related people living together as one unit a 'corporate' family. Living together in this way is not simply a matter of dwelling arrangements but also of economic solidarity and social control. One way of looking at the family in simple and agrarian societies is to see the conjugal family as being less independent of the wider kinship structure than it is in industrial societies. Its formation through marriage, its economic position, and the behaviour of its members are all governed to a greater degree by elder relatives. In most pre-industrial societies such control is facilitated by the 'joint-household' which arises when the newly married couple are required to live with the parents of one or the other partner. But a conjugal family may, although not occupying the same household with relatives, share so much of their daily lives that they and their relatives do in effect constitute one domestic unit, one 'composite' family. We use the term corporate family to apply as much to a wider kinship group living together thus as we do to a conjugal family and relatives who are occupying the same household all the time (the 'joint-household'). Again the Bemba provide a good example of the composite family: here the corporate family is composed of separate conjugal families housed in huts in the same village and not fenced off in any way from the rest of the community; but because the daughters' households are so closely linked with that of their mother, it must be reckoned as forming one domestic unit.

Given that in non-industrial societies the corporate family is typical, several consequences follow which are conducive to high fertility. Age at marriage is young because there is no implication that the husband must be able to support a wife and family before he gets married. Marriage is in no way made contingent on the possession of separate property by the newly married pair. In the patrilocal joint-household the bride simply joins her husband's family and the groom continues to live there. The bride can contribute to the joint economy even though young, and the groom is not required to be financially independent. In India in 1891 nearly a fifth of all girls below 15 years of age and 89 per cent of those aged 15–19, had been married. Even in 1951 nearly 10 per cent of Indian girls under 15 and three-quarters of those 15–19 had been married. In countries like Korea and Turkey practically no women between the ages of 20 and 24 are single. Early marriage represents the maximum possible insurance against the possibility of the disappearance of the family line in societies where not only is the annual death-rate high but the danger of sudden catastrophic increases in mortality is ever present. If the age of entry into marriage is late, the potential fertility that is lost may never be recovered: other things being equal, the younger the age at marriage, the higher the ultimate fertility.

In societies where the corporate family system prevails, marriages are usually arranged by the elders who make the arrangements early in the lifetime of the prospective mates. It is not difficult to see why this occurs. If the system is one of patrilocal residence, for example, a grown daughter remaining in her parental home is an anomaly. Her presence runs counter to the normal division of labour by sex which assumes the complementarity of husband and wife. Moreover, she must adjust to the wives of her brothers coming into the household. The daughters, then, must be married off as early as possible. Moreover, the daughter is most in demand as a prospective wife when she is young not only because she then has a greater potential fertility ahead of her and is more attractive sexually but also because she fits more easily into a subordinate status in her husband's parental home.

The corporate family system also encourages the early marriage of sons. The authority of the elders continues after marriage in China, India, rural Africa and many other agrarian areas. The father in China, for example, maintains his authority over his married sons and over the family property until death. The marriage of his sons is not, therefore, a threat to his authority and consequently he has no incentive for postponing the marriage. On the contrary, his authority is extended when his son brings a wife into his household and when she has children. Moreover, a marriage represents an alliance with another family and strengthens the position of the family in the wider community. The necessity of getting one's children married is an essential means of extending one's lineage and is frequently viewed as a religious and moral obligation. Consequently fewer persons go through life without marrying in agrarian than in urban-industrial societies. In India in 1891 a higher proportion of women aged 20–4 had been married (97·3 per cent) than were ever married at all in Western European countries. It is mainly in urban-industrial societies that the proportion of women never marrying by the end of the reproductive period exceeds 10 per cent. In Sweden in 1945 the figure was as high as 20·9 per cent, in Switzerland in 1941 20·1 per cent, in England in 1931 16·8 per cent and in Belgium in 1930 13·3 per cent. In non-industrial societies a very different picture emerges. In India in 1931 it was only 0·6 per cent, in Ceylon in 1946 3·4 per cent, in Malaya in 1947 3·3 per cent.

Once married the young couple in non-industrial societies are motivated to have offspring as early as possible and in considerable number. The economic cost of rearing children does not impinge directly on the parents to the extent it does in those societies where the conjugal family system prevails. With a common household and economy the child draws upon the resources of the kinship group as a whole not upon the parents' income alone. The inconvenience and effort of child care do not fall so heavily on the parents alone. The corporate family enables young mothers to work long hours in handicraft or in the fields while older women or older children look after the infants. The young married woman has every incentive to have children. She arrives in the patrilocal family as a stranger among her husband's relatives; her newness and her youth ensure her a low position in the family hierarchy. The birth of a son proves her contribution to her husband's line, gives her extra standing in her husband's eyes, and improves her status in the family as a whole. The corporate family rewards not only the mother's but also the father's reproduction. Numerous children help to strengthen the family as well as ensuring the continuation of the patrilineage. The household gains economic and political strength by the sheer weight of numbers: further, the more children the parents have the greater the security for their old age.

The roles of men and women tend to be sharply segregated in traditional agrarian societies. Women are confined to the household and to agricultural tasks of a menial kind and their lives revolve around home and children. There are no other careers open to them. The childbearing and rearing role is their main role. Moreover, women have a subordinate status in most agrarian societies. Although they may resent the physical burden and danger of childbearing the husband is unlikely to co-operate in any way to limit the size of the family. The husband usually views reproduction as his prerogative involving simple compliance on the wife's part.

This type of family structure is well adapted to a peasant mode of life. Apart from land, human labour is the main instrument of production. Hence the larger the family, the more labour is available. To learn the skills involved in this work no formal education is required: all that is necessary is observation and practice. Children can start earning a living at a very early age. Women can work in the fields and in the household handicrafts without much hindrance from constant childbearing.

In attempting to explain why fertility is so high in non-industrial societies it has been necessary to focus upon the social structure and in particular the family structure of these societies. It is, of course, true that most agrarian societies do not have the necessary technology to produce effective means of chemical or mechanical birth control. Some of them lack even elementary knowledge of the physiology of reproduction; others do not possess enough knowledge of chemistry to give command over materials. Where techniques of contraception are employed (usually in extramarital sexual intercourse) the methods tend to be hit-or-miss with folklore, rather than science, guiding the choice of means. Even the methods that would actually accomplish contraception are apt to be clumsy, sexually unsatisfactory, or even unhealthy. The technology and economy of preindustrial societies are not equal to the task of producing chemical or mechanical contraceptives

which would be at once cheap, readily available, effective, and satisfactory. But although techniques like withdrawal, intercourse without penetration, and heterosexual 'perversions', which are not dependent upon scientific and technological progress, are known and practised in nearly all societies, they do not represent major forms of fertility control in underdeveloped areas. The fundamental reason why fertility is so high in agrarian societies is that people are not motivated to limit the size of their families; the institutional structure provides incentives for having many children not for practising birth control.

However, almost all non-industrial societies practise abortion and infanticide as means of reducing the number of children at certain times— for example when food is short and the family is faced with starvation, or when the family is forced to migrate, either to escape from attack or to find new supplies of food, and only those who can be transported can survive. Abortion and infanticide have the advantage over contraception that they are always effective. At time of intercourse there is always the chance that pregnancy will not occur, and if events subsequent to intercourse make the birth of a child undesirable abortion or infanticide are effective remedies. Infanticide, of course, has the especial advantage over contraception that it allows children to be selected. In many underdeveloped societies it was the practice to kill or to allow to die many more female than male children. Infanticide allows offspring to be selected according to physical characteristics, weeding out those with deformities, bad health, or other unacceptable characteristics. Sometimes infanticide is practised when the circumstances of birth are considered abnormal and taboo. Twins, children born by breech birth, or on unlucky days, are typical victims.

The decline of fertility in industrial societies

The contrast between the fertility levels of industrial and non-industrial societies is very marked. This contrast can be illustrated by comparing the crude birth-rates of selected countries around 1955.

(*a*) *Non-industrial societies*

Ceylon	37·8
India	40
Malaya	43·5
Burma	45

Egypt	45
Ecuador	45
Mexico	45·9
Venezuela	46·6
Pakistan	50
Philippines	50
Guatemala	50·5

Range 38–50 live births per 1,000 population

(*b*) *Industrial societies*

United Kingdom	15·6
Belgium	16·7
Denmark	17·5
Netherlands	21·6
Australia	22·7
New Zealand	24·6
Norway	18·6
Sweden	14·9
USA	25·2

Range 15–25 live births per 1,000 population

The societies now characterized by low birth-rates formerly had far higher rates. In Scandinavia where birth-rate data are available for the longest period, the birth-rate averaged 31–4 per 1,000 between 1733 and 1800. With minor fluctuations the crude birth-rate was maintained at this level until after 1870. Between 1880 and 1884 the average crude birth-rates in these societies were:

England and Wales	33·82
Belgium	31·09
Denmark	32·26
Netherlands	35·01
Australia	35·09
New Zealand	37·57
Norway	30·83
Sweden	29·35
USA	36

The long-term decline of the birth-rate is one of the most complex problems in the demography of industrialized societies. The decline is known to have begun early in the nineteenth century in both the USA and France. In Sweden a slight downward trend became apparent during the first half of the nineteenth century, and in Ireland the birth-rate seems to have declined since around 1850. In the other industrializing countries the decline probably began later. For most countries it is not possible to determine the exact date at which decline began as the birth-rate fluctuated considerably from year to year and the registration of births was unreliable.

In most of the now industrial countries the level of the birth-rate in the 1870s was around 30 per 1,000 or higher. The downward trend began around 1880 and continued without any significant interruptions up to 1914. This decline proceeded at a rather modest pace up to 1900 but thereafter it became more pronounced. At the outbreak of the first world war the birth-rate had declined to less than 25 per 1,000 in all the now industrialized countries except Finland, Germany, the Netherlands and the countries of Southern Europe. The first world war saw a sharp decline in the birth-rate particularly in countries most directly affected by the war, such as Belgium, France, Germany and Italy where the birth-rate was reduced by 1919 to around 50 per cent of the pre-war level. The separation of men from their homes and families prevented many marriages and many births within existing marriages. In other countries like Finland, Britain, New Zealand and Switzerland, the decline was more moderate but still amounted to around 20–25 per cent. In Australia, Denmark, the Netherlands, Sweden, and the USA, there was only a minor decline.

Immediately after the war a brief period of recovery in the birth-rate was experienced in all countries. The peak rates were experienced in 1920 or 1921: but by 1923–4 the level of the birth-rate in all industrial societies was below the pre-war level. By the early 1930s the crude birth-rates were:

United Kingdom	15·8
Belgium	17·6
Denmark	17·9
Australia	17·6
New Zealand	17·5
Norway	15·7
Sweden	14·4
USA	19·7

The widespread economic depression with its accompanying unemployment and the general political instability of the 1930s acted as a deterrent to marriage and to childbirth. The lowest birth-rates observed between the two world wars in any of the industrialized societies occurred in Austria (12·8 in 1937) and in Sweden (13·7 in 1939). However, in southern Europe, Canada and the Netherlands the birth-rate did not fall appreciably below 20 per 1,000.

The break in the downward trend appeared first in northern Europe and Oceania around 1935: in central and southern Europe and North America the decline in the birth-rate continued until 1936 or 1937 and in Spain and Portugal until

1941. The birth-rates remained fairly stable for several years and even the outbreak of the second world war did not introduce a sharp decline in rates. Indeed rates began to rise noticeably in most European countries even while the fighting continued; the 'recovery' of the birth-rate was well under way by 1942 and 1943. The different patterns of development of the birth-rate during the two war periods were due to the fact that the general level and the underlying long-term trends of the birth-rate were different. Whereas the fluctuations around the first world war were superimposed upon a generally declining trend in an often still very high birth-rate, the trend around the second world war was almost stationary or showed even a slight increase in a very low rate. The average birth-rate for the period 1939–45 was, in most industrial countries, above the pre-war level.

The peak in the 'recovery' of the birth-rate after the 1930s was reached in most advanced societies in 1946 or 1947: the birth-rate at this point had not been as high since the years immediately following the 1914–18 war. Indeed in Finland and New Zealand an equally high rate had not been recorded since before 1914 and for the Netherlands it is necessary to go back to 1900 to find a birth-rate as high as that recorded for the period 1946–50. Since the early post-war years, however, the birth-rate has again declined in most countries: in Denmark, Britain, the Netherlands, and Sweden it declined by 25–30 per cent from the post-war peak of 1947 to 1954. In Australia the birth-rate has fallen from 23·6 per 1,000 in 1946 to 19·4 in 1967. The slight 'recovery' of the birth-rate in industrial societies from some time in the late thirties to about 1947 is likely to be a result of people getting married earlier and of a higher proportion of people getting married rather than of any increase in completed family size.

Why has there been a long-term decline in the birth-rate? Why has the general level of fertility fallen as the societies become increasingly urban and industrial? The answer lies in the ever increasing proportion of the population within these societies adopting the practice of family limitation by contraception. It is, of course, theoretically possible that there has been some decline in the physical capacity of men and women to produce children in industrial societies. It has been suggested that various factors in urban-industrial life have reduced reproductive capacity: increase in alcoholism and in venereal disease, employment of women in factories, excessive practice of sports by women, frequent bathing with soap (an effective spermicide), even bicycle riding (reputed to harm the female reproductive organs) have been mentioned. It has also been alleged that the nervous strain of modern life lowers the intensity of sexual energies and thus reduces the frequency of intercourse. Such arguments need not be taken seriously. All the evidence points to a decline in alcoholism and venereal disease since the eighteenth century: no one has attempted to show how women's sports or employment in factories lessen reproductive capacity. As for bicycle riding, this practice is most common in the Netherlands which has the highest birth-rate in Western Europe. Certain features of modern industrial societies have probably *improved* reproductive potentialities—better health, better nutrition, increased knowledge of the reproductive process, better obstetrical care. Women certainly suffer less from serious deformities of the pelvis than in the past and this must to some extent have increased their capacity to have children. In fact the inquiry into family limitation and human fertility carried out by Dr E. Lewis-Faning for the Royal Commission on Population (1949) demonstrated convincingly that present-day couples in Britain would experience no difficulty in having as many children as Victorian parents had if they so desired. The overwhelming weight of the evidence supports the view that family size has declined in industrial societies as a result of the deliberate use of birth control techniques. The salient factor in the secular decline of the birth-rate over the past hundred years has been a radical change in attitude towards parenthood. People no longer wish to have the large families which were customary in pre-industrial society.

In attempting to explain this phenomenon the experience of England and Wales may be taken as generally illustrative of that of Western Europe, the United States and other industrial societies. It is important to emphasize that the fall in family size has not proceeded uniformly throughout all sections of society. It began first and continued most rapidly among the highest socio-economic groups. The earliest signs of a decline in fertility in England took place among the families of military and naval officers, clergymen, lawyers, doctors, authors, journalists and architects. Not far behind them came civil service officers and clerks, law clerks, dentists, schoolmasters, teachers, professors and lecturers, people employed in scientific pursuits, and accountants. In general the decline in family size in England began as an upper- and middle-class phenomenon at some time in the 1870s. It was not until much later that the decline occurred in less privileged social groups. The inverse relationship between income and fertility is still marked today. Persons in the more highly paid, more desired, and more difficult to enter occupations have smaller families than people in the lower income and status positions: 'the rich get rich and the poor get children'.

During the period 1850–70 there was a very marked increase in the number of middle-class people in England. The number of occupations with middle-range incomes increased enormously. Proportionately more people than in the past were able to afford to live in the middle-class manner. They felt secure and looked forward to ever increasing prosperity and progress. Such optimism gave rise to ever increasing aspirations. The rise in real incomes made higher levels of living possible for the successful and the necessary status symbols of the middle class became increasingly elaborate and expensive. Larger houses, costly food and wine, more servants, carriages, expensive furniture, travel, holidays abroad—these were becoming the marks of middle-class living. This period was also a period of marked social mobility: people from lower-class origins were moving into middle-class occupations. The display of material possessions emphasized the achievement of new status. Then came the so-called great depression of 1870–90. Although the middle-class standard of living was never seriously threatened during this period most people who gained the public ear talked as though it was. The feeling of increasing prosperity, the confidence of the 1850s and 1860s, was shattered. In this situation the members of the middle class chose deliberately to reduce the size of their families rather than give up their newly acquired taste for those material comforts which had become a recognized part of their style of life.

The growing emphasis on personal achievement led to increased preoccupation with the competitive nature of life. It was felt necessary to struggle to keep one's job and one's position in the social hierarchy. Children came to be regarded as a liability, as a severe handicap in the race up the status ladder. The number of children had to be limited, not only because expenditure on them handicapped parents in their own efforts to maintain a middle-class style of life, but also because the fewer the children the more could be spent on each child and the better the start in the competitive struggle the child would have. By 1870 'giving the children a good start in life' was becoming an increasingly expensive affair. It meant providing a long and costly education. The qualifications for entering medicine and the law were tightened. Patronage in the army and the civil service was abolished making entry now by competitive examination. Entrance to the professions thus became more formal and easier to understand. This widened the field and made parents doubly anxious to provide the education necessary for their sons to enter the 'gentlemanly' jobs. It is not surprising that this period marks the great expansion of public school education. Nor is it difficult to see why the idea that children were sent by God gave way to the notion that it was not immoral to prevent them from coming if their future prospects, as members of the middle class, were less bright than those of their parents had been.

Once the process of family limitation got under way it became one of self-sustained momentum. The gap between those with large families and those with small families widened and the advantages of family planning became obvious. For women the advantages were considerable. It freed them from the perpetual risk, burden, and inconvenience of childbirth and child rearing. It enabled them to take advantage of the increasing opportunities to make a career outside the home. The use of birth control was thus a factor in the emancipation of women: at the same time the changing power position of women, and their attainment of greater equality with men, was one of the factors furthering the decline of the birth-rate.

In Britain manual workers were slow to follow the middle classes in adopting family limitation. Although a few skilled workers were enjoying rising wages in the last decade of the nineteenth century, about a third of the total population of the industrial cities was living in poverty. Poverty and overcrowding are not conducive to the foresight and planning which contraception involves: nor are they the conditions which favour a break from tradition and the introduction of new practices. The subordinate role of the manual worker's wife tended to make her feel helpless at the prospect of successive unwanted pregnancies and unable to take the necessary steps to prevent them in the face of opposition from a husband who might regard the use of contraception as a threat to his virility. The separate and largely segregated activities of members of manual workers' families defined children as the wife's responsibility. Husbands paid over a fixed wage to their wives who had to do the best they could with it. The increasing affluence of the manual worker since 1950 has been accompanied by the predictable decline in family size.

Sometimes the fall in family size is explained entirely as the consequence of the improvement and increased dissemination of contraceptives and contraceptive knowledge. Yet sheer knowledge of a technique and its easy availability are not enough to induce people to use it: people will only make use of a technique if it serves their needs. Increased contraceptive knowledge and improved methods of contraception have clearly been a major *means* of limiting fertility since 1870, but the *causes* of family limitation must be sought in the changes in social structure which led to attitudes favourable to smaller families.

Ageing of populations

With few exceptions, every society has persons of all ages in it, but societies differ from one another in their age composition (that is, in the proportion of the total population found in each age group). Where these differences are large they may be of great importance both as factors limiting further demographic changes and also in influencing social and economic development.

Table 5.4 The age structures of different types of society

Country	Year	Age composition of the population (% of total in each age group)			
		0–14	15–44	45–64	65+
Non-industrial societies					
Guatemala	1950	44	43	11	2
India	1951	37	46	13	4
Egypt	1947	38	45	14	3
Highly industrialized societies					
Britain	1951	22	43	24	11
Sweden	1950	23	43	23	11
Austria	1951	23	40	26	11
Transitional industrializing societies					
Britain	1851	35	46	14	5
	1901	32	48	15	5
Sweden	1850	33	46	16	5
	1900	33	42	17	8
Austria	1869	34	46	16	4
	1900	34	45	16	5

Source: *The Aging of Populations*, Population Studies, No. 26, New York: United Nations, 1956.

Table 5.4 shows the age distribution of different types of societies in the middle of the twentieth century and of some highly developed countries in the past. By comparison the highly industrialized societies have low percentages of children, high percentages of old people, and a relatively large intermediate age group (sometimes called 'the working age group', 15–64). As far as we know, the age structure of the non-industrial societies has undergone little change in the past hundred years or more. In the now highly developed countries the age structure has, by contrast, undergone marked changes during the last fifty to a hundred years. The direction of this change has been an increase in the proportion of elderly people and a decline in the proportion of children. This process is known as the ageing of the population. In France, for example, the proportion of persons over sixty-five has increased from 6·5 per cent of the total population in 1851 to 11·8 per cent in 1950; Belgium the increase has been from 5·9 per cent in 1846 to 10·7 per cent in 1947; and in the United States the percentage has changed from 3·4 per cent in 1880 to 8·1 per cent in 1950. The present differences between the industrial and non-industrial countries can be put in this way: in France one person in eight is over sixty-four, in Sweden and Britain one in ten and in the United States one in twelve; whereas in Guatemala only one person in fifty is as old as that and in Ghana only one in sixty-six. In France, England, and Sweden half of the population is over thirty-three, thirty-six and thirty-seven respectively: in Pakistan, on the other hand, half of the population is under eighteen, in Brazil under nineteen, and in the Congo under twenty.

What accounts for these differences and these trends in the age distribution of populations? The age structure of a population is governed by demographic factors alone, at least directly. Although it is true that demographic variables are themselves influenced by the social structure, it is through the demographic variables that the social structure affects the age composition. Or to put it a different way, it is only to the extent that changes in social structure produce changes in births, deaths, or migrations that they modify the age structure. The demographic variables—fertility, mortality, migration—may be regarded as independent, at least within a certain range of variation. Changes in fertility may take place without any variation in mortality, and vice versa. Similarly, changes in reproductive behaviour may occur without affecting migratory movements. It is evident, however, that all these variations are independent only within certain limits. If the death-rate in a country with a high level of fertility declines steadily, there will be an increase in population such that sooner or later fertility will decline in turn. Accordingly it may be said that this decline in fertility is not independent of the decline in mortality. It is easy to conceive of situations in which variations in mortality and fertility would ultimately give rise to migratory movements. However, before the stage is reached at which movements are necessarily interdependent, there will be a period when mortality, fertility and migrations may vary independently of one another.

The problem to be solved may therefore be stated as follows: if two of the three factors are held constant, what effect will the variations of the third have on age structure? Let us confine ourselves to a particular example, the population of Britain. There is a long series of good censuses, equally spaced in time, which provide the necessary data. In the last hundred years both fertility and mortality have declined substantially. Mortality has declined since the end of the eighteenth century, though the decline has been most rapid since 1900. Fertility declined from 1870 to the 1930s, then rose slightly, and now appears to be at a level slightly above the 1930s' point. Migration can be ignored here since it has not occurred on a scale large enough to affect significantly the age structure of Britain. The influence of fertility on age composition must now be separated from that of mortality. This can be done by first taking the actual age structure of Britain in 1861 and in 1951, as revealed by the census. Two hypothetical populations are then calculated. The first is the population of Britain in 1951 as it would have been had fertility remained constant at the 1861 level while mortality followed its actual course between 1861 and 1951. The second projection is based on the assumption that mortality remained constant at the 1861 level while fertility followed its actual course.

The resulting age structures are shown in Table 5.5. From this it is clear that the main factor responsible for the ageing of populations is declining fertility. The fall in the birth-rate from the 1870s, if experienced without any change in death-rates, would have led to a trend in age structure following somewhat closely that which actually occurred (cf. columns 4 and 2). Had the mortality decline of the last hundred years been experienced without any change in fertility the

Table 5.5 Age structures of Great Britain, 1861 and 1951 (per cent)

Age	Actual 1861 census	Actual 1951 census	Hypothetical 1951: projected from 1861 on assumptions of (a) fertility constant at 1861 level (b) actual mortality 1861–1951	Hypothetical 1951: projected from 1861 on assumptions of (a) mortality constant at 1861 level (b) actual fertility 1861–1951
0–14	35·68	22·38	39·07	20·87
15–59	56·83	61·93	53·71	63·85
60+	7·49	15·69	7·22	15·28

Source: N. H. Carrier, 'Demographic aspects of the ageing of the population', in A. T. Welford et al., Society, London: Routledge & Kegan Paul, 1962, pp. 457–68.

proportion of children in the population would have remained much higher and the proportion of aged persons would have been much lower (cf. columns 3 and 2). The effect of a decline in mortality alone would have been to keep the age structure much as it was in 1861 (cf. columns 3 and 1). The reduction of mortality, to which ageing of populations has so often been attributed, does in fact lead to rejuvenation not ageing. The reason for this is that the decline in mortality has been very much a decline in infant and childhood mortality, with relatively little improvement at older ages. Thus the population of Britain has become older since 1861 because of falling fertility; but falling mortality (with its tendency to produce a younger population) has prevented it from becoming older still.

Every individual inexorably gets older as time passes. How old he gets depends on how long he avoids death. Populations, on the other hand, can get older or younger. They get older primarily as the result of declining fertility, and younger primarily as the result of rising fertility. It is the small number of children born per woman that explains the high average age found in industrial countries and the high birth-rate of non-industrial countries that accounts for their young populations.

There has been a widespread tendency to exaggerate the effects of ageing of populations.[3] The increase in the proportion of old people in highly developed societies has been considered the cause of many social problems which are, in fact, the result of other changes in social structure. Much of the alarm about ageing is unjustified. The recent rise in the birth-rate in all industrial societies will lead gradually to a decline in the proportion of old people, unless some epoch-making discovery, like a cure for cancer, reduces mortality in the old age groups. The talk about 'the crippling burden of old age' ignores the fact that the youthful age structure of non-industrial societies entails a very high rate of population growth and is concomitant with a large dependent child population.

Whether the aged constitute a problem depends not so much upon their number as on their social situation. All societies assign status, ascribed rights and duties, according to age. In simple societies and in agrarian societies the aged command great respect and power. In traditional societies like ancient China and India, the old had greater authority and prestige than any other age group. In an illiterate society where knowledge depends on memory and habit, the old are the wise ones. In a relatively static society where learning is traditional the old are more proficient than the young: their accumulated knowledge is not displaced by new techniques, new theories, new facts. 'With the ancient is wisdom, and in length of days understanding.' In a society in which the corporate family is the norm the head of the family has great authority. His authority extends over a wide kinship group and is buttressed by his close and long association with other members of the family since their infancy. This creates in them ingrained habits of respect and subordination towards him. In ancient China the family religion (incorporating so-called ancestor-worship) also bolstered the position of the aged. Respect for the aged while alive was closely akin to worship of them after death. In traditional agrarian societies the aged are no problem: they are not pitied or shoved aside, and are not treated as objects of charity and special concern. Their status is very high. An old Chinese proverb puts the matter clearly, 'My father is all-wise but my father's father is even wiser.'

It is only in a changing, mobile, urban, industrial society that birth-rates fall so markedly as to produce ageing of the population. At the same time this type of society also alters the status of the aged. It makes them obsolescent, useless, insecure. For in highly industrialized societies the emphasis is on change, innovation, new ideas, new techniques, new knowledge, new skills. The sheer speed of social change puts a premium on flexibility, on the recency of what has been learnt: and hence the whole emphasis is on youth. The old, with habits and fundamental notions acquired forty years or more ago are out-of-date. What was new and revolutionary forty years ago is regarded as antiquated and conservative today.

An important feature of industrial societies which helps to make the aged a social problem is the conjugal family system—the type of family in which husband, wife, and children live apart as a separate unit and have a high degree of independence from parents and other relatives. This conjugal family structure excludes aged parents because by the time the parents have reached an advanced age the children have gone out to found independent homes of their own. Aged parents must therefore live by themselves or with other old people. In the United States in 1940 only 9·4 per cent of men, and only 20·7 per cent of women aged 70–4 were living in the home of a son or daughter. In interpreting this data it must be realized that, on the average, each old person has more than one grown-up offspring with whom he could live. Even if all persons aged seventy or over lived with a son or daughter, this would still mean that relatively few married couples would have an older person living with them. The spatial and mental separation of parents from children is heightened in industrial society by the fact that the fertile period in each woman's life is tending to begin and end earlier. Women have their first child earlier than was usual in the nineteenth century, and they tend to have all they are going to have at an earlier age, usually before they reach thirty. Thus not only are parents having fewer children but they are experiencing a longer period of life after their children have become independent. The isolation of aged parents from their children is aggravated by the high level of geographical mobility, which often separates parents and children by hundreds of miles, and by the high degree of social mobility which often places parents and children in different social worlds. This high degree of geographical and social mobility is a concomitant of a high degree of industrialization.

Bureaucratization and the shift to large-scale organizations also affect the status of the aged. In farming and in small businesses the owner, as he gets older, can gradually reduce the amount of his work and confine himself increasingly to a supervisory role. He can ease off at his own discretion; he can retire gradually. But in the large enterprise emphasis is placed on efficiency, on standardized bureaucratic rules, and on impersonality. Such conditions preclude gradual retirement. A rigid retirement age is fixed and the change is abrupt and taken without regard to individual capacity. An individual is suddenly separated from his work. Despite a lifetime's experience, he is of no more use. Even before retiring age, the speed of economic change in highly industrial societies creates difficulties for the older worker. Structural changes in industrial employment, a necessary and fundamental feature of highly developed societies, affect the older worker far more than the younger. Older workers will have specialized skills or certain routines which if they become obsolescent are not easily discarded. Younger workers are more easily retrained—and are more readily accepted for retraining—than older men. They also tend to be more adaptable and mobile. Older people are likely to have built up strong ties within a community which act as a deterrent to moving to new developing areas. Unemployment statistics reveal that workers over forty have much longer durations of unemployment than younger men.

It is often argued that an ageing population will produce a conservative society: that economic, cultural, and political progress is retarded where the population is composed of a relatively large proportion of aged persons. This might be true if the aged had more power than other groups in industrial societies. In fact they seem to be one of the most powerless groups—unable, indeed, even to secure for themselves a reasonable standard of living. But quite apart from these considerations, the world's most conservative regions are those with a very young population, the non-industrial countries. In India, for example, the greatest justification for any practice has always been that it was always done that way in the past. The kind of society that can reduce its fertility to the point where there is a great proportion of old people in the population is necessarily a developing society. It must have cities, industrial technology, and science: it must be a constantly changing society.

The Royal Commission on Population (1949) argued that ageing of populations restricts social mobility:[4]

In the nineteenth century the older and more experienced workers were relatively scarce. A high proportion of them obtained superior positions, and promotion tended to take place at relatively young ages.

Nowadays the seniors are considerably thicker on the ground; other things being equal, there would not be the same pressure to promote young men, and a larger proportion would tend to miss promotion altogether. With still further ageing the competition for promotion must be expected to increase. . . . the tendency will be for only the most exceptional of the younger people to be promoted. The prospects for the younger may become so poor that a powerful sense of frustration may arise.

This paragraph contains a whole series of fallacious statements. It may well be true that if the top posts in a hierarchy were filled by persons chosen at random from the population, a society with a high proportion of old people would be more likely to have elderly leaders than a population with a low proportion of old people. But whether posts are filled by young persons or old persons depends upon the way in which office-holders are recruited. It also depends on whether the number of such posts is stationary, declining, or increasing. In an expanding economy where the demand for doctors, engineers, managers, teachers, and other high level people is increasing, the number of opportunities for promotion and social mobility will also increase. A highly industrial society is characterized by an increasing middle class and by a high rate of social mobility. In such a society the prospects for social mobility are far greater than in a non-industrial society with a young population. After all, the very process of ageing implies that the proportion of young people is declining: this should surely reduce competition among the young not increase frustration.

Another conceivable consequence of an ageing population is the economic drain of old-age dependency. In sheer numbers, however, the increased proportion of the aged has been counterbalanced by a decreased proportion of dependent children. Compared with 'under-developed' societies, industrial societies are in an advantageous position so far as the ratio of economically active (15–64 age group) to dependent age groups (0–14, and over 64) is concerned. Of course the weight of the dependency burden is determined not only by the ratio of dependants but also on the amount spent for the support of each dependant. Thus a reduction in the proportion of children in the society does not necessarily mean a proportionate decrease in the costs of childhood dependency. Children may be given better and longer education, improved medical care, better diet. The essential point to be remembered is that those societies which have a low proportion of children and a high proportion of old people are those with the highest productivity and the highest national income per capita. These societies can afford to carry a high burden of dependency, and they have, indeed, raised the standard of what is considered appropriate for children and for old people—higher levels of nutrition, education, housing, and medical care.

Notes

1 This section is based on Kingsley Davis, 'The world's population crisis' in Robert K. Merton and Robert Nisbet (eds), *Contemporary Social Problems* (3rd ed.), 1971, pp. 363–405.

2 This section is based on Kingsley Davis, 'Institutional patterns favoring high fertility in under-developed areas', *Eugenics Quarterly*, 2, 1 March 1955, pp. 33–9.

3 This section is based on Kingsley Davis and J. W. Combs, 'The sociology of an aging population', in *The Social and Biological Challenge of our Aging Population*, Proceedings of the Eastern States Health Education Conference, 1949. New York, 1950, pp. 146–70.

4 *Report of the Royal Commission on Population*, (Cmd 7695), London: HMSO, 1949, pp. 119–20.

Reading

Banks, J. A., *Prosperity and Parenthood*, London: Routledge & Kegan Paul, 1954. An excellent sociological study of family planning among the Victorian middle classes.

Cipolla, Carlo, *The Economic History of World Population*, Harmondsworth: Penguin, 1962. Brief, inexpensive, and valuable.

Davis, Kingsley and Blake, Judith, 'Social structure and fertility: an analytic framework' in *Sociology, The Progress of a Decade*, edited by S. M. Lipset and N. J. Smelser, pp. 356–77, Englewood Cliffs: Prentice-Hall, 1961 and the Bobbs-Merrill Reprint Series in the Social Sciences, S–371. Another of the many excellent articles by Kingsley Davis on the sociology of population.

Freedman, Ronald (ed.), *Population, The Vital Revolution*, New York: Doubleday Anchor, 1964. A well-chosen selection of short essays by leading American demographers.

Petersen, William, *Population*, London: Collier-Macmillan, 1969 (2nd ed.). In many ways the best textbook. Students will have no difficulty in recognizing those sections which are marred by Petersen's commitment to US capitalism.

Wrong, Dennis H., *Population and Society*, New York: Random House, 1967 (3rd ed.), The best short introduction to the sociology of population: includes a useful chapter on migration.

Further reading

Birmingham, W. B., Neustadt, I., and Omaboe, E. M. (eds), *A Study of Contemporary Ghana, Volume II: Some Aspects of Social Structure*, London: Allen & Unwin, 1967. The first four chapters on population, pp. 17–200 by Dr J. C. Caldwell are outstanding: one of the best studies of the population of a non-industrial society.

Davis, Kingsley, *The Population of India and Pakistan*, Princeton University Press, 1951. The other outstanding study of the population of an under-developed area.

Hawthorn, Geoffrey, *The Sociology of Fertility*, London: Collier-Macmillan, 1970. A stimulating critical review of the literature with an excellent annotated bibliography.

McKeown, Thomas, *Medicine in Modern Society*, London: Allen & Unwin, 1965. Part I, pp. 21–58, is the best discussion of the decline of mortality and population growth in England and Wales 1750–1900.

Susser, M. W. and Watson, W., *Sociology in Medicine*, London: Oxford University Press, 1971 (2nd ed.). The first chapter, pp. 1–54, contains much useful data.

The Department of Economic and Social Affairs (formerly the Department of Social Affairs) of the United Nations Organization, New York, has been responsible for the publication of many admirable studies of population. Students will find *Preliminary Report on the World Social Situation* (1952), and *Report on the World Social Situation* (1957, 1961, 1963, 1967, 1970) extremely useful. *The Determinants and Consequences of Population Trends* (1953) is a very thorough and lucid summary of all the important theories and facts about population up to 1952. *The Aging of Populations and its Economic and Social Implications* (1956) and *Recent Trends of Fertility in Industrialized Countries* (1957) are useful. *A Summary of the World Population Situation in 1970* (1971) is a very brief (36 page) survey of the field. *Demographic Yearbook* is the standard secondary source of world population statistics. It is indispensable for advanced study.

6 The family

The structure of the human family

For as far back into history as we have evidence human beings have lived in families of one sort or another. But family forms are not uniquely human; they can also be found in some other mammal species. The main difference is that the family forms of lower mammals are biologically conditioned whereas the human family has an immense variety of types and the particular form it takes is largely the outcome of social factors. The relationship between infants and other members of the species is especially important with human beings, partly because of the relative immaturity of the human infant at birth, and partly because human self-sufficiency is much more dependent upon learning processes than is that of most animals.

Perhaps the most important of these relationships is that between the infant and the mother. In birds and the lower mammals (for example, rats), the mother and the offspring are bound together by mechanisms which appear to be largely biological and 'instinctive'. The glandular processes of a pregnant rat drive her to build nests and, after the birth of her offspring, to perform the activities necessary for feeding and protecting them. These actions are performed in a highly standardized and stereotyped way which characterizes the whole species. At the level of monkeys, however, there is evidence to suggest that such maternal behaviour is no longer entirely biological and automatic, but dependent on complex learning processes. This is even more the case at the level of human beings, where the mechanisms binding the mother to the offspring are cul-tural and not biological. Rather than a universal 'maternal instinct' resulting in a standard form of maternal behaviour there is a wide variety of ways of treating children, ranging from neglect and selective infanticide in some societies, to the highly protective, child-centred household of modern Western society. Even the degree to which women want to have children (as well as how many they want) varies from society to society —a variation which itself can only be explained in terms of other aspects of the society: in some societies there are religious and economic rewards for having large numbers of children; in other societies there are religious and economic penal-ties. In short, although there is a physical relation-ship between a woman and her offspring, maternal behaviour is largely learned from the customs, values and beliefs of the society; as these differ so do the relations between mother and child.

Marriage

The biological link between the father and the offspring is less direct and less ostensible than that of the mother and child, but nevertheless in most societies there is a bond between a man and the woman-infants unit. In some societies the bond of marriage is a permanent one; in others it may be dissolved at will. In some societies one partner dominates the relationship; in others there is equality between the spouses. In some societies sexual relations are crucial to marriage; in others they are much less important. And so one could go on; marriage relationships are as variable as those between mother and child. In all societies, however, marriage (or some recognized form of man-woman union) has the support of law, custom and religion and in many societies it is highly valued. There are two factors which help us to understand why this is so and at the same time help to account for some of the variability of marriage relations from society to society. One is the economic division of labour between the sexes; and the other is the prohibition on incest.

Modern industrial society is historically unique in that a clear division of labour between the sexes does not prevail. Such a division of labour has been a feature of all previously existing societies and is also present in contemporary non-industrial societies. The nature of the tasks allocated to the two sexes, however, is variable. The allocation of domestic duties to women and 'bread-winning' tasks to men which characterized some sections of European society in the recent past, and is still held by many to be the ideal state, is only one of many variants. In most hunting and gathering societies the men are the hunters and the women are the food gatherers. In some other simple societies the division is between hunting and cultivation. In many West African societies women engage in trade and commerce, men in hunting and trapping, and agricultural tasks are systematically divided between the sexes. The consequences of such economic specialization for life in such societies are well illustrated by the following example related by the anthropologist Lévi-Strauss:[1]

> One of the strongest field recollections of this writer was his meeting, among the Bororo of central Brazil, of a man about thirty years old: unclean, ill-fed, sad, and lonesome. When asked if the man was seriously ill the natives' answer came as a shock: What was wrong with him?—nothing at all, he was just a bachelor, and true enough, in a society where labour is systematically shared between man and woman and where only the married status permits the man to benefit from the fruits of woman's work, including delousing, body painting, and hair-plucking as well as vegetable food and cooked food (since the Bororo woman tills the soil and makes pots), a bachelor is really only half a human being.

Clearly in such a society the benefits to be derived from having a complementary partner in social and economic tasks provide a very considerable incentive for men and women to get married and this helps us to understand the support given to marriage by law and custom.

The almost universal prohibition upon marriage or sexual relations with close relatives highlights another important function of marriage. As with the division of labour between the sexes, however, the precise form of marriage prohibition and of the incest taboo varies from society to society. In all known societies (with the exception of the royal houses of a few historical societies—the best known being ancient Egypt) sexual relations between parent-child and brother-sister are prohibited. Some societies have no further prohibitions; others prohibit sexual relations between different classes of cousins; yet others extend the ban to the whole lineage or clan. On the whole, marriage prohibitions follow similar patterns. There is some reason to believe that sexual unions between close kin may, in certain circumstances, have an undesirable genetic effect. But it is by no means unknown for human societies to adopt habits and to cling to them for centuries even though they are biologically harmful: witness the prohibition of beef to starving Indian peasants, or the ritual denial of meat, fish, eggs and milk to pregnant women and growing children in several East African tribes. Biological arguments are not a very satisfactory explanation of the universality of the taboo on incest; and they are no explanation at all of the variations from society to society of the relatives who shall be included in the prohibition.

Whatever the explanation of the incest taboo and the prohibitions on marriage that accompany it, its major function is to compel the young adult to participate in social groupings other than that of the parents. If the individual family is to be related to the wider society, if familial dependence and co-operation is to be incorporated into a wider social division of labour, then the offspring must form ties to families other than their own. This is particularly important because, in most societies, marriage is not the individual man-woman affair of Western industrial society, but essentially a bond between the families, lineages or clans providing the husband and wife. Thus 'marriage out' becomes a method of forging links of material obligations between groups. The importance of this is illustrated by a New Guinean view of marriage; to them the real purpose of getting married is not so much to obtain a wife, as to secure brothers-in-law. Which relatives are included in the marriage ban depends upon the structure of the wider society. In industrial societies, where family ties are not involved in wider societal organization, incest and marriage prohibitions only apply within the immediate family. On the other hand, in societies such as the Tonga of East Africa, where there are no specific laws or political institutions to settle disputes and govern, marriage with any member of the same clan is prohibited. Marriages must therefore be between clans and they form reciprocal obligations which give everyone an interest in other clans and so enhance economic co-operation. The result is that disputes are more likely to be settled without resort to open warfare and a measure of political stability is achieved.

These two factors give us a different perspective on marriage from that usually held. Whatever the motivations of the individuals involved, marriage provides a way of participating in the larger society; of forging bonds and reciprocal obligations between groups and individuals. It is also an avenue for engaging in the economic division of labour.

The focus of the family

It has already been suggested that family forms differ widely from society to society. One of the major variations is in the size and nature of the residential unit which is of crucial importance because it suggests where the major focus of the family lies. We can distinguish two major types of family unit along these lines: the 'conjugal', where the residential unit consists of husband, wife and children and is relatively independent of wider kinship connections; and the 'corporate', where several generations, their spouses and offspring, form a residential unit. The occurrence of one or other of these types in the societies of the world is not haphazard; on the contrary, it is systematically related to variations in other parts of the society.

Economic organization is particularly important and different types of economic pursuit are found in conjunction with characteristic types of family organization. The conjugal family type tends to occur at two widely separated levels of economic development. Advanced industrial economies and simple hunting and gathering economies both facilitate a relatively independent conjugal unit. In industrial societies people make their living outside the family, in specialized institutions— factories, offices and the like—where the pattern of organization rests on an impersonal, contractual basis. Kinship connections are, for the most part, relatively unimportant, both in getting a job and in carrying it out. Neither the laws and cus-

toms of property ownership and landholding, nor the organization of labour, are such as to hold one adult generation to the other. On the contrary, geographical mobility and social mobility are characteristic of industrial societies and both facilitate the emancipation of the child from the family in which he grew up. Similarly, hunting and gathering societies do not provide economic bonds for holding the generations together and are characterized by a conjugal family unit. Subsistence is usually too meagre and dispersed to support a large number of people in one economic unit. Further, the economic pursuits of hunting and gathering usually require constant seasonal mobility which prevents a residential concentration of kin. In the exceptional hunting and gathering societies where food is plentiful or where big-game hunting, necessitating organized co-operation, is a feature of the economy, a community of kin in a corporate family unit does tend to develop.

Large, corporate families tend to occur in societies where the generations are tied together by economic bonds. This is usually the case in agricultural economies with peasant cultivation where family land-holding and the need for organized co-operation hold the generations together around collective economic production and consumption. The limits to the expansion of such families are set by the size and productivity of the communal land and by the availability of alternative opportunities for making a living. Thus, in rural India, although the large corporate family is held to be the ideal form, the average family size seldom exceeds five or six people. This is because the peasant holdings are very small and, in addition, there is a demand for labour on larger estates. More recently there has been the additional possibility of migration to the towns which further hinders the achievement of the ideal. For these reasons it has only been among the prosperous peasants and the large landowners that the ideal of the large, corporate family has been realized.

Power and authority in the family

Another important way in which family structures differ is with regard to the distribution of authority. In some societies one member of the family (usually the father or the eldest male) may hold all property rights and may control the life of other members in the smallest detail. He can determine whom they shall meet, whom they should marry, what work they may do and how they shall behave in public. His permission may even be necessary before they can speak at table or leave the house. A family structure of this kind we call 'patriarchal'. A good example is the *paterfamilias* of ancient Rome, who derived his power and dominance from the ownership and complete control of land. In early republican Rome all other members of the family were dependent upon him for their subsistence and social standing. This dominance was embodied in the law of early Rome. For example, other members of the family had no property rights and the father had the power of life and death over them. However, with the development of Roman society, and particularly with the growth of occupational and career opportunities in its military and administrative ranks, this paternal monopoly of control over life chances broke down. This shift in the power situation is reflected in the development of the patrician family in the late Empire. Some laws relating to the family were changed; others were increasingly ignored. Considerable autonomy and freedom were enjoyed by wives and adult children.

Family relationships and sexual practices can often best be understood as manifestations of the distribution of power in the wider society. Thus, when there are wide disparities in wealth and power within a society, more powerful men can monopolize for themselves a large number of women. This can happen either through the practice of polygamy—or strictly speaking, polygyny—(as in Islamic societies) or through concubinage (as in Imperial China). In some societies, however (Christian societies for example), there are religious and/or legal pressures which make polygamy and formal concubinage impossible. In these cases powerful men resort to informal practices like that of 'taking mistresses' in the noble courts of Europe. Further, whenever older males have full control over the life chances of their women and juniors, they can impose sexual constraints which redound to their own advantage. If the dependants subsequently gain some degree of power, then this constraint is mitigated. In the noble Roman family already cited, for example, marriage became a way of establishing family alliances for political and financial ends. Increasingly the married woman became part of the power game and herself acquired power through the crucial position she occupied in alliances. She was able to defy the constraints imposed on her by the man-made laws and customs so that the relative sexual freedom of noble

women during the later empire was partly due to this increased power. A similar process can be observed in the European (particularly French) aristocracies of the seventeenth and eighteenth centuries where again one finds a combination of marriage alliances and easy virtue. The increased sexual freedom of young people, particularly women, in contemporary industrial societies can be explained in terms of the increasing access of the young to sources of economic independence. The enforcement of the dual standards of Victorian middle-class morality in the nineteenth-century England was contingent upon the helplessness and dependence of women and young people and on the dominance of older men. Occupational opportunities for a woman were strictly limited and she had no legal right to hold property. Her legal personality, in so far as it existed at all, was incorporated in that of her husband. The young man, in order to assume a respectable middle-class position, had to undergo long periods of training and needed considerable financial help. In this he was largely dependent on his family. The recent expansion of occupations, particularly of tertiary occupations, created opportunities for women and younger people which had never previously existed. Because they were carried on in impersonal institutions which were independent of family power, such occupations afforded economic independence, or at least the possibility of such independence, from the family. Women and young men were able to rebel against the dual standards of morality which demanded from them standards of behaviour different from that demanded of the head of the household. More generally, the authoritarian relationship between the father and his family gave way to a more egalitarian relationship.

Conjugal stability

The distribution of power within the family is also relevant to the stability of marriage. The more a wife has sources of power and status independent of her husband, the greater is the likelihood of marital disputes or dissolution. Two very different examples demonstrate something of the range of marriage arrangements which make it possible for the wife to derive power and status from outside the conjugal household. In modern industrial societies the wife's power lies in her relative economic and social independence. The relatively open and impersonal labour market extends a wide range of employment opportunities to women and so gives them an autonomous social and economic base (see page 86). Moreover, with the relatively individualistic view of marriage common in such societies, there is a correspondingly great emphasis on romantic love and the mutual compatibility of husband and wife. Compared with most non-industrial societies, the marriage relationship is relatively independent of (and supported by) the wider structures of kinship and community. Because of this more fragile foundation, marital tensions and disputes are more likely to arise, and when they do arise, they are more likely to culminate in separation or divorce. As the social and economic autonomy of women has grown, and as marriage has become a more individual affair, there has been a progressive relaxation of divorce laws. This has put divorce within the reach of almost everyone by making it both easier and cheaper. In addition, the long-term trend is for more and more people to avail themselves of the opportunity offered by the new laws. The resultant increase in rates of divorce during the twentieth century is illustrated in Table 6.1.

Table 6.1 Divorce-rate per thousand marriages in selected industrial societies 1900–60

Country	1900	1910	1920	1930	1940	1950	1960
USA	75·3	87·4	133·3	173·9	165·3	231·7	259·0
Sweden	12·9	18·4	30·5	50·6	65·1	147·7	174·6
Australia	13·5	12·9	22·6	41·7	41·9	98·2	88·9
France	26·1	46·3	49·4	68·6	80·3	106·2	82·4
England and Wales		2·2	8·0	11·1	16·5	86·1	69·5

Source: William J. Goode, *World Revolution and Family Patterns*, New York: Free Press, 1963, p. 82.

Marital instability of a different nature characterizes some simple societies in which the lineage and clan organization conflict with the marriage relationship. In the traditional Ndembu society of Central Africa, for example, descent is traced through the mother's line; the kinship organization is matrilineal. When a man takes a wife he pays a bride-price to her brothers. The wife goes to live with the husband's family group, thus depriving her brothers of her labour and transferring this asset to her husband's group. Children of the marriage have divided allegiance between their mother's brothers, to whom they 'belong' and must eventually return, and their father's group with whom they are growing up. The mother, too, owes her primary allegiance to her brothers. They want her and her children back as their labour is of great economic value and their numbers add to the political power of the group. So there is a perpetual conflict between the woman-giving and the woman-receiving groups. In such a situation marital problems frequently culminate in the breakdown of the marriage. In the Ndembu situation, then, the wife can draw upon the power and status of her matrilineage, which is in conflict with her husband's kinship group precisely over the issue of her marriage.

Patriarchal families of all kinds provide a contrast to these two examples. As we have seen, in patriarchal families the eldest male controls the life chances and the status of the women and the young. A wife or a daughter in such a family has no opportunities outside her husband's or father's household; she is entirely dependent. A variety of cases, from the agricultural corporate families of India and China to the middle-class family of Victorian England illustrate the point. In such societies the severe consequences of divorce or separation for the woman lead to her acquiescence in the marital situation and her subjugation induces relative harmony. In addition marital stability is reinforced by the pressures and requirements of the wider kin or community to which both spouses are subjected. Exceptions to this general rule occur when the customary and legal powers of the husband over the wife are so great that he can divorce her at will. This has been the case in traditional Islamic societies and in Japan. In the latter case the legal protection of the rights of the wife, which came with industrialization, has led to a decline in the divorce rate.

To sum up: the structure of the human family is subject to considerable variations. The focal point of the whole family varies, and even within a single residential type—say the conjugal family —there are wide variations of structure according to the particular relationships between husband, wife and children. All of these variations are closely related to the structure of the wider society, and as the society changes so does the family structure.

The family in early stages of industrialization

Non-industrial societies, based as they are on an agricultural economy, are often characterized by a corporate family structure. As we have already seen, however, this is related to the *particular* form of economic production—namely peasant agriculture—which is dominant in most non-industrial societies. For peasant holding or tenancy tend to involve the wider kin in working on the land and sharing its products, thus holding them together as a unit. This system of cultivation was characteristic of most parts of pre-industrial Europe and is still typical of many parts of the world. But there are also non-industrial societies based on forms of agriculture other than peasant land-holding. The wage-labour systems characteristic of much of eighteenth- and nineteenth-century England, or of many parts of the West Indies today, concentrate production on large farms or estates and do not provide the kind of economic bonds between kinsmen which require common residence. In addition, such wage labour is a very insecure, often seasonal, form of employment which is poorly paid. The agricultural labourer also has to be prepared to travel in search of employment. Poverty, insecurity and mobility combine to make the upkeep of a corporate family group difficult or impossible. Sometimes, indeed, the labourer is not even able to support a conjugal group on his wages. Where this is the case (and it is a common situation among labourers in many parts of the West Indies), men are no more than occasional visitors to the household and the family unit is likely to be 'matrifocal'—that is the adult women are the heads of the family which they support as best they can.

The changes in family structure which are brought about by industrialization vary according to the nature of the family structure in the pre-industrial situation. Industrialization involves the transfer of the focus of economic production from agriculture to manufacture. The early stages of industrialization make little difference to the focal point of the agricultural wage-labourer's family; usually it merely transfers him from a rural situation of poverty, insecurity and mobility to a similar situation in the overcrowded slums of the town. When agriculture has previously been based upon peasant cultivation, however, the changes in family structure are more fundamental. The transfer of production from the domestic setting to specialized factories and workshops disrupts the cohesive productive function of the corporate family and heightens the importance of the conjugal type of family.

The disruption of the corporate family, however, does not lead to the total demise of wider kinship bonds. In England, Japan and the United States, for example, the wider kinship network has survived and continues to play an important part as a kind of mutual aid society for members. But the larger kinship group is no longer the dominant unit; it seldom has the economic production functions and the residential unity of such a group in most non-industrial societies. The conjugal group does become the principal form of family organization. An example of such a change in family structure can be seen below in the discussion of Japan.

As the first society to embark upon industrialization England is an important, although not necessarily typical, case. Pre-industrial England was *not* characterized by the large corporate family and, consequently, changes in family structure were perhaps less drastic than in some other industrializing societies. Developments in Britain since the Civil War had led to a transformation of agriculture from the traditional feudal system of small-holding tenant cultivation to a much larger scale of farming on farms and estates worked mainly by wage labour. This process must have weakened any larger kinship units which existed earlier and the individuation of labour involved in the transformation laid the foundation for the predominance of the conjugal family unit. At this time manufacturing crafts were carried out within the household, but in England these craft households were also characterized by the conjugal rather than the corporate family unit. The life of the pre-industrial rural worker has often been romanticized as one in which leisure and freedom to work at one's own pace provided conditions for the good life surrounded by loving kinsmen. Contemporary writers, however, painted a rather different picture. For example, a country parson wrote:[2]

> I could not but observe with concern their mean and distressed condition. I found them in general but indifferently fed; badly clothed; some children without shoes and stockings; very few put to school; and most families in debt to little shopkeepers. In short, there was scarcely any appearance of comfort about their dwellings, except that the children looked tolerably healthy. Yet I could not impute the wretchedness I saw either to sloth or wastefulness.

This shift of labour from agriculture and domestic industry to mining and manufacturing industry, from rural poverty to the emergent slums surrounding the new factories and mines, while not bringing about a change in the focus of the family, nevertheless had important consequences for family structure in other ways. In particular, women and children were more susceptible to the rigours of factory discipline and control than were men. They could also be paid lower wages, a possibility which predisposed some factory owners to employ women and children almost exclusively. The unemployment of men and the gross exploitation of women and children which followed from this provided a powerful motive for a variety of social and political agitations. Unlike rural misery, the new urban situation was geographically concentrated and readily visible to other social groups. This concentration of large numbers of workers in transparently exploitative conditions also facilitated the organization and growth of movements of discontent ranging from sporadic violence and destruction of factory machinery to the secret organization of rudimentary trade unions. These movements were among the forces which led to legislative reforms protecting women and children from the grossest forms of work exploitation. The reforms also had the indirect effect of excluding women from certain types of heavy work, thus ending the situation of exclusive male unemployment.

The precise effect on the family of these changes was variable and often depended on local conditions. One common feature, however, was the separation of family members from one another during working hours. Farm labour and domestic crafts had usually been carried out by members of the family working together; the long hours of factory work were spent apart. Economic survival was no longer dependent on family solidarity and stability. Such stability now depended much more on ties of affection; and such ties were not always present. A contemporary wrote of the situation in London:[3]

> Marriage as an institution is not fashionable in these districts. Ask if the men and women living together in these rookeries are married and your simplicity will cause a smile. Nobody knows. Nobody cares. Nobody expects that they are. Those who appear to be married are often separated by a mere quarrel and they do not hesitate to form similar companionships immediately.

The first stages of industrialization also transformed the middle classes and gave rise to new entrepreneurial strata. The pre-industrial middle classes carried out their trading and manufacturing activities largely within the domestic household. Women and children were often active in these business activities. But with the coming of factory production, and even with the earlier expansion and elaboration of trade and finance, business activities were increasingly carried out in specialized institutions. The middle-class household, and particularly the wife, were no longer involved in production and business. The family became merely the sphere in which the prosperous middle classes consolidated their financial gains in status display. The middle-class wife was relieved from domestic chores by the employment of servants; the numerous children she bore were taken off her hands in infancy by nursemaids and (after about 1850) in the later stages of childhood and youth by the public schools. Increasingly she became a powerless and almost functionless ornament. These changes in the location of economic activities lay behind the patriarchal pattern of the Victorian middle-class family: the active, dominant husband; the submissive, passive, virtuous wife; and the good children who were seen but never heard. The men controlled the economic life chances of their women and younger dependants (a control which was supported by the man-made laws of the land) and consequently could dominate and subordinate them socially.

The family in later stages of industrialization

The changes in the structure of the family that occur in the later stages of industrialization are primarily to do with the structure of the conjugal family, although there are also some changes in relationships with the wider kin. All these are related to the wider processes of social change; to continued individuation, bureaucratization, and urbanization, and to the persistence of geographical and social mobility. The later stages of industrialization invariably involve developments in all these spheres but the changes do not take place to the same degree in all industrializing societies. Variations in the wider processes of change are reflected in differences in the structure of the family from industrial society to industrial society.

In addition to the continuation of earlier changes which affect family life, the later stages of industrialization are characterized by three relatively new factors which have important implications for the family. (1) There are urban/industrial communities which have been established for several generations; the apparent transience of urban community and family life has in many places given way to stability. At the same time, however, in other parts of the society there is a re-ordering of city life—the drift to the suburbs—which provides a different environment for family life. (2) Bureaucratization and the associated growth of tertiary occupations leads to an unprecedented demand for administrative and clerical labour, which can usually only be satisfied by the employment of women in these jobs. 'Middle-class' occupations are increasingly available for women and a *career* (as distinct from a job) becomes a possibility for them. In turn this process is related to the political and social emancipation of women, a factor which continues to be crucial to changes in family relationships as it was in the earlier stages of industrialization. (3) Part of what we mean by bureaucratization is that a substantial proportion of the population is employed in jobs which have some sort of career prospects. The pursuit of a career frequently involves a high incidence of movement from job to job. This is especially the case in the USA where often the 'organization man' has to change his job several times in his life if he is to make the most of his career opportunities. This, too, has ramifications for family structure.

The highly industrial society is more complex than its predecessors, partly in that it encompasses a greater variety of social situations, including a greater variety of family situations. There is the family in the suburb; the family in the slum; and the family in the countryside. There is the family that spends all its days in one community; and the family that moves to a different town every two or three years. And there are (as there always have been) rich families and poor families; upper-class families and lower-class families. Some of the effects of industrialization are widely distributed throughout the society. The independent employment of women, for example, creates conditions throughout industrial societies in which social independence is a *possibility*; and yet some employed women remain subject to their husbands. The relationships within the conjugal family vary according to the nature of the relationships of husband and wife to their wider kin and to the wider community. These in turn are related to the degree of residential stability or mobility that exists. So finally, to put some order into the variety of family structures we must relate them to the question of mobility.

Changes in employment opportunities for women

We have seen how, in the early stages of industrialization, the position of women in the family was determined to a considerable extent by their economic position. In nineteenth-century England women of the lower classes had even worse pay and conditions than their menfolk. Property laws gave the husband the *right* to the earnings of his wife, even in cases where he had deserted wife and children. The wife's dependence, as well as her general physical dilapidation, was heightened by frequent pregnancies and births. Thus the economic activity of working-class women did not form a basis for a challenge to male dominance in the family. Among the middle classes the position was even more clear cut since most women did not work at all.

Changes in occupational distribution, particularly the growth of tertiary occupations, created a very different situation; the demand for white collar labour was such that it could only be met by employing women in these occupations and the exodus of large numbers of men for the battlefields of the first world war accentuated the process. The clerical, administrative and professional ranks which were gradually opened to women offered much greater power, prestige and independence than the occupations which had formerly been available and the employment situation was reflected in the gradual social and political emancipation of women. Closely related to these changes was the decline in size of middle-class families. Successful family limitation is dependent upon joint consultation between husband and wife and/or a position of considerable feminine power. In turn, relief from the drudgery of continual child-bearing enhances the woman's independence from her husband and provides opportunity for a more active life. These economic and social changes provided the possibility of a marriage relationship very different from the earlier one of male dominance and female subservience.

Individuation and marriage choice

The first stages of industrialization had involved a separation of economic production from the domestic setting. The dominance within the family of the father, however, normally preserved his influence over the marriage of his children. With improved employment opportunities for young people and the concomitant changes in the power structure of the family, young people gain more and more autonomy in this sphere. For the most part men and women choose their husbands and wives with little interference from wider kinship groups; marriage is more a matter between individuals and less one between two family groups than in non-industrial societies. Perhaps this statement is least true of the highest social classes where there is considerable family pressure upon young people to find 'suitable' marriage partners, thus maintaining status exclusiveness (and sometimes 'appropriate' patterns of inheritance). Take as an example, a recent statement by the Prince of Wales:[4]

> You've got to remember that when you marry, in my position, you are going to marry somebody who perhaps one day is going to become Queen. You've got to choose somebody very carefully, I think, who could perform this particular role; the one advantage about marrying a princess, or somebody from a royal family, is that they do know what happens.

In all social groups, however, people are more likely to marry members of the same locality, the same social class, the same ethnic group and the same religion. This is less due to any belief that this is right and proper (although such beliefs may still be very strong—for example, with regard to inter-racial marriages) than to the fact that people are more likely to meet marriageable members of their own groups than of other groups. Courting in Western industrial societies is usually carried on (or at least introductory meetings are effected) at dances, parties, schools and colleges, workplaces, coffee bars and the like. These situations have a tendency to be homogeneous in terms of locality, class and so on. So, in the language of demographers, one is exposed to a greater 'risk' of marriage to members of one's own group; in practical terms, the 'marriage market' is a very restricted one—although less so than in the homogeneous rural society.

Long-term residential stability

In some situations a residential pattern emerges in which the household is composed of the conjugal family but where wider kin are to be found in the immediate neighbourhood. This pattern is to be found where a family has lived in a neighbourhood for several generations and may occur in rural or urban areas. The conjugal family is the dominant unit but ties with more distant relations are far from unimportant. In urban areas the neighbourhoods characterized by this pattern are usually homogeneous in their class composition and are most likely to be working-class areas, partly because multi-generational residence in a neighbourhood is more characteristic of the working class than of other groups, and partly because these patterns are enhanced by poverty. The best known of them (best known because they have been studied by sociologists) are Bethnal Green in London, Ship Street in Liverpool, and 'Ashton' (a fictitious name for a small mining town) in Yorkshire, but many towns and cities have such an area.

The most important way residential stability influences the structure of the conjugal family is that there is no necessity for a couple to break off their pre-marital friendships. Marriage usually takes place between two people from the locality; it is consequently superimposed upon the existing friendship patterns of the couple. Each partner retains his or her group of friends and does not become exclusively dependent upon the conjugal relationship. Close and frequent relationships with parents remain possible after marriage and these communities are marked in particular by ties of co-operation between the mother and her married daughter. Because they live close to each other they are able to share the chores of daily life, particularly those to do with child care and child rearing. These two factors—the strength of the mother/daughter relationship and the retention of pre-marriage friendship patterns—form the basis for a close, co-operative community of women, who work together, gossip together and bring up their children together. Bringing up children is not restricted to the home but is shared with kinswomen in the locality and sometimes is carried out by the community as a whole. The child, like the whole family becomes 'neighbourhood centred' and grows up with the constant companionship of the other children of the neighbourhood. Children thus have considerable influence upon each other's beliefs, values and activities as they grow up; the peer group is an important agent of socialization and social control. Nevertheless, an important part of bringing up children is carried out by adults who are likely to use physical punishment to discourage undesirable behaviour that comes to their attention. But, because of the neighbourhood situation, no one adult is in constant contact with a child and so a lot of such behaviour goes unnoticed. The result is that punishment, while effectively controlling 'external' behaviour of children, has little effect on the formation of 'internal' guilt mechanisms.

The friendship groups of men, similarly, are single sex groups—a result, or sometimes a legacy, of poverty, poor housing conditions and long working hours, which alienated the man from his home and disposed him to seek the little leisure and pleasure he had in the company of his mates in the pub or club. In areas dominated by 'traditional' industries—mining, fishing, dock work— the physical and collective nature of the work in gangs or teams welded the men into loyal groups. Add to this fact that work-mates invariably lived close to each other and had grown up together and one is hardly surprised to find that the solidarity of the work group is carried over into the neighbourhood and reinforces the bonds of community. Hard times and poor facilities also enhanced the functions of the 'women's co-operative' in the neighbourhood, the women helping each other out in times of special need. With the improvement in standards of living and housing conditions which has recently come about in Europe and North America, the rigidity of these patterns of sexual separation is modified and there tends to be greater contact and co-operation between the conjugal pair. Men are likely to spend more time in the now more congenial home, a trend that has been accelerated by the advent of television. But these changes only modify the pattern; in spite of greater conjugal closeness and reciprocity, the main pattern of 'women's co-operative' and male comradeship persist as long as this kind of neighbourhood persists. It is only likely to change when, for one reason or another, young people no longer remain in the district to work and marry.

New towns, suburbs and estates

Many of these stable communities have been broken up by the movement of people from the city centres to suburbs and estates on the periphery of large towns or to newly created towns. This has been due, partly to rehousing schemes involving slum clearance in the city centres, and partly to government attempts to locate new industries away from the existing city centres. Families who move from a stable residential area to a new suburb, new estate or new town are in a very different family situation from that we have just described. The difference is especially acute for the first

generation to move to the new area. There is likely to be very little mixing; little co-operation between neighbours; and in some cases there may be a covert, or even active, hostility between neighbours. The geographical distance separating the newly mobile family from their wider kin places a considerable strain on kinship relations. The change in the mother/married daughter relationship is particularly significant, for the older generation frequently remains in the old district. Although considerable efforts may be made to maintain frequent contact, the nature of the relationship necessarily changes fundamentally. With neither kin nor long established neighbours to rely on for day-to-day help, the wife becomes more dependent both materially and emotionally upon her husband.

The basis for the old patterns of male friendship groups are also undermined: the type of work available is less likely to be in one of the traditional industries than in a modern mass production industry, such as the motor industry. The work is mainly on the assembly line, each worker having his own task to perform. There is little of the solidaristic co-operation so characteristic of work gangs in mining or the docks. For the individual worker there is little emotional involvement in the work group. Added to this, workers are recruited from all over the country and have no common background and no common local culture. Studies of workers in the motor industry in England show that there is little sociability between work-mates outside work. Nor are work-mates normally neighbours; they live in different localities and neighbourhoods. This lack of congruence between work groups, neighbourhood groups and friendship groups contrasts strongly with the near identity of these groups in areas of residential stability. It coincides with and enhances the individualism of the work situation. So the man, too, relies more on his home and his wife for entertainment and companionship.

With this new situation new patterns of leisure activities emerge. Both men and women spend most of their leisure time in the home; there is little 'going out', little visiting and little entertaining. The home, rather than the neighbourhood or the pub, becomes the focus of people's lives; and the conjugal family, rather than the community or friendship groups, becomes the centre of people's activities. In short, people become more home-centred.

All this has important implications for the relationship between parents and children. The more home-centred the family becomes, the more child-centred it becomes as well; the child's welfare, behaviour and education become a focus for the parents' attention and concern. Furthermore, the child is brought up primarily within the conjugal family. Grandparents are usually too far away to exert day-to-day influence and the influence of the neighbourhood on the growing child is relatively unimportant. This is particularly the case in neighbourhoods of mixed or uncertain class composition, where children are often discouraged from playing with neighbours' children. The peer group consequently tends to be school-centred rather than neighbourhood-centred and does not become crucial in socialization until later in the child's life when, often enough, the parents of childhood friends do not know each other. In the early years the child, as well as the parents, is dependent upon the conjugal family and is in continual contact with his parents. There is, therefore, the possibility of non-physical means of controlling his behaviour. This requires, however, a level of verbal skill not always possessed by the parents. This is especially so with working-class parents with the result that the ways in which the child is disciplined are likely to be inconsistent and unpredictable.

We have suggested that this pattern is likely to be particularly noticeable among the first generation in a new area, but it is likely to be a semi-permanent form of family and social life. Certainly it is unlikely that the old type of communal life will ever be established in the new areas, for the housing estate poses problems different from those in the traditional communities and it affords new facilities. It consequently requires new adaptations. At the material level, the new house presents a challenge for the newcomers. They feel they must live up to it by furnishing it according to certain standards, tending the garden and acquiring domestic gadgets. In this respect the standards are already set by the neighbourhood; what the other houses have is an unspoken norm for the newcomers to keep. To quote from one study of such an area:[5]

> People struggle to raise their all-round standards to those of the home, and in the course of doing so, they must look to their present neighbours for guidance. To begin with, the first-comers had to make their own way, but the later arrivals have their model at hand. The neighbours have put up nice curtains. Have we? They have their garden planted with privet and grass seed. Have we? The new arrivals watch the first-comers and the first-comers watch the new arrivals.

To this end a substantial amount of family earnings is invested in hire purchase payments on furniture and appliances. The home becomes a comfortable place in which to spend leisure time, and one on which a good deal of maintenance work needs to be done. The television set facilitates this home-centredness.

In the new situation there are new expectations and new standards; different qualities and activities are highly esteemed. An action that would have been applauded in the old district may be derided in the new, and vice versa. Adjusting to these new values may be very difficult, for it may involve people in changing their self-image. Young and Willmott make this point well when they compare traditional Bethnal Green with a new housing estate they call Greenleigh:[6]

> In Bethnal Green, people belong to a close network of personal relations. They know intimately dozens of other local people living near. . . . In this situation, Bethnal Green is not, as we see it, concerned to any marked extent with what is normally thought of as status. It is true, of course, that people have different incomes, different kinds of jobs, different kinds of houses—in this respect there is much less uniformity than there is at Greenleigh—even different standards of education. But these attributes are not so important in evaluating others. It is personal characteristics which matter. The first thing they think of about Bert is not that he has a 'fridge' and a car. They see him as bad-tempered, or a real good sport, or the man with a way with women. . . . He is judged, if he is judged at all, more in the round, as a person with the usual mixture of all kinds of qualities, some good, some bad, many indefinable. He is more of a life-portrait than a figure on a scale.
>
> How different is Greenleigh . . . where nearly everyone is a stranger, there is no way of uncovering personality. People cannot be judged by their personal characteristics: a person can certainly see that his neighbour works in his shirt sleeves and his wife goes down to the shops in a blue coat, but that is not much of a guide to character. Judgement

must, therefore, rest on the trappings of the man rather than on the man himself. If people have nothing else to go by, they judge from his appearance, his house, even his Minimotor. Once the accepted standards are few, and mostly to do with wealth, they become the standard by which status is judged.

In the absence of small groups which join one family to another, in the absence of strong personal associations which extend from one household to another, people think that they are judged, and judge others, by the material standards which are the outward and visible marks of respectability.

These differing criteria of social evaluation, then, are the indices of a different kind of relationship to the neighbours; a more competitive and, to a certain extent, a hostile relationship. However, status competition does not necessarily rule out friendliness and sociability. Indeed, studies of American middle-class suburbs indicate that status competition is displayed within the context of intense neighbourhood sociability. The areas we are considering, however, are very largely working-class areas and we must take note of differences between the classes with regard to attitudes to friendship and with regard to certain technical skills that are necessary to sociability. To the working classes a friend is given, not 'made'. A friend is someone you grow up with, know at school, work with, and so on. He is someone with whom you share a common background and common assumptions about the world. To *make* friends who are not given in this way presupposes an ability to converse and to join in common activities with people where there is no common background. Linguistic and conceptual skills are necessary to elaborate common interests and recreations between people whose experience, assumptions and local cultures are not necessarily shared. Such skills are more characteristically middle-class. Moreover, activities which make for sociability—like mutual entertaining and joining recreational clubs and associations—are also more characteristic of the way of life of the middle classes.

The combination of all these factors—movement away from kin and long-established neighbours, work relationships which do not carry over into after-work hours, a competitive way of life in which some traditional working-class life styles and attitudes (especially those towards friendship) survive—produces a family structure

with a distinctive combination of characteristics. There is a focus on the conjugal relationship and the parent/child relationship, a concentration of leisure activities in the home, and combined with this, a low level of sociability and neighbourliness.

Residential mobility

The way of life of modern industrial societies also produces a section of the population who frequently move their home, often from one part of the country to another and sometimes even from country to country. This is especially the case for those who undergo higher education; their education itself usually takes them away from their parents' home and they often enter the kind of occupations where moves are essential if they are to make the most of their opportunities. Consider the typical example of a young man in this situation. He spends his childhood and youth in the locality where his parents live and goes to school there. He goes to college in another area, and starts his first job in yet another. He is likely to move subsequently, following employment opportunities for career advancement. At some stage in his career, perhaps while at college, he meets his future wife; she is likely to have had a similar mobility pattern. Both of them make friends at every stage of their careers; and sometimes these are, from the start, joint friends. People undergoing this pattern of mobility have no firm psychological anchorage in a community, nor any stable network of informal social relationships, with the consequence that marriage and the conjugal relationship assume crucial importance. The conjugal family becomes the only relatively permanent point of reference and there is a great deal of emotional involvement and interdependence between husband and wife. Decisions are made jointly; household tasks are shared without rigid role allocation; finances are jointly administered.[7] Such couples tend to emphasize the importance of personal and sexual compatibility for the success of a marriage.

The career pattern of these groups is also important for the sociability pattern it entails. Friends are made by each spouse (or both) in their schools, colleges or jobs. But their friends are hardly ever neighbours; on the contrary they tend to be widely dispersed. Friendship is, therefore, distinguished by entertaining at home and, to a lesser extent, going out with friends. In this kind of sociability, the couple, and not the individual partner, is the friendship unit. Past friends of one partner who prove to be incompatible with the other are likely to be abandoned. Whether such a couple will also make friends with neighbours depends very much on the nature of the neighbourhood. If neighbours are of a similar occupational and social status level, then neighbourhood sociability is likely to develop. If, on the other hand, the neighbourhood is socially mixed, or if there is substantial ambiguity of social status in the district, then there will be very little neighbourhood sociability.

In these mobile families, too, the child is often the focus of parental attention and grows up largely within the confines of the conjugal family. The normally high educational level of the parents, however, ensures a high level of verbal skill which is invariably used in the disciplining and control of children. Physical punishment invariably takes a minor place and is sometimes not used at all. The parents have effective alternatives at their disposal and are in a position to make a choice.

The greater wealth of these families enables them to maintain contact with their more distant relatives if they want to. The motor car, the telephone, the postal service all facilitate regular contact in spite of distance; strong emotional ties can be maintained and are reinforced by family visits which are made possible by increased leisure time. Even in highly industrial societies kinship groups often serve as a kind of 'mutual benefit association' in which help and support is exchanged between the members. This is often particularly crucial for newly married couples who depend a great deal on their parents and older relatives for support and guidance and sometimes for financial help. In the poorer social groups, given the housing problems in most industrial societies, an initial roof over the heads of the newly married couple is often provided by the parental home. Nor is help to older family members entirely a thing of the past. While it is not extended to such a wide range of kinsmen as formerly, people normally feel some responsibility for the well-being of their aged parents.

In all family situations in highly industrial societies, then, the major changes of individuation and bureaucratization have left their mark on the structure of the family. The influence of geographical mobility is more variable. The greatest differences in family structure are between those families characterized by long-term residential stability and those (predominantly middle-class)

families characterized by frequent moves. There are, however, significant differences between these latter families and those of the new estates and new towns, even though mobility has been characteristic of both. These differences are largely due to differences in the style of life between middle-class and working-class families and, in particular, to differences in sociability which derive from educational and occupational differences.

Modernization and the family

The diversity of family forms to be found in industrial societies is more than mirrored in the contemporary modernizing societies of Africa, Asia and Latin America. The variety of the traditional situation has been compounded by differential contact with the industrial world which has variously affected the structure of the family. In some of the more remote areas of Africa and Asia family relationships are little changed; in the mushrooming towns and cities they have changed drastically in the last half century. Two processes which have particularly important consequences for the family are urbanization and the growth of new occupations. And these are processes which not only affect the people who are themselves moving into the cities or changing their jobs, but which also have far-reaching consequences for the whole society. The fact that there are employment opportunities in government bureaucracies, commercial companies, mines and plantations—all areas which lie largely outside the sphere of family influence— affects the family relationships, attitudes, and behaviour even of those people who do not pursue such opportunities.

The single most important consequence of these processes is the individuation of labour and of economic opportunity. In traditional, predominantly agricultural, societies the family is the major unit of production. In such situations, as we have seen earlier, family power can be maintained partly through control over the economic opportunity of its members. Large-scale economic changes, resulting in the growth of new occupations located mainly in towns and cities, lessens the importance of the family as a productive force and consequently weakens the family's control over the life chances of its individual members. In addition these changes increase the incidence of geographical mobility. Where migration is a temporary phenomenon (as is the case with a good deal of mining and agricultural labour throughout tropical Africa) it invariably leads to a separation of the man from his wife, children and other family members. This may be a separation of a few weeks or of several years. Where the migration is more permanent (as with most forms of urbanization) the conjugal family usually moves together. In either case, however, while the *nature* of relationships between kinsmen and family members is transformed, economic dependence on the family may acquire new and more subtle forms.

The city provides a bewildering and hazardous experience for the rural migrant. He lacks the social skills and the contacts of the urbanite and therefore needs backing and 'sponsorship'. This is frequently provided by earlier migrants from his village to the city, some of whom are likely to be kinsmen. Former ties—including those of kinship—are thus by no means irrelevant. The economic insecurity of life in most modernizing societies also helps to sustain bonds of kinship. In the towns unemployment is often rife; in the rural areas there is frequent under-employment. The economies of these countries are often dependent upon world prices for one or two basic commodities and are consequently subject to wild fluctuations. Political instability sometimes contributes to the general economic insecurity. In this situation the maintenance of kinship obligations can provide at least some degree of security. If the worst comes to the worst the destitute urban dweller can go back to his kinsmen in the village and receive such support as they are able to give him. Conversely, when he is in employment he may remit some of his pay to his kinsmen.

It is, however, easy to overstate the mutual obligations of kinsmen in, say, contemporary West Africa. With continued economic and social development individual dependence on the family gradually weakens and the willingness to honour traditional obligations tends to decrease. This is especially so if a society is able to maintain high levels of employment, job stability and security—either through industrialization or through other forms of economic development.

Japan provides a good example of a society in which modernization has taken the form of successful industrialization. The traditional Japanese family ordered every aspect of the lives of its members and was supported in this by laws which upheld the authority of family heads. Laws of inheritance were also important. All household property, including the family's means of subsis-

tence such as land or business, was passed on from the father to the eldest son. This led to a system that has become known as the 'stem family', the stem consisting of the line of eldest sons, who perpetuated the family name and property. Younger sons, on getting married, were expected to start a separate household and these, together with their descendants, are known as the 'branches'. Although they formed separate households these branch families were still dependent upon the stem families. The father or elder brother was expected to help the younger brothers to start their households. Typically, a propertied stem family would give a piece of land or a small part of a trading business to their 'branches' for this purpose. The decisions and dictates of the head of the stem household remained binding on the actions of other family members (although in the case of large and important families a council of household heads assumed this authority). In this stem and branch system the conjugal family of any given member was entirely subordinated to the larger family authority. Filial and fraternal bonds (especially to the eldest brother: note that the Japanese word for 'parents' means father, mother and elder brother) were much stronger and much more highly valued than marriage relationships.

In the early stages of industrialization in the last quarter of the nineteenth century, economic and political conditions were little more stable than in pre-industrial Japan and family dependence, particularly the dependence of the branch on the stem, continued. The newly urbanized worker needed the support and sustenance, however meagre, which his larger family could provide in difficult times. With the attainment of industrial maturity, however, the modern sector of the Japanese economy was increasingly able to offer subsequent generations of urban workers a considerable degree of security and stability, thus lessening their dependence upon traditional kinship connections. Indeed, the twentieth century has witnessed the gradual emancipation of the individual and the conjugal family from the hegemony of the corporate family. This emancipation has occurred both in law and in fact. There were legal and political struggles between the traditionalists and the reformers; the traditionalists claiming that the corporate family system lay at the very basis of society and as such must be protected by law; the reformers arguing that such a system is incompatible with a modern progressive society. Various compromises were reached in the legal reforms enacted in the post-second-world-war Japanese constitution and finally legal protection of traditional corporate ties was abandoned and the importance of conjugal family ties was emphasized.

However, even though the traditional family pattern as a mode of organization has largely disappeared, some of the affectional ties and the habits of thought associated with them still persist. This is particularly true of relations between men and women and the attitudes to female employment. Although women account for a substantial proportion of the labour force in Japan, most of the women at work are young and unmarried. Only a small, albeit increasing, proportion of married women are in paid employment. Moreover, there remains a strong current of opinion (especially, but not exclusively among men) which disapproves of married women working, particularly if they are mothers. In spite of this, however, the proportion of working married women is increasing. This suggests that the growth of employment opportunities, together with the influence of the wife's wage on the family's standard of living, are gradually changing the traditional patterns even in this area.

So far we have scarcely distinguished between the different groups in the societies under discussion. There are, of course, considerable differences in the life patterns and experiences of the different classes and groups whether in traditional societies, in modernizing societies or in industrial societies. For example, where the traditional family structures were patriarchal, there are indications that male domination was much greater and more firmly entrenched among the wealthier and more powerful strata. Among the poor, such domination was mitigated by the fact that the wife shared in the ardours of labour and shouldered much of the burden of poverty.

In modernizing societies there are, perhaps, greater differences to be observed than in any other societies. The development of modern occupations and of formal education and their co-existence with traditional patterns ensures a greater variation in social relationships and styles of life. In different parts of the same society there exist widely different family structures. And because of the peculiar recent history of many modernizing societies—with their recent independence from colonial rule and their recent and rapid development of a 'modern' sector—there are many persons who were themselves brought up in a corporate family or kinship group and find themselves parents in conjugal families of a very different structure. Since these changes are so recent, family relationships are often exposed to very considerable strain. Many young, educated West African men, for example, engage in a style of life quite different from that of previous generations. They are quite likely to be married to women who are themselves educated and who expect to have their own career and a considerable degree of independence. While it is by no means a new thing for women in West African societies to work, the modern, bureaucratic work situation lends support to their claims to an autonomy that the menfolk (because of the retention of a traditional orientation favourable to themselves) are often reluctant to concede. The relative rarity of educated women and the value placed upon having an educated wife for a go-ahead bureaucrat or businessman gives the educated woman an additional weapon in the battle of the sexes. For only such a wife is able to maintain the 'Western' style of life and engage in the patterns of sociability that are expected by the husband's working colleagues. Thus we have a contemporary example of the changing distribution of power between the sexes that we have earlier described in ancient Rome, eighteenth-century France, nineteenth-century England and twentieth-century Japan.

Conflicts may also arise between the educated man and his kinsmen in societies in which different sectors have very different expectations of mutual help. Those who occupy the positions of relative wealth and power that education can buy are frequently expected to honour their obligations to kinsmen by financial or other help to younger members of the kinship group. They are expected to use their influence to get them desirable jobs; to make substantial payments towards their education; and so on. Such traditional obligations may place a considerable burden on the relatively high, but not unlimited, income of educated men and women. Moreover, they conflict with the demands and requirements of the 'new' urban, conjugal family, and with the financial pressures of maintaining a 'modern' style of life.

Similarly, as in the industrializing societies of the Western world, the way in which marriage partners are chosen is changing. In some more extreme traditional cases, marriage had to be with a particular category of relative; thus in many African tribes some variant of marriage between cousins was the normal thing. Most traditional patterns, however, allow some individual choice, while restricting this choice to certain ethnic, tribal or village groups. Invariably the final authority for the choice lay with the parents or with the whole kin group. As we have already noted, however, there are now strong pressures encouraging the educated to marry among themselves and it is often difficult for a man to find a partner who is 'appropriate' in both the traditional and the modern sense. Increasingly, among this group, the choice is made in terms of the new rather than the old criteria of what constitutes a suitable partner.

These conflicts are characteristic of the rapidly changing situation of contemporary modernizing societies. They arise from the contradictory pressures and discordant expectations which result from the contact between industrial societies and relatively simple societies. In so far as economic and social development proceed in modernizing societies, we may expect the older patterns of family relationships to give way. However, as long as there remain substantial areas where the traditional agricultural sector is prominent the patterns of the corporate family and the wider kinship group will remain.

Notes

1　C. Lévi-Strauss, 'The family', in H. L. Shapiro (ed.), *Man, Culture and Society*, London: Oxford University Press, 1956, p. 269.

2　Rev. Davies, 'The case of labourers in husbandry', quoted in R. Fletcher, *The Family and Marriage*, Harmondsworth: Penguin, 1962, p. 74.

3　Rev. A. Mearns, *The Better Cry of Outcast London*, 1883, quoted in R. Fletcher, op. cit., p. 104. Note the similar situation in many Latin American and African towns of today. See, for example, O. Lewis, *Five Families*, New York: Mentor, 1959.

4　*Listener*, 82, 210, 3 July 1969.

5　M. Young and P. Willmott, *Family and Kinship in East London*, Harmondsworth: Penguin, 1962, pp. 159–60.

6　Ibid., from pp. 161–4.

7　This pattern has been elucidated by Elizabeth Bott in her book *Family and Social Network*, London: Tavistock, 1957.

Reading

Goode, W. J., *World Revolution and Family Patterns*, New York: Free Press, 1963. An account of changes in the structures of the family in the contemporary world. Includes chapters on the West, Japan, Africa, India, and China.

Harris, C. C., *The Family*, London: Allen & Unwin, 1969. A comprehensive textbook.

Klein, Josephine, *Samples from English Cultures*, London: Routledge & Kegan Paul, 1965. Contains summaries of a number of studies of family and community in England.

Lévi-Strauss, C., 'The family', in H. L. Shapiro (ed.), *Man, Culture and Society*, London, O.U.P., 1956. A good general essay on the nature of the family with particular reference to simple societies.

Lewis, Oscar, *Five Families*, New York: Mentor, 1959. Case studies of five Mexican families. Written by an anthropologist in the style of a novel.

McGregor, O. R., *Divorce in England*, London: Heinemann, 1957. In pursuing its main theme this very readable book also provides a good description of the Victorian family in England.

Queen, S. A., Habenstein, R. W., and Adams, J. B., *The Family in Various Cultures*, New York: Lippincott, 1961. Description of the family in a dozen different pre-industrial societies—European, African, Asian and American Indian.

Further reading

Ariès, Philippe, *Centuries of Childhood*, London: Cape, 1962. A perceptive and readable account of the development of the family in Europe since the middle ages.

Banks, J. A., *Prosperity and Parenthood*, London: Routledge & Kegan Paul, 1954. This study of Victorian family planning gives considerable insight into the Victorian middle-class family.

Edwards, J. N. (ed.), *The Family and Change*, New York: Knopf, 1969. A good collection of articles focusing upon the relationship between the family and the processes of industrialization and urbanization.

Goode, W. J. (ed.), *Readings on the Family and Society*, Englewood Cliffs: Prentice-Hall, 1968. Another useful collection of articles.

Laing, R. D. and Esterson, A., *Sanity, Madness and the Family*, Harmondsworth: Penguin, 1970. This collection of case studies of the families of schizophrenics has interesting implications for the social psychology of the family more generally.

Radcliffe-Brown, A. R. and Forde, D. (eds), *African Systems of Kinship and Marriage*, London: O.U.P., 1950. Anthropological studies of kinship in nine traditional African societies and an important introduction by the editors.

7 Socialization

The effects of isolation in childhood

At birth the human baby is completely helpless and absolutely dependent on others. Indeed, strictly speaking the infant is not a 'human' being in the fullest sense but rather a little 'animal' without speech or self-control, two of the most important attributes of the normal adult member of any human society. The term 'socialization' refers in a general way to the process of growing up into a human being, a process which necessitates contact with other people. It is through this process that the growing child acquires the language and standards of the social group into which it has been born.

Some indication of the necessity of human contact for the normal development of the child is furnished by the several cases of children who have been found living wild. One of the most striking of these cases was the so-called 'Wild Boy of Aveyron' who was found roaming in a French forest in the year 1799. He had apparently been eking out a precarious existence on what he could find to eat in the woods, although it was impossible to say how long he had existed in this way. Although he appeared to be about eleven he could not talk and simply grunted like an animal. This naked, dirty, scarred creature was taken to Paris where a young doctor named Itard devoted five years of his life to the boy's education. Considerable progress was made for, after a couple of years, the boy was clean, affectionate, able to read a few words and able to understand much that was said to him. Despite all Itard's efforts, however, the boy never learned to speak more than two words and in this respect the attempt to humanize him was a failure.

An even more dramatic case is that of the two Indian children who were reported to have been discovered in a wolf-den in Bengal in 1920. The den was excavated and the two children—girls about two and eight years old—were taken to an orphanage where they were cared for by a minister, the Rev. J. A. L. Singh, and his wife. The younger of the two, Amala, died soon after but the other girl, Kamala, lived in the orphanage until November 1929 when she also died. What Kamala's behaviour was like and the extent to which she had become humanized can be judged from a letter that the Rev. Singh wrote towards the end of 1926.[1]

At the present time Kamala can utter about forty words. She is able to form a few sentences, each sentence containing two, or at the most, three words. She never talks unless spoken to, and when spoken to she may or may not reply. She is obedient to Mrs. Singh and myself only. Kamala is possessed of very acute hearing and evidences an exceedingly acute animal-like sense of smell. She can smell meat at a great distance. Never weeps or smiles, but has a 'smiling appearance'. Shed a single tear when Amala died and would not leave the place where she lay dead. She is learning very slowly to imitate. Does not now play at all and does not mingle with other children. Once, both Amala and Kamala somewhat liked the company of an infant by the name of Benjamin while he was crawling and learning to talk. But one day they gave him such a biting and scratching that the infant was frightened and would never approach the wolf-children again. Amala and Kamala liked the company of Mrs. Singh, and Kamala, the surviving one of the pair, is much attached to her. The eyes of the children possessed a peculiar glare, such as that observed in the eyes of dogs or cats in the dark. Up to the present time Kamala sees better at night than during the daytime and seldom sleeps after midnight. The children used to cry or howl in a peculiar voice, neither animal nor human. Kamala still makes these noises at times. She is averse to all cleanliness, and serves the calls of nature anywhere, wherever she may happen to be at the time. Used to tear her clothes off. Hence a loin-cloth was stitched to her in such a fashion that she could not open or tear it. Kamala used to eat and drink like a dog, lowering her mouth down to the plate, and never used her hands for the purpose of eating or drinking. She would gnaw a big bone on the ground and would rub it at times in order to separate the meat from the bone. At the present time she uses her hands for eating and walks straight on two legs, but cannot run at all.

Thus, after six years in the orphanage, Kamala showed some human characteristics. Although she apparently never talked spontaneously, she did have a limited command of language, and, what is particularly important, she had developed a definite emotional attachment to Mrs Singh and was obedient to her. In many other respects, however, Kamala was still relatively unsocialized and the Rev. Singh came to believe that the apparently animal-like features of her behaviour were due to her supposed contact with wolves. In this he was probably mistaken. It should be noted that the circumstances in which the children were found are not entirely clear; no one actually knew how they might have got into the wolf-den in the first place, nor how long they might have been there. Even if it were established beyond any doubt that the children had been found together with wolves, it does not follow that they had been *reared* by these animals. To suppose this without further evidence is sheer conjecture, however attractive it may be to the imagination. What one can say is that the two little girls were not human beings in their behaviour when they were found, and that Kamala would not have become even as humanized as she did without the efforts of the Rev. Singh and his wife. The same may be said about the 'Wild Boy of Aveyron' who would certainly not have made as much progress as he did without the unsparing efforts of Dr Itard. Of course, in these cases we do not know whether the children suffered from any inborn defects which might have limited their capacity to become fully human beings but, assuming they were not defective in this way, it seems reasonable to regard their lack of humanity as due to isolation from other human beings during critical periods of their lives.

Further insight into the effects of social isolation in childhood can be gained from a consideration of those cases where a child is deliberately isolated by the parents. For instance, in 1938 a girl of more than five years of age was found locked up in a room on a lonely farm in America. Apparently she had been incarcerated in this room from babyhood because she was illegitimate. When she was finally discovered and removed from the room she could not walk or talk and was in very poor physical shape altogether. After nearly two years in an institution 'Anna' could at least walk, feed herself and understand simple commands, but she still did not speak. In August 1939 she was taken to a private home for retarded children where she made much more progress. By July 1941 'Anna' had acquired firm habits of personal cleanliness and her feeding habits were normal, except that she still used a spoon as her sole implement. She could dress herself except for fastening her clothes. The most striking thing of all, however, was that she had finally begun to speak and could construct a few complete sentences. She made a little more progress during the following year but then died in August 1942. As in the cases previously considered, the absence of adequate social relationships in early life had resulted in a creature that was hardly recognizable as a human being. The human contact in the two institutions made some socialization possible, particularly in the areas of speech and self-control, but even so the final level reached was very low. Again it is impossible to say with any precision what 'Anna' would have been like if she had received a more normal upbringing from birth but she would almost certainly have reached a higher level of mental development than she did. Again there is the snag that the girl may have been feeble-minded and, in this particular case, there is some evidence that the girl's mother was mentally defective to some degree.

It is particularly instructive to compare the case of 'Anna' with that of another American girl, 'Isabelle', who had also been kept in seclusion because she was illegitimate. 'Isabelle' was discovered nine months after 'Anna' was found and at the time of discovery she was about six and a half years old. Her mother was a deaf-mute and apparently the two of them had spent most of their time together in a dark room shut off from the rest of the family. The girl did not speak and communicated with her mother only by means of gestures. Her behaviour towards strangers showed considerable fear and hostility and, like 'Anna', she was in poor physical shape. At first it was hard to tell whether she could even hear or not, and even when it was definitely established that she was not deaf the specialists thought that she was feeble-minded.[2]

In spite of this interpretation, the individuals in charge of Isabelle launched a systematic and skilful programme of training. It seemed hopeless at first. The approach had to be through pantomime and dramatization, suitable to an infant. It required one week of intensive effort before she even made her first attempt at vocalization. Gradually she began to respond, however, and, after the first hurdles had at last been overcome, a curious thing happened. She went through the usual stages of learning characteristic of the years from one to six not only in proper succession but far more rapidly than normal. In a little over two months after her first vocalization she was putting sentences together. Nine months after that she could identify words and sentences on the printed page, could write well, could add to ten, and could retell a story after hearing it. Seven months beyond this point she had a vocabulary of 1,500 to 2,000 words and was asking complicated questions. . . . In short, she covered in two years the stages of learning that ordinarily requires six. . . . The speed with which she reached the normal level of mental development seems analogous to the recovery of body weight in a growing child after an illness, the recovery being achieved by an extra fast rate of growth for a period after the illness until normal weight for the given age is again attained.

When the writer saw Isabelle a year and a a half after her discovery, she gave him the impression of being a very bright, cheerful, energetic little girl. She spoke well, walked and ran without trouble, and sang with gusto and accuracy. Today she is over fourteen years old . . . Her teachers say that she participates in all school activities as normally as other children.

Thus, compared with 'Anna', 'Isabelle' obviously made enormous progress, none of which, of course, could have been made without the stimulation of the adults who took such great pains over her training. 'Isabelle' probably had a greater inborn potential than 'Anna', although it must not be forgotten that she received a far more intensive and effective training as well. Moreover, the emotional relationship between 'Isabelle' and her mother seems to have been much more positive than that between 'Anna' and her mother, and this may well have resulted in a greater willingness to learn. The case of 'Isabelle' also suggests that, up to a certain age at least, deprivation of normal social contacts may be made good to quite a substantial degree by the provision of suitable contacts later on, although there is probably a limit to the degree of recovery. If 'Isabelle' had been ten or older when she was found it would have been even harder to teach her to speak and, above a certain age, it might have been impossible. It is significant that the 'Wild Boy of Aveyron', who was estimated to be about eleven when he was found, did not learn to speak although, as we have already noted, we cannot rule out the possibility that he was mentally defective at the outset.

Despite the numerous qualifications one has to make, all these cases show that deprivation of human contact in early life inhibits the development of normal social responses. All human beings, except those born with severe physical handicaps, have the inborn capacity to become fully mature members of society but, in order for this capacity to be realized, the child has to have adequate social relationships with others. *Social behaviour in humans is not inborn; in a very important sense we have to 'learn' to be human beings.*

Variations in patterns of socialization

In the normal course of events, every child grows up in a particular society in direct contact with particular people. He gradually takes on the characteristics of those people and becomes one of them. He learns to speak their language; he learns to think in terms of their concepts; he internalizes their standards of good and bad, right and wrong, and so on. There are, however, enormous variations in the patterns of socialization from one society to another; growing up in an African tribe is quite different from growing up in Britain. Even within a society there may be marked differences in the pattern of socialization. There is, for instance, a considerable difference between growing up in a large industrial city and growing up in a small village; and in the city, too, there is all the difference in the world between growing up in a rich and exclusive suburb and growing up in a poor neighbourhood.

The variations in patterns of socialization show us just how malleable so-called 'human nature' really is. Furthermore, knowing how people behave in societies different from our own enables us to take a fresh look at the way *we* behave, and to increase our understanding as a result. Many beliefs and forms of conduct which we take for granted and unconsciously assume to be universal are a part of the fabric of a particular society and may not be found in other societies. For example, all of us have certain ingrained ideas and opinions about the essential differences between 'masculine' and 'feminine' characteristics. We may believe that girls are 'naturally' submissive, intuitive, and unpractical, but even if most girls in a particular society are actually like this it does not follow that these traits are inborn and universal. Indeed, in other societies the definition of femininity and masculinity may be quite different. Thus, in a survey of the native inhabitants of what used to be British Central Africa it was found that spinning, weaving and sewing were very definitely regarded as men's work.[3]

> the men, in general, are neat-fingered and take to these things almost instinctively, while to their wives, who are gathered into sewing classes at the missions, by way of making them 'womanly', they are mostly pain and grief.

In some societies women do much of the manual labour, while in others cooking, housekeeping and looking after babies are regarded as proper male activities. Hunting is frequently regarded as an essentially masculine pursuit, but amongst the Aboriginal inhabitants of Tasmania seal-hunting was definitely women's work. They swam out to the seal rocks, stalked the animals and killed them with clubs. And finally, the idea that men are 'naturally' more aggressive than women is hardly born out by the practice of warfare, which is certainly not an exclusively male sphere. For instance, in some of the traditional societies of Africa regiments of women were occasionally formed. These women were specially trained to be warriors and enjoyed a considerable reputation for their proficiency and ferocity. And here one might also refer to the legendary Amazons who, whether legendary or not, have provided us with the word 'Amazonian' which means a strong, aggressive, or ironically enough, 'masculine' woman.

In any society there are widely shared conceptions as to how males and females should behave. These conceptions serve as models to which the growing child is expected to conform. Moreover, we generally come to accept the patterns of behaviour which are current in our own society as morally right. This makes it difficult for us to understand and appreciate people whose behaviour differs considerably from our own; there is the quite natural feeling that 'ours is the best way'. As we have just seen, however, there is likely to be considerable variation in what is regarded as 'the best way'. To the sociologist *all* varieties of human behaviour are worthy of study and it is no part of his task as a scientist to try to decide which pattern of conduct is the best.

Apart from the question of the behaviour of the different sexes, the comparative study of human societies indicates striking differences in many other aspects of social life, for instance in attitudes towards property. In some societies, our own for example, the emphasis tends to be on individual ownership, so much so that many people feel that common ownership is contrary to 'human nature'. On the other hand there are societies in which collective ownership is the norm, and people in these societies would in turn feel that individual ownership is 'unnatural'. These different attitudes are well illustrated in an essay by the anthropologist W. H. R. Rivers:[4]

> When I was travelling in 1908 on a vessel with four Polynesian natives of Niue or Savage Island, and took the opportunity of inquiring into their social organization, they retaliated in a manner I am always glad to encourage by asking me about the social customs of my own country . . . one of the first questions was directed to discover what I should do with a sovereign if I was fortunate enough to earn one. In response to my somewhat lame answers, they asked me the definitely leading question whether I should

share it with my parents, brothers and sisters. When I replied that I might do so if I liked, but that it was not the usual custom, they found my reply so ridiculous that it was long before they left off laughing. It was quite clear from their ejaculations that their amusement was altogether due to the incongruity with their own attitude of my conduct with regard to my earnings.

One can readily see that *sharing* would be completely taken for granted by these Polynesians, and their children would be taught to accept it as the right and proper thing to do. In fact, an ethic of sharing is quite common in many of those societies we would describe as 'primitive'. Among the Eskimo and similar peoples in Siberia any seal or whale killed by an individual is shared with the other members of the community. In such communities the successful hunter is morally bound to share his spoils with the unsuccessful. 'The hunter kills, other people have', say the Yukaghir of Siberia. In these societies food must always be made available to others on pain of ostracism and *giving away*, particularly at times of scarcity, is regarded as a moral duty. (Although the present tense is used here it should be noted that many of these communities are undergoing radical change as their members become increasingly involved in larger economic and political systems.)

It is clear that this behaviour does not conform to our stereotype of 'economic man' who is supposed to maximize his profit and minimize his loss, and it follows that we cannot understand the behaviour of primitive hunters and food gatherers in terms of our categories of economic analysis. This highlights the extremely important point that the socialization process in which we have participated and the consequent concepts and standards that we have internalized may act as a major obstacle to the understanding of a way of life which is radically different from our own. We are not normally aware of the relativity of our outlook and we unconsciously judge other peoples in the light of our own standards. Thus the missionaries in the example quoted earlier felt that sewing was *naturally* women's work and set about trying to teach the native women to do this, imposing their own values on people with different values. It may also happen that failure to appreciate the way in which our outlook has been shaped by growing up in a particular society may have rather surprising consequences in certain situations. For example, we tend to take it for granted that our desire for a higher standard of living and our acceptance of economic incentives are universally shared, and probably reflect some basic trait of 'human nature'. However, the importance we attach to these things is a fairly recent development:[5]

In earlier centuries wants were stable in the West and this led to widespread complaints, for example in England, that the result of giving workers higher wages was not a better but an inferior quality of industry, not more but less labour. As needs could be satisfied with a shorter period at work, many skilled labourers who were able to earn as much money as they required in less than the conventional work week spent only three or four days at their jobs and the rest in idleness. The generalized desire for more goods and therefore a higher income and the increasingly accepted demand for a disciplined labour force have lessened the frequency of this type of reaction in the West in the twentieth century.

In the poor countries, the desire for a higher standard of living developed at a later date, and indeed, is only now growing in many areas. In Burma at the turn of the century, rice fields were often left unharvested after the wants of the farmers had been satisfied, despite the existence of markets in which the grain could have been sold. The recruitment of a labour force for a textile factory in the middle of a poor agricultural district in Guatemala proceeded with great difficulty, although the wages offered by the factory were substantially higher than those in agriculture—it took fifty years to build a relatively stable labour force.

From the point of view of our standards, the above reaction to increased income and employment opportunities might seem to be 'irrational', but it must be remembered that from the different perspective of the people involved they would appear to be eminently 'rational'. Some evidence on the way in which these differing standards are already internalized in childhood is provided by a series of essays written by twenty-six children in Guatemala and twenty-six in Iowa, USA. The subject of the essays was 'My home, what I like about it, what I do not like, my ambitions for my home in the future'.[6]

Twenty-two of the twenty-six children from Iowa mentioned the importance of material facilities and none of those from Guatemala; twenty-three out of twenty-six from Guatemala mentioned love and peace in the home as compared to thirteen in the USA, and eighteen from Guatemala mentioned the importance of space as compared to three in the USA.

It goes without saying that the children from Guatemala would consider their standards to be the best, and that the American children would consider their standards to be the best. From a sociological point of view the really important thing is that the standards and values are different. and then the problem becomes one of trying to explain why they are different.

The development of human behaviour

The examples we have discussed show that most of the differences in the patterns of behaviour of people in different countries, or between different classes and sections within a country, are not inborn in any biological sense; they are *acquired* patterns of behaviour. What is inborn in the biological sense is *the capacity to be different*, the capacity to respond in a different way if circumstances change. It is this that makes man such a flexible creature able to adapt to wide variations in environment. Apart from certain reflexes, human beings have very few fixed reactions at birth; human behaviour is something which *develops* in the context of social interaction. Of course there are inborn physical dispositions with respect, for instance, to temperament and intelligence, but the way in which these dispositions are woven into the texture of behaviour is largely patterned by social interaction. And even very basic 'biological needs' such as hunger and sex are everywhere overlaid by social influences. Thus, in every human society, sexual impulses are hedged around by a whole variety of customs and rules, and similarly, food habits vary enormously from one social group to another.

While granting that human behaviour patterns show remarkable flexibility, the question remains as to whether there are any *universal* features of the process of socialization. The results of socialization vary enormously but are there any common features which can be found in all societies? What are the underlying processes whereby the growing child learns to speak and

think and take over the attitudes and values of the members of the group into which he has been born? We have seen that in the most general sense these processes are bound up with social interaction, and our earlier discussion of the effects of social isolation in childhood suggests that the crucial thing is the relationship that normally develops between the child and those that care for it (usually the biological parents, but not necessarily so). This relationship comes to have a strong emotional content; the child normally comes to need the love and affection of those that care for it as well as the satisfaction of its more physical needs for food, etc. In the world of the small child, emotional and physical needs are closely interwoven as can be seen by the fact that disturbances of feeding are often an indicator of emotional disturbance, and, indeed, the actual development of the need for love is very much bound up with experiences of feeding and handling.

Once the need for love and affection has begun to develop there exists a powerful lever for socialization; *in order to satisfy its emotional needs the growing child will come to accept the 'do's and don'ts' of those that care for it*. It is by no means self-evident to the small child that cleanliness is any better than being dirty; as a matter of fact small children evidently enjoy being dirty! Nevertheless, most children learn to accept the standards of cleanliness that the adult members of their society hold. Why is this if the child's spontaneous tendency is in an opposite direction? Putting it briefly, the answer is that being clean results in parental approval and being dirty results in parental disapproval; to the child who needs the continuing affection of those who care for it, learning to be clean is the required 'price' it has to pay. This goes for many other detailed forms of behaviour, for example the countless ways in which children normally imitate their parents. This vital process of imitation revolves around a basic emotional identification with the parents, as if the child were acting on the principle 'I want to be like my father and mother.' Of course, a child may want to be more like one parent than the other and this is directly encouraged by the different expectations parents have of boys and girls. It is through these reciprocal identifications and expectations that the patterns of behaviour appropriate to each sex are gradually exhibited.

The general truth of all this is born out in those cases where the child fails to behave according to parental requirements. Children are usually extremely ambivalent (i.e. have mixed feelings of love and hate) towards those that care for them. If the balance of the child's ambivalence is tilted towards hate it may well exhibit behavioural abnormalities and difficulties of various kinds. There may be regression in feeding and toilet habits, or the child may be generally difficult and intractable for a time. Even more drastic than this are those cases where there is something fundamentally abnormal in the relationship between the child and those who care for it. Consider the following case of an eight-year-old adopted girl who had got into trouble for telling lies and stealing:[7]

> After an illegitimate birth, the child was shifted about from one relative to another, finally brought to a child-placing agency, and then placed in a foster-home for two months before she came to the adoptive parents. . . . The parents described the child's reaction to the adoption as very casual. When they took her home and showed her the room she was to have all for herself, and took her on a tour of the house and grounds, she showed apparently no emotional response. Yet she appeared very vivacious and 'affectionate on the surface'. After a few weeks of experience with her, the adoptive mother complained to her husband that the child did not seem able to show any affection. The child, to use the mother's words 'would kiss you but it would mean nothing'. The husband told his wife that she was expecting too much, that she should give the child a a chance to get adapted to the situation. The mother was somewhat mollified by these remarks, but still insisted that something was wrong. The father said he saw nothing wrong with the child. In a few months, however, he made the same complaint. By this time, also it was noted that the child was deceitful and evasive. All methods of correction were of no avail.

In this case it appears that the instability of the child's early relationships with adults have prevented the formation of the normal emotional attachments of parents and children. Without these attachments the child has great difficulty in developing the generalized need for the approval of other people which is the basis for the acquisition of standards of right and wrong. There is, as it were, an inability to love or feel guilty, and one could say that the development of 'conscience'

has been impaired. There are a number of situations which may have this result; apart from instability of relationships in early life, actual rejection of the child by the parents may have similar consequences. Socialization depends upon a reciprocity of affection between children and adults, and, without this, normal development does not occur. We might recall at this point our earlier discussion of the cases of 'Anna' and 'Isabelle'. 'Isabelle' did spend quite a lot of time with her mother and they did communicate, if only by means of gestures: 'Anna', by comparison, seemed to have been largely rejected by her mother. These differences in mother-child relationships may well have been part of the reason for the very difference responses of the two girls to subsequent training. In certain cases, like that of the eight-year-old girl quoted above, the inability to love or to feel guilt may lead the child to become delinquent, although it does not follow that *all* juvenile delinquency can be explained on this basis.

In considering the way in which socialization takes place, the important general point is that what are at first external standards imposed by the parents or other adults are gradually internalized by the child and become part of his own personal way of behaving. This process rests on the normal existence of a need to be accepted by others and ensures some degree of conformity to their expectations. The process can also be seen at work outside the immediate family, for instance among children and young people of the same age group, i.e. one's 'peer group'. The growing child learns some very important lessons in social conduct from his peers and, in this sense, socialization continues beyond and outside the family situation. Children's games, for example, provide an important context in which the concepts of 'fair play' and the 'rules of the game' can be acquired.

One famous study of Swiss boys traced the development of their grasp of the rules of the game of marbles.[8] At first the small child of two or three simply enjoys playing with the marbles without any conception of there being a 'game' with 'rules' which has 'winners' and 'losers'. At four or five, however, the child begins to understand the notion of 'rules'. Thus, you must draw a square of a certain size; you must stand outside this square; you must pitch one marble at a time, and if your marble goes outside instead of hitting that of your opponent, you have lost. At this stage the rules are usually regarded as fixed and unchangeable, but at seven or eight this begins to give way to a more flexible view in which the rules may be modified, providing everybody agrees. Finally, in the pre-adolescent period, considerations of equity may enter in to modify strict application of the rules; for instance, a boy with a physical handicap may be allowed certain advantages over the others by way of compensation.

If the growing child does not conform to the 'rules of the game' he may well be subjected to criticism or even ridicule by his peers. Conformity to the standards of one's peers is an extremely important process in societies like our own where peer groups play an important part in the social development of the child. In this connection it is important to note that what many people regard as the rebelliousness of teenagers in our society (in other words their frequent nonconformity to the standards of their parents) does not mean that they do not conform to *any* standards. On the contrary, they are probably just as conformist as their parents, possibly even more so, for in order to be accepted by the teenage peer group they must exhibit the characteristic attitudes, the likes and dislikes, and the modes of speech and dress which are current in that group.

Socialization, then, is not a process confined to the immediate family, although it is there that certain very basic social characteristics are acquired. The process continues beyond and outside the family into the peer group, and beyond that into adulthood. An extremely important part of this later socialization is the internalization of the standards and attitudes characteristic of one's occupational group, a process which is well described in the following passage:[9]

> Already at the age of twenty-five you see the professional mannerism settling down on the young commercial traveller, on the young doctor, on the young minister, on the young counsellor-at-law. You see the little lines of cleavage running through the character, the tricks of thought, the prejudices, the ways of the 'shop', in a word, from which the man can by-and-by no more escape than his coat-sleeve can suddenly fall into a new set of folds.

In a highly complex society like our own, socialization is indeed an intricate process. Apart from parents, peers and the members of one's occupational group, there are many other people who are directly and indirectly involved in shaping the outlook of the individual as he develops into a particular kind of person. There are the teachers at all levels of the educational system, and there are all those who are involved in the production of books, magazines, newspapers and television programmes. In less complex societies socialization is itself relatively less complicated. This is necessarily so, for to describe a society as less complex can be regarded as a shorthand way of saying that social life is less differentiated, that there are fewer distinct kinds of social groupings. In the simplest kinds of human society, activities like raising a family, getting a living, the maintenance of law and order, politics and religion are not sharply separated from each other as they are in more complex societies with the distinct social groupings of families, firms, political parties and churches. And, apart from these sorts of distinctions, more complex societies are frequently divided into different social classes which are differentiated from each other by inequalities of wealth and power. These class differences, in so far as they involve differences in outlook and standards, also entail diversification of patterns of socialization. The general point to note is that the more differentiated the society the greater the number of possible agencies and modes of socialization.

Socialization and social change

This picture of socialization as a continuous process extending into adulthood and involving interaction with different sets of people can help us to resolve a problem which has been implicit in much of what has been said so far. There is a temptation to over-emphasize the way in which socialization brings about *conformity*. If children were perfectly socialized to accept the standards of their parents, then how could *change* come about? There is a tendency to think of socialization as inherently conservative and orientated towards the past, with the individual as an essentially passive object being moulded to fit into society. From this point of view, deviance from current social norms is almost bound to be seen as undesirable. Yet, as we have seen, one must recognize that human beings have the capacity to be different, to innovate, to create something new. Innovation frequently involves some deviation from standard practice, and many great innovators have, as a matter of fact, found themselves in conflict with social traditions; for example, thinkers like Galileo, Darwin and Freud whose views brought them into sharp conflict with established ideas and values. So, deviance may be a positive, if painful thing without which new ideas and practices are impossible.

People frequently break with tradition because they are forced to in order to cope with changed circumstances, and herein lies part of the answer to our problem. If the world into which children grow up is changing, then many of the things they learn will lead them to have a different outlook from that of their parents. The consequent estrangement of the generations can be illustrated by what is happening today in those economically underdeveloped countries where large numbers of young people leave impoverished rural areas to seek work in towns and cities. These young migrants move into a new world where the standards and values are usually quite alien to those of parents and other kin in the tribe or village. In the process of adapting to the urban milieu, the migrant inevitably develops an outlook which is more or less foreign to that of the older generation rooted in rural ways of life. Even if the parents accompany or follow the young people to the urban area, the relationship between the generations is altered. The parents are usually strangers to urban ways of life and cannot effectively prepare their children for adulthood in the new environment. It is the children who are quicker to adapt to the new situation, and this can easily lead to loss of respect for the traditional wisdom and authority of the parents. However painful it may be for the people involved, conflict between generations is probably inevitable in periods of rapid social changes.

In industrial societies, too, there are many ways in which wider social changes bring about conflict between parents and children. Perhaps the most obvious of these is, as we previously noted, where the code of conduct of young people is at variance with parental conceptions of correct behaviour. More specifically one can readily see how the opportunities for personal advancement *via* higher education may lead to the estrangement of children from their parents. In a society with increasing equality of educational opportunity, an increasing number of boys and girls receive an education which enables them to 'climb the social ladder' and move a long way away from the world of their parents. This type of social mobility, however, is not usually achieved without some degree of personal conflict for the individuals involved. Thus, in order to become accepted in 'middle-class' society, the 'working-class' boy or girl is forced to acquire new standards of behaviour which often clash with old ones. In some cases this process is acutely painful. Here the process of socialization entails conflict between standards and values internalized in the context of home and neighbourhood and those embodied in the educational system.

These remarks on the way socialization may entail conflict between the generations lead us directly to the conclusion of this chapter. Socialization is a process which usually involves both continuity and discontinuity. Continuity is made possible by the internalization of traditional values which represent the past. Discontinuity occurs because the members of each new generation may have to reject some of the heritage of the past in order to cope with a changing present and an imagined future. The development of both individual and society depends upon the balance of these inherently opposed but inter-related tendencies.

Notes

1 Quoted in a note by P. C. Squires in *American Journal of Psychology*, vol. 38, 1927, pp. 314–15.
2 Kingsley Davis, 'Final note on a case of extreme isolation', *American Journal of Sociology*, vol. 52, 1947, pp. 436–7.
3 Alice Werner, *The Natives of British Central Africa*, London: Constable, 1906, pp. 196–7.
4 W. H. R. Rivers, *Psychology and Politics*, London: Kegan Paul, 1923, pp. 36–7.
5 R. Theobald, *The Rich and the Poor*, New York: Mentor, 1961, pp. 30–31.
6 Ibid., pp. 31–2.
7 Case quoted in J. Bowlby, *Child Care and the Growth of Love*, Harmondsworth: Penguin, 1953, pp. 33–4.
8 Jean Piaget, *The Moral Judgement of the Child*, London: Routledge & Kegan Paul, 1932.
9 Margaret Knight, *William James: A Selection from his Writings on Psychology*, Harmondsworth: Penguin, 1950, pp. 78–9.

Reading

Brim, Orville G. Jr and Wheeler, Stanton, *Socialization after Childhood: Two Essays*, New York: Wiley, 1966. These essays are rather advanced, but the interested student might usefully tackle the first one which gives a comprehensive picture of 'Socialization through the Life Cycle' from a sociological point of view.

Elkin, F., *The Child and Society: The Process of Socialization*. New York: Random House, 1960. A short but fairly systematic introduction to the topic. Ideal for the beginner.

Lindesmith, A. R. and Strauss, A. L., *Social Psychology* (3rd ed.), New York: Holt, Rinehart & Winston, 1968. A good textbook for sociology students. Part 4, 'Socialization and Interaction', contains several excellent chapters in which socialization is consistently viewed in relation to the pattern of social relations of which it is part. This section includes a useful chapter on adult socialization.

Mead, Margaret, *Coming of Age in Samoa*, and, *Growing up in New Guinea*, Harmondsworth: Penguin, 1943 and 1942. Detailed accounts of growing up in societies very different from our own.

Piaget, Jean, *The Moral Judgement of the Child*, London: Routledge & Kegan Paul, 1932. A classic study of social relations among children as a factor in the development of moral judgment. Although Piaget possibly overstates his case, his approach is a useful reminder that socialization is not simply a matter of parent-child relations. The beginning student may well find Piaget a little difficult to follow but it is worth making the effort.

White, R. W., *Live in Progress* (2nd ed.), New York, Holt, Rinehart & Winston, 1966. A stimulating discussion of the development of personality based on detailed case histories of three very different people. The book brings out the real complexity of human growth and the many and varied factors involved in becoming a particular kind of person. The broader implications of the case histories are discussed in several very good theoretical chapters.

Further reading

Brown, Roger, *Social Psychology*, New York: Free Press, 1965 (see part 3, 'The Socialization of the Child'). A sophisticated textbook discussion which brings out the importance of symbolic processes in socialization; includes a good introduction to the work of Piaget and his colleagues on cognitive development.

Clausen, John A. (ed.), *Socialization and Society*, Boston: Little, Brown, 1968. This book is the outcome of the work of a special Committee on Socialization and Social Structure appointed in 1960 by the Social Science Research Council of America. It is concerned with the inter-relationships between social structure, socialization processes, and personality formation; particularly useful in so far as it brings together the psychological and sociological approaches to the study of socialization.

Goslin, David A. (ed.), *Handbook of Socialization Theory and Research*, Chicago: Rand McNally, 1969. A comprehensive collection of advanced essays on various aspects of socialization; particularly good on theoretical issues. The term 'handbook' is misleading; this is a very substantial volume of over 1,000 pages!

Isaacs, Susan, *Social Development in Young Children*, London: Routledge & Kegan Paul, 1933. A psycho-analytically oriented study of the emotional aspects of social relations in childhood, based on detailed observational records of the social and sexual development of children.

Parsons, Talcott, *Social Structure and Personality*, New York: Free Press, 1964. The first part of this collection of essays contains the author's various attempts to place Freudian theory in a sociological context. See particularly 'The superego and the theory of social systems' and 'The incest taboo in relation to social structure and the socialization of the child'. Several other essays in the book are also relevant to the topic of socialization, notably 'The school class as a social system'.

Zigler, Edward and Child, Irvin L., 'Socialization', in volume 3 of Gardner Lindsey and Elliot Aronson (eds), *The Handbook of Social Psychology* (2nd ed.), Reading, Mass.: Addison-Wesley, 1969. A useful review of the literature and the current state of research.

8 Education

The development of education

In simple societies education is synonymous with socialization. The homogeneity of the society and the relatively low level of technology enable the social skills necessary for adult life to be taught to the child informally, as part of his everyday contact with his elders. Consequently there are no special teachers entrusted specifically with the training of young people. Typically, boys learn the skills of hunting or farming from their fathers or other adult males; girls learn how to cook, sew, and perhaps farm from the women of the community. In this way the process of education (or socialization) is carried out through a loose form of apprenticeship and, as we have already seen, this informal learning process is present and important in all societies. In the more complex societies of the industrial world, however, where there is more division of labour and a large number of different adult roles, there are persons who specialize in educating the young. In intermediate stages of development this task is often given to the priests, and education becomes closely connected with religion, as in ancient Egypt, ancient India and medieval Europe. In the latter case, for example, the clergy held a monopoly of the skills of literacy and consequently were the only persons capable of carrying out educational tasks involving reading and writing. Gradually schools emerge as separate institutions specializing in education, and teachers emerge as a separate occupational group. Thus there grows up a new complex of institutions—an educational system—specially designed to perform an important part of the process of socialization. But in addition to the function of socialization an educational system has many other functions—some of them unintended and sometimes not even recognized. In other words the process of preparing young people for adult life has many side effects some of which may even be contrary to the stated aims of the educators.

The highly complicated systems of compulsory education that are to be found in industrial societies today did not emerge overnight. When the occupational roles demanding literacy are few, the specialized system of education remains the preserve of a minority, while for the majority 'education' is carried on as before. In England, it was not until the nineteenth century that it was thought necessary to provide formal education of any sort for the mass of the population. Prior to the eighteenth century 'young gentlemen' were tutored privately in the art of gentlemanly behaviour; a few of the sons of the rich attended the older of the public schools (the name by which they were later known); a few received education in one or other of the schools attached to the cathedrals; and a very few (including in this case the sons of 'commoners') were taught by the local parish priest. For the most part, however, all learning was in the hands of parents or others with whom the young people worked.

Such a system, with father teaching son, was geared to agricultural rather than industrial conditions and, although it could be adapted to the 'cottage' type of industry where parents and their children normally worked alongside each other, later changes made it unsuitable. With the changing nature of industry in the late eighteenth and early nineteenth centuries, and in particular with the accelerating growth of large towns, the drawbacks of this 'apprenticeship' type of system became more obvious. For some time the exploitation of children in the factories was so intense that there was not time for education of a more general sort. With the passing of the Factory Acts, however, education became a possibility. Indeed the Factory Acts themselves represent the earliest legislation directly related to education. The Factory Act of 1802, for example, required employers in the cotton industry to provide adequate instruction in reading, writing and arithmetic for at least four of the seven years of apprenticeship. The earliest schools of industry had been founded a hundred years before this legislation and such schools, although few in number, did provide the opportunity for some children to earn their keep while attending school part time.

In addition to this stimulation from the growth of industries there were in the late eighteenth and early nineteenth centuries important changes in the intellectual and political climate—changes which themselves were later to be encouraged by the spread of mass schooling. More egalitarian ideas were spreading to England from revolutionary France, and the gradual extension, throughout the nineteenth century, of political power at home gave increasing control to groups whose commercial interests made them more favourable to the spread of education than the landed gentry had been. There were, of course, counter-influences, often stemming from the same sources. For example, there was the fear of the ruling classes, most eloquently expressed in the writing of Edmund Burke, that education for the majority of the people would result in political unrest and perhaps even in a revolution similar to that experienced in France. For the most part, however, the idea of training the poor only to poverty was dying.

Even so, for the greater part of the nineteenth century education, in common with all activities not directly connected with law or defence, was not considered to be a realm appropriate for government action. Throughout the first part of the century educational development was exclusively in the hands of non-governmental agencies, and of these the most important were the churches. The breakdown of the moral and religious control by the churches which occurred when villagers moved to towns, combined with the religious enthusiasm of the middle classes during much of the nineteenth century, not to mention the rivalry

between the Anglicans and the Nonconformists, provided a fertile ground for the initial growth of schools. In particular, the Nonconformist emphasis on the importance of being able to read the Bible for oneself led to a high evaluation of literacy. This religious interest in education was reflected in the Sunday School movement—a movement which frankly acknowledged the industrial conditions of the day by giving instruction on the only day of the week when the children were not labouring in the factories—and more systematically in the formation of the National Society for Promoting the Education of the Poor in the Principles of the Established Church, and the British and Foreign School Society (a Nonconformist run society whose schools were to contain no denominational teaching). But in the second half of the century, when enough growth had taken place to bring these groups into direct competition for the *same* pupils and when the possibility of substantial government grants arose, jealousy and suspicion between them hindered further growth and prevented the systematization of education. The 'religious question' exhibited a a regular pattern throughout the years of the struggle. Whenever there was a proposal before parliament to give financial support to denominational schools it was blocked by the Nonconformist group (as, for example, with the 1843 Education Bill), because such a measure would benefit the Anglicans with their greater number of schools. Whenever the plan was to assist 'non-denominational' schools from public funds there was Anglican opposition (as, for example, with the 1839 Education Bill). The consequent position of stalemate over the extension of state aid to education, which had begun in a small way in 1833, can thus only be understood in the light of the religious divisions in the country.

Christianity has also played a decisive role in the development of education in some other countries. In most European colonies and ex-colonies, for example, the agencies through which Western education was spread were initially the Christian missions. Indeed, the educational scene of much of English-speaking Africa bears a striking resemblance in this, as in other respects, to the English educational system a hundred years ago. In spite of a general upsurge of government activity in the years since independence many of the schools are still run either by local churches or foreign missions. But the emergence and continuance of these Western-style schools cannot be explained simply in terms of religious or humanitarian goodwill, any more than such an explanation is sufficient for the development of the English system. In the latter case the transformation from a situation where schooling was a luxury granted to very few to its establishment as a normal practice for all children was very closely connected with the whole complex of industrialization and urbanization. But the churches were the only non-governmental agencies capable of organizing on anything like the national scale required to meet the need for education although other bodies could and did provide a sprinkling of schools here and there.

In the same way, in many African societies before their contact with the West there was no need for a Western type of educational system. Literacy itself was a skill that had little relevance to traditional ways of life. Consequently when missionaries tried to start schools the response was one of apathy. On the west coast of Africa, for example, there were attempts of this kind over a period of more than three hundred years, but the only schools which met with even partial success were those catering for the children of the Europeans living in the coastal castles. It was not until the establishment of trading posts along the coast and a consequent re-orientation of the values of the indigenous peoples that any local interest was shown in the schools. Then it became increasingly evident that schooling provided a gateway to a new kind of job, as clerk or assistant to a European trader or missionary, and this occupational relevance of education began to popularize the schools.

From this example it is clear that religious zeal is not, of itself, sufficient to establish formal education. Only when the economic conditions are suitable for such development is pioneering action in education effective. Especially important in this respect is the emergence of occupations demanding a high level of literacy. The importance of religion in the development of the Western type of formal education was in the provision, through its denominations and its missionary societies, of a sponsoring organization for education at times when government action in the field of education was minimal.

Political considerations form a further element in the growth of educational systems. Reference has already been made to some of the political changes in nineteenth-century England which were especially relevant to education. The extension of political power to wider groups—or more accurately the passing of legislation which made such an extension a possibility even if not an actuality—gave the expansion of elementary education a boost in the expectation that it would in turn provide an educated, or at least a literate, electorate and perhaps also in the desire to exert some control over this newly influential group. The saying 'we must educate our masters' was a cynical formulation of this new attitude towards popular education. A rather more remarkable appreciation of the interaction of the economic, political and educational spheres was demonstrated by Mr W. E. Foster during the parliamentary debate on the 1870 Education Bill: 'Upon the speedy provision of elementary education depends our industrial prosperity ... upon this speedy provision depends also, I fully believe, the good, the safe working of our constitutional system. ... Upon this speedy provision of education depends also our national power.'[1]

Similarly, in modernizing societies political life has not been without relevance for the educational system. The rewards offered to educated people through the occupational structure of both industrial and modernizing countries provide what is perhaps the dominant motive of individuals when they seek education for themselves or their children. But once such motivation is present it becomes possible for other institutions to influence the extent to which it is satisfied. So it was impossible for the newly independent governments of Africa, dependent as they were in the early stages of independence upon popular support, to oppose the wishes of an education-seeking population by restricting education in the way that their colonial predecessors had done. The legislation of the first year after independence invariably includes measures to expand the educational system in one way or another. The governments of newly independent countries typically aim at compulsory, free primary education in the shortest possible time, partly from a genuine idealism and sense of social justice, and partly because they are pressed into such action by a pro-education electorate.

Thus it would appear that economic, political and religious factors are all important in determining the timing and pace of the emergence of education. But so far all our attention has been focused on primary education; what of the secondary schools? In England separate institutions for secondary and university education had existed even at the beginning of the nineteenth century albeit under the wing of the Church of England and, in a few cases, the

Nonconformist denominations. The universities of Oxford and Cambridge, however, were little more than places for rich young men to squander their wealth ostentatiously, and the schools—the endowed grammar schools and other independent foundations—attracted few pupils and had low physical and academic standards. Moreover, the Nonconformist academies which had, in the eighteenth century, been an important source of scientific innovation had subsequently declined into insignificance.

There was, however, a growing need for 'higher' education, so that when reforms occurred in some of the schools there was a rapidly growing clientele to make use of them. In spite of their wealth, the rising class of industrialists and businessmen were not accepted by the landed aristocracy on terms of equality. This helps to explain the eagerness with which they sought education for their children; for the reformed public schools, together with an increasing number of new foundations, provided an education which was at the same time a training for political and professional activities (the gentlemanly activities) and a means by which the sons of the *nouveaux riches* could learn the customs and habits of the upper classes and thus eventually attain the respectability denied their fathers. Furthermore, the improvements in transport—and especially the growth of the railways—which took place in the middle of the century enabled these schools to become national institutions, drawing their clientele from all over the country rather than from a single locality.

As was the case with the early primary schools, the first secondary schools were founded and controlled by non-governmental agencies, and the secondary school revival of the nineteenth century was also a revival of independent schools. This must be borne in mind when we look for an explanation of the *type* of secondary system of education which eventually grew up in England, for these schools attained a position of high prestige and a virtual monopoly over entry to powerful positions in the country. Consequently, when the state came to establish a system of secondary education at the beginning of the twentieth century it merely copied the established pattern of providing secondary education only for a minority. There were, however, forces other than imitation which influenced the establishment of secondary schools, and one of the most important of these has been the class structure.

Even a casual glance at English education in the nineteenth century makes it clear that it consisted of two *separate* streams rather than a unified system. There was elementary education—the education which was provided for the working classes, initially as an act of charity by voluntary organizations such as the churches, and after 1870 increasingly by the state. There was, second, the growth of the public schools and grammar schools for the sons (and in the latter part of the century the daughters as well) of the middle classes. It was this second sector that came to be known as 'secondary' education, and the division between elementary and secondary was in effect a division between two parallel systems, one being for the poor and one for the rich, with few links between them. This class basis of education was frankly recognized at the time and is implicit in the reports of all the major committees and commissions on education. A good example is the Taunton Commission which was set up in 1868 to investigate all secondary schools other than the nine chief public schools (which had been investigated separately). The Taunton Commissioners recommended that three types of school should be established, but the content of the report is perhaps of less interest than its phraseology. The first type of school, they said, should be for the sons of men of ample means or good education; the second for those whose means were 'straightened' but who wished to enter one of the professions; and the third for the 'sons of the smaller tenant farmers, the small tradesmen, the superior artisans'.

Towards the end of the century and for the first years of the twentieth century there was increased pressure for more secondary education, pressure which had its origin in industrial, political and other social changes. In particular the extension of the franchise in the last third of the nineteenth century had led to a more vocal condemnation of the economic and social inequality which showed itself in the class structure and which had previously always been taken for granted. The rise of the Labour party provided a national political party to voice this disquiet which eventually (after the first world war) took shape as the Labour party's campaign for 'secondary education for all'.

During the 1890s the demand for more 'higher' education was met largely by the growth of 'higher elementary' schools, created through the upward extension of some of the existing elementary schools. There was also some expansion of grammar schools. With the incorporation of secondary education into the state system after the 1902 Education Act, most of the higher elementary schools were converted into secondary schools and therefore they provided a similar education to the old grammar schools, although sometimes with more emphasis on science. But the entry of the state into the secondary field did not alter the basic pattern of an educational system split into separate elementary and secondary streams. Throughout the first half of the twentieth century social and economic conditions increasingly demanded that more and more children should stay longer at school. In response to this demand two things happened. First, the age of finishing compulsory school attendance was raised and attendance was more strictly enforced; second, greater provision was made for children to transfer from the elementary to the secondary stream by means of scholarships. But secondary education was still generally viewed as the education of a particular group rather than as a stage— the post-primary stage—in the education of all children.

The new view of secondary education as the education of an *age* group was developed by the various committees who were asked to report on post-primary education between the wars and during the second world war (the Hadow committee, 1927; the Spens committee, 1939; the Norwood committee, 1943). Each of these committees recommended the provision of separate types of secondary education for different groups of children. This pattern of secondary education, so important in later developments received a pseudo-theoretical justification in the report of the Norwood committee who submitted that there were three types of children: one type 'is interested in learning for its own sake'; the second type has abilities which 'lie markedly in the field of applied science or applied art'; and the third type 'deals more easily with concrete things than ideas'. This classification of the 'types' of children's mind was, claimed the committee, based upon 'common sense'. One might point out that it was also contrary to psychological evidence available to, but ignored by, the committee. As Professor Barnard has written:[2]

the history of English education is full of examples of theoretical arguments advanced to justify an already existing state of affairs. The *a priori* classification outlined by the Norwood committee fitted in excellently with the scheme of post primary education laid down in the Spens report; and that in turn

had been moulded largely on a system which had grown up in this country and had been determined mainly by historical, political and economic conditions.

In spite of its questionable foundations the Norwood report provided the initial justification for the practice of tripartitism (or dualism as it turned out in practice) which dominated English secondary education in the twenty-five years since the second world war. The dualism between grammar schools and secondary modern schools was, in effect, a continuation under new names of the old secondary-elementary dichotomy which itself originated in the class structure of the nineteenth century. Thus to a considerable extent the structure of the system of secondary education which emerged from the war reflected the class structure of a previous century.

The major change in the structure of secondary education since the war has been the movement towards 'comprehensive' secondary schooling. Even with the basic framework of the dual system, however, a number of significant changes have taken place. The most important of these has been the considerable increase in the average length of formal schooling. The minimum school leaving age was raised to fifteen in 1947, but since that time an ever-increasing number of young people have been continuing their full-time education beyond this minimum. In January 1947 there were 39,000 pupils over the age of seventeen in school; twenty years later the figure had risen to 164,000. Moreover, the tendency to stay on at school has been observable in all types of schools, although it has been most marked in those offering pupils an opportunity to sit for the General Certificate of Education. This represents an extension and an acceleration of changes which have been visible throughout the century. It is partly connected with the fact that the increasing complexity of industrial societies demands a longer period of learning, but in England much of this learning process has traditionally been carried on outside the schools and colleges through the institution of apprenticeship. (This is one of the reasons for the lower enrolment in English education after the age of compulsory school attendance when compared to the United States of America.) More closely related to the extension of education, and especially to the extension of the academic education which has characterized the grammar schools and higher education, have been the changes in the occupational structure represented by the growth of the professions and of white collar occupations such as clerks and typists.

The traditional association of secondary schools with occupations receiving high economic reward and prestige remained when these schools gradually opened their doors to the children of the lower classes. In addition, the increasingly bureaucratic nature of society made it more and more difficult for persons of working-class origin to achieve upward social mobility through success in business or industry; the best jobs went to those with the highest educational qualifications. The result was that the educational system—and particularly the grammar schools—became important as a channel through which young people of lowly origins could make their way to more respected, more highly remunerated and more prestigious occupations. In other words they became a major channel of social mobility. The secondary school, and the grammar school that replaced it, increasingly appeared as the only opportunity that working-class children had of rising to the ranks of the middle-class 'salariat' and it has been ambitious parents who have provided one of the driving forces behind the expansion of secondary education. In the years since the second world war the awareness shown by middle-class parents of the vocational relevance of grammar schooling spread to many working-class parents, and places at such schools come to be valued primarily for their occupational potential.

This also explains the strange history of the secondary modern schools. Designed for the children who 'deal more easily with concrete things than ideas', their early career was marked by curricular experiments, experiments in methods of teaching and a general emphasis on 'learning by doing'. Within a few years, however, many of them were training their children for GCE 'O' level examinations which involved a reversion to traditional curricula and teaching methods, and for those pupils who could not manage 'O' level another set of public examinations (the Certificate of Secondary Education) was introduced. Curiously enough it was the children and their parents who forced these changes, often against the opposition of teachers and educationalists, and curiously again, it is by the provision of such courses that secondary modern schools have increased their public appeal and been able to persuade pupils to stay at school beyond the statutory leaving age. It is the occupational relevance of these examinations, clearly seen in the demand of employers for paper qualifications, and the perception of this relevance by children and their parents that have been supremely important. Such occupational considerations dictated the direction of the development of secondary modern schools no less than they determined the expansion of the grammar schools.

There are, of course, other factors than the class structure and the occupational structure which help to determine the structure of education. In contemporary modernizing countries, as in the industrial countries in the past, the amount of money available for education is important in determining what type of educational system emerges. Where money is scarce it may be impossible to provide universal primary education and it will certainly be impossible to provide universal secondary education. In such a situation education can only be provided for a small proportion of school age children. Consequently immediate economic pressures are such as to encourage minority education. The growing educational systems of these countries are also open to influences from other countries, both through the examples offered by the existence of education elsewhere and more directly. Many of them had their first experiences of formal education while they were under colonial rule and frequently an educational system similar to that of the colonial power was grafted on to them irrespective of local conditions. Where this happened, the explanation of many facets of education lies outside the country altogether and can only be understood by an appreciation of conditions in the metropolitan country. Perhaps even more important than this, however, has been the world atmosphere of egalitarianism and democracy into which the newer countries have been born. The contemporary world is one in which widespread government action in the field of education is both expected and positively valued, so that most younger governments feel obliged to intervene to attempt to provide something akin to equality of educational opportunity. Partly because of this, there is government intervention at a much earlier stage in the development of the educational systems of the new countries than was the case in the now industrial countries.

One further difference between the 'new' and the 'old' countries needs mentioning. At the time when education was being grudgingly extended to the lower classes of the nations of Western Europe these countries had been in the process of industrializing for a hundred years or more. The contemporary modernizing countries, by contrast, have hardly started upon the road of industrialization. Thus, in the case of the 'old' countries, the growth of educational systems was a spontaneous response to the changing social conditions of industrializing societies, whereas in many modernizing societies there has been no such spontaneous development. Both the educational systems themselves and the factors giving rise to a local demand for education have been imported from other societies, and in this situation there has been a tendency for educational expansion to outrun other social changes. This in turn has important implications for further economic development, for unemployment, and even for political stability.

Socialization in schools

As we have already pointed out, socialization is only one of the functions of formal systems of education. It is nevertheless important and should not be ignored. In favourable circumstances the educational system provides an efficient processing machine, turning out its clients with particular skills, values and attitudes. One of the best examples of this was the work of the American schools, in the days of widespread immigration, in assimilating young people from diverse national origins into a single nation with a strong sense of their common nationhood. It was very largely through the educational system that the second and third generation of immigrants became fully American, a process which often necessitated a disruption of their ties with their parents. Socialization of the young generation into a new America could only be achieved by breaking down the values and customs of the immigrant community. Much the same was true in the USSR prior to the education reforms of 1958. Here the situation was more complex in that the problem of welding several nationalities into a single unit conflicted with the need to mollify the suspicion of Russian domination entertained by other ethnic groups. One of the concessions made was to give non-Russians the opportunity to receive their education in their native language, which in turn served to strengthen local sentiment. The consequent limitations on their ability in the Russian language limited the career prospects of many non-Russians but, on the other hand, this concession made the political aspect of some of the curriculum more palatable than it would otherwise have been and, in this way, smoothed the transition to a socialistic society tightly controlled from the

centre. In other words, in the American case and to some extent in the case of the Soviet Union, the socializing influence of the school worked in the opposite direction to the socializing influence of the family. This illustrates a more general point that where a modern educational system is grafted on to a relatively simple society its socializing influence, and indeed its very existence, may be disruptive rather than supportive of the old society. The new educational system acts as an agent of socialization not into the existing society (i.e. the immigrant communities of America or the regions of the Soviet Union) but into the new *modern* society which sponsored the educational system in the first place.

The clearest examples of this are to be found in non-Western countries which have adopted a Western pattern of education. Throughout Africa and Asia the growth of educational systems and the gradual establishment of an occupational sector based upon educational qualifications has helped to destroy the traditional patterns of authority as well as the old customs and beliefs. Members of the new (educated) élite, who monopolized the important positions in the modern occupational sector and were invariably given such positions of responsibility as were delegated by the colonial powers, owed their position to their education not to tradition. Indeed, the pre-independence politics of many of these countries consisted of a struggle for power between the educated and the traditional rulers. This alienation from the traditional patterns of life was partly due to the nature of the socialization process within schools. But the most important thing about education was that it resulted in the introduction of a new element—an educational system—into the social structure. The very implications of formal education, especially the setting up of academic qualifications as a source of authority and a means of occupational selection, were incompatible with the assumptions of the traditional societies. It mattered little *what* was taught in the schools; the important thing was that they existed.

In colonial countries the establishment of schools also provided a training ground for those who were later to challenge the legitimacy of colonial rule. The leaders of the independence struggles of the middle decades of the twentieth century have invariably been the products of mission or government schools—often highly gifted persons who had received higher education in Western universities. Once again the important factor was not so much *what* they learnt at school or university, as the part played by educational institutions in the emergence of a new type of society; a society in which educated leaders had sufficient power successfully to challenge foreign supremacy.

Education and economic development

Contemporary modernizing societies also provide us with the opportunity of making contemporary observations of the part played by education in the early stages of economic development. Ever since social scientists first became interested in these problems in the 1950s it has generally been held that education plays a key part in determining economic growth; certainly this has been the expressed opinion of many practising politicians. The experience of industrial countries is often cited to suggest that educated personnel are needed to further the process of industrial development and that therefore expenditure on education can be a form of investment. Without such an investment, it is argued, industrial developments will prove unattainable. Those charged with planning educational policy have almost always advised vast expansion schemes which have, for political reasons, been attractive to governments. Our discussion of the growth of English education, however, has already cast some doubt over the dominance of education in economic change. Certainly the early stages of industrialization in England owed little to formal education for it was these very changes which created the major need for mass education. Closer observation of the economic problems of Africa, Latin America and Asia will lead us to further scepticism. Perhaps the major problem of economic growth in these continents is a shortage of capital for investment in power projects, factories, the modernization of agriculture and so on. Money spent on educational developments is money diverted from such directly productive investment. In the past it has been considered to be a praiseworthy diversion— an investment in manpower which while reducing the immediate benefit would pay ample dividends in the long run. It is now being realized, however, that excessive investment in education may actually retard economic development by using up a disproportionate amount of the available capital. In some countries, for example in Western and Eastern Nigeria prior to 1965, up to 40 per cent of all government expenditure has been on education. Many economists are now of the opinion that in purely economic terms direct investment in industry produces higher returns at this level of industrial development than a similar investment in education. Of course, it is necessary for the educational system of these countries to turn out enough educated persons to man the commercial and industrial sector of the economy: it is as inefficient to produce factories with nobody capable of running them as it is to produce managers, foremen and semi-skilled workers with nothing to run. But the size of the modern sector of the economy in such societies is very small— invariably less than 10 per cent of the total employed population and often very much less. In order to provide manpower for such a small sector it is not necessary to mount the huge compulsory education programmes that typify newly independent countries. A relatively small educational system would suffice for such a task. In purely economic terms growth beyond this minimum, far from stimulating industrial development, actually retards it.

In the contemporary modernizing countries, then, as in Western countries in their early stages of industrialization, education has little power over the economy and certainly much less than is commonly ascribed to it. At later stages of industrialization, however, education becomes a more powerful instrument of promoting or retarding further economic development. The modern industrial world is not short of capital, and massive investment in education need not prejudice the continued growth of industry or commerce. Indeed, the increasingly technological nature of society requires, for its very maintenance, a great increase in the type of training that can only be carried on within formal institutions of higher education. The educational systems and the economies of countries such as the USA, the USSR, and Great Britain are more highly *inter*-dependent that was the case a hundred years ago. A level of industrial development has been reached where the educational system has become an essential element in society, and further developments in the technology of such societies are dependent upon a continued supply of research scientists. Innovation thus becomes part of the very fabric of society.

Occupational selection

In industrial societies, then, the task of socialization through the educational system (the task of educating the young as it is called in everyday speech) involves, in particular, the preparation of young people for the jobs they are going to do in later life. In the early stages of industrialization in England the task of sorting out which people were best fitted for which jobs presented no problems; a person's first occupation, and consequently the education necessary to prepare him for it, was prescribed by his father's class position, while any social mobility took place through achievement *on the job*. Nowadays, however, social mobility takes place predominantly through achievement in education, since occupations are allocated largely according to educational merit. Thus the educational system performs the task of *occupational selection*; of selecting at a fairly early age which people are most likely to be suited to a given type of occupation and providing them with appropriate training.

This process of selection can be seen at work most clearly in the traditional English type of educational system, in which children are sent to different types of secondary schools to prepare for different types of jobs. But *all* educational systems of industrial societies (and those of societies industrializing or attempting to industrialize through the adoption of bureaucratic methods of appointment) are selective in this way; the difference lies in the point at which the selection is made. Where only a tiny minority receive any education at all (for example, throughout much of Africa in the first half of the twentieth century) it is possible for those with only three or four years of elementary schooling to monopolize clerical occupations. The important thing here is whether one has been to school or not. In Britain at the beginning of the century, however, or in tropical Africa today, the majority of children receive some elementary education and clerical posts are only open to those who have completed a more extensive schooling. What has happened in such situations is that the educational system has grown faster than the number of white collar jobs with the result that higher qualifications are now required for entry into a given occupation.

In England, the first major point of selection has until now been upon entry to secondary schools which have offered differential training for different types of occupations. Where comprehensive secondary schools predominate (as in the USA and elsewhere) a larger part of the selection process is carried out in the secondary school and a good deal of selection is delayed until the school leaving age or later. Entrance to college or university is another significant point of selection especially where a majority of children stay at school after the minimum school leaving age. In the USA further selection is made during the college course with the result that many students leave college without completing the course.

Education, social mobility, and the class structure

In societies where job allocation is made on grounds of educational qualifications (and this includes all societies with highly developed educational systems), this type of selection will always be an important function of education. In modern societies, however, it is usually considered important that the 'best' person should be selected for a given position irrespective of where he lives, what he looks like, what he believes and who his parents are. The selection processes are therefore designed to pick out the academically most able children to proceed to the next stage or to be trained for the top jobs. One of the main concerns of sociologists interested in education has been to measure how far the selection process is successful in selecting the most able children irrespective of their social background. Do educational systems in fact select the most able candidates for important and difficult jobs or do they function primarily to place the children of the élite in high occupational positions themselves? Do modern educational systems favour particular class, residential, religious or ethnic groups? The short answer is that in most countries the educational system *both* acts as an agent of social mobility *and* tends to reinforce inherited social positions, but to varying degrees in different countries and at different times. In many countries the position is complicated by the existence of an important private sector of secondary schools. The public schools in England have in the past performed the function of reinforcement—of passing on high status from father to son. The high fees charged have, for the most part, excluded the less wealthy members of society and even when, after the second world war as an outcome of the Fleming report on public schools, a few free places were made available to the working classes, these groups showed little inclination to send their children away to boarding schools to be educated. For the few working-class children who have taken up such scholarships, however, the very nature of education in a boarding school with an overwhelmingly middle-class clientele has facilitated the assimilation of middle-class values and behaviour patterns. At the other end of school life, the public schools have usually been able to place their pupils in prestigious and remunerative jobs, and, in addition, their close links with some of the Oxford and Cambridge colleges have given their pupils further advantages. A further important function of the minor public schools has been in the provision of an alternative line of 'academic' education for those sons of wealthy parents who have failed to gain entry to the grammar schools. This has been particularly important for the reinforcement function of the system since it has enabled such children to avoid *downward* social mobility through the educational system. This function of the public schools is likely to survive any schemes of reform designed to 'broaden' the public school entry. In the USA the private secondary schools play an essentially similar, if less extreme, part through their association with the Ivy League colleges. As with the English public schools, however, this link with higher education is now of decreasing importance.

Within the state sector of education, whether the selection process operates primarily as an agent of social mobility or primarily as a mechanism of status maintenance depends largely upon its accuracy in sorting out the most able from the rest. As has already been stated, the major point of selection in England in the past has been upon entry to secondary schools, and (public schools aside) the greatest opportunities to achieve positions of high income, status and power have been available to those who have gained entry to the grammar schools. How far has access to these schools been open to all classes? Formerly the grammar schools were very largely middle-class schools since their fees put them beyond the reach of the lower classes. In spite of the changes which have taken place since the entry of the state into the field of secondary education in 1902, many studies in the last decade or so have shown that children of the middle classes are still over-represented in the grammar schools and in the 'academic' streams of comprehensive schools. The earlier studies of this problem in the 1930s and early 1940s explained it simply in terms of poverty. Although it had become more possible for working-class children to gain entry to secondary schools, for many of them this never became a real possibility as their parents could not afford the extra expense involved even if they won a scholarship. The continued possibility of buying places in the secondary schools further explained the preponderance of middle-class children shown in these early studies. In 1944, however, fees were

finally abolished and after that time it was only possible to attend the grammar schools by passing a test of ability of one kind or another. These tests were designed to select the most able children, and in order to do so various combinations of written examinations, intelligence tests and primary school teachers' reports have been used.

The abolition of fees and the introduction of selection tests of one kind or another did increase the representation in grammar schools of the sons of manual workers (compare Table 8.1, columns 1 and 2). Whatever the method of selection used, however, the grammar schools have invariably contained a higher proportion of children of professional workers and a lower proportion of the children of manual workers than has the population as a whole (compare Table 8.1, columns 2 and 3). Furthermore, the children of

Table 8.1 Occupational distribution of the fathers of boys entering grammar schools in England and Wales and of the male labour force (per cent)

Father's occupation	G S entrants 1930–41[1]	G S entrants 1946–51[2]	Total male population aged 20–64, 1951[2]
Professional and managerial	40 ⎫	26 ⎫	
Clerical and non-manual	20 ⎬ 60	18 ⎬ 44	28
Manual	40	56	72

Sources: (1) J. Floud, 'Social class factors in educational achievement', in A. H. Halsey (ed.), *Ability and Educational Opportunity*, OECD, 1961, p. 97, and (2) *1951 Population Census of England and Wales*, London: HMSO.

the working classes have shown a tendency to make less progress at school, and in particular tend to leave school at an earlier age than do their middle-class contemporaries. At the university level this social selection is even more acute. In the 1960–1 academic year only 25 per cent of the undergraduate population was the children of manual workers—a proportion which had hardly changed in thirty years despite dramatic university expansion. Table 8.2 shows in more detail the social background of undergraduates at university in 1961. A study of this table will show that occupational class I has about four times the representation among undergraduates in universities as it would have under a random distribution. At the other end of the scale class V would have about nine times *more* representa-

Table 8.2 Occupational distribution of undergraduates' fathers and of the male labour force, 1961 (per cent)

Father's occupation	Undergraduates 1961/2[1]	Male labour Force 1961[2]
I Higher professional	18	3·9
II Other professional and managerial	41	14·4
IIIa Clerical	12	11·0* ⎫
IIIb Skilled manual	18	38·8* ⎬ 49·8
IV Semi-skilled manual	6	19·9
V Unskilled manual	1	8·6
Unclassified	4	3·4

*estimated from previous census

Sources: (1) *Higher Education*, Appendix 2(b) *Students and their education*, London: HMSO. Cmnd 2154, II–I, Table 5, p. 4, (2) *Population Census 1961*, London: HMSO.

tives in the universities were the distribution random. The position seems to have changed very little since that time. While the newer technological universities are not so exclusive in terms of social background as the others (especially Oxford and Cambridge where more than three-quarters of the students still come from professional and managerial backgrounds), the chief gains in this respect have been made by the children of 'white collar workers' rather than by those of manual workers. Moreover, in the university sector as a whole there has been, at most, a marginal change in the social background of students. Despite the post-Robbins expansion of universities, what we have called the reinforcement function of education still prospers at the expense of the mobility function.

How far is this a result of the division of English secondary education into secondary modern and grammar schools? This division has been the centre of the major politico-educational controversy of the second half of the century—the debate concerning the merits of the comprehensive system of secondary education against those of the dual system. The educational arguments in favour of a retention of grammar schools (only rarely have arguments been put forward to 'save our secondary modern schools') centre upon the need to safeguard the high academic standards for which the grammar schools have become noted and upon which the economic well-being of the country depends. The arguments in favour of comprehensive schools focus on the wastage of human talent through early and often inadequate

selection; the unfortunate effects of selection upon the primary schools; the encouragement which comprehensive schools are thought to give to less able pupils; and upon the academic results which have been achieved in 'comprehensive' schools in some areas. Underlying the controversy, however, and accounting for much of the emotionalism and irrationality which often enter it, is the hope or fear that a new type of educational system would bring about radical changes in the nature of English society—particularly in the class structure.

As was pointed out earlier, the grammar school retained the old secondary school's function of preparing people for essentially middle-class positions in society. Changes during this century enabled some children of lowly origins to gain entry into the grammar schools, and thus climb the educational ladder to some of the highest positions in the land. The term 'meritocracy' has been given to this type of society where stratification is still important but positions are allocated not by birth or wealth, but by merit as measured by educational success. Many people see the existence of separate secondary schools for those destined for different positions in the occupational structure as a form of organization which will both reduce the amount of social mobility through education and intensify the differences between occupational groups and thereby perpetuate the existing differences.

Many who find the existence of social classes abhorrent have turned to comprehensive education as a way of overcoming these divisions. They argue that the education of all children in a common secondary school would allow children from different family backgrounds to mix socially. In this way the growth of separate sub-cultures would be minimized. Such a view, however, overstates the power of the educational system to alter the social structure and seems to stem from the popular confusion of class distinction with 'snobbery'. It is conceivable, although by no means certain, that the introduction of comprehensive schools might lessen status consciousness, but it is hardly likely that such educational changes would influence the distribution of economic and political power on which the class structure is equally dependent.

A sociological appreciation of the history of English education suggests that the class system has had a considerable influence on the type of education system which eventually emerged. The reciprocal influence of the educational system on the class structure has, however, been confined in the main to the partial preservation of the *status quo*. It is, then, highly doubtful that the extension of comprehensive education will initiate significant changes in the class structure. But the problem need not be left entirely at the level of conjecture for there are industrial societies with systems of comprehensive secondary education where we can see how such systems function.

A good example is the USA where there is both comprehensive schooling and a strong commitment to equality of educational opportunity. The early high schools in the USA were designed for the needs of the predominantly higher-class children who intended to enter professional or similar occupations. Their curriculum was consequently somewhat similar to that of their counterparts in England. As the numbers of children undergoing secondary education increased, and especially after the introduction of compulsory secondary education, it was felt that this highly academic curriculum was not suitable for the whole of the high school clientele, many of whom had no intention of entering professional occupations nor of going to college. The result was the establishment, alongside the academic or 'college preparatory' curriculum, of alternative courses variously called vocational, commercial or general courses. There is a considerable body of evidence to show that the children of parents with high occupational positions are very likely to take the college preparatory curriculum—the line that leads to higher education and/or high status employment, while the children of manual workers are much more likely to find themselves in one of the other streams. There is, in effect, a situation essentially similar to that in England whereby the type of schooling received by children tends to confirm them in the same class positions as those occupied by their parents. It is even possible that the comprehensive school in Britain may be less well suited to the task of promoting the social mobility of working-class children than the old grammar school. For one of the consequences of the élitist assumptions of the grammar schools was that they operated relatively efficiently as agencies of socialization into middle-class values. The comprehensive school may prove less well suited to persuading clever working-class children to raise their levels of aspirations.

Despite the comprehensive high school, the children of members of the American lower classes tend to finish their education and go out to work full time earlier in their lives than do the children of the upper classes. An American sociologist, Robert J. Havighurst, has demonstrated the way in which virtually all upper- and upper-middle-class children graduate from high school, while many lower-class children (more than one-half in some areas) fail to complete the high school course. He also shows that, in 1960, 85 per cent of upper- and upper-middle-class young men and 70 per cent of the young women entered college, while only 10 per cent of the males and 5 per cent of the females in what he calls the lower class did so. At the same time he points out that this represents a change from 1940 when virtually no lower-class children went to college, a change that is part of a vast absolute increase in college places between 1920 when 8 per cent of the appropriate age group were attending college and 1960 when more than one-third entered college.[3]

Again, in the USSR in 1958, nearly 70 per cent of the students in higher education in Moscow were the children of members of the intelligentsia or of the upper levels of the bureaucracy. In contrast with the West, however, this proportion had been rising for twenty years, a reaction against the extreme attempts to 'proletarianize' education during the 1930s. In a highly bureaucratic society like the Soviet Union, a person's future occupation depends almost entirely upon his education, with the result that here, too, education was operating largely to maintain the children of the present élite in positions of wealth and influence. This situation, which accorded so ill with the ideology of the government, was one of the important motivations behind the campaign begun in the late 1950s to establish boarding schools throughout the country. By 1964, 2,000 of these had been established and were attended by some 700,000 pupils drawn mainly from *lower*-class children. They thus represent an attempt to increase social mobility by providing better educational opportunities for lower-class children. The aim was that the boarding schools should eventually dominate Soviet education, thus removing the children from parental control and so shielding them from traditional values and influence, especially those reflecting status consciousness in any form. In this way it was hoped that the influence of the family in the eventual placement of the child would be minimized. This attempt to eliminate the influence of the family on a child's education and subsequent occupation was a more thorough attempt to provide equality of opportunity than any undertaken in the Western world, and if it had been carried through, might have been expected to yield more in the way of results. The magnitude of the task, however, was such that the scheme was never fully implemented, so the assumptions upon which it was based have still to be tested.

We may feel justified in concluding that whenever there are differential opportunities in education the most attractive types of schooling (in terms of the rewards offered) will be dominated by the children of the privileged sections of the society. Moreover, this appears to be the case at all levels of development where a formal educational system exists, irrespective of the *type* of educational system and irrespective of the political system. Indeed, it has been estimated that there is no country in which the working classes achieve more than one-half of parity, while in some of the less developed countries the lower occupational groups achieve considerably less than this.

Region, race and residence

But class is not the only important factor; there are also differences in educational opportunity between other groups. It has been shown that in a number of societies, both industrial and non-industrial, there are considerable differences in the chances that children have of reaching a given level of education according to where they live. Data from such diverse countries as the USA, France, Ghana, the USSR, and India show that *regions* of educational underprivilege are a worldwide problem. Within a given society the areas of greatest educational opportunity are the areas of highest economic development. Thus, for example, in the USA the southern states are both economically and educationally backward when compared with the northern states, while in West African coastal countries the coastal areas are both economically and educationally more advanced than the hinterland. Similarly, in all countries urban children have greater educational opportunities than rural children, for it is in the towns that a concentration of population makes both for pressure to provide schools and for ease in administering them. Contemporary modernizing societies clearly show how, in the early stages of educational development, school building tends to be concentrated in the large towns. But in highly industrial societies one finds similar, if less extreme, differences. In addition there are differences within the towns—suburban areas usually providing better opportunities than the city centres. These factors are closely related to the social-class composition of the various areas but also exercise some independent influence. In England, where the Local Education Authority has decided important matters of educational policy (including, for example, the number of grammar school places to be made available), the location of one's home one side or the other of a local government boundary, local government politics, or an accident of history have often been the deciding factors in a child's educational career. For example, in 1964 only 13·1 per cent of the eleven-year-old children in the south of England were offered places in grammar schools compared with 28·6 per cent of the same age group in Wales. In 1968 some local authorities had nearly 40 per cent of their children in grammar schools; others had more than 80 per cent in secondary modern schools. The same startling difference between local authority areas can be seen at the sixth-form level. In 1968 approximately 33 per cent of the seventeen year olds in Cardiganshire were still in school compared with only 8 per cent for the county borough of Middlesbrough.

In societies where there is a racially diverse population there are also differences in the educational chances of the different races. This can be seen most clearly in southern Africa where the educational system, and the positions of wealth, power and prestige in the society as a whole, are dominated by the white minority. In the Union of South Africa in 1962 only one-half of the Bantu population aged 6–16 was at school, compared to 77 per cent of the 'coloured' population and 100 per cent of the white population. In 1966, about one in 30,000 of the non-white population was attending university while for the white population the figure was one in eighty. Much of this differential opportunity derives from the policy of apartheid but racial differences, although less extreme than those in South Africa, can still be seen in countries with an ideology of equal educational opportunity between the races. Thus in the USA in 1962, for example, 13·1 per cent of the total 25–9 age group had completed four years of college education but only 4·2 per cent of the non-whites in the same age group had done so.

Perhaps the universality of findings referring to social selection is the more surprising in view of the fact that the various systems of education use quite different criteria of selection. In systems where fees are charged for secondary education, as was the case in the early stages of the educational development of industrial countries and is now the case in most modernizing countries, it is hardly surprising to find the channels to high occupational positions dominated by the children of the higher classes since they alone can afford the luxury of education. Where no such fees have been charged for many years, however, such dominance is harder to account for. In most parts of England since the second world war, intelligence tests have played a large part in the selection process and yet middle-class children have still been over-represented in the grammar schools. In America, on the other hand, there is considerable freedom of choice of curriculum in the junior high school but the results are similar to those in England. Are we to conclude that the children of the middle classes are inherently better suited to an academic type of education than are lower-class children? Certainly the English experience suggests that they do better at intelligence tests. But how far do such tests measure something which is inborn and how far do they measure something which has been developed by the process of socialization? It is now generally held that an important part of what we call intelligence is dependent upon the influence of the social environment, and the available evidence suggests that the same factors are likely to affect performance in the primary school, performance in written examinations, or even in the child's free choice of type of education. In any case, even at a given level of measured intelligence, selection still seems to operate in favour of some groups of children against others. Thus the Robbins report found that the proportion of middle-class children who enter grammar schools is higher than the proportion of working-class children *of the same measured ability* who do so. Consequently whether selection is based upon intelligence tests, teachers' reports, written examinations, or parental preferences the child's chances of selection are likely to be influenced by his social environment.

We must therefore ask what it is about working-class life, life in rural areas, life in economically depressed regions, and life in racially underprivileged communities that handicaps a child educationally. Where there are no legal barriers (such as those in South Africa or in the southern states of the USA before de-segregation) and no serious financial barriers (such as those which exist wherever education is not free), one important factor is the way in which education is viewed by the parents and by other members of the community. A number of community studies in working-class areas in English towns have suggested that such communities have viewed education as something 'not for the likes of us' and that a child attending a grammar school or college from such a community has been likely to be a lonely figure. Indeed, until recently there were frequent reports of children from such areas refusing grammar school places. After the statutory school leaving age there are further pressures to give up education, particularly the knowledge that one's contemporaries are earning wages and are now 'adults'. In this situation the encouragement of the parents is likely to be crucial in the decision to continue education, but parental commitment to education is not a notable characteristic of most such communities. That this situation has only recently begun to change is a reflection of the fifteen or twenty years that it has taken for these parental and community attitudes to adapt to the new situation initiated by the 1944 Education Act. Furthermore, the increased affluence of some sections of the working classes means that the attraction of an extra young wage earner in the house is of less importance and longer term considerations can be taken into account.

Another factor which may influence a child's educational chances is the size of the family into which he is born. Many studies, for example the Scottish Mental Health Survey, have shown that there is an inverse correlation between measured intelligence and family size, and on the whole working-class and rural families are larger than middle-class and urban ones. The larger the family, the less contact a child is likely to have with adults in his early years, and this tends to retard verbal development. This in turn handicaps the development of thinking which is dependent upon language. The American sociologist, A. Davis, has also found verbal retardation to be common among twins and suggested that this is because they tend to communicate with each other non-verbally and consequently have less need to develop verbal communication with adults. Moreover, some parents teach their children to verbalize their feelings and develop a pleasure in the use of words while other children acquire only a limited vocabulary and learn only a language of authority, not one of reason. Many classroom difficulties stem from this since the language of the teacher has no meaning for these latter children and there is a consequent breakdown of communication.

Thus family and community life appear to be the important factors which differentiate between the educationally privileged groups on the one hand and the educationally underprivileged on the other. Consequently attempts to eliminate inequality of educational opportunity by removing the child from the influence of the family (like the Russian attempt) are on the face of it likely to be more successful than changes in the structure of secondary education (such as the current English changes to comprehensive schools). It is equally clear, however, that such changes are unlikely to be implemented, or even seriously considered, in most industrial societies where they would offend other, deeply held, values.

Notes

1 Hansard, 3rd series, vol. cxxix, London, 1870, p. 466.
2 H. C. Barnard, *A History of English Education*, University of London Press, 1961, p. 264.
3 Robert J. Havighurst, 'Social class influences on American education', in Nelson Harvey (ed.), *Social Forces Influencing American Education*, University of Chicago Press, 1961.

Reading

Adams, D. and Bjork, R. M., *Education in Developing Areas*, New York: McKay, 1969. A useful survey of its field, combining wide coverage with brevity.
Banks, O., *The Sociology of Education*, London: Batsford, 1968. By far the best of many textbooks on the subject.
Bernbaum, G., *Social Change and the Schools 1918–1944*, London: Routledge & Kegan Paul, 1967. A sociological discussion of an important period in the development of English education.
Douglas, J. W. B., *The Home and the School*, London: Panther, 1967. A study of the relationship between family structure, and the ability and academic success of primary school children in England.
Eggleston, S. J., *The Social Context of the School*, London: Routledge & Kegan Paul, 1967. A clear survey of the literature relating the school to the local and national environment.
Grant, N., *Soviet Education*, Harmondsworth: Penguin, 1964. A very readable description of the Soviet educational system.
Sexton, P., *The American School*, Englewood Cliffs: Prentice-Hall, 1967. The relationships between the school, the educational system, the community, and the wider society are discussed in a clear general survey which includes an analysis of power in, and control over, education.

Further reading

Anderson, C. A. and Bowman, M. J. (eds), *Education and Economic Development*, London: Cass, 1965. A wide range of papers analysing the relationship between education and economic development, with evidence from American, English, Russian and Japanese history as well as from contemporary modernizing societies.
Banks, O., *Parity and Prestige in English Secondary Education*, London: Routledge & Kegan Paul, 1955. A sociological analysis of the development and major functions of English secondary education in the twentieth century.
Coleman, J. S. (ed.), *Education and Political Development*, Princeton University Press, 1965. Nine general papers relating to individual countries, and a number of more specific contributions on particular aspects of education. The whole is linked by a series of introductions by the editor.
Halsey, A. H., Floud, J. and Anderson, C. A. (eds), *Education, Economy and Society*, Chicago: Free Press, 1961. A useful and comprehensive collection of articles but limited in the main to Britain and the USA.
Hansen, D. A. and Gerstl, J. E., *On Education: Sociological Perspectives*, New York: Wiley, 1967. A variety of sociological essays on education. Includes essays on the relationship between education and social stratification and mobility, and an essay on education as a social institution.
Hargreaves, D. H., *Social Relations in a Secondary School*, London: Routledge & Kegan Paul, 1967. An analysis of the social structure of a school, including teacher-pupil relationships, relationships between pupils within a class, and relationships between streams.
Havighurst, R. J. (ed.), *Comparative Perspectives on Education*, Boston: Little, Brown, 1968. Sociological essays on aspects of education in France, the Soviet Union, Japan, Brazil, China, Ghana, Tudor England, South Africa, New Zealand, the Netherlands, the Sudan, and among the Hopi Indians.
Lawton, D., *Language, Social Class and Education*, London: Routledge & Kegan Paul, 1968. A critical survey of the literature on the relationship between language skills and the educational development of children.
Rosenthal, R. and Jacobsen, L., *Pygmalion in the Classroom: Teacher Expectations and Pupils' Intellectual Development*, New York: Holt, Rinehart & Winston, 1968. A study of how teachers' expectations affect school performance.

9 The professions

The word *profession* conjures up a wealth of images: of security, public service, respectability, independence, prestige and even wealth. Furthermore, the occupations we regard as professions—medicine, law, architecture, accountancy, science—are popularly accorded high prestige in comparison with other occupations. Today, both in industrial societies and in non-industrial societies, education for a career in one of the professions is increasingly regarded as the gateway to the good life. To the individual, it is worth the long and sometimes arduous years of training; and to many new occupational groups the lure of professional status is worth the self-discipline and expenditure of resources which may lead to eventual public recognition.

In recent decades large industrial corporations, both public and private, have become more and more dominant in the economic life of industrial societies. One important effect of this development has been the reduction of opportunities for individual success in business entrepreneurship. It has become increasingly difficult for the small businessman and the self-made man to compete with the industrial giants. One result of this is that a career in the professions is becoming a more important object of individual ambition. Such a career is equally attractive in contemporary modernizing countries where large-scale state dominance of business and industry has given high status to bureaucratic and professional occupations. The rapid expansion of professional occupations in industrial societies has been partly due to the expansion of existing professions, but the crystallization of new occupational tasks has also been important. These include many activities which are based upon the application of scientific and technical knowledge to new social needs. The emergence of new occupational tasks, such as those of the probation officer, the metallurgist, the radiographer and the atomic physicist, has diversified the field of professional practice and raises problems in the use of the term profession itself.

What is a profession?

Professional occupations are regarded as special in some way. They are said to have some unique characteristic which sets them apart from other types of occupation; to have highly important functions to perform in industrial societies which, to a large extent, explain the prestige, power and wealth they command. Interest in these 'unique characteristics' is by no means new, but it is only in industrial societies that a predominant social role has been claimed for professionals. In their capacity as experts they are sometimes feared to be taking over the leadership of societies to the exclusion of all others. On the other hand, they have also been counted among the 'bulwarks' of democracy by those who see the professional association as a model of collective control by members. It has also been claimed that, by virtue of their independent status, professions stand as a 'bastion' against state control of the individual; that, because of their corporate organization, they are a check upon the worst excesses of individualism; and that their ethic of public service enables them to cut across disruptive class ideologies.

These three features—their corporate organization, independence and ethic of public service—

are often said to characterize the professions. In recent years, however, the phenomenon of the salaried, dependent professional has increasingly dominated the professional scene; more and more professionals are employed within large organizations rather than working as independent or solo practitioners. An 'idealized' view of the professions, stressing the importance of independence and community service cannot account for this modern phenomenon of the 'bureaucratized' professional except as a pathological aberration resulting from the evils of big business and/or state intervention. Nor can such an idealized view account for the great disparities in power, prestige and income which exist between and even within professional groups. In all industrial societies teachers, for example, are significantly differentiated from doctors and lawyers, while great diversity exists within all three professions. What are the special characteristics which professional occupations share and why is it that some of them do not share the social and material benefits of others?

The crude distinction between 'brain' and 'brawn' is not a satisfactory criterion of a profession as against other occupations. Surgeons have remained essentially manual workers, yet they have grown steadily in prestige since their separation from the Barbers' Guild in seventeenth-century England. We have already pointed out that independent professionals relying upon fees from individual clients are a dwindling proportion of professionals as a whole. Thus, independence cannot be taken as a useful criterion. Nor can the professional be regarded in any way as unique in being organized within an association, for professional associations share many functions in common with trade unions. Professionals comprise a minority of those employed in occupations providing a service; more and more occupations today demand high-level, long-term periods of training and, in any case, craft apprenticeships have always been similar to professional training in this respect. And so we could go on: but any attempt to list the occupational characteristics which would enable us to recognize a profession is likely to prove unsatisfactory.

The sociologist, however, is interested in explaining a social phenomenon such as the professions in terms of social structure—that is to say, in terms of the patterned and persisting relationships which exist between professionals and their clients, between professionals and the wider society and among professionals themselves.

Can we explain the importance of professional ethics, status and prestige in society in these terms? Certainly, it is true that all the so-called professions give a service, whether the client be an individual, a private corporation or a government department. It is also true that in giving such a service the professional is making use of his training; he is applying a body of knowledge in response to the needs of the client. But the crucial aspect of this relationship is that the client or layman finds it difficult to *judge the quality of the service* he is getting. The practice of a physician is not open to evaluation by the average layman; we have to take his diagnosis and treatment on trust. If we recover from an illness after seeking the advice of a doctor it is often difficult to know whether the treatment was successful or whether recovery would have been spontaneous. Similar problems exist when we consult an accountant, a solicitor or an architect; we remain dependent upon the judgment of the professional.

Thus the nature of the professional-client relationship is such that there is an inherent tension, resulting from the client's inability to judge the service provided. This problem does nor exist to the same extent with all services nor with most market transactions involving material goods. For example, if a corporation dustman inadequately performs the service of emptying our dustbins this is readily testable through our sense of smell; if a baker sells stale or inferior bread we can feel, taste, and perhaps see the inadequacy. In neither case are we dependent upon a guarantee of integrity. By contrast, conflict is built into the professional-client relationship because of the expertise of the professional and the ignorance of the client. As a result, various institutions have arisen to control this relationship.

One such form of control has been the professional association—such as the British Medical Association, the Law Society, or the Chartered Institute of Accountants. These bodies guarantee the integrity of their members (partly by enforcing a professional code of ethics) while in return their members gain control of the relationship with the client in such matters as fee-setting. This way of controlling the relationship between the client and the professional has frequently been regarded as the natural end-product of the dilemma created by the ignorance of the client. Carr-Saunders and Wilson, for example, claimed that no profession is a 'true' profession until it throws up an 'autonomous corporate association with the function of guaranteeing the competence, honour and security of its members'.[1] If, however, we were to apply the principle of autonomy to the professions in England today only barristers could be regarded as a 'true' profession. Moreover, many occupations which are in a position to exploit their ignorant clients are not, and never have been, organized in autonomous associations. This is because the tension which exists between a professional and his client can be resolved in a number of ways and through a variety of institutional forms.

A brief consideration of the way in which the professions have developed historically reveals, broadly speaking, three ways in which the tension has been resolved. In some cases, the members of an occupation have been able to determine who should receive their services—perhaps through the mechanism of a fee scale—and, by virtue of their recognized expertise, they have been able to set the standards of the service given. This is exemplified by the control over various services exerted by the autonomous professional associations which arose in the nineteenth century largely as a product of industrialization. Professional autonomy was linked to the increasing power of the urban middle class and was most nearly attained by the occupations of medicine and law. This professional domination of the relationship with the client is what we would normally refer to as *professionalism*, and involves various forms of colleague control which will be discussed later. A second way of resolving the tension between the client and the professional is where the client, because of his position in society, has the power to define his own needs, the way in which they are to be met, and the professional standards expected. This typically occurs in societies where a powerful group, such as an aristocracy, is the main consumer of professional services. This type of professional-client relationship we may call *client control*. Finally, both client and professional attempt to define the relationship which may be subordinated to external demands and definitions, such as those imposed by the church in medieval Europe, or the activities of modern states which regulate professional services in the process of extending various forms of welfare to all citizens or to special groups who are defined as being in need. The welfare state has, then, entailed the emergence of new forms of *third party control* over the professional-client relationship.

These alternative solutions to the problem of controlling the professional-client relationship provide a framework for the classification and analysis of professional occupations.

The professions in pre-industrial societies

In the simplest of societies the only forms of the social division of labour which exist are those between the sexes and between the young and old. Where there is division of labour between the sexes or between generations only, specialized occupations such as those we are calling 'professions' do not exist. Caring for the sick and infirm, for instance, is an activity which is incidental to other roles, such as a wife or mother. In societies where disease is attributed to 'bad magic' the care of the sick may devolve upon magical specialists but in many simple societies even this capacity to do harm or good by magical means is diffused through the whole community. Among the Dobuans, a Melanesian people who live on a small island north east of New Guinea, there is a belief that the only causes of disease are witchcraft and sorcery; that supernatural forces affect the health of individuals through the agency of other members of the Dobuan community. Illhealth is attributed to jealousy or a desire for revenge on the part of neighbours and is directly caused by ritual incantations. Healing is therefore possible only when the sorcerer recants and the cause is removed. In this manner all Dobuans have the potential capacity to cure as well as cause disease; there is no specialization involved.

The major limitation upon the development of specialized occupational tasks in simple societies is the subsistence economy; members who are not themselves food producers cannot be fed. Only when an economic surplus is produced can specialized occupations be supported by the community. In the evolution of human societies, among the first specialized activities to emerge were those of magical specialists and priests. Where people understood and explained their physical and social environment in terms of the intervention of supernatural beings or forces, knowledge and the rituals associated with it often came to be monopolized by a priesthood which was, in a number of senses, the archetypal profession. Like the modern medical profession it monopolized an area of knowledge vital to the health and general fortunes of the society as a whole: and, as is the case with many modern professions, it closely controlled entry into the occupation. Often the priesthood became an hereditary caste, entry being monopolized by a single family or a clan.

Even in the complex civilizations of Greece and Rome the practice of law and medicine did not give rise to specialized independent professional associations such as we know today. The physician in Greece was regarded as a craftsman who served an apprenticeship under a master and sought custom in the market place along with other craft specialists; in Rome he was typically a slave attached to a rich man's household. The Roman lawyer was not a specially trained advocate practising before a qualified judge, but more likely, the litigant's friend speaking to the litigant's equals, while in Greece, the practice of law was not differentiated from other more general forms of social control such as ethical custom, religious doctrine and public opinion. In such a situation the advocate in a dispute might be any man known for his oratory, and the business might be conducted by any literate man or scribe.

The development of professions in England

The church and the professions—third party control

For long periods in the history of many societies religious organizations have been so powerful that, as new specialized occupational tasks emerged, these organizations were able to maintain control over the relationship between the practitioner and his client. The power of the priesthood derived not only from its monopoly of knowledge but also from its control over a large slice of the economic surplus and sometimes from military power as well—as was the case with the warrior-priest kings of the ancient Mesopotamian city-states. In Europe the church enjoyed a monopoly of knowledge during the Middle Ages: a monopoly which was reinforced by its importance as a landholder in an agrarian society. The basis of all knowledge was contained in the 'revealed truth' of the Bible, and the Church's control of access to this truth enabled it to control man's interpretations of the universe, while attempting to exclude what it defined as heretical. The Church contained within its organization the specialists in thinking and in the application of knowledge. There were few specialist occupations in existence, but those which did exist were controlled and administered by the Church. Indeed the earliest meaning of the verb 'profess' noted by the *Shorter Oxford Dictionary* refers to taking the vows of a religious order. Until the twelfth century, medicine was the preserve of the monastic orders and later, when medical practice was forbidden to monks, it was taught only in the cathedral schools of Salerno in Italy and Montpellier in France. The activities carried out by physicians, lawyers, civil servants and educators were all performed under the aegis of the Church. The Church provided training and educational centres; the Church provided a system of rewards and statuses. Professionals typically took clerical orders and were rewarded with a canonry or rectory.

It was the Church which defined the manner in which professionals were to serve clients and, by virtue of its functions as a welfare agency, it also defined the needs of the clients themselves. Thus, the way the sick were treated was affected by the biblical injunction that clerics should not spill blood. As a consequence, surgery was excluded from the field of medicine for several centuries and was practised separately within the barber-surgeons' craft guild. Indeed, the surgeons craft was practised mainly on the battlefield.

Similarly, law was administered by the Church. Trials were not so much an investigation of the facts as a revelation of the judgment of God. Yet the emergence of the common lawyer in England provided an increasingly significant exception to the rule of Church control. One result of the growth of trade and commerce in the late medieval period and the processes of urbanization and centralization associated with them, was that the monarch gained power at the expense of the Church. The gradual secularization of law, whereby judgments proceeded from custom and precedent rather than from 'revealed' knowledge, and the emergence of the common lawyer to apply this secular knowledge, were related to these changes in the power structure. The services provided by the common lawyer were related to the administrative needs of an increasingly powerful monarch; they were related to the needs of the central administration itself; and they were related to the economic needs of an urban élite which was prospering under conditions of commercial expansion.

The period in which the relationship between the professional and his client was mediated and controlled by the Church was formally brought to a close by the Reformation. The Inns of Court, the university of the common lawyer, were already established in the fifteenth century. The victory of common lawyers over canon lawyers, which resulted in the exclusion of ecclesiastics from common law practice, was a process characteristic of the transition of any professional occupation from one form of institutional control to another.

A new occupational group providing a new service to meet new client needs came into conflict with entrenched professional groups who still exhibited the organization and values of the old order. By the sixteenth century medicine, too, had become a secular profession, although ecclesiastics remained as prominent members of the Royal College of Physicians until the end of that century. Church control of the relationship between the professional and his client was giving way to a new institutional form—that of patronage.

Patronage and the professions—client control

In England at the time of the Reformation a good deal of ecclesiastical wealth passed into private hands, a process which further diversified the sources of professional patronage. Those contemplating a professional career were no longer forced to take holy orders and, by the seventeenth and eighteenth centuries, secular professions were, by and large, servicing a small aristocratic élite and the landed gentry. In these new conditions the client came to dominate the relationship with the professional, defining his own needs and dictating the manner and content of the service. This dominance was clear cut in the case of the Royal College of Physicians whose limited membership serviced a small élite group, but it can also be seen in the case of lawyers where the patronage of the aristocracy was channelled through the political parties. The political control of medicine was also important as is shown by Charles II's exclusion of Papists and foreigners from Royal College Fellowships in 1676.

It was during this period in English history that the ideal of the professional gentleman arose. Membership of the Royal College of Physicians and a liberal education at an English university were the essential background of the cultured physician. Technical qualification was less important than social acceptability. The intimate relationship with a patron made it imperative that the medical doctor should be *socially* qualified to take his place in 'the ample life of the great houses'. A contemporary comment makes the point clearly:[2]

> The character of a physician ought to be that of a gentleman, which cannot be maintained with dignity but by a man of literature. If a gentleman engaged in the practice of physic, be destitute of that degree of a preliminary

and ornamental learning, which is requisite; if he do so speak of any subject either in history or philosophy, is immediately out of his depth; (this) is a great discredit to the profession.

This particular injunction was directed against the claims of apothecaries who were, at the end of the eighteenth century, threatening the monopoly of the Royal College of Physicians. It illustrates one of the consequences of patron dominance—the way in which the professional's prestige was based not upon his professional knowledge or technique but upon the degree to which he conformed to the values and customs of a consumption-oriented leisure class. The great physicians of the eighteenth century—men like Garth and Arbuthnot—were known not so much for their medical skills as for their wit and elegance. The successful lawyer had to be politically sound as well as socially acceptable. Technical competence in law practice played only a minor part in entry to the profession; residence at the Inns of Court was no longer a necessity. Students were either the sons of gentlemen acquiring a vocation or party men in receipt of preferment and, by the eighteenth century, the Inns had become known for their 'masques and revels' rather than for law education.

Where the professional was in no position to control the relationship with his client on his own terms the type of knowledge accentuated by the profession was also affected. Medical knowledge of the day emphasized therapies (such as blood letting) which were guided by simple, single-factor explanations of disease. This type of knowledge reflected the physician's need for certainty and to do what was required of him without demur. Uncertainty is the prerogative of those who have power. Moreover, it was not possible for the physician to experiment upon a man of social position and it was only with the founding of hospitals for the poor that experimental medicine began to make headway.

Industrialization and professionalism—colleague control

Until the last quarter of the eighteenth century not more than half a dozen professional occupations existed in England. By the end of the century, however, nascent industrialization and the growth of commerce were bringing new forms of professional service into being. The growing complexity of trade and financial transactions made mercantile accounts and exchange procedures so intricate that they required the skilled services of a calculator or accountant. By the end of the eighteenth century an accountant of some kind, whether he was a lawyer specializing in financial affairs or the qualified apprentice of a 'writing master', was to be found on the staff of many large mercantile firms. It is estimated that, even by 1775, five hundred young men were studying accounting techniques in the City of Glasgow alone; and accountants were only one occupational group among many which were emerging. Industrialization opened the floodgates of professional growth. Developments in science and technology crystallized into techniques which provided the basis of new professional occupations such as civil engineering and, later, mechanical and electrical engineering. The new large-scale enterprises which were associated with changes in manufacturing technology, and the rapidly growing towns were the location of more new professional occupations. This development is most spectacularly demonstrated by the growth of civil service bureaucracies. The expansion of professionalism was so great that the period between 1841 and 1855 alone saw the foundation of six new professional associations.

This growth was only partly due to the creation of new scientific and organizational techniques; new social needs (and new definitions of 'need') were also important. Industrialization brought the rise to power of the urban middle class and it was members of this class who increasingly took up professional practice and who provided an expanding market for professional services. Demands which previously had been restricted to the upper stratum of society filtered down and outwards so that professional occupations such as medicine could no longer maintain themselves as small, socially prescribed cliques servicing a small group of patrons. They were in process of becoming large associations with a technically qualified membership servicing competing status groups of equals or near equals.

One example of transitional conflict which arose during the Industrial Revolution was that between the Royal College of Physicians and the apothecaries, which led to the Apothecaries Act of 1815 and later to the foundation of the British Medical Association in 1851. In this case the conflict between 'insiders' and 'outsiders' reached an intense form. The College of Physicians—entrenched, select and functioning in relation to the patronage system—was challenged by the growing power of the apothecaries, who had originally separated from the Grocers' Guild in 1617 to become dispensers and compounders of drugs. It has been claimed that general medical practice by apothecaries was established during the Great Plague of 1665 when the physicians fled London. In any case the physicians' charge that apothecaries were unlawfully treating patients was already familiar by the end of the seventeenth century. It was not until the eighteenth century, however, that large numbers of apothecaries were known to practise medicine. The expansion of medical practice by apothecaries was said by a contemporary to be the result of:[3]

> an increase of sickness among people, the 'middle orders' who were unable to produce medical aid by feeing Physicians as often as their situation required medical care, and the Members of the Royal College of Physicians having made no diminution in their accustomed fee, to meet the actual wants of persons in this class of society they were compelled to resort to others for advice.

Apothecaries, then, provided medical services for the rising middle class who were excluded by cost from the physician's consulting room. The middle classes were also the main source of recruits for apothecaries. The poet John Keats, for example, was one of the first to be licensed under the Apothecaries Act of 1815 which gave apothecaries the legal right to practise medicine.

So, once again, we see a new professional group coming into conflict with entrenched interests. In the case of the apothecaries the conflict was resolved by the new group taking on specialist tasks within the general field. This was to be a common pattern in the development of the medical profession. In the mid-nineteenth century, for example, such conflicts were resolved by the creation of the complementary groups of consultant physicians, surgeons and general practitioners. As we shall see, the twentieth-century development of several professions has followed similar lines.

During the nineteenth century the professional-client relationship took on a new form; one in which the professional himself increasingly dominated. It was in this historical period that *professionalism* emerged, with the creation of monopolistic and autonomous professional associations. Two factors were important in the development of this monopoly and autonomy. First, the professionals shared in the growing power of the middle class and were thus able to protect and enhance their interests, in particular through political pressure leading to state registration. At the same time the growth in size of the middle class provided a growing market for professional services, so reducing the professional's subservience to a patron. Second, the relationship between the professional and his new middle-class client was characterized by social distance deriving from the increasing technical authority of the professional; professional expertise became a more significant aspect of the relationship.

The competence and integrity of individual professionals came to be guaranteed by a self-disciplining, internally-regulated professional body. The autonomy of the professional association allowed the professionals themselves to determine who was to receive the service (by regulation of fees) and the manner in which clients' needs were catered for (by virtue of the establishment of an ethical code and the control of recruitment, training and entry into the profession). A by-product of professional control of this kind was a change in the character of professional knowledge. It was during this period of increasing professional control that knowledge began to be characterized by its scientific or systematic nature. In law, for example, the great systematization of common law and precedent was embarked upon and the lawyer gained prestige as a result of his forensic skill. More generally, the professional's prestige depended more upon his technical competence in a group of equals and less upon his social graces. The professions became the 'repositories of special knowledge', stressing research and rationality.

The professions in the contemporary world

The era of *professionalism* in England was short-lived. Even at its peak, at the end of the nineteenth century, the seeds of its decline were already present and gaining in force. Paradoxically, the creation of professional monopolies by Acts of Parliament in the nineteenth century was the precursor of state intervention which, in the twentieth century, has transformed the professional-client relationship once again. Industrialization has brought with it a new form of *third party control*, namely control by the state. And this is partly a result of increased working-class power. Second, industrialization has created new forms of *colleague control*, stemming largely from specialization within

the professions, and differentiation of clientele. A third outcome of industrialization which has greatly affected professional services has been the growth of large-scale organization in both private business and public administration. As a result, the salaried career and employee status have become the normal expectation for large numbers of professionals, who are thereby subject to new forms of *client control*.

New forms of third party control

The professional occupations which exist in contemporary societies have emerged at different times and under varying social conditions. Because of this professional occupations not only vary in their organization from society to society but even in the same society they exhibit marked organizational differences which are a consequence of their historical development. A professional occupation which emerged in association with the rise of middle-class power in England brings with it into the twentieth century certain features which characterized the period of *professionalism*, even though increasing state control is characteristic of the present period. Today, in most industrial societies, the trappings of *professionalism* are present even though professional control in its purest form is, in most cases, a thing of the past.

Professionals who provide services for individual members of the public through a state agency are an increasing proportion of all professionals, but the degree to which they are dependent upon state regulation varies. In some cases the state defines not only who is in need of the service but also the manner in which these needs are to be met. This may be regarded as the nationalization of a profession and results in a minimum of autonomy for the profession. In many countries the teaching profession has been a familiar example. In England, the existence of school governors representing local interests and an agency such as the inspectorate of schools are symbolic of the teachers' lack of autonomy, although today the inspectorate is less an agency of central control than it was. A more recent addition to the 'nationalized' professions in industrial societies has been social work.

In some cases, however, the state merely defines who is to receive the service, leaving the profession to regulate the conditions and standards of the service. Such is the case with the British National Health Service. The creation of the National Health Service, which brought virtually all general practitioners into a state medical scheme, was not an abrupt loss of independence for the medical profession. Even in 1933 half the doctors had panel practices under the National Insurance Scheme. Nor has the National Health Service resulted in complete loss of autonomy for doctors. The profession itself still controls the manner of practice and, rather than receiving direct salaries from the state, members of the profession are paid from a pool which the profession itself administers. In some societies, however, the USSR for example, the medical profession is 'nationalized', in the sense referred to above, and this further loss of autonomy has led to a decline in the power and status of the occupation. At the other extreme is the United States of America where the medical profession, which has maintained a high degree of autonomy, has for many years successfully fought attempts by the federal government to introduce various forms of 'socialized medicine'.

The occupations we usually grouped together under the label 'social work'—for example, probation officers, psychiatric social workers, medical social workers, child care officers and so on—have grown directly out of the state's attempts, through legislation and the use of state funds, to rationalize and make more effective the 'philanthropic' response to social problems associated with industrialization. The state has also created new occupations in response to new social problems (the post of community relations officer is one recent example in Britain). As the task of aiding the 'deserving poor' was gradually taken over by statutory bodies, social workers found themselves the salaried agents of government. Social workers, like teachers, are therefore dependent professionals who have rarely been in a position to set up in independent practice. Furthermore, the fact that social workers are both members of a professional group and employees of a state agency may mean they are subject to conflicting expectations in carrying out their job, particularly where professional training stresses the need for a personal relationship with the client. Stressing the needs of the client may, for example, bring the probation officer into a head-on collision with the demands of the law courts of which he is legally an officer. His training and knowledge of his client may tell him that one course of action is necessary whilst the law may demand another.

All social work groups in Britain and the United States lay stress upon the importance of 'casework' in their jobs. In other words they emphasize the manipulation of their personal relationship with the client as a means of overcoming any social and/or emotional difficulties the client may be experiencing. Casework is considered to be the core of professional activity and any reform which threatens to weaken or reduce the possibility of this personal relationship is regarded as a threat to professional status. However, the areas of competence of the various social work groups in Britain and the lines of demarcation between them are not clearly defined. As a result conflict within the profession of social work centres upon attempts by the various sectors to define an area of competence and control within the casework relationship. Although the importance of 'liaison' between social workers is always stressed such co-operation is often fraught with hostility and 'demarcation disputes'.

New forms of colleague control

(a) *The professional community* The term colleague control is usually used to refer to the extent to which professionals are equal members of a homogeneous, self-disciplining professional group. It implies that the professions have many of the characteristics of a community. Professionals are bound by a sense of common identity, and a professional career involves a continuing status and permanent relationships with others. The professional career is a source of identity which has become increasingly important in modern society as other sources of identity (such as the family, village or locality) have become less important. The professional community controls its members in so far as it brings sanctions against those who deviate from the community rules and customs. These sanctions are enforced by the professional associations through their executive councils. Control over members also stems from the regulation of entry into the community. It is within the training period—characteristically long for professional occupations—that recruits are both taught the theory and techniques of practice and experience an intense period of adult socialization. They are inculcated into the values of the community and learn a common language which is only partially understood by 'outsiders'. One of the major concerns of emergent professional occupations is to agree upon a standardized terminology. This has, for example, been a continuing effort within the accountancy profession in both Britain and the United States. Standardized terminology makes for easier communication with the professional group and, equally significantly, it excludes outsiders from participating in the group's activities.

There are, in all societies, common and sometimes extreme reactions to the 'community' aspects of professional organization. The high development of colleagueship leaves the layman with the feeling of a Kafkaesque hero; helpless in the face of professional silence, solidarity and ritual. George Bernard Shaw expressed this feeling well when he wrote in *The Doctor's Dilemma*: 'All professions are conspiracies against the laity.' In his later *Doctor's Delusions* he claimed that the success of this conspiracy depended upon 'dogmas of omniscience, omnipotence, and infallibility, and something very like the theory of the apostolic succession and kingship by anointment'.

There is, however, another face to professional solidarity—namely the guarantee it provides for the layman who cannot judge the quality of the service provided. Thus, within the professional community, the competence of all, from the newly qualified recruit to the practitioner who is about to draw his pension, is guaranteed. All are accorded equal competence. This fiction of equal competence (expressed, for example, in ethical rules with regard to advertising) maintains the service orientation of the professional man whilst protecting his interests. In this way the professional-client relationship is removed from the disruptive consequences of individualistic competition. The code of ethics of a profession prescribes the duties of members to each other and to the public. In addition, however, it usually reflects the interests of an historically powerful segment of the profession. Thus the codes express and reinforce a double fallacy: first, that there is always the possibility of an inclusive professional interest and, second, that this interest can at all times be harmonized with the public interest.

An over-concentration on the community aspects of professions minimizes the importance of a number of recent trends. As well as the proliferation of new professional occupations industrialization has also involved the diversification of single professional occupations. Many professions have become constellations of intensive and narrow specialisms and the various sub-groups do not necessarily share a common interest. The existing codes of ethics which formally control their behaviour may operate to the benefit of some sub-groups at the expense of others. Community identity and colleague equality is likely to be minimal in a heterogeneous group, as the case of the teaching profession illustrates.

Many modern professional occupations are loose amalgamations of specialists rather than close-knit communities of equals. Each specialist group pursues different objectives in different ways. Wherever such specialization occurs it results in cleavages in organization and differences of interest. Each speciality sees itself as having a 'unique mission' of supreme importance within the profession as a whole.[4] General medical practitioners and public health officers may be members of the same profession, but their 'missions' are quite different and often in conflict. They have different tasks and use different methods and techniques. There are physicians who continue to think of the surgeon as 'knife happy', and there are psychiatrists who differ from general practitioners about the importance of psychological as against physical causes of illness. Furthermore, different segments of a profession may service different ranges of clientele; the dock brief lawyer and the famous Queen's Counsel have different clients and in many cases differing interests result. The segments also have a different range of colleagues; psychiatric social workers and probation officers are fellow professionals, but the colleague network of the probation officer includes officers of the law courts while that of the psychiatric social worker also contains hospital staff. In many cases this gives these different professional workers differing views of the problems which need to be solved.

(*b*) *Professional hierarchies* As a result of this increasing heterogeneity new forms of colleague control have arisen in highly industrial societies. The growth in complexity of the organizational environment in which the professional finds himself and the expanding demand for professional services have led to new forms of professional organization—part of what the American sociologist, C. Wright Mills, has called 'the commercialization of the professions'. There are, for example, the 'law factories' in the United States of America and the accountancy partnerships which have developed into large-scale management consultancies. A comparable development in medicine is that of the private medical clinic of the USA and the state-run clinic of the USSR. In all such organizations the professional man is no longer 'free and independent'. Increasingly, he is fitted into new hierarchical organizations. Intensive and narrow specialization has replaced self-cultivation and wide knowledge; assistants and sub-professions perform routine, although often intricate, tasks while successful professional men become more and more the managerial type'.[5] In this situation new forms of colleague control arise in which some practitioners, by virtue of their position at the head of an organizational hierarchy, have authority over their professional colleagues.

By convention, English barristers cannot practise in partnership. Each barrister has an individual practice, although a group may share 'chambers', a clerk and a small secretarial staff. A solicitor, however, may practise in partnership or as an assistant to a principal. In England more than half the solicitors in private practice are in partnership, and nearly one-fifth work as salaried assistants to other solicitors. In the United States, by contrast, where the legal profession is not divided and the qualified lawyer performs all legal duties including that of barrister or counsellor, nearly 70 per cent are in solo practice while only 5 per cent are assistants. The remaining 25 per cent are in partnership which is a rapidly expanding form of organization among lawyers. There is no legal limit to the number who can enter a partnership and at least one New York law firm has more than a hundred partners.

The 'law factory' is still atypical of law practice but is securing a rapidly increasing proportion of the business. This shift in form of organization reflects a shift in the major functions of the lawyer. The lawyer who, as an officer of the courts, carries out a wide variety of tasks in response to an equally wide range of problems, is giving way to the specialist whose task is to shape the legal framework of public and private corporations. It is increasingly these specialist jobs in large enterprises that are the greatest attraction for the bright, young recruit. The large law firms of New York, for example, are able to be highly selective and draw 71 per cent of their recruits from the high-prestige law schools of Yale, Harvard and Columbia.[6] The firms' partners employ salaried lawyers who do the routine work in highly specialized departments. At times specialization is so intense that a team of lawyers, working under the supervision of a partner, is engaged continuously upon the solution of one type of legal problem or upon problems presented by a single client. The partners are essentially the 'business getters', providing work for the associates and assistants.

The form of colleague control which has developed in these firms illustrates a more general trend. The relationship between professionals is, in many areas, being transformed from one of colleagueship to one of hierarchical rankings. Increasingly, authority derives not from technical competence but from ownership of the firm and bureaucratic position within it.

In medicine, too, increased specialization (there are more than fifty listed medical specialisms in Britain) has given rise to new forms of professional organization; hierarchies of authority are imposed upon and modify the professional colleague system. The hospital in Britain, and the clinic in other countries, have superseded general practice as the foci of medical treatment, providing the technology and facilities without which modern practice could not be achieved. These developments have reduced the functions of the general practitioner, who is now the main agent in a formal referral system. In the United States even this function has declined drastically, with about 5 per cent of American physicians in general practice.

The development of the team of medical specialists has resulted in a situation where some doctors perform services dependent on diagnostic decisions made elsewhere. In large-scale organizations such as hospitals, the dependent position of these professionals is accompanied by relatively low status and pay and has, in recent years, led to the militancy of junior hospital doctors in England. In other words, increasing diversification of authority within a profession is likely to be related to diversification in status and reward.

Hierarchical forms of colleague control, such as are found in the modern hospital, have supplemented but not entirely replaced the older forms based upon social difference rather than technical competence. In one area of Canada, for example, the successful medical career has, in the recent past, been dependent upon gaining admittance to an 'inner-fraternity' whose members sponsored the careers of socially acceptable newcomers.[7] This inner-fraternity of Anglo-Saxon Protestants maintained itself as a stable, self-perpetuating group, controlling post-graduate training opportunities and the 'plums' of medical practice. No doctor was able to succeed as a specialist unless he gained entry to this inner-fraternity and accepted his subsequent obligations to other members and their protégés. Hospital appointments were crucial to the successful specialist career and the inner fraternity controlled these as well as the lucrative practices. In this way informal relationships, based upon non-medical criteria, were effective in controlling professional relationships and careers.

(*c*) *The marginal professions*   Yet another form of colleague control gives rise to the phenomenon of the *marginal* profession. Many occupations— some of them old, such as nurse or midwife, and others new like probation officer or psychiatric social worker—are marginal in the sense that they share a number of characteristics with the classical professions yet fail to achieve similar status and rewards.

Some of these groups are marginal because they are auxiliary to, and are controlled by, another and more powerful professional body. Nurses, for example, are aides to the medical profession. Nursing care follows the doctor's diagnosis and his determination of the necessary treatment; the nurse may not act independently. Yet the relatively low status and rewards of nursing are not entirely a result of medical control. They also stem from a dependent status within the hospital administrative hierarchy and, in most societies, from the wider social disadvantage of being largely a woman's profession.

Other medical auxiliaries include almoners, health workers of various kinds and members of the 'professions supplementary to medicine'— physiotherapists, radiographers, dietitians, medical laboratory technicians, occupational therapists, remedial gymnasts and so on. In Britain the Medical Act of 1961 gave these practitioners formal recognition and a measure of control over internal discipline and training. In spite of this they remain subordinate to the medical establishment because they may only accept their patients from members of the medical profession and their treatment is subject to medical supervision. Other auxiliary professions include legal executives (formerly managing clerks) and book-keepers, who provide services for the solicitor and the accountant respectively, as well as pharmacists, who again are subordinate to the prescribing physician. The auxiliary status of the pharmacist may be further complicated by his involvement in business as a chemist. The ambiguity of his position is such that the American public is almost equally divided between those who think of pharmacists as professional workers and those who think of them as businessmen.

In the course of the historical development of professional occupations, auxiliary groups have often entered into direct competition with the established professions. We have already seen how the apothecaries (originally druggist-shopkeepers) successfully established themselves as medical practitioners in the face of fierce opposition from the Royal College of Physicians. Similar examples of successful competition with the established professions have been provided within the last hundred years by the development of accountancy. A number of accountants' associations originated in the attempts of book-keepers and clerks to provide accounting services (perhaps after working hours) for social groups who could not afford the fees of the established professionals. The process of fission in professional groups, where specialist and competing bodies hive off from the main body is the result of two concomitant processes. First, it results from changes in the social structure whereby new needs arise. For example, small-scale businessmen more and more demanded the services of lawyers and accountants to deal with the increasing complexities of business life—to guide them through the intricacies of taxation, of licensing law, and local government regulations. The great significance of international relationships has also led to the crystallization of specialist functions such as those of the international lawyer, the space lawyer and the United Nations diplomats. A second factor affecting this process of fission is the dynamic nature of a body of knowledge itself, the development of which creates a basis for the emergence of new occupational groups. Advances in the physical sciences lie behind the emergence of electronics engineering and computer programming; advances in the biological and social sciences lie behind the growth of psychiatry.

Other professional groups are marginal in the sense that their practice is of a limited nature. Again, there are examples of the limited professions in the medical field where pediatrists, chiropodists, audiologists and dispensing opticians have the area of their expertise defined by the medical body as a whole, although they retain control over the treatment given within their specialism. Dentists are the most fully established in their independence of all these groups, chiefly because the practice of dentistry has always been largely independent of medical control. This independence might be explained by the fact that until very recent times, that is until the development and application of anaesthetic and dental technology, the practice was regarded by physicians as a rather degrading manual occupation.

It is the goal of established professional associations to control, or where necessary eliminate, the competition of marginal groups, preferably by a legal restriction of practice to their own members. The greatest threat to the established professional is usually perceived as coming not from the creeping 'takeovers' of the auxiliary and limited professional groups, but from the frontal assaults of what are sometimes called the fringe or quasi-professions. This form of marginality stems from attempts to exclude groups whose practice is based on a body of knowledge which differs from that sustaining the established profession. Osteopaths, chiropractors, naturpaths, herbalists, homeopaths and hypnotherapists differ from auxiliaries in the medical field in that they lay claim to an explanatory system which they hold to be in some way superior to established medical knowledge. Thus the difference between the osteopath and the physiotherapist is that the osteopath claims to be able to diagnose and treat patients in his own right, whereas the physiotherapist remains subject to the physician's diagnosis and supervision. Attempts to bring bone manipulation within general medical practice in Britain have foundered on this difference; osteopaths refuse to enter the National Health Service on the terms accepted by physiotherapists. A recent study of 'fringe medicine' makes the point very clearly.[8]

> The physiotherapist is a medical auxiliary, the 1961 Act accorded (him) official recognition as a member of a Profession Supplementary to Medicine, but only so long as he agreed to treat only such patients who were referred to him by doctors and to treat them along the lines doctors suggested. The Osteopath rejects the implication that doctors are qualified to diagnose the right cases for, and supervise, manipulative treatment. On the contrary, he argues, they are disqualified by their lack of the appropriate training.

Osteopathy and chiropractice are far more widespread in the USA than in other industrial societies. American chiropractors treat about thirty million cases a year. This is partly a result of the high degree of specialization within the medical profession, which has left the field of general practice relatively open to the chiropractor and osteopath. Even so, the incorporation of osteopaths into the medical profession in the State of California in 1962 was only achieved in the face of bitter (and continuing) opposition from their colleagues in other States.

New forms of client control

(a) *Client choice* We have seen how, in eighteenth-century England, client control of professional activity was effective through a system of patronage. Client control as it exists in contemporary societies operates through other channels. The most obvious of these channels is client choice. The lawyer, the doctor and the accountant are all subject to the vagaries of client choice which often results from an informal system or referral in the community. The newcomer sooner or later gets round to asking friends, work-mates or colleagues: 'Do you know a good dentist?' or 'Which doctor do you go to?' Such judgments are necessarily based on non-technical criteria; a 'good' dentist may be defined in terms of social acceptability, good looks, religion and so on. To the degree that choices are extra-professional, some control over the professional man's activities passes to the client. Client choices are likely to work most effectively in relatively homogeneous village communities where few professionals would risk setting up in practice without strong local connections. The greater anonymity and the most specialized nature of social relationships in towns increases the importance of colleague referral systems. Even in towns, however, non-technical choices may be an important constraint on the professional. For example, a negro doctor in a white neighbourhood in the United States, or an Indian doctor in Britain may find successful general practice eludes them.

(b) *The employed professional* A more specific form of client control is found where professionals are directly employed by public or private organizations. Accountants, lawyers, architects, engineers and scientists are today employed in large numbers by business firms. Under this contemporary system of patronage the independent status of the professional is, in large part, a fiction, but it is a significant fiction. As a result of his socialization into the profession, the organization lawyer or accountant may identify more with the profession than with the firm. This ambivalence in the role of the employed professional involves tensions and conflicts. Such tensions, for example, are inherent in the position of the industrial scientist, who may be subject both to professional demands for publication and to commercial demands for secrecy. Similarly the government-employed architect may be subject both to professional aesthetic requirements and to utilitarian demands from his employer.

In all highly industrialized societies the proportion of professionals in independent practice is declining; in the underdeveloped world the professions have, to a much larger extent, been brought into being by state action, and their members are today employed by government agencies. In neither case is the typical professional an independent practitioner. In Britain in 1960, for example, only one-third of accountants were in private practice. In the case of surveyors the figure was 27 per cent; architects 25 per cent; actuaries 4 per cent; and engineers 2 per cent. Solicitors were unusual in that a majority (62 per cent for England and Wales) was engaged in private practice.[9] In the United States independent professionals make up about 1 per cent of the employed population. The proportion of salaried professionals, however, has risen to at least six times that number. This illustrates how the recent expansion of professional workers in industrial societies has taken place within bureaucratic employment. In other words, not only has bureaucracy invaded the professions—in the form of the law firms, the medical clinic, the management consultancy, and the mass university—but the professionals have infiltrated the bureaucracies. In Britain, the flow of accountants into business bureaucracies, and later into controlling positions on the boards of the corporations, was initiated by the Companies Act of 1867 (paralleled in the United States in 1896). This Act was a major step towards making audit by a qualified accountant compulsory for public companies. By the first world war accountants were joining the ranks of management in significant numbers. Later, in the great economic depression of the 1930s which resulted in the breakdown of *laissez-faire* economic policies, the services of accountants were at a premium. Their special talents as 'fixers', in working out the financial details of mergers, takeovers and price fixing, were in great demand as they have been ever since. Since the 1940s cost accountants have also become an important part of management as the techniques of budgetary control have been developed. Similarly, research and development needs of the large mass-production firm have increased the importance of the scientist and engineer who have, in their turn, begun to advance

up the ladder of bureaucratic control to join the accountants on the boards. Latest in the line, but increasingly to be found in the higher ranks of management, are the men versed in the mystique of sales and market research—for the expensive, modern automated plant is built only when market research is complete and potential sales are known. This places the market expert at the heart of the decision-making process.

The professionalization of the business bureaucracy may occur not only as a result of the infiltration of the professional, but also through the growing claims to expertise and professional status of general managers. The authority of the general manager does not derive from technical competence but from the position he occupies in the managerial hierarchy. There is, however, an increasing tendency for such managers to call themselves professionals and to behave like professionals, instituting lengthy training schemes and creating professional bodies such as the British Institute of Managers, which was incorporated in 1947. This trend is partly the result of the growing size and complexity of business firms and the rapid rate of technological change. Under these conditions the skills needed to operate the organizational machine are difficult to acquire 'on the job' and cannot be passed from father to son. The claim to professional status, however, is usually limited to the managers of large firms in which corporate solidarity is conspicuous, where decision making has important consequences for the community at large, and the ethic of service has some relevance. Attempts to implement some kind of incomes policy in a number of industrial societies today appear to be founded on the belief that the manager (and the union official) has obligations to the public which should be recognized when wages, prices and profits are under consideration. Perhaps symbolic of these changes is the recent modification of the Rotary motto from 'He profits most who serves best' to 'Service above self'.

Another aspect of management's claim to professional status is that it now shares with established professions a dependence upon a complex body of knowledge. Aspects of psychology, economics, sociology and other disciplines are now incorporated into the syllabuses of business studies courses—a rapidly expanding sector of higher education. The extent of professional training for business managers in the United States is indicated by the fact that in 1958 there were 300,000 students enrolled on business administration courses at the undergraduate level alone. Formal management training of this kind is by no means as advanced in other countries but is expanding rapidly.

The professional society?

The great expansion in the numbers of professionals and the increased demand of many new occupational groups for a degree of self-control over their work activities are trends which are often thought to be transforming the nature of industrial societies. It is argued, for example, that as professionals make up a larger and larger proportion of the labour force so the peculiarities of professionalism will exert a more pervading influence leading ultimately to a society dominated by professionals. Our analysis of the character of the professions would lead us to challenge some of the more extreme claims associated with this line of argument.

Is industrial society increasingly dominated by professionalism? Certainly many occupations are developing some of the characteristics associated with professionalism. Some would argue that even manual workers are becoming professionals to the extent that manual occupations may involve a specialized technique and provide a career. There may also be an 'ethical code' in the form of conventions of fair practice—for example, rules of behaviour developed in management-union negotiations and in arbitration procedures. Similarly, business management is said to be becoming more professional, partly as a result of the inclusion of professionals in management but also through the development among managers of codes of ethics and specialisms which are based upon a theory of management practice. Our scepticism of the claim that we are witnessing 'the professionalization of everyone' is based on an appreciation of the variety of forms of control characterizing contemporary occupations that are called professions. Their practice may be controlled by a professional association, by the state, by their clients, or by a combination of these. Today control by the professional body alone is not a common means of regulating an occupational activity. This is most evident in the growth of large-scale organizations which employ experts of one kind or another. In a large hospital the task of co-ordination is carried out by specialist administrators. To do their job successfully they must have considerable authority and this reduces the independent authority of the salaried medical specialists. Consequently arguments to the effect that professional expansion will counter the bureaucratic impersonality and arbitrariness of large-scale organizations must be treated with caution. The work situation of the typical professional is no longer independent practice and the typical professional association is now as likely to be concerned with the pay and conditions of its members as with the maintenance of professional standards and conduct among solo practitioners. So the expansion of the professions need not necessarily result in the growth of professionalism.

These changes in the nature of professional organization must also be borne in mind when considering claims that a professional ethic increasingly permeates the institutions of modern industrial societies; that the humanistic and individualistic creeds of the professions provide a source of independent criticism in the face of 'monolithic, bureaucratic impersonality'. It has been suggested that the traditional 'personal service professions'—medicine, law and the clergy—allied with the new 'counselling' professions, such as social work, are influencing the moral ethos of our society.[10] The personal service ethic, it is said, will spread from the professions to society at large and will become the ideology by which many decisions of the ruling groups are justified. As planning and welfare become central to the modern industrial state so the personal service ethic, stressing collectivistic and altruistic considerations will become more relevant to the decision-making process. But the fact that most of the 'new' professionals and an increasing proportion of the 'old' are employed by public or private organizations should alert us to the possibility of changes in the functions and image of professionals. There is, for example, reason to doubt that professional codes and the service orientation will remain significant where the professional is subject to bureaucratic rules and authority. Moreover, the fastest growing professions are not those providing a service for an individual client but technologists, record keepers, and planners—engineers, auditors, accountants, town planners, computer programmers and so on.

This increasing application of specialized skills to all kinds of social and personal problems has been made possible by a massive growth in what has been called 'the knowledge industry' and has given rise to problems of control over new occupational groups. In addition the proliferation of sales techniques, the growth in house ownership, the development of mass tourism, all provide 'control' problems of the sort we have been discussing. The layman is equally incapable of judging the technical expertise of a television repair man or a garage maintenance mechanic; the advice of a tourist agent or house agent; and the work of a solicitor or physician. Who is going to provide the guarantee of integrity, competence and honour? The practitioner? The public? The state? The practitioners have an interest in maintaining a monopoly, but the state has the power to impose alternative forms of control and has done so in some cases. In recent years the public, too, has begun to play a more positive part in attempts to control a variety of services. Consumer bodies of various kinds are flourishing. Perhaps one consequence of the changes we have outlined will be the growing importance of 'consumer politics'. Whatever the outcome, it is certain that the development of these occupations, which enjoy high status and not a little power, will be of great significance in the future development of industrial societies.

Notes

1 A. M. Carr-Saunders, *Professions: Their Organisation and Place in Society*, Oxford: Clarendon Press, 1928, pp. 3–31.
2 From a pamphlet written in 1794 by the Medical Director of York County Hospital, quoted in Bernice Hamilton, 'The medical professions in the eighteenth century', *Economic History Review*, 4, 1951.
3 Robert Masters Kerrison, *Observations and Reflections on the Bill now in Progress through the House of Commons for Better Regulating the Medical Profession as far as regards Apothecaries*, 1815, pp. 18–19.
4 See R. Bucher and A. Strauss, 'Professions in process', *American Journal of Sociology*, 66, 1961, pp. 325–34, for a discussion of this point.
5 C. Wright Mills, *White Collar*, London: Oxford University Press, 1956, p. 112.
6 See O. Smigel, 'The impact of recruitment upon the organization of a large law firm', *American Sociological Review*, 25, 1960, pp. 56–66.
7 See O. Hall, 'The informal organisation of the medical profession', *Canadian Journal of Economics and Political Science*, 12, 1946, pp. 30–44.
8 Brian Inglis, *Fringe Medicine*, London: Faber, 1964, p. 109.
9 *Report of the Royal Commission on Doctors' and Dentists' Remuneration*, Cmnd 939, London: HMSO, February 1960, Table 14.
10 See Paul Halmos, *The Personal Service Society*, London: Constable, 1970.

Reading

Elliott, Philip, *The Sociology of the Professions*, London; Macmillan, 1972. An analysis of the development of professional occupations in terms of the move from traditional 'status professionalism' to 'occupational professionalism' associated with modern industry and commerce.
Lees, D. S., *Economic Consequences of the Professions*, London: Institute of Economic Affairs, 1966. A fifty-page pamphlet in which an economist looks at the monopoly position of professional associations and argues that it operates to the detriment of new entrants to the profession and 'consumer welfare'. Contains a brief case study of lawyers.
Lewis, R. and Maude, A., *Professional People*, Harmondsworth: Penguin, 1953. A great deal of useful information is presented in a value laden manner. The book is dominated by a spirit of nostalgia for the old independent professions as against the modern trends toward bureaucratization and state involvement.
Millerson, Geoffrey, *The Qualifying Associations*, London: Routledge & Kegan Paul, 1964. The significance of the qualifying associations in the development of professional occupations in England: their organization and functions in the provision of education and control over professional conduct.
Reader, W. J., *Professional Men*, London: Weidenfeld & Nicolson, 1966. A study of the changing structure of the traditional professions and the emergence of new professions associated with the development of the English middle classes in the nineteenth century.

Further reading

Carr-Saunders, A. M. and Wilson, P. A., *The Professions*, London: Cass, 1964. A thorough pioneering study first published in 1933.
Etzioni, A. (ed.), *The Semi-Professions and Their Organization*, New York: Free Press, 1969. Separate studies of elementary schoolteachers, nurses, and social workers in the USA and a commentary upon the dominance of women and the high levels of bureaucracy in these 'semi-professions'.
Halmos, Paul, *The Personal Service Society*, London:

Constable, 1970. An attempt to evaluate the social significance of the professions, arguing that the ideology of the 'personal service professions' has seeped into general belief systems and is in process of becoming the dominant ideology of industrial societies.

Jackson, J. A. (ed.), *Professions and Professionalization*, Cambridge University Press, 1970. A collection of essays presenting a variety of 'new' approaches to the study of the professions.

Johnson, Terence, *Professions and Power*, London: Macmillan, 1972. An evaluation of the present state of sociological theory relating to the professions and a theoretical discussion in elaboration of some of the approaches suggested in this chapter.

Prandy, K., *Professional Employees*, London: Faber, 1965. A study of engineers and technologists, and the effect of their situation as employees upon their status and power in society as a whole.

Vollmer, H. M. and Mills, D. L. (eds), *Professionaliza-tion*, Englewood Cliffs: Prentice-Hall, 1966. A wide selection of readings relating to such subjects as the concept of professionalization, the social context of professionalization, professional asso-ciates and colleague relations, professionals as employees, professionals and government, etc.

10 Social stratification

Wherever there is a systematic division of labour in economic and political life there are also differences in men's access to power. Where there are specialist occupations some specialists invariably manage to gain control over the lives of others, and to monopolize the surplus of production over consumption at the expense of others. The composition of this dominant group varies from society to society. In some societies the most powerful men are warriors led by a warrior king; in others they are priests; in others, landowners, merchants, or industrialists. In most industrial societies power is shared between two or more groups in such a way that it is difficult to locate it with any precision. In all complex societies, however, a minority of the population exercises power out of all proportion to its numbers.

How is it that some groups manage to control the distribution of the economic surplus and keep a major part of it for themselves? Why is the dominant group able to sustain a huge difference in life styles between themselves and the masses in some societies but not in others? What factors explain the differences from one society to another in the relationships between the powerful and the powerless? How can people pass on their privileged position to their children? The task of this chapter is to suggest some answers to these questions by looking at the development of social stratification in a variety of societies.

The emergence of social stratification

There are some human societies where there are no differences in power, where wealth is shared equally, and where high social standing is dependent entirely on ability and carries with it no economic or political 'perks'. In other words there are some societies where there is no social stratification. These are societies in which all persons of the same sex engage in the same tasks. It may be hunting; it may be the cultivation of small plots; it may be fighting. The differences in social standing and decision making which do exist are based upon age (which eventually comes to all and therefore provides no basis for semi-permanent differences in status position), or upon the universally recognized skills and abilities of an individual. A man who is especially skilled in a common activity—say, hunting—may be influential in directing the movements of the band, and his skills may win him a position of high honour. The nature of such a position of prestige may be gauged from the following description of the leader of a Bushman band.[1]

> Nobody ever contested Toma's position as leader, for it was not a position Toma held by force or pressure, but simply by his wisdom and ability, and people prospered under him. No Bushman wants prominence, but Toma went further than most in avoiding prominence; he had almost no possessions and gave away everything that came into his hands. He was diplomatic, for in exchange for his self-imposed poverty, he won the respect and following of all the people there.

There are very few material possessions in hunting societies, partly because the migrant nature of the band places severe restrictions on the accumulation of property. Consequently, ideas of ownership tend to focus very closely upon ownership of food, and there are invariably detailed rules concerning the obligations of ownership. It is generally obligatory to give food to all other members of the band when a kill has been made. In societies where the hold over life is so precarious, such customs 'spread the risk' of failing to make a kill. The members of hunting societies are well aware of this function of their sharing customs. As one anthropologist writes of the Eskimo: 'he knows that the best place for him to store his surplus is in someone else's stomach, because sooner or later he will want his gift repaid.'[2] The really important thing to note, however, is that 'ownership' does not mean the right to do what one likes with the game. There are deep-seated social obligations to give most of it away, and the man who fully honours his obligations is highly esteemed. The reward of the successful hunter is prestige, not meat. Wealth does not accumulate in the hands (or even in the stomachs) of the successful alone, so there are no significant differences in wealth. Moreover, the prestige accorded the successful and generous hunter relates primarily to his hunting prowess and generosity. In so far as it does become more general, it only gives him influence as long as the other members of the society willingly accord him a position of influence—as long, that is, as he is able to *persuade* them to follow him, and this is usually conditional upon his continued success as a hunter.

Some horticultural and pastoral societies are similar to hunting bands in that, despite a more complex technology and a more certain food supply, their economies produce only a very small surplus. Wherever there is little or no surplus of production over subsistence it is not possible for any person or group to secure a more than equal share of the products without pushing others below the line of subsistence. Since these are also societies which have not developed legal monopolies of force (i.e. a state form of organization) this is unlikely to occur. Moreover, everyone has to engage directly in the production process; none can be released from this labour. There is therefore little occupational specialization to provide a basis for the coalescence of dominant and subordinate groups.

Settled cultivation and pastoralism, however, do have potentialities for the creation of an economic surplus that are absent in all but the most fortunately placed hunting and gathering societies. The grains and roots produced by cultivators are suitable for storing and so can be accumulated,

and the preservation of meat 'on the hoof' is simpler and more effective than the preservation of dead animals—especially in tropical areas. It is therefore in these societies that the phenomenon of accumulation first appears. The accumulation of a significant surplus over and above the small reserve required for security presents a society with the economic problem of what to do with it. One solution to this problem that is common among known simpler societies is the development, out of the egalitarian society, of the economic organization associated with chiefdoms. The major economic task of the chief is one of redistributing the surplus produce; of receiving, as gifts, produce of different sorts from the people, and redistributing it—often in 'wasteful' feasts. The chief possesses no power to coerce his fellow men into giving up their surplus, and his own position in the early stages of the development of a chiefdom would seem to be based entirely upon his ability to give more than others. This in turn is often based upon his greater capacity for hard work, so that the chief is not necessarily released from food production. There is rarely any accumulation of wealth by the chief so, although there is a strong tendency for the office of chief to be monopolized by a single lineage, there is no concomitant economic gain. Indeed, the chief's influence and prestige stem from his generosity; a man's 'wealth' only brings him prestige and influence if he fulfils his obligation to give it away.

As the size of the surplus increases, the chief and his close kin gradually become released from their obligations as food producers and increasingly become full-time distributors of produce and organizers of labour. Here we have social stratification in embryo. But this is not yet a stratified society. The chief has little power to organize people against their will. He lives in much the same way as his people, although he probably has a grander dwelling and the exclusive right to certain ornaments. Moreover, the whole population benefits from the redistribution process, although the chief and his kinsmen usually benefit somewhat more than others. All members of the society still have unrestricted access to the basic essentials of making a living. In some societies, Ashanti and other West African chiefdoms for example, land (the basic resource in a cultivating society) was held corporately by the lineage, and the chief's control over the use of land was a control exercised on behalf of the corporate group. As chiefdoms develop so the powers of the chief become more extreme. In many Polynesian societies, for example, the chief could re-allocate land on his accession. While chiefs rarely denied men access to the land they needed they could, and more frequently did, deny access to the equally crucial irrigation schemes which had been built, under chiefly direction, by communal labour. The higher level of techno-logical development of these relatively complex chiefdoms thus gave greater powers to the chief, for he controlled the distribution of water which was vital for successful cultivation.

The greater gap between the chief (and his relatives) and the common man in highly devel-oped chiefdoms is illustrated by the elaborateness of the taboos surrounding the paramount chief of Hawaii in the days before significant Western contact.[3]

> The following is only a partial list: it was prohibited for a man's shadow to fall on the paramount's house, back, robe, or any possession; it was prohibited to pass through his door, climb his stockade, to put out in a racing canoe before him, to put on his robe or his bark cloth; it was required that one kneel while he ate, not appear in his presence in a wet bark cloth, or with mud on one's head. . . . Even the ground the chief walked on became charged with mana and was avoided by others. In the presence of the paramount, all had to prostrate themselves on the ground in a posture of extreme humility and obeisance.

Early European travellers to Hawaii, reporting on these chiefly taboos, tell us that the usual punish-ment for a breach was death, but that the punish-ment would not be exacted if the wrongdoer had 'influential friends'. Similar inequality before the law occurred in Tonga, where there was no vengeance for the kinsman of a commoner killed by a chief, and in Tahiti. It is an inequality more typical of stratified societies, where a small group monopolizes the means of violence, and indeed, societies like Hawaii stand on the boundaries between 'rank' societies and stratified ones. Extreme exploitation, however, was lacking, largely because of the presence of the 'redistribu-tive ethic'.

It is with the emergence of a state structure that social stratification in its full sense appears, for stratification involves the wielding of *power* by some groups at the expense of others. A small group uses its power over others to build a style of life more grand than the life styles of the mass of the population. In non-industrial societies there is a tendency for the very great bulk of the eco-nomic surplus to be used for the benefit of the rulers or those that serve them directly. As increases in food production allow a progressive division of labour, most of the specialists—goldsmiths, builders, domestic servants and the like—provide services only for a very limited section of the population. In other words, the surplus production, far from being equally divided, supports a few in lives of relative luxury. The larger the surplus, the greater the luxury and the greater the differences between the rich and powerful and the poor and powerless.

How does the ruling minority manage to keep such an unequal share of the society's wealth for its own use? Why does the majority continue to produce a surplus when it does not enjoy the benefits? Pre-industrial examples provide two broad answers: the rulers either gain their privi-leged position by physical coercion or by super-natural coercion. Either they establish their dominance by conquest and maintain it by the threat of physical violence, or they obtain it by controlling access to the gods and spirits whose goodwill is thought to be necessary for the well-being of the society. In the first case, the ruling stratum tends to be one of warriors; in the second, one of priests. In addition these two groups often combine in a ruling alliance.

Of the two oldest states one (Mesopotamia) developed an upper stratum of priests, and the other (Egypt) was based upon conquest. In Mesopotamia the surplus was drawn from the cultivators by priests, whose proximity to the deities gave them special knowledge of the require-ments of the gods. The gifts of food and other goods to the gods were administered by the priests; the building of the temples to the glory and honour of the supernatural powers was directed by the priests. Their task of interpreting the divine will gave them an authority which placed them at the heart of the decision making process and made it right and proper that they should enjoy certain privileges not available to the ordinary man. Their privileged position was based upon a monopoly of knowledge which enabled them to control the thoughts and actions of men. For example, they alone recognized the regularity of climatic conditions. Their ability to predict such events as the annual floods conse-quently appeared to ordinary men to represent power over natural phenomena—a power which could not be ignored.

The early development of social stratification in middle America was also based upon religion (although later, military might became an equally important factor). About 900 BC the simple farming community gave way to a society of greater economic complexity, yielding a larger surplus on the basis of more diverse crops. At about the same time there is the first evidence of a social gulf between members of the society. Archaeological evidence from burial sites shows a priesthood set apart from ordinary men by differences in dress, deportment and skills. The organization of the society underwent a major change with the priest emerging as the dominant figure. The priests were specialists in organization as well as religious practitioners and could therefore exact tribute as well as worship from the rest of the population. The temples were also centres of political power and, since markets were attached to them, of economic activity. Priestly authority, however, ultimately derived from the task of mediation between human beings and the supernatural. Obedience was commanded in the name of the gods. The tight ideological control exercised by the priesthood seems to have rendered warfare largely unnecessary. Control over the population and the extraction of the greater part of the economic surplus from the majority was achieved through supernatural terror rather than physical terror.

The second type of domination—that based upon military might of one kind or another—is more common in pre-industrial societies. The stratification systems of Egypt, Mexico after AD 900, ancient Rome, and many of the African kingdoms of the eighteenth and nineteenth centuries, all seem to have arisen directly out of conquest or to have been substantially modified by conquest. In Egypt, for example, although religion played an important part, the first centralized accumulation and concentration of foodstuffs resulted from the conquest of the Nile delta by Menes, the king of Upper Egypt. The conquest placed Menes in control of comparatively vast resources, first as booty from the campaign and subsequently as a continuing revenue in the form of tribute. Much of the surplus was used to support labourers and craftsmen who worked on the construction of the royal tombs, and in obtaining the foreign material with which they were so lavishly constructed. A contemporary estimate suggested that 100,000 men were fully employed for ten years simply on quarrying stone for the great pyramid. The power of a ruler who could

successfully organize such an enterprise is beyond dispute. Indeed, the pharaohs were considered divine. Other persons of high position in ancient Egypt merely absorbed some of the reflected glory of the king. They were, moreover, appointed by him and held office only as long as they continued to please him. One of the consequences of this absolutism was that persons from humble origins whose ability caught the eye of the pharaoh could be elevated to positions of very considerable power. Thus the Israelite Joseph, sold into slavery in Egypt as a boy, rose to become second only to the pharaoh in all the land. The chance of such a dramatic rise to power came most frequently (but still very infrequently) to those who were the household servants of the pharaoh, for it was they who came into most frequent contact with him and therefore had the opportunity to impress. It was a hazardous business, however, and there was a much higher chance of being condemned to death than of being promoted, as is shown by the fate of Joseph's fellow servants.

If we look at many of the traditional states of East Africa we find a distribution of power involving similar absolutism and also seemingly based upon conquest. These states also demonstrate the potentialities for clear-cut stratification even where the economic surplus is relatively small. Reconstructions of the history of the part of Africa lying between the great lakes suggests a southwards movement of tall, Nilotic, nomadic pastoralists who conquered the existing cultivators and set themselves up as a ruling group. A number of traditional kingdoms in this area— Rwanda; Ankole; Toro; Nyoro—have roughly similar structures, with the pastoralist and ethnically distinct minorities (usually about 10 per cent of the total population) ruling over agricultural serfs.

The kingdom of Ankole provides the least complicated example. The positions of the Bahima (pastoralists) and the Bairu (agriculturalists) were legally, politically, economically, and socially unequal. In economic terms, the domination of the Bahima was manifest in the compulsory tribute which had to be paid in food or labour by all Bairu. While only the king or the chiefs could levy this tax, all Bahima benefited from it since much of the produce was used by the king in feeding and provisioning his Bahima visitors. There is a significant difference here from the process of redistribution in a chiefdom which we observed earlier. In most chiefdoms the commoners could withhold their gifts to the chief if they were not satisfied with his behaviour, and even in the most highly developed chiefdoms like Hawaii, where this was not possible, everyone benefited to some extent from the redistribution through ceremonial feasts. In stratified societies, such redistribution as takes place is much more limited and benefits only a few. In the case of the Ankole, it was the Bahima who gained from this system of taxation.

A further economic difference between the two major groups lay in the prohibition of Bairu ownership of productive cattle, for cattle were the main form of wealth. Prohibitions of a non-economic kind furthered the difference. Bairu were not allowed to engage in military activities—a common prohibition placed upon conquered peoples, and one which clearly retains control of the means of force in the hands of the dominant stratum. They were also debarred from high official positions and were thus unable to bring any political influence to bear upon the king. The two groups stood in different legal positions in the sense that punishment depended upon which group one belonged to more than upon the nature of the offence. Bairu, for example, were not allowed to kill a Muhima under any circumstances. Without this right of blood revenge they were unprotected against any physical violence which the ruling group might direct against them.

As in many African states, the power of the Ankole king was very great and could be exercised arbitrarily. Part of the Bahima's high standing derived from their closeness to the king. The relationship between the king and his Bahima followers was one of clientship; that is to say, the king offered protection in return for certain services and homage payments (usually in cattle) from his clients. Such cattle were added to the royal herds which were used to replenish the stock of Bahima herdsmen in distress. In this, one can see the essential difference between the homage payment of the Bahima, which was freely paid in return for certain benefits, and which even in itself acted as an insurance against hard times, and the obligatory tribute exacted from the Bairu, who benefited hardly at all from the payment.

Social relations in traditional Ankole, then, were dominated by the distinction between Bahima and Bairu. Ultimately, the unequal relationship was maintained by a monopoly of the effective use of force and it probably had its origin in conquest. But naked power was overlaid with ideas about ethnicity and rights of cattle ownership. This is demonstrated by the ease with which conquered Bahima from neighbouring territories were assimilated into the dominant stratum. The Bairu of conquered areas fared less well, for some of them were taken as slaves to serve in the households of the king and chiefs. These slaves had no legal status whatsoever; they were the property of the master and he had the power of life and death over them. Their lowly position was summed up in the common practice of cutting off their ears so that they could be easily recognized as slaves if they escaped. For Ankole Bairu there were bounds to legitimate exploitation, and it was part of the task of the king to see that these were not exceeded. No such limitations were placed upon the treatment of slaves by their masters.

As societies grow more complex so their systems of stratification become more complex: new strata emerge and relationships between existing strata undergo subtle but important changes. Economic development creates an increasingly efficient economy and thus potentialities for greater differences between the strata. These changes may be observed in the social development of republican Rome, although access to political power remained crucial, as in all the societies we have considered so far, and the significance of military might and conquest grew more rather than less important. The unusual feature of the Roman republic is that it was not governed by an absolute ruler. Hence, the designation 'citizen' had considerable force and introduced a further complication into the relations between strata. This is not to say that all citizens were equal, and from the earliest records Roman society is divided into patricians and plebeians.

In the early days of the republic there was little difference of wealth between the two groups. The difference was essentially a legal and political one. As the military might of Rome grew and her frontiers expanded, the relations between the strata underwent a number of changes. The most important of these related to the increased prestige and wealth of senators; the growth of tribute from the provinces; the influx of slaves; the growth of trade; and ultimately, the development of a professional army under 'permanent' commanders who were increasingly an independent political force. It was a complex process and provides a good illustration of the fact that the gain of a state may not be equally shared by all its members (or even by all its citizens). Indeed, the growth of Rome as a world power was paralleled by a polarization of the upper stratum and the commoners.

One of the most decisive steps towards world

dominance—the conquest of Carthage—serves as an admirable illustration of one of the ways in which this happened. The Carthaginians were worthy military opponents and the Punic wars were long and costly. In the course of Hannibal's invasion of Italy enormous damage was done to the farming land around Rome. Added to years of neglect, brought about by the absence of the bulk of the male farmers on military service for lengthy periods, this made the problem of reconstruction after the war a colossal one. The peasant farmers who survived the war returned to find that their soldiers' pay was not sufficient to cover the necessary outlay in seed, stock and equipment, and they were forced into debt at ruinous terms. As a result, the small farms around Rome fell into the hands of those few who had the capital to re-stock them. The concentration of landownership was exacerbated by the state making over large tracts of public land in repayment of war loans, for it was the same wealthy people who had financed the costly war with Carthage. In this way the huge ranch-type farms of the Roman landed aristocracy developed, for pasture provided the landowner with a higher profit than agriculture. In addition, the wars had resulted in a huge influx of slaves, providing cheap labour which was especially suited to work on large estates.

The position of a substantial section of the farming citizenry was thus undermined by these twin processes resulting from the wars. They were forced to seek refuge in Rome itself where their position was little better. Here, too, the free labourer competed with slave labour. By the time the Republic came to an end there were some 200,000 slaves in Rome—one-fifth of the city's total population. The majority of these were domestic slaves, but there was a number of skilled craftsmen among them and this depressed the wages and living standards of the free artisans. That Julius Caesar found it expedient to pacify the citizens with a corn 'dole' is perhaps less significant as a sign of the value of citizenship than as a commentary upon the economic position of the townsman. The plight of the non-citizen freeman, who did not qualify for this state aid, was even worse.

The slaves themselves constituted the lowest stratum of Roman society. Although a few individual slaves exercised considerable influence (through their advisory position in the household of a great man) and one or two managed to become fairly wealthy, the general position of the slave must have been unenviable. His position in society is evidenced by the fact that in a Roman law court evidence from a slave was only admissible if it had been extracted under torture! Perhaps the best evidence of the deplorable life of slaves is the frequency of slave revolts—the actions of desperate men, with enormous odds against success.

There were also, of course, those who derived great benefit from Rome's wars. Tribute from subject peoples made taxation obsolete and, while this may have benefited the rich more than others, it also helped freemen who had achieved modest economic success, and perhaps it even provided some consolation for the unemployed who would otherwise have had taxation imposed upon their other burdens. The greatest direct beneficiaries from the wars, however, were those who conducted them and, to a lesser extent, those who subsequently ruled over the conquered peoples. It was loot, slaves, and tribute (as well as the effect of war upon landownership) that enabled the senatorial families to raise their standard of living so much above that of the common man. In the days before the Punic wars there had been a positive embargo on senatorial wealth, and any spoils of war had been faithfully paid into the Treasury. The ambition was not to be rich but to be powerful. In the days of world dominion, however, things were somewhat different. The sole compensation for a year's posting as governor to one of the provinces lay in the common expectation that this year's service of the state would put one in funds for life. The lower ranks of the army serving under such a governor made more modest, but still worthwhile, profits. When, as happened from time to time as with Cicero's appointment to Sicily, a governor was appointed whose sense of justice prevented him from operating this extortion, the provincials 'regarded him with speechless astonishment'.[4] We can imagine that the army under his command viewed him with similar astonishment but less gratitude. It is evident that great wealth was often associated with military success. In the latter days of the republic, especially, the great fortunes were made by military commanders like Pompey and Julius Caesar.

Another group to profit economically from Rome's military supremacy, however, was the rising stratum of *equites*. Part of their profit came from the flourishing business life of the Mediterranean and the favourable trading position they enjoyed under the sponsorship of Rome. By their very involvement in these profitable activities, however, they renounced all claim to the political life and thus to real power and prestige. For landownership alone of economic activities carried some *social* distinction, and business and trade was forbidden to men of senatorial rank. Such political influence as was exerted by individual men of this stratum (and it was sometimes considerable) was achieved through the financial backing they were able to provide for politicians. In spite of the 'dishonour' of their involvement in business, the most successful of them met senators socially on terms close to equality, and intermarriage was sought by both sides for their mutual advantage.

The emergence of the *equites* marks the development of a new stratum with an essentially economic base. Such a stratum is common in the more highly developed agrarian societies. Traditional Japan, Imperial China, Mughal India and medieval Europe all had a stratum of merchants whose wealth was often in excess of their social status and political power. Some of them became very wealthy (wealthy enough to underwrite the expenses of an aristocratic patron) although the majority were much less successful. In these traditional societies the merchants, to a large extent, stood apart from the dominant power relationship—that between landlord and tenant. Their own activities, especially in the economic sphere, were less easily controlled by landowners and rulers, and so they usually had a good deal more freedom of action than the peasants and tenant farmers.

There were also quite wide dissimilarities in the position of merchants from one agrarian society to another. In some societies, such as Mughal India, the merchants were unable to use their wealth to make even moderate political and social gains. Indeed, they often had the utmost difficulty in retaining their wealth. In some other societies they gradually managed, as a group, to exert political influence and to raise their social position. In the later Middle Ages in Western Europe, for example, the merchants were instrumental in securing the 'freedom of cities', sometimes through force, more often by purchasing privileges from the king. A number of English boroughs were established in this way and within them the wealthier and more powerful merchants to all intents and purposes constituted the government. This further stimulated trade and enhanced their position in the wider society, thereby paving the way for the great expansion of commerce in the fifteenth and sixteenth centuries. In turn, this 'commercial revolution' further enhanced the position of 'bourgeois' groups and helped to

establish the springboard from which industrialization was later launched. Before the Industrial Revolution, however, the landed gentry were still socially and politically dominant. It was not until the rise of the industrial society that the rising economic stratum was able to capture political power, and ultimately social power as well.

Industrialization and the development of social classes in England

The process of industrialization had a crucial significance for social stratification. Relationships between existing strata—landowners, merchants, tenant farmers—underwent changes, but of far greater importance were the new strata thrown up by the fundamental processes of social change. The dominant economic position of the landowners, which had been challenged but not supplanted by the growth of commerce and trade, was substantially undermined by the economic success of a new breed of men—the industrial entrepreneurs. In many ways the interests of these men were fundamentally opposed to landed interests, and the creation, through industrialization, of this 'industrial middle class' paved the way for a gradual transfer of political power as well. Subsequently, as the scale of industrial enterprises increased, it became less easy for one man or one family to control the enterprise. Joint stock companies emerged in which managers were appointed to run the firm on behalf of shareholders. By the beginning of the twentieth century the typical industrial firm was no longer a family concern, but a bureaucratic institution operated by managers. The mode of earning a livelihood and the way of life of the mass of the population has also been completely changed by industrialization. The decline in the number engaged in agricultural labour has been balanced by an increase in industrial labour. And while the mid-nineteenth century was still characterized by a great deal of 'domestic' manufacture and craftsman production from small workshops as well as by factory production, it was the latter that was to become dominant. In addition there was, in the second half of the century, a growth in the number of miners as the industrial demand for coal rose, and an increase in dockers, stevedores and the like as the volume of international trade increased. The twentieth century has seen, in mass production, yet another change which has brought about the expansion of a previously relatively insignificant group—the semi-skilled factory workers.

It is these technological and social changes in the organization of work that lie behind the changes in stratification of the last two hundred years. Whatever the cause, however, it was so apparent to contemporaries in early industrial societies that the nature of the relationships between strata where changing, that a new terminology was evolved to describe the changed situation. Whereas writers in eighteenth-century England wrote of 'ranks' and 'orders', those of the nineteenth century increasingly spoke and wrote of 'classes'. By 1834 J. S. Mill could write that social commentators habitually distinguished three classes in society—landlords, capitalists and labourers. Yet, as we shall see, these three great classes were far from being homogeneous.

The rulers of pre-industrial and early industrial England were aristocrats and gentry. That is to say, they owed their position to their ownership of land (and, to some extent, to possession of a title). As landowners their economic fate was overwhelmingly linked to the prosperity of agriculture, although urban land rents were an important source of income for some. The ancestors of many of those with urban land had been merchants who, having achieved wealth from trade, bought estates and a title, retired from commerce, and, adopting the aristocratic style of life, lived off their land. This relative openness of the English aristocracy, the relative ease with which new groups were continually being assimilated, and the eagerness with which they married their sons and daughters to the hiers and hieresses of commercial fortunes, was one of its most important characteristics. It encouraged successful merchants to aspire to membership of the aristocracy and to identify with them. It did not necessarily, however, indicate a willingness to compromise with commercial or industrial interests for, unlike the later 'industrial peers', those adopted into the aristocracy before 1800 gave up their stakes in the world of commerce and trade and became part of 'the landed interest'. It is true that there were a number of landowners who made substantial profits from the mineral rights of their land, and whose economic and political interests did not coincide with those of their fellow landowners. They were joined after 1856 by industrialists, railway magnates and others who remained active in industry or commerce, and whose estates merely represented their surplus assets. By and large, however, in the early years of the century the economic interest of the rulers was wedded to agriculture. The political expression of this was the passing, in 1815, of the Corn Laws, imposing restrictions on the import of American corn and thus maintaining a high price for home farm produce. The close link between economic interest and political action has rarely been clearer. In a single action the ruling group demonstrated beyond all doubt their intention to govern in their own interest. The higher price of food which the Corn Laws entailed forced up the level of the subsistence wage and thus reduced industrial and commercial profits. The result was that the industrialists and merchants, who up to that time had shown little inclination to become permanently involved in politics, were driven to protest by political means. The experience drew the various industrial and trading elements closer together and gave them a common cause around which to unite. The campaign for the repeal of the Corn Laws and agitation for parliamentary reform, then, was the crucible in which the English middle class was formed. For campaign purposes a tactical alliance was made with some groups of manual workers, but this was abandoned in the settlement that led to the Reform Bill of 1832. Thereafter the political as well as the economic power of the middle class grew steadily and middle-class consciousness prospered.

The politics of compromise, by which the landowners extended political participation to the middle class but to them alone, enabled the aristocracy to continue to dominate political life. Furthermore, the mystique of the aristocracy retained some force long after the middle class could have assumed political as well as economic power. Industrialists, for example, often shared the view that the landed gentry were 'natural' rulers— that only they could maintain order and stability in the country. 'For we believe, we men of the middle class,' said one of them, 'that the conduct of national business calls for special men, men born and bred to the work for generations. . . .'[5] This is, perhaps, a peculiarly English form of social deference that is still far from dead and remains one of the more subtle aspects of the power relationships between classes. The relationship between gentlemanly behaviour and government and administration was to remain. Gradually, however, the belief spread that these attributes could be learned and, in particular, the public schools were viewed as the great training grounds for political leadership. Since the rich middle-class boy mixed with the sons of the landowners in the public schools, such an education gradually enabled non-gentry to play a fuller part in government. The purely social mystique of the aristocracy, however, survived their relative political decline.

In the course of the nineteenth century, then, the middle class gradually came to a larger share of power—first through pressure on a mainly aristocratic parliament, later by direct representation. It was this struggle to establish the political conditions within which industrial capitalism could thrive which, more than anything else, established them as a class. The solidarity thus formed was both demonstrated and strengthened by later struggles with their employees.

The power of employers over their employees had been apparent from the very beginning of factory employment. But, to begin with, it had been very much a local phenomenon—the power of a factory master over the factory hands. Very often the total subjection of the employees extended to all spheres of their lives. There is ample documentation of the miseries of factory conditions in the early nineteenth century, but this relationship between employer and employed is not necessarily symptomatic of the new 'class' society. Employers had exploited their workers long before industrialization. But there were differences in the new situation. Two stand out in their significance.

First, the newly dominant middle class had a philosophy of life which was different from that of the old aristocracy of the eighteenth century. Especially significant was the different view held of the poor and needy. The old view is well expressed by Bishop Butler in a sermon to the London Corporation in 1740:[6]

> He who had distributed men into these
> different ranks, and at the same time united
> them into one society . . . has by this
> constitution of things formally put the poor
> under the superintendency and patronage of
> the rich. The rich, then, are charged by natural
> providence, as much as by revealed
> appointment, with the care of the poor.

To the landed gentry, God has ordained the division into rich and poor *and* charged the rich with the care of the poor. Such a view was not accepted by the successful and often self-made industrialists. They held that the poor were poor because of a lack of self discipline, hard work and initiative. They saw their own success as a reward for these virtues. It followed that the poor must not be indulged in their indolence – a view which lay beneath that policy of the work-house which

suggested that it should, as one Poor Law Commissioner put it, be as much like prison as possible. The middle-class view of poverty as indicative of *moral* inferiority was an important part of the changed relationship between the dominant stratum and the mass of the population. It provided a convenient justification for the neglect, or even the ill-treatment, of the poor.

The second significant difference in the new situation was that, after about 1815, it became increasingly an urban situation. In the towns the 'exploitation' of the workers was more transparent (if little worse) than that in rural industry and agriculture. And, as Karl Marx pointed out so clearly, the urban situation was one in which the workers became aware of their common situation. It took many decades, however, for the class consciousness of workers to develop fully—that is to say, for them to become aware of their position *and* to develop the organizations by which they could take economic and political action to change it. One reason for this was that it took a long time for solidarity to develop among the workers. The least privileged labourers are confronted as much with the relative prosperity of their more skilled (or more fully employed) fellows as with the riches of the landowners, rulers or factory owners. This is most striking to rural labourers who compare the factory workers' lot with their own. Agricultural labourers in nineteenth-century England might well have agreed with the views of the Sardinian soldiers brought to Turin to deal with strikes.[7]

> 'We have come to put down the gentlefolk
> who are on strike.'
> 'But these are not gentlefolk: they are workers
> and they are poor.'
> 'These chaps are all gentlefolk: they all wear a
> collar and tie and earn 30 lire a day. I know
> the poor folk and what they are dressed like.
> In Sassari they are poor; and we earn 1 lira
> 50 a day.'

For reasons such as these 'the working class' is generally held to be an urban-industrial phenomenon. Rural workers, even when they are wage earners but especially when they are peasants, are, at most, marginal in their membership. Their scattered situation does not easily lend itself to collective organization and action. Their chief significance to the developing class society of nineteenth-century England lay in the fact that they provided a constant stream of new recruits to the towns and thus acted as a depressant on urban wages.

Even in the towns and within industrial employment, however, there had always been very considerable differences in wealth, way of life, and social status. Henry Mayhew, writing in mid-century, describes some of the differences graphically:[8]

> In passing from the skilled operatives of the West End to the unskilled workers of the Eastern quarter of London the moral and intellectual change is so great that it seems as if we were in a new land, and among another race. The artisans are almost to a man red-hot politicians. They are sufficiently educated and thoughtful to have a sense of their importance to the State. The unskilled labourers are a difference class of people. As yet they are as unpolitical as footmen, and instead of entertaining violent democratic opinions, they appear to have no political opinion whatever.

Mayhew draws our attention to significant political differences between skilled and unskilled workers. Elsewhere in his volume he dwells upon the misery, hunger, and squalor of the casual (and often unemployed) worker which contrasts with the relative prosperity and security of the artisan. The social relationships between the groups, too, often read like those between strata. A writer of a decade earlier points out the status distinctions within the craft industry of carriage-making.[9]

> The body-makers are the wealthiest of all and compose among themselves a species of aristocracy to which the other workmen look up with feelings half of respect, half of jealousy. They feel their importance and treat the others with various consideration: carriage-makers are entitled to a species of condescending familiarity; trimmers are considered too good to be despised; a foreman of painters they may treat with respect, but working painters can at most be favoured with a nod.

The awareness of their difference from labourers was also expressed in the artisans' organization in unions. For these craft unions, even in factories, were more a protection for their members against competition from unskilled labour than against exploitation from employers. Yet it was union organization which first enabled manual workers to have some say in politics and, since they alone were unionized, the 'labour aristocracy' played an important part in the growth of the working class. It is the trade unions, gradually extending downwards through the hierarchy of labour, that are the mark of the nascent working class of the nineteenth century. They represent the disciplined organization through which the energies spent on sporadic and often desperate mob violence in the eighteenth and early nineteenth centuries were channelled into concerted action towards clearly defined political and economic goals. It was through the unions that the power latent in the large numbers of manual workers was partially realized through the Reform Bill of 1867. The result was a decade in which more industrial legislation favourable to workers was passed than in the whole of the previous hundred years. Such was the improvement that in 1895 Engels, writing a new preface to his *The Condition of the Working Class in England*, could include factory workers in the 'aristocracy of the working class':[10]

> A permanent improvement can be recognized for two 'protected' sections of the working class. Firstly, the factory hands. The fixing by Act of Parliament of their working day within relatively rational limits has restored their physical constitution and endowed them with a moral superiority, enhanced by their local concentration. They are undoubtedly better off than before 1848. . . . Secondly, the great Trades' Unions. . . . The engineers, the carpenters and joiners, the bricklayers, are each of them a power, to that extent that, as in the case of the bricklayers and bricklayers' labourers, they can even successfully resist the introduction of machinery. That their position has remarkably improved since 1848 there can be no doubt, and the best proof of this is in the fact that for more than fifteen years not only have their employers been with them, but they with their employers, upon exceedingly good terms. They form an aristocracy among the working class; they have succeeded in enforcing for themselves a relatively comfortable position, and they accept it as final.

For the great majority of non-union, unskilled labour, however, the position was very different. Engels continues his comments:[11]

> But as to the great mass of the working people, the state of misery and insecurity in which they live now is as low as ever, if not

lower. The East end of London is an ever spreading pool of stagnant misery and desolation, of starvation when out of work and degradation, physical and moral, when in work.

Lest it should be thought that Engels was exaggerating the position for the sake of political advantage one might point out that he is supported from diverse sources. Religious leaders, such as Archbishop Tait of the Church of England and General William Booth of the Salvation Army reported on the London scene in almost identical terms to those used by Engels. The social scientists, Seebohm Rowntree in York and Charles Booth in London, concluded from their investigations that one-third of the population was living in poverty—that is, they simply did not have sufficient income to feed, clothe and house themselves.

For the 'great mass' of unorganized, unskilled labour there was little permanent gain until their own unionization—the 'New Unionism' as it was called—which was already well under way as Engels was writing in 1895. More significantly, the reaction of the middle class and the government to the New Unionism, and the gradual whittling away of trade-union rights granted in the legislation of the 1870s drew the skilled and unskilled workers together for the first time. Beginning with the dock strike of 1889 there is an increase in anti-union press comment; a growing tendency to employ the police and armed forces in strike-breaking; better organization in recruiting labour described variously as 'free' or 'blackleg' depending on the point of view of the writer; and, above all, a growing flood of judgments against the unions in the law courts. This culminated in the Taff Vale Judgment of 1901 which declared that a union could be held corporately liable for damages arising from the actions of its members. While it was the tactics of the New Unionism (in particular their use of the strike—the only effective weapon of men with no control over the abundant supply of labour) which provoked the reaction, the implications of the judgments were also critical for the older, more conservative skilled unions. Differences were therefore largely buried in the face of the common threat. The result was political action on behalf of *all* working groups—skilled and unskilled—and this led to the increase of direct representation of labour in parliament and to the Trade Disputes Act of 1906.

At the turn of the century, then, English society exhibited the characteristics of a 'class society' more clearly than at any earlier time. That is to say there were substantial differences in wealth and power which had some degree of inter-generational stability and, allied to an awareness of these differences, there were feelings of solidarity promoting economic and political action which reflected class interest and which encompassed the great majority of the population. Finally, the strata were in some real sense social entities, exhibiting different styles of life and feelings of group superiority and/or inferiority. Their members showed great selectivity in limiting significant social interaction on terms of equality to members of their own class. All this is not to say that all differences within the classes had disappeared. Rather that, as T. H. Marshall put it, class provides 'a force that unites into groups people who differ from one another, by over-riding the differences between them'.

Social classes in contemporary industrial societies

There have been a number of changes in the structure of social stratification in twentieth-century industrial societies. Two sets of changes have been especially significant. First, there have been important changes in occupational structure resulting from technological changes and the nature of economic developments. Second, in the years since the second world war, industrial societies have sustained marked increases in overall income which, together with changing patterns of residence, have had a marked effect upon ways of life—especially among manual workers. These economic changes have mingled with political and other social changes, part cause and part effect, so that the industrial world exhibits some marked differences in social stratification as well as some marked similarities.

One of the most substantial changes stemming from technological and economic developments has been a change in the distribution of occupations. One important aspect of this has been a steady expansion, since about the 1880s in Britain and America (a little later elsewhere), of what are usually called 'white collar occupations'. In Britain in 1851 clerks formed rather less than 1 per cent of the labour force; by 1966 they comprised some 13·5 per cent. In the USA the increase has been even more rapid; from 0·6 per cent in 1870 to more than 16·5 per cent in 1969. In twentieth-century Britain, the expansion has been from less than 5 per cent of the total occupied work force in 1911 to 13 per cent in 1961. On the face of it, this is just the type of change, creating a high rate of expansion of non-manual occupations relative to manual ones, which gives rise to upward social mobility. A closer look at the expansion of clerical jobs, however, shows that the proportion of the *male* labour force working at this level has expanded much more modestly—from 5·5 per cent in 1911 to 7 per cent in 1961. More than one-quarter of the *female* working population in 1961 was in the clerical grade. We must therefore be careful how we interpret such statistics. For, while the occupational position of single women has considerable bearing on their class position, the social class of *families* is much more closely related to the occupation of the father than of the mother. This has remained true in industrial societies despite the increase in the number of working wives. The type of work carried out by the wife/mother remains a minor determinant of class position and its main contribution is usually through the generation of additional family income. For this reason Table 10.1 is confined to the occupational distribution of the male population. The changes in percentage distribution between 1911 and 1951 are, on the

Table 10.1 Percentage distribution of the male occupied population of Great Britain 1911–51

	1911	1921	1931	1951
Higher professional	1·3	1·4	1·5	2·6
Lower professional	1·6	2·0	2·0	3·2
Employers and proprietors	7·7	7·7	7·7	5·7
Managers and administrators	3·9	4·3	4·5	6·8
Clerical workers	5·5	5·4	5·5	6·4
Foremen, supervisors and inspectors	1·8	1·9	2·0	3·3
Skilled manual workers	33·0	32·3	30·0	30·4
Semi-skilled manual workers	33·6	28·3	28·9	27·9
Unskilled manual workers	11·6	16·7	17·9	13·8

Source: Guy Routh, *Occupation and Pay in Great Britain, 1906–60*, Cambridge University Press, 1965, table 1, pp. 4–5.

whole, quite small, yet with the male labour force standing at 16 millions, a change of 1 per cent in a category signifies a changed occupational position for some 160,000 families. The changes shown in Table 10.1 which are of greatest rele-

vance to social stratification are a decline in the relative numbers of semi-skilled workers (largely accountable in terms of movement out of agricultural activities which are included in this category) and a steady increase in professional and managerial occupations.

The growth in managerial employment and the decline, since 1931, in the proportion of 'employers and proprietors' is generally indicative of a change in the organization of industry. 'The employers and proprietors' who made up 5·7 per cent of the working population in 1951 consisted almost entirely of small-scale proprietors. Most of them were engaged in trade or services—only one in twenty was concerned with manufacturing or mining. The enterprise owned and run by a single individual or a single family is no longer typical. There has been a proliferation of experts whose expertise is made necessary by the complexities of technological developments, and there has been a continuation of the growth, already well in evidence at the turn of the century, of the joint stock company and of relatively bureaucratic management.

Nearly three-quarters of both British and American companies are corporately owned—some of these with many thousands of shareholders. The growth of the joint stock company has resulted in what is usually called a separation of ownership and control—a process whereby the owners relinquish the day-to-day running of the enterprise which they place in the hands of professional managers. The significance of this change for the nature of the industrialist group lies not so much in the changed outlook of the new rulers of industry (which it is easy to exaggerate) as in the different patterns by which such industrial leaders are recruited. The self-made owner/manager of the early nineteenth century was often a man who had risen from the ranks of master craftsmen or small traders—a man who had, in his working life, significantly altered his social and economic position. He had engaged in a type of social mobility called 'intra-generational' mobility. This type of social mobility was able to continue during the growth of family firms and in the early days of the joint stock company. Frequently the man chosen as manager at whatever level was a man who had proved his abilities in the industrial situation—perhaps as a foreman, perhaps as an office supervisor. Even the giant corporations of the early decades of the twentieth century witnessed some careers of the 'office-boy to managing director' type. Gradually, however, with the increasing specialization of industry, the rise of 'the expert' and the growth of 'scientific management', it has become more difficult to learn the skills of management on the shop-floor and such meteoric careers have become less common. This is not to say, however, that there is necessarily less upward social mobility. New job requirements have produced new patterns of recruitment. Recruitment of 'management trainees' is increasingly recruitment of university graduates or of young people with other formal educational qualifications. Industry has thus undergone a bureaucratization of its recruitment activities. The expansion of education and the gradual opening of the educational system to members of all classes has consequently opened the way for a new type of upward social mobility—one which is achieved through the educational system rather than through promotion on-the-job, and one in which mobility is largely complete (or at least assured) by a relatively early age—say 25–30. The result of these industrial changes has been a decline in intra-generational mobility and an increase in inter-generational mobility. Whereas previously the process of upward mobility often occupied a large part of a man's working life, today, since the main channel of social mobility is the educational system, chances of mobility are very poor after the early twenties. Administrative occupations have an even greater tendency to recruit bureaucratically—that is, on the basis of paper qualifications. Since the great expansion of these positions has taken place this century, this has added to the trend from intra-generational upward mobility to inter-generational upward mobility.

The growth of the joint stock company has also increased the number of 'owners' of industry. Whereas in the heyday of the owner/manager there were few more owners than there were enterprises, there are now hundreds of thousands of persons with some stake in industry. In the USA in 1959, for example, 8 per cent of the population owned stock. In Britain in the middle of the 1960s, the figure was 5 per cent. The majority of such 'owners of industry', however, are small-scale stockholders. In the USA in 1953, the concentration of ownership within the stock-holding group was such that a mere 1 per cent of the population owned three-quarters of the stock. In Britain the concentration was even more extreme—more than 80 per cent of the stocks and shares being held by 1 per cent of the population (1954).

In terms of their control over American industry, a very small group of men (estimated at about 2,500 in 1959) dominate the 200 leading corporations. These 200 in turn, dominate the rest of industry through their corporate ownership of 43 per cent of the assets of the smaller companies. There is considerable identity between this group and the very rich. In Britain, too, there is considerable evidence to suggest that a small group of men exercises disproportionate control over industry, and that this group is one of the wealthiest in the country. In the 1950s there were five companies where the average value of the directors' shares exceeded £100,000, and a company director is still more likely than a member of any other occupational group to hold a substantial number of industrial shares. (Interestingly, the landed aristocracy rank after company directors as the group most likely to hold industrial shares and in the middle 1960s owned some 15 per cent of such shares.)

The change to corporate ownership, then, does not signify any great change in the power-holding group in industry (except that in Britain it provides an illustration of the economic adaptability of the aristocracy) nor even any very significant alteration in the degree of concentration of ownership. Both in terms of ownership and in terms of the exercise of power, a small minority has remained in control. Yet the concentration of wealth is not quite so extreme as the figures relating to ownership of stocks and shares would suggest. While shareholding is perhaps the most significant form of wealth in industrial societies and is largely the prerogative of the wealthy few, other forms of wealth—cash and bank deposits, government securities, land, buildings, and the like—are not quite so unequally distributed. When all such forms of capital are taken into account for Britain in 1960 we find that 42 per cent was owned by 1 per cent of the population and 83 per cent was owned by 10 per cent of the population. (It should be noted, however, that since these figures are compiled from estate duty returns they exclude the smaller holdings and therefore overestimate the concentration of wealth —perhaps by as much as 35–40 per cent.) Table 10.2 shows the distribution of wealth liable for estate duty in Britain for selected years between 1911 and 1960, and indicates that the share of wealth held by the richest 1 per cent has been declining since 1911 when it stood at 69 per cent of the total. The share of the richest 10 per cent, however, has fallen much less sharply—a fall of

Table 10.2 Percentage distribution of wealth in Britain, 1911–60*

	1911–13	1924–30	1936–8	1954	1960
Wealthiest 1 per cent of adult population	69	62	56	43	42
Wealthiest 5 per cent of adult population	87	84	79	71	75
Wealthiest 10 per cent of adult population	92	91	88	79	83

* These figures represent something of an exaggeration of the degree of concentration of wealth since they are compiled from estate duty returns and therefore exclude smaller holdings.

Source: A. B. Atkinson, 'The reform of wealth taxes in Britain', *Political Quarterly*, 42, 1971, p. 46.

Table 10.3 Percentage of United States national personal income (before tax) received by each income-tenth

	1910	1921	1929	1934	1941	1945	1959
Highest 10%	33·9	38·2	39·0	33·6	34·0	29·0	28·9
11–20%	12·3	12·8	12·3	13·1	16·0	16·0	15·8
21–30%	10·2	10·5	9·8	11·0	12·0	13·0	12·7
31–40%	8·8	8·9	9·0	9·4	10·0	11·0	10·7
41–50%	8·0	7·4	7·9	8·2	9·0	9·0	9·2
51–60%	7·0	6·5	6·5	7·3	7·0	7·0	7·8
61–70%	6·0	5·9	5·5	6·2	5·0	6·0	6·3
71–80%	5·5	4·6	4·6	5·3	4·0	5·0	4·6
81–90%	4·9	3·2	3·6	3·8	2·0	3·0	2·9
Lowest 10%	3·4	2·0	1·8	2·1	1·0	1·0	1·1

Source: G. Kolko, *Wealth and Power in America*, London: Thames & Hudson, 1962, table 1, p. 14.

9 per cent in the fifty-year period. Indeed, if one excludes the wealthiest 1 per cent, the share of the remainder of the richest tenth has *risen* from 23 per cent of the total wealth to 41 per cent. This pattern of redistribution of wealth has continued along the same lines during the 1960s. It is a pattern which suggests that the bulk of the redistribution has been from the very rich to the moderately rich. As with the ownership of industrial stock, the concentration is rather less extreme in the USA where in the 1960s the wealthiest 1 per cent of the population owned 24 per cent of the personal capital.

The position between the two countries is very similar with regard to the distribution of income, even though the highest salaries in British industry bear no comparison with those in America. In both countries there has probably been some redistribution of income in the present century, but, as with the redistribution of wealth, this has taken place mainly between the upper and middle levels of the income range. Table 10.3 shows the changes in income distribution in the USA between 1910 and 1959. In his persuasive commentary upon these figures, Kolko argues that taxation makes little difference to the distribution (never more than a 3 per cent reduction in the highest tenth) and suggests that the decline in the share of the richest tenth since 1941 may well be due to an increase in the non-declaration of income (for purposes of tax avoidance) and that the real decline is much less. In addition the highest income group has a variety of 'hidden' incomes. Take, for example, the view of the *Wall Street Journal*:[12]

> Hidden hunting lodges are one of the 'fringe benefits' awaiting officials who succeed in working their way up to the executive suite of a good many US corporations. Other impressive prizes: sharing use of yachts, private planes and railroad cars, jaunts to exotic watering places and spectacular soirees —all paid for by the corporation. . . . In this way, a good many executives whose fortune-building efforts are impaired by today's high taxes still are enjoying the frills enjoyed by the Mellors, Mongers and Baruchs.

Such perks are of particular significance to the study of social stratification because they enable a small group to maintain a style of life whose luxury cuts them off even from the well-to-do middle classes.

In Britain in the financial year 1968–9 there were some 7,000 pre-tax incomes in excess of £20,000 and a further 37,000 between £10,000 and £20,000. In the same year there were more than 10 million incomes below £1,000 and nearly 3 million below £500. The distribution of income in Britain for selected years between 1938 and 1963 is shown in Table 10.4. As in America, the highest income-tenth received about 29 per cent of the total income in 1959 and also in 1963 (the proportion was slightly lower in 1969). And as with the American figures there are doubtless distortions due to the non-declaration of income, and a variety of non-monetary benefits exist which make for further inequalities. The change in

Table 10.4   Percentage of personal income (before tax) in Great Britain received by various percentile groups

Percentile Group	1938	1949	1957	1959	1963
Highest 1%	16·2	11·2	8·2	8·4	7·9
	(11·7)	(6·4)	(5·0)	(5·2)	(5·2)
2–5%	12·8	12·6	10·9	11·5	11·2
	(12·5)	(11·3)	(9·9)	(10·6)	(10·5)
6–10%	9·0	9·4	9·0	9·5	9·6
	(9·5)	(9·4)	(9·1)	(9·4)	(9·5)
11–20%	12·0				
	(12·8)	34·9	37·5	38·4	39·0
20–40%		(37·0)	(38·5)	(39·8)	(39·5)
41–70%	50·0	19·2	23·1	22·5	22·6
	(53·5)	(21·3)	(24·1)	(23·8)	(23·5)
Lowest 30%		12·7	11·3	9·7	9·7
		(14·6)	(13·4)	(11·2)	(11·8)

Figures in brackets refer to incomes after tax.

Source: R. J. Nicholson, 'The distribution of personal income', *Lloyds Bank Reviews*, January 1967, pp. 14 and 16; and H. F. Lydall, 'The long term trend in the size distribution of income', *Journal of the Royal Statistical Society*, 122, 1959, tables 6 and 7, p. 14.

distribution of income observable between 1938 and 1963 is partly due to a number of wider social changes (for example, since in official figures incomes of husband and wife are treated as a single 'income unit', the trend towards earlier marriage and the growing practice whereby wives continue to work after their marriage has inflated the incomes of the lower placed 'income units'). Nevertheless, some redistribution—although rather more modest than that shown in Table 10.4—has taken place in the years since 1938. The major trends shown in Table 10.4 are for the richest 1 per cent *and the poorest 30 per cent* to receive a lower proportion of the personal income. The degree of redistribution of income through taxation can be assessed by comparison with the figures in brackets in Table 10.4 which refer to incomes after tax. For the highest income-tenth in 1963 taxation reduced their proportion of the total income from 28·7 per cent to 25·2 per cent. The lower income groups have a modestly higher proportion of the total income after tax than before tax but had a smaller share of the total post-tax income in 1963 than in 1949.

There is still a considerable concentration of income, wealth and economic power and it is evident that there remains, in both Britain and the USA, a small, powerful and highly privileged minority. In addition to this concentration of economic power the members of this 'new upper class', as it might well be called, are able, to a considerable extent, to pass not only their wealth but also their high occupational position on to their children. These élite groups recruit primarily from amongst their own number. For example, in Britain in 1958, 80 of the 149 directors of large insurance companies had been to the 'top' *five* public schools (46 had been to Eton alone), and 83 of the 166 directors of the Bank of England and the five other leading banks had been to these five schools (50 were Old Etonians).[13] None of the members of these powerful groups had working-class origins.

In terms of political power, however, the undoubtedly great influence of wealth and 'the industrial interest' has been tempered by the exercise of citizenship rights by substantial sections of the population. The gradual growth of the political participation of the working classes has brought Western industrial societies closer to political equality, in the sense that governments have to take some account of their wishes. In some countries, like Britain and Sweden, the development of 'the Welfare State' and the rise to power for substantial periods of Labour governments, which have been sympathetic to certain working-class grievances even if they have not governed in class interests, have significantly changed the condition of life of the majority of the population.

Rather more important in changing styles of life, however, has been the post-second-world-war prosperity enjoyed by industrial societies. In all Western industrial societies real incomes have risen steadily in a quarter of a century of relatively full employment. Thus, although the proportion of the national personal income of the USA received by the poorest tenth of the population has declined, this does not represent an absolute decline in living standards. The extent of poverty is no longer as great as at the time when Rowntree and Booth could conclude that one-third of the population of Britain was in a state of primary poverty. It is clear from Table 10.3 that there has been little change in the distribution of income in the USA in the post-war years of growing affluence. But if the cake is still divided in approximately the same proportions, nevertheless it is a larger cake. Moreover, there have, in these years, been some changes in the relative income of various occupational groups. In particular, the earlier income differential between the lower white collar jobs and the better paid of the manual occupations has been first eroded and then reversed. The emergence of the 'affluent workers' in an age of high mass consumption, allied to changes in industrial organization and patterns of residence, has lessened the sharpness of the differences between working-class life and middle-class life. The traditional pattern of working-class life in close-knit and densely populated communities is no longer typical (and was never universal). The relative political solidarity, forged in the discrimination of the nineteenth century and hardened in the continued poverty of the inter-war years, has given way in Britain to support for a Labour party which has become a moderate party. And the spread in industrial societies of something more nearly akin to equality of educational opportunity has brought about important changes in manual workers' attitudes and aspirations for their children. Such aspirations, even if they are frustrated more often than they are realized, are of considerable significance for relations between the strata. In these and other ways the 'affluent' section of the working class has inherited the mantle of the artisan rather than that of the labourer.

But there are some groups in modern industrial societies that have been by-passed by affluence. In Britain in 1970, two and three-quarter million persons were living below the standard of living at which Supplementary Benefit was given. In 1966, a Ministry of Social Security report concluded that 280,000 families with two or more children fell below the National Assistance standard. In the USA in 1953, 7 per cent of American families incurred medical debts of more than 20 per cent of their annual income. In 1964 the *Annual Report of the Council of Economic Advisers* informed President Johnson that there were 40 million Americans—'one-fifth of the nation'—living in poverty.

Of course, many of the causes of poverty are only indirectly related to social stratification. Old age is perhaps the commonest cause in societies where the basic pension is frequently inadequate and at times even falls below the current scales of Public Assistance. There is also, especially in America, an increasingly large number of families whose head is a woman, and women as a category are low earners. Even in these cases, however, it is old people and women in the working classes who are most likely to fall into poverty. But there are other reasons for poverty which are more directly related to class. Unemployment for instance, is almost entirely a working-class phenomenon, and large families (another factor in poverty) are more

common among the working class. For these people in poverty—even if the poverty is, in absolute terms, less bad than in the nineteenth century—the affluence of the majority is a mockery which makes their position all the harder to bear. Moreover, the chance of them *or their children* escaping from their position is slight.

Social stratification and communism: the case of the USSR

The industrialization of the Western world brought about the rise of the class society and, despite significant changes, the stratification systems of the industrial West still have a basically class character. Political and social power, as well as economic power, continue to be based to a considerable extent upon wealth and economic position. Nor is economic position, in terms of occupation, in any way irrelevant in the stratification systems of communist countries. Here, too, different occupational groups have differential access to power and command different incomes and social esteem. The children of members of these groups have differential opportunities to make good in life. Yet a closer control is exercised by the political authorities over these economic forces than in the Western world. This, together with the fact that the political leadership is committed to a socialist ideology, has had an important effect upon the precise forms social stratification has taken and is taking. The other major factor which has influenced the development of social stratification, in the Soviet Union especially, has been the remarkably rapid industrialization during the half century since the revolution (particularly during the Stalin era).

Industrialization inevitably involves dramatic changes in the occupational structure, whatever the political regime under which it occurs. In the USSR the rapid growth (especially after 1928) in numbers of factory workers, engineers, scientists, administrators and white collar workers transformed a largely agrarian society, which was still in a relatively early stage of industrialization, into a highly differentiated industrial society (albeit one which still has a large rural sector). During the first two five-year plans (1928–37) the number working in industry multiplied by more than two and a half times. Yet the expansion was greatest in the most highly skilled occupations. For example, in the same period, the number of managers increased by four and a half times, the number of scientists by six times, and the number of engineers by nearly eight times. Such rapid occupational changes involved a substantial number of people in moving from one job to another and provided a wider spectrum of occupational opportunities. Peasants migrated to the towns and became industrial workers. Factory workers were promoted to the expanding ranks of supervisors and some, especially during the first five-year plan when political reliability was a major qualification for high office in industry, were promoted to the level of factory management. The nature of this social mobility, and perhaps also its degree, was somewhat similar to that which occurred in nineteenth-century England when a similar industrial expansion was taking place (although rather less rapidly), and may be viewed as an adjunct to such industrialization. The more than proportionate expansion of relatively high status occupations necessitates considerable upward mobility. Typically, mobility at this stage is intra-generational. Writing of the same phenomenon in the early (and rapid) stages of industrialization in Poland, a Polish sociologist states: 'The family no longer plays the traditional role as the elementary unit of social class: at the birthday table in a peasant's house an engineer and a miner, a junior or senior executive and an army officer, a peasant and a physician sit together.'[14] It is easy, however, to exaggerate the amount of social mobility in a society simply because those who are upwardly mobile are so noticeable. Doubtless the situation described is as rare in communist societies as in capitalist ones. In the Soviet case there were also exceptional factors which influenced social mobility and thus stratification. In the first place, the huge losses of the second world war created a chronic manpower shortage throughout industry which facilitated upward mobility during and after the war. Second, the frequent purges of the Stalin era created many vacancies in political circles, often at high levels. As a result, these circles were unusually open to members of the lower levels of the bureaucracy and army. This aspect of mobility in the Soviet Union at that time bears a closer resemblance to the non-industrial absolutist states discussed earlier in the chapter than to other industrial societies.

The close control of the political leaders over the distribution of economic and political power has resulted in a uniquely uneven development. Initially, after the revolution, there were attempts to establish the 'dictatorship of the proletariat' and to raise the position of the manual workers.

Deliberate discrimination in favour of industrial workers, peasants and 'employees' in such crucial things as the allocation of ration cards and housing led to a sharply stratified society in which the old order of privilege was reversed. Those who had previously occupied positions of high status were made to suffer the indignities of the poor and the powerless. Furthermore, until 1930 only workers were admitted to membership of the party—the chief organ of political power. The political direction of revolutionary leaders is apparent in all these changes.

The subsequent periodic shifts in policy relating to income differences and party membership have emphasized the continued significance of central direction in these important spheres. Soviet history in this respect is remarkable chiefly for its oscillations. The period of 'war communism', with its drive towards economic equality and the political primacy of the workers, was followed in 1923 by the 'new economic policy' under which wage differentials were widened, private peasant agriculture was reinstated (allowing the reappearance of the Kulak or wealthy peasant), and the factories were largely managed by their former owners. The beginning of planned industrialization in 1928, however, brought a renewal of the revolutionary spirit. Many of those who had managed to retain or recover high position during the previous ten years were dismissed. A few lost their lives. The Kulaks were liquidated, and manual workers received preferential treatment in appointment to managerial positions and in selection for educational institutions. Stalin's speech of 1931 in which he condemned 'equality mongering' heralded another change with its contention that the workers' state needed its own intelligentsia. Income differentials were increased in favour of non-manual workers, party membership increasingly became dominated by the intelligentsia, and education became substantially the preserve of the wealthy through the re-introduction of tuition fees. Stalin defended the material aspects of these measures in the following terms:[15]

The kind of Socialism under which everybody would get the same pay, an equal quantity of meat and an equal quantity of bread, would wear the same clothes and receive the same goods in the same quantities—such socialism is unknown to Marxism. . . . Equalitarianism has nothing in common with Marxist socialism.

The political and educational aspects of the policy, which ostensibly accord so ill with the objectives of the revolution, may be explained in terms of Stalin's need, in a time of rapid industrialization, for an industrial élite which was loyal, efficient, and well motivated. At the same time, the existence of this stratum provided the political leaders with some insulation from the mass of the industrial and agricultural workers upon whom the burdens of heavy investment in capital industries, with its consequent low consumption, fell most heavily. The political danger to the rulers of such a policy, however, lay in the increasing autonomy, and thus the potential opposition, of the élite group. The post-Stalin attempts at renewed social and economic levelling were in part a curb on a group that was beginning to acquire a basis for power independent of the party. Particularly important were Kruschev's attack on the high-handedness of managers and administrators, the drive to recruit workers and peasants to the party, the introduction of higher wages for the lowest paid groups (and a decrease in pay for some of the highly paid), and the abolition of tuition fees. In education, moreover, there was an attempt to give children from 'disadvantaged homes' preferential admission into some educational institutions. Total equality, however, was no more a part of Kruschev's policy than it was of Stalin's. As he told the Twenty First Party Congress: 'Under Socialism inequality of classes is excluded.[16] There remains only the inequality of the share one receives in the distribution of the products.[17]'

Table 10.5 Average (mean) monthly wages in roubles of three categories of occupations

	1940	1950	1960	1966
Manual workers	32·3	68·7	89·9	104·4
Engineering and technical workers	68·9	120·8	133·0	150·1
White collar workers	35·8	63·6	73·2	88·2

Source: David Lane, *Politics and Society in the USSR*, London: Weidenfeld & Nicolson, 1970, p. 402.

Table 10.5 shows the average monthly wages for various occupational categories in selected years between 1940 and 1966. Rather than any radical equalization of incomes, the *relative* incomes of the main occupational categories have remained more or less constant. The only significant change has been some gain by manual workers relative to white collar workers. It should be noted, however,

that a similar change has occurred in the industrial West where there is no ideology of the superiority of manual work. Income figures, however, have a rather different significance than in the Western world and do not give an entirely satisfactory picture of inequality in the USSR. Because of the shortage of consumption goods, scarce resources are more likely to be allocated by the party than sold on the open market. In such cases the political control over the distribution of consumption goods is clearly apparent.

The frequency of these changes in policy, and the resultant variations in group incomes further illustrate the relative ease with which economic factors can, in the Soviet Union, be manipulated by those in political power. The variations in the access of different occupational groups to the party—the main channel for the exercise of political power—are therefore crucial and they, too, illustrate the political dominance of the ruling élite. The members of the élite have been able to maintain their own power, and, at the same time, through their control over party membership and party offices, they have determined who shall occupy the middle and lower levels of political power.

This highlights the main difference in the stratification systems of East and West. Yet there are also striking similarities. In the USSR, as in the West, industrialization has been associated with bureaucratization. One important aspect of this is the close link between occupational placement and possession of educational qualifications. Where this is the case, and where income, status and, to a large extent, political power depend upon occupation, educational opportunity becomes crucial in determining the degree of rigidity of the stratification system. Herein lies the significance of the educational policies discussed earlier. Such meagre evidence as is available suggests that access to higher education (and thus to desirable occupations) is perhaps slightly more open to the children of manual workers in the USSR than in Western industrial countries (with the possible exception of the USA). One of the reasons for this is the greater and more systematic provision in the Soviet Union of facilities for part-time higher education. On the other hand, the serious and universal underprivilege of rural workers in this respect is more significant in the USSR since they make up a much larger proportion of the working population.

The success of the political leadership in shaping ideas on social status, however, appears to be more limited. The ideology of communism concerning the value of industrial manual work has had some effect, at least to the extent that, in all communist countries for which we have information, such occupations are more highly regarded than in the Western world. But this is also partly due to the ready comparison with the much larger agricultural sector which is characterized by largely unskilled and unmechanized work for relatively poor economic rewards. There is some indirect evidence to suggest that a good deal of the old prestige order of occupations has remained. For example, the frequent exhortations from party officials concerning the value of manual work and the mobility of physical labour, not to mention the castigations of those who 'desert' the ranks of the workers for the pleasures of life in the intelligentsia, testify at least as much to the popular retention of the old 'bourgeois' scale of values as to the determination of the political leadership to wipe them out. It is clear too that there is considerable motivation to undertake higher education and it is reasonable to assume that this is not unconnected with the desirability of the non-manual occupations to which such education leads. There is also some evidence of a non-scientific kind (especially in the writings of recent Soviet novelists) of the existence of fairly widespread status distinctions. Take, for example, a passage in Solzhenitsyn's *Cancer Ward* on the question of 'suitable' marriage partners.[18]

> He was such a naive boy, he might be led up the garden path by some ordinary weaver girl from the textile factory. Well, perhaps not a weaver, there'd be nowhere for them to meet, they wouldn't frequent the same places. . . .

Look at Shendyapin's daughter, how she'd very nearly married a student in her year at teachers' training college. He was only a boy from the country and his mother was an ordinary collective farmer. Just imagine the Shendyapin's flat, their furniture and the influential people they had as guests and suddenly there's this old woman in a white headscarf sitting at their table, their daughter's mother-in-law. . . . Thank goodness they'd managed to discredit the family politically and save their daughter.

The probability is that such feelings of social superiority (and reciprocal inferiority?) cannot be discounted, even after more than fifty years of communist party rule. The order of precedence of occupational groups may vary in detail from those of other industrial societies, but this cannot be determined as long as social scientists work only within an official ideology which ignores all such status distinctions.

In Soviety society, then, social stratification does not rest primarily on an economic basis. Rather, as in pre-industrial societies, it rests upon a monopoly of political power and the legitimate use of force—on control of the state apparatus. While the political leaders have not been entirely successful in controlling the status dimension of stratification, they have been able to control access to major and minor positions of economic and political power. Changing patterns of privilege during the Soviet era represent the manipulations of the political leaders in their (successful) attempt to prevent any other group from achieving a position of independence, cohesion and self-consciousness.

Notes

1 Elizabeth Marshall Thomas, *The Harmless People*, Harmondsworth: Penguin, pp. 179–80.

2 Peter Farb, *Man's Rise to Civilization*, London: Secker & Warburg, 1969, p. 43.

3 M. Sahlins, *Social Stratification in Polynesia*, Seattle: University of Washington Press, 1958, pp. 20–1.

4 See F. R. Cowell, *Cicero and the Roman Republic*, Harmondsworth: Penguin, 1956, p. 293.

5 Quoted in S. G. Checkland, *The Rise of Industrial Society in England, 1815–1885*, London: Longmans, 1964, p. 284.

6 Quoted in Asa Briggs, 'Middle class consciousness in English politics, 1780–1846', *Past and Present*, 9, 1956.

7 Quoted in E. J. Hobsbawm, *Labouring Men*, London: Weidenfeld & Nicolson, 1964, p. 302.

8 Henry Mayhew, *London Labour and the London Poor*, London: Griffin, Bohn, 1861–2, vol. III, p. 243.

9 W. B. Adams, *English Pleasure Carriages* (1837), quoted in E. J. Hobsbawm, 'Custom, wages and work-load in nineteenth century industry', in A. Briggs and J. Saville (eds), *Essays in Labour History*, London: Macmillan, 1960, p. 116.

10 F. Engels, *The Condition of the Working Class in England*, London: Panther, 1969, p. 31.

11 Ibid., p. 31.

12 *Wall Street Journal*, 18 March 1958, quoted in G. Kolko, *Wealth and Power in America*, London: Thames & Hudson, 1962, p. 18.

13 See W. L. Guttsman, *The British Political Elite*, London: MacGibbon & Kee, 1963, table III, p. 336.

14 Z. Bauman, 'Economic growth, social structure, élite formation: the case of Poland', in R. Bendix and S. M. Lipset (eds), *Class Status & Power*, London: Routledge & Kegan Paul, 1967, p. 537.

15 J. V. Stalin, Talk with Emil Ludwig, *Collected Works*, London: Lawrence & Wishart, 1952, vol. 13, pp. 120–21.

16 To Soviet politicans and officials (and social scientists) classes are defined in strict Marxist terms—that is, in terms of ownership. According to the Soviet view, therefore, there are only two classes in the USSR: the workers and the collective farmers. Collective farmers are conceptualized as a separate class because they own their seed and the produce of their labour. Included in the official category of workers are the 9 million agricultural workers on State farms, the 7 million forestry workers and the 'intelligentsia' (comprising white collar workers, scientists, politicians, and other 'mental' workers). This categorization bears little relationship to the ways of life, standards of living, or life chances of the Soviet people, but it is necessary to understand it if one is to make any sense out of Soviet statistics or official pronouncements.

17 N. Kruschev, speech to Twenty First Party Congress, quoted in A. Brodersen, *The Soviet Worker*, New York: Random House, 1966, p. 171.

18 A. Solzhenitsyn, *Cancer Ward*, quoted in David Lane, *Politics and Society in the USSR*, London: Weidenfeld & Nicolson, 1970, p. 410.

Reading

Beteille, A. (ed.), *Social Inequality*, Harmondsworth: Penguin, 1969. Extracts from eighteen sources on social stratification in simple societies, agrarian societies and industrial societies.

Bottomore, T., *Social Classes*, London: Allen & Unwin, 1965. A brief and clearly written introduction.

Domhoff, G. W., *Who Rules America?*, Englewood Cliffs: Prentice-Hall, 1967. An analysis of the distribution of economic and political power in the modern USA.

Lockwood, D., *The Blackcoated Worker*, London: Allen & Unwin, 1958. An excellent study of the social position of clerks in Britain, with special reference to problems of class consciousness.

Macquet, J. J., *Power and Society in Africa*, London: Weidenfeld & Nicolson, 1971. The middle chapters deal with social stratification in traditional Africa, with special (but not exclusive) reference to Rwanda. There is also some discussion of modern Africa.

Perkin, H., *The Origins of English Society, 1780–1880*, London: Routledge & Kegan Paul, 1969. A book by a social historian on industrialization in England, paying particular attention to the development and growing importance of social classes.

Zinkin, T., *Caste Today*, London: Oxford University Press, 1962. A brief discussion of the nature of caste as it was in traditional India and of some recent changes. Clearly and simply written.

Further reading

Bendix, R. and Lipset, S. M. (eds), *Class Status & Power*, New York: Free Press, 1966 and London: Routledge & Kegan Paul, 1967. This edition is the largest and most comprehensive collection of both theoretical and empirical articles.

Cowell, F. R., *Cicero and the Roman Republic*, Harmondsworth: Penguin, 1956. A general discussion of the Roman republic by an historian which contains a good deal of material relevant to questions of stratification.

Goldthorpe, J. *et al.*, *The Affluent Worker in the Class Structure*, Cambridge University Press, 1969. An analysis of changes in the patterns of life among wealthier sections of the working classes in Britain in the 1960s, including a demolition of the thesis that such workers are 'becoming middle class'.

Lane, David, *The End of Inequality? Stratification Under State Socialism*, Harmondsworth: Penguin, 1971. A brief and useful discussion of the 'official' communist views on stratification and of the evidence relating to stratification in Soviet Russia and Eastern Europe.

Lenski, G., *Power and Privilege*, New York: McGraw-Hill, 1966. A mammoth comparative study of the distribution of wealth and power in different types of societies. Full of examples.

Miller, S. M., 'Comparative social mobility', *Current Sociology*, 9, 1960. A 'trend report' and bibliography which provides not only invaluable comparative information on social mobility but also a sophisticated conceptual discussion of social mobility.

Tuden, A. and Plotnicov, L. (eds), *Social Stratification in Africa*, New York: Free Press, 1970. Fourteen articles on social stratification in traditional societies of Africa.

11 Race relations

Relations between 'racial' groups pose some of the most urgent and intractable problems in the world today. The United States, South Africa, Rhodesia, Uganda, and many other countries are currently facing serious, often mounting, racial tension. Brazil appears to be one of the few racially heterogeneous societies which *may* be avoiding severe problems of this sort. Not so long ago, it was widely thought that Britain was immune to them. Now, with the relatively large-scale influx of West Indians, Indians, Pakistanis, and East African Asians, problems of racial tension have become one of the central political issues in British society.

A constitutive feature of 'race relations situations' is the fact that members of the groups involved tend to adhere strongly to exaggerated, often erroneous, beliefs about the biological, behavioural and social differences between the groups. They also tend to perceive such differences as inherited genetically. The findings of modern science, however, suggest strongly that behavioural and social differences between human groups—for example, in intelligence, temperament and customs—are *learned*. The only differences which are *known* to be transmitted genetically are differences in physical characteristics such as skin colour, eye colour, hair form, lip and nose shape. It follows that 'racist' beliefs and the patterns of social relations to which they correspond have to be explained in sociological terms.

In many ways, racial groups are types of social strata, that is, groups with differing access to wealth, status and political power. There are, however, two main differences between racial and other forms of social stratification: first, beliefs about the genetic inheritance of group characteristics tend to be stronger and more deeply entrenched in the racial forms of stratification, though, of course, they are not entirely absent in the 'non-racial' forms; second, physical traits such as skin colour, lip and nose shape, because they are transmitted genetically and unalterable by the individual, can serve as marks of more or less permanent inequality and give a 'caste-like' rigidity to a society in which they are stressed. Movement out of a racial group is much more difficult because the marks of membership are so much clearer.

The emergence of 'white domination'

The most serious problems of race relations in the modern world have arisen in relations between 'white' and 'coloured' peoples, not because of any biologically inherited qualities of these groups, but simply because it was members of 'white' European countries who achieved world dominance and the possibility of subordinating other races. The social development of Western Europe, even as early as the Renaissance, made available means of transport (especially efficient sailing ships), scientific knowledge (for example, the knowledge that the world is round), and technical inventions (such as the lodestone and the sextant), which facilitated the exploration and circumnavigation of the earth. Growing economic surpluses enabled voyages of exploration to be financed and military developments, such as the invention of firearms, enabled Europeans to control and dominate newly discovered territories and peoples. In its turn, colonial expansion increased the wealth and power of European societies and, in some, proved to be a key factor in their further development. In the case of Britain, the first country to industrialize, there is reason to believe that the gradual development of the modern urban-industrial-nation-state was heavily dependent on extensive colonization. Subsequently, industrialization made possible further colonization and a more effective domination of colonial peoples. Contemporary problems of relations between white and coloured peoples have developed from the relations between racial groups established through colonization and industrialization. These processes, therefore, form an essential starting point for an understanding of modern race relations.

Some of the territories over which Europeans gained control were already heavily populated and many of these provided markets which were crucial to England's early industrialization. Others, for example in the West Indies and the Americas, were only sparsely populated. In these territories, Europeans who wished to extract minerals, or produce and sell tropical crops such as sugar, tobacco and cotton, were faced with an acute labour shortage. At first they forcibly recruited natives. Before long, however, the native inhabitants of the West Indies had been practically wiped out—partly as a result of the conditions under which they were forced to work, partly through the ravages of diseases brought by the Europeans. The Amerindian populations of Central and South America fared little better. The difficulties faced by the Spanish and Portuguese, the first to establish colonies in the 'New World', were further increased by Jesuit opposition to the enslavement of the people they had come to convert to Christianity. In this, the Jesuits were supported by the Spanish and Portuguese kings. Similar objections, however, were not raised, at least on a significant scale, to the importation of Africans as slaves. As is well known, it was these negro slaves who came to provide the bulk of the labour force, not only for the Spanish and Portuguese, but also for the other European colonies in the New World. At first, slave labour was supplemented by convict labour and by the labour of poor, white, indentured servants (often working out a service contract in return for their passage to the New World). Such men, however, often had aspirations to independence that made them bad plantation workers. Negro slaves were more amenable to the discipline and rigid control of the plantations,

partly because their capture and transportation had disrupted their lives and social organization to such an extent that they found it difficult to organize effective resistance. Above all, negro slaves provided a cheaper labour force. A planter could buy a negro for life with the money that would secure a white man's services for only ten years. As a Governor of Barbados put it, the planters on that island soon discovered that 'three blacks work better and cheaper than one white man'.

For three and a half centuries, beginning in the middle of the sixteenth century, the Atlantic slave trade supplied the labour force for the plantations of the West Indies and the Americas. Some 15 million Africans arrived at their destination. Many more died or committed suicide on the march to the sea and during the 'middle passage'. In the eighteenth century, Britain emerged as the dominant colonial power and the slave trade came to form part of the extremely lucrative 'triangular trade'. This involved the purchase of negroes in Africa with British manufactures, their transportation and sale to the colonial plantations where they produced sugar, tobacco and cotton for shipment to Britain where, in turn, new industries grew up to process the raw materials. The slave trade played an important part in the development of several British ports (between 1783 and 1793 Liverpool alone put 878 ships into the slave trade and Liverpool merchants received a net income of more than £2,300,000 solely from this trade). 'The profits obtained', wrote Eric Williams, 'provided one of the mainstreams of that accumulation of capital in England which financed the Industrial revolution.'[1] However, the importance of slavery for the beginnings of industrialization lay more in the fact that it was the slave plantations which furnished the raw material on which the Lancashire cotton industry was built. It is significant that this industry became established in the hinterlands of Liverpool —the greatest of the slave trading ports. At first, its raw material was principally provided by the slave plantations of the West Indies but after 1790 a virtually unlimited source of supply was provided by the slave plantations of the Southern United States which became, in part, an economic dependency of Lancashire. In this manner, the most advanced centre of production in the world at that time helped to preserve and extend plantation slavery in the American South.

White domination and planter society in the American South

Some of the harshest and most exploitative forms of dominance over a subject group even known developed on the slave plantations of the American South and in the 'planter society' that emerged with them. American negroes have still not fully succeeded in overcoming the effects of plantation slavery on their culture, personality and institutions. To understand contemporary race relations in the USA it is therefore necessary to look first of all at social relations in the Old South.

Most of the slaves in the South at the height of the 'Cotton Kingdom'—there were nearly four million in 1860—were owned by a rich 'planter aristocracy'. This class dominated Southern society through their ownership of property (land and slaves), through their control of politics and state governments, and by serving as a 'model' for small owners and poor whites (non-slaveowners who constituted three-quarters of the one and a half million free families in the *ante-bellum* South). The large plantations were usually characterized by a simple division of labour between household slaves and field slaves, the latter subject to control by a white overseer. Since the slaves had little or no incentive to work, force often had to be employed. Frequent whippings, use of the stocks, and imprisonment in the plantation jail were common. Runaways were hunted with dogs and, when caught, they were clapped in irons, branded with their master's mark and even castrated. As an Arkansas planter expressed it in 1860:[2]

> Now, I speak what I know, when I say it is like casting pearls before swine to try to *persuade* a negro to work. He must be *made* to work, and should always be given to understand that if he fails to perform his duty he will be punished for it.

The master had virtually absolute power over his slaves and this power was supported by law. Writing in 1856, George M. Stroud, an abolitionist, condensed the legal nature of the master–slave relationship into the following twelve propositions:[3]

1. The master may determine the kind and degree, and time of labour to which the slave shall be subjected.
2. The master may supply the slave with such food and clothing only, both as to quantity and quality, as he may think proper or find convenient.
3. The master may, at his discretion, inflict any punishment on the person of his slave.
4. All the power of the master over his slave may be exercised not only by himself in person, but by anyone whom he may depute as his agent.
5. Slaves have no legal rights of property in things, real or personal; but whatever they may acquire belongs, in point of law, to their masters.
6. The slave, being a *personal chattel*, is at all times liable to be sold absolutely, or mortgaged or leased, at the will of his master.
7. He may also be sold by process of law for the satisfaction of the debts of a living, or the debts and bequests of a deceased master, at the suit of creditors or legatees.
8. A slave cannot be a party before a judicial tribunal, in any species of action against his master, no matter how atrocious may have been the injury received from him.
9. Slaves cannot redeem themselves, nor obtain a change of masters, though cruel treatment may have rendered such change necessary for their personal safety.
10. Slaves being objects of *property*, if injured by third persons, their owners may bring suit, and recover damages for the injury
11. Slaves can make no contract.
12. Slavery is hereditary and perpetual.

The slave stood at the mercy of the master's whims. The only effective restraint lay in the economic interests of the master. It is recorded that on one occasion, on a plantation in Mississippi, a slave attacked an overseer and almost killed him, yet went unpunished. Had the master executed the slave for this 'crime' he would have lost a valuable 'piece of property' in which he had invested a considerable sum of money.

According to a Georgia slaveowner writing in 1854, punishment did not make the negro revengeful but tended 'to win his attachment and promote his happiness and well-being'.[4] Although this sounds rather far-fetched, it may have contained a grain of truth. It is not uncommon for people under conditions of harsh oppression to identify with their oppressors and even, in a way, to 'love' as well as to hate them. If, from birth, their independence is systematically crushed, they have no models to identify with other than that of the masters. In this way, many slaves tended to see white culture as superior, to regard the (white) law as right and to believe in the legitimacy of their masters' rule and power to punish.

A central corollary of the near absolute power of the master was the almost total and permanent dependence of the slave. 'The negro', wrote John Pendleton Kennedy in 1832, is 'a dependent on the white race; dependent for guidance and direction even to the procurement of his most indispensable necessaries. Apart from this protection he has the helplessness of a child—without foresight, without faculty of contrivance, without thrift of any kind.'[5] 'I love the simple and unadulterated slave', wrote Edward Pollard in 1859, 'with his geniality, his mirth, his swagger and his nonsense. ... The Negro, in his true nature, is always a boy, let him be ever so old.'[6] The stereotype of negroes expressed in these statements was, no doubt, an ideology which facilitated their exploitation. Such statements were written, at a time when the system was under severe attack, in order to justify slavery and to 'prove' that negroes could not be awarded independence. But they probably had some basis in reality as well. The slave had few opportunities to develop the personality traits and modes of behaviour thought appropriate by adult Southern whites. Like a child, he had only limited possibilities for initiating independent action. Unlike a child, his dependence was total, permanent and maintained by powerful sanctions. From the slave's point of view, moreover, the plantation was a closed system, a kind of 'total institution' in which virtually the whole of his life was encapsulated. He was hardly able to broaden his experience by contact with the outside world and by exposure to models different from those of his master.

Statements of the kind made by Kennedy and Pollard also suggest that identification between masters and slaves was a two-way process, that masters often grew fond of their slaves—provided, of course, that they kept to their 'proper' place. But just as the slaves' feelings for their masters tended towards ambivalence so, reciprocally, did those of the masters for their slaves. Affection probably mingled with guilt over treating human beings as property and the whole relationship was overlaid with a more or less constant fear of slave uprisings. That there were so few of these may well have had something to do with the ambivalent nature of the master–slave relationship, comprising, as it did on both sides, elements of affection as well as hate, identification as well as rejection.

The abolition of slavery and the emergence of 'colour caste'

Just as England's industrialization was crucial in the development of American slavery, so the development of industrial capitalism in the United States was instrumental in changing the pattern of relations between black and white. For the increasingly powerful industrial capitalists of the North East, and the dependent, increasingly market-oriented farmers of the Middle West, had interests which conflicted strongly with those of the 'planter-aristocrats' who were dominant in the Southern states. The differences were rooted in the two differing socio-economic systems and at first took the form of a struggle to control the federal government. Later the conflict led to the attempted secession of the South and so, in 1861, to the civil war which resulted in the abolition of slavery. Slavery formed a focus of the conflict largely because it marked a crucial difference in the *economic* structures of North and South. The South wanted to expand the plantation system into the new Western states, partly because of the profitable ventures that those regions promised and partly because their methods of agriculture tended to impoverish the soil. The North wanted to encourage the growth of independent farming in the West, partly because this would expand the market for Northern products. Moral revulsion against slavery, and sympathy for negroes, also played a part in the growing movement for abolition, but *anti*-negro prejudice was a more decisive factor. As early as 1835, Alexis de Tocqueville noticed that 'the prejudice of race appears to be stronger in the states that have abolished slavery than in those where it still exists; and nowhere is it so intolerant as in those states where servitude has never been known.'[7] In 1856, in a referendum conducted in Kansas—it was boycotted by those in favour of slavery and therefore |confined to anti-slavery groups—1,287 voted to exclude negroes from the territory and only 453 voted against the proposition. One of the chief arguments used against slavery, there as elsewhere, was that it would eventually produce a free negro population.

The North was more interested in preserving the union than in abolishing slavery and tried, to the last—although unsuccessfully—to effect a compromise with the South. Civil war broke out and, two years later, abolition was declared by federal decree. Even though they lost the war, the Southern states continued to regard negroes as a form of property—a fact attested by the 'Black Codes' in which most of the restrictions on the behaviour of slaves, and the punishments for breaches of these restrictions, were re-enacted with reference to free negroes. Even the First Reconstruction Act (1867), which placed the South under military rule in an attempt to guarantee negroes the right to vote, was ineffective. This was partly because of the vehemence of Southern opposition, and partly because of the unwillingness of the federal government and the Northern industrialists to spend the considerable sums of money needed to make the Act effective.

Moreover, the majority of negroes at that time were, by themselves, incapable of solving the problems which they faced. They were very poor and had to devote most of their energies simply to keeping alive. Slavery had kept them dependent upon whites and emancipation led to widespread demoralization and aimlessness among them. Such a condition was not conducive to the formation of the well-organized, politically conscious groups which alone could effectively have challenged the dominance of the whites. So slavery was replaced by a system of domination in which negroes, although nominally free, continued to be controlled and exploited by whites. On the economic level this took the form of 'sharecropping' and similar forms of 'debt peonage' whereby the propertyless negro was given a tract of land for growing cotton in return for a fixed proportion—usually a half and sometimes as much as three-quarters—of the crop. The landlord, however, marketed even the tenant's share and the latter had no means of ensuring that he received a fair price. The poverty of the tenants continually placed them in debt to the landlords for seed, tools, clothing and food, and for most of the year they were forced to live on credit at a high rate of interest. In these and other ways the landlords were guaranteed a more or less permanent supply of cheap labour.

Yet it was not only negroes who were placed in this position. The concentration of the best land in the hands of the wealthy few also forced more and more poor whites to become sharecroppers, and for a time, during the 1880s and 1890s, a united movement of the poor of both races seemed a possibility. A political movement known as 'Populism' arose and appealed for such a

united front. In the words of Tom Watson, who was one of its leaders, speaking in Georgia in 1892:[8]

> ... the People's Party says to these two men, 'You are kept apart that you may be separately fleeced of your earnings. You are made to hate each other because upon that hatred is rested the keystone of the arch of financial despotism which enslaves you both. You are deceived and blinded that you may not see how this racial antagonism perpetuates a monetary system which beggars you both'.

But the legacy of dependence on the planter-aristocracy made negroes poor political partners. They were prey to political manipulation by the dominant planter class and the Populists turned against them. The majority of poor whites retained the racism from which they derived considerable social satisfaction. For, even though they were poor and stood at the bottom of the *white* social hierarchy, they were not at the bottom of the *Southern* social order. It was to protect this position from 'negro domination'—about which they developed unrealistic, exaggerated fears—and from the economic competition of negroes, that they formed a number of secret societies such as the Ku Klux Klan which terrorized negroes into acceptance of their subordinate position. In their campaign against negroes, the poor whites received support from most sections of the white population. A variety of devices were used to circumvent the fifteenth amendment to the Constitution (which, in 1870, had established that 'The rights of citizens of the United States to vote shall not be denied or abridged by the United States or any State on account of race, colour or previous condition of servitude') and these virtually disenfranchised the negro once again. In Louisiana, for example, there were in 1896, 130,334 registered negro voters; by 1904 there were only 1,342.

In 1890, an act was passed, also in Louisiana, legalizing the segregation of railway carriages. It was declared constitutional by the Federal Supreme Court in 1896 in the case of *Plessy* v. *Ferguson*. This was a crucial decision upholding the provisions of the Southern constitutions whereby transport, residential areas, schools and shops were increasingly segregated. Such segregation secured important gains for whites. For the white upper classes, it helped to remove the threat of a racially united working class. For the poor whites, it buttressed their feelings of superiority and secured important gains in fields such as education, for state funds were systematically diverted to 'white' schools with a resultant improvement in the education, and thus the life chances, of white children.

'Segregation', however, never meant a cessation of all contact between the races—this would have made economic and other forms of exploitation impossible—but rather that contact should take place within a context of ritual which emphasized the subordinate position of the negro. As under the old slave regime, negroes were expected to address a white person as 'Mr', 'Mrs', or 'Miss' or by a title such as 'Cap'n' or 'Judge'. In return, he would be addressed as 'boy' or 'uncle' or by his first name. A negro was not allowed to contradict a white and was expected to give way to him on the street. If he addressed a white man in 'proper' English, this was regarded as an insult, as tantamount to a claim to equality. Breaches in such rules of inter-racial etiquette were swiftly and severely punished and negroes as a group were insufficiently powerful and too insecure and dependent to resist the pressures of white domination. They continued, by and large, to accept the white man's notion of negro inferiority. In these and other ways, the abolition of slavery resulted in a rigid, caste-like system of white domination and not in the emergence of racial equality.

The urbanization of American negroes

As the nineteenth century drew to a close, the position of the United States as the world's chief producer of cotton began to be challenged, particularly by Egypt and China. Prices started to fall, a trend which was reinforced as artificial fibres came increasingly into use in textile manufacture. The response of the Southern states was twofold; they attempted firstly to diversify their economy by embarking on a process of industrialization and secondly to cut labour costs by mechanizing the growing of cotton. Negroes began to be pushed into towns (in the North and West as well as in the South) as a result of declining employment opportunities in rural areas and were simultaneously attracted to them by the growing demand for factory labour. In the course of this process of urbanization, negroes began to be transformed from a regional peasant group into a segment of the national urban working class.

The pattern of negro migration to the towns between 1900 and 1950 is shown in Table 11.1.

As this table shows, in 1900, 90 per cent of the American negro population lived in the South. By 1950, this figure had fallen to 68 per cent. Ten

Table 11.1 Distribution of the US negro population by region and urban-rural residence, 1900–50 (per cent)

	1900	*1920*	*1940*	*1950*[1]
South[2]	90	85	77	68
Rural	74	64	49	35
Urban	16	21	28	33
Other regions	10	15	23	32
Rural	3	2	2	2
Urban	7	13	21	30
Total rural	77	66	51	37
Total urban	23	34	49	63

[1]Because of a change in the census definition of 'urban' between 1940 and 1950, these figures are not exactly comparable with earlier data.
[2]Alabama, Arkansas, Delaware, Florida, Georgia, Kentucky, Louisiana, Maryland, Mississippi, North Carolina, Oklahoma, South Carolina, Tennessee, Texas, Virginia, Washington D.C., West Virginia.

Source: Eli Ginzberg, *The Negro Potential*, New York: Columbia University Press, 1956, p. 15.

years later, just over 50 per cent remained within that region. The table also shows the northward and westward movement which corresponded to the growing demand for factory labour in the cities of the North and West.

During the second half of the nineteenth century, the demand for unskilled and semi-skilled factory labour in the rapidly industrializing Northern states had been satisfied mainly through migration from Europe. The first world war and the strict immigration controls established after the war reduced this flow to a trickle. Northern industrialists were forced to draw on the large reservoirs of surplus labour that had been building up for some time in rural areas, particularly in the South. Negroes were especially valuable to employers: they were willing to work for low wages, ready to submit to the employers' authority and could be used as strike breakers. They showed little inclination to join trade unions and when they tried to do so they were usually prevented. But employers were not the only group to benefit from the addition of negroes to the urban work force. Landlords were able to charge high rents for overcrowded accommodation, the white middle classes were supplied with cheap domestic servants, and the white working classes benefited from the distinction which grew up between 'white' and 'negro' jobs – the latter being poorly paid and/or unpleasant.

The majority of negro migrants settled in the city centres, partly because these areas were cheaper, partly because negroes were usually excluded from more desirable residential areas by discriminatory practices. The result, hastened by the movement of the more affluent whites to the suburbs, was the growth of 'black belts' in most American cities. By 1960, New York had over a million negroes in the Harlem, Bedford Stuyvesant and Bronx ghettos; Chicago had 890,000 in its 'black belt' on the South Side; Los Angeles had 334,000 primarily in crowded suburbs such as Watts. By 1960, too, negroes constituted 14 per cent of the population of New York, 23 per cent of Chicago, 26 per cent of Philadelphia, 29 per cent of Detroit, 34 per cent of Newark (it has since risen to over 50 per cent), 35 per cent of Baltimore, 37 per cent of New Orleans and Memphis, 38 per cent of Atlanta and 54 per cent of Washington D.C.

This urban concentration enabled negroes to organize themselves more effectively for collective action and so had important consequences for the balance of power between black and white. Under these conditions peaceful protest and riot were effective weapons and, gradually, negroes began to 'slough off' the sense of inferiority (and its corollary, the belief in white superiority) which they had inherited from slavery. They began to be able, as a group, to stand up to whites and to reject their own subordinate status.

An important part of this process was the emergence and expansion of the negro middle class—the 'black bourgeoisie'. The emergence of this class was centrally connected with the ghetto mode of living which most negroes were forced to adopt. Residential segregation and the rising income of the urban negro (in absolute terms although not relative to whites) gave rise to an increasing demand for the services of teachers, ministers of religion, doctors, lawyers, owners of hairdressing and beauty salons, undertakers and newspaper proprietors, all catering to the special needs of the segregated community. Businessmen and professionals such as these have come to stand at the apex of economic, political and other forms of social power within the negro community, yet they are in a marginal and ambiguous position. On the one hand, they are distinguished from the majority of negroes—with whom they have little in common other than race—by their income, education and style of life. On the other, they

have been systematically rebuffed by whites of comparable income, wealth and occupation (although this may be decreasing somewhat at the present time), and forced to live a segregated life. This ambiguity has led to an ambivalent identification with both the white middle classes and the negro masses. In spite of their relatively high occupational positions, their awareness of themselves as negroes makes them a more radical group politically than is usually the case with persons in similar positions in the white social hierarchy. Historically, members of the black bourgeoisie have been prominent in forming and supporting protest organizations such as the National Association for the Advancement of Coloured People (founded in 1909), and in providing leaders for the struggle for civil rights. Their education has given them the ability to articulate, publicize and explain their objectives. Their comparative affluence has enabled them both to finance such organizations and to focus upon long-term objectives rather than short-term gains. Thus, although the NAACP and similar bodies have substantial white membership and get some of their funds from white philanthropists, they owe their existence, their permanence and their policies primarily to the 'black bourgeoisie'.

The political and legal pressures of the NAACP have met with some success, most notably in 1954 when they secured the reversal, by the Federal Supreme Court, of the 'separate but equal' doctrine in public education. This success spurred negroes to a new militancy in their struggle for civil rights but also stimulated white opposition, especially in the South where federal troops had to be sent to Little Rock, Arkansas and Oxford, Mississippi to secure implementation of the Supreme Court decision. It was in the South, too, that the early militant negro protests occurred. Sit-ins at segregated establishments, marches and 'freedom rides' were organized by the Southern Christian Leadership Conference which was led, after his role in the highly successful bus boycott in Montgomery, Alabama in the winter of 1955 and 1956, by Martin Luther King. The relative stability and integration of the negro community in Southern (as opposed to Northern and Western) towns, and the organizational basis provided by the negro churches, enabled such movements to keep tight control over their members. This control enabled a non-violent campaign to be sustained which was influenced equally by New Testament ethics, the philosophy and political methods of Mahatma

Gandhi, and a realistic appreciation of the tactical hopelessness of the use of violence on a large scale by a small and relatively powerless minority group. Demonstrations were planned in detail and carefully organized. Potential demonstrators were thoroughly screened and trained not to retaliate, even in the face of severe white provocation.

This non-violent protest movement was fed by the growing affluence of the better-off part of the negro population and by their (partly consequential) improved chances of obtaining higher education. In 1930, there were only 27,141 negroes in college in the whole of the USA; by 1960, the number had risen to more than 200,000. In the colleges, especially in the segregated ones, large numbers of young people were gathered together in a situation relatively free from parental restraint. This facilitated the discussion of grievances and the organization of collective protest, and helps to explain why negro college students were so prominent in the demonstrations of this period. The success of the non-violent protest movement began to raise the confidence and self-respect of negroes as a group (which was one of its primary aims). It was aided in this by the emergence, in the late 1950s and the 1960s, of independent black African states and the appearance in Washington and New York of black diplomats and politicians.

The Civil Rights Acts of 1957, 1960 and 1964 mark the success of protest in that period in securing better employment opportunities for negroes, in realizing their voting rights on a local level (which was especially important in the South) and in forcing the desegregation of public facilities. But the mass of poorer negroes were too involved in the business of making a living to be over-concerned with niceties such as the desegregation of restaurants and art galleries. Moreover, the changing employment policies of the white establishment, which increased the number of white collar and managerial jobs available to negroes, only benefited the educated. For the vast mass of poorer, less well-educated negroes, the successes of the civil rights movement served only to raise vain hopes that they, too, would share the affluence of the post-war USA. Martin Luther King recognized this and saw why some negroes were turning against non-violent protest. Commenting on an incident in 1966, in which he was booed by 'black power' activists, he wrote:[9]

For twelve years I, and others like me, had

held out radiant promises of progress. I had preached to them about my dream. I had lectured to them about the not too distant day when they would have freedom, 'all here and now'. I had urged them to have faith in America and in white society. Their hopes had soared. They were now booing because they felt that we were unable to deliver on our promises. They were booing because we had urged them to have faith in people who had too often proved to be unfaithful. They were now hostile because they were watching the dream that they had so readily accepted turn into a frustrating nightmare.

This rising disillusionment was connected with the worsening employment situation of poorer negroes. Automation made it difficult for those who were ill-educated, many of them only recent migrants to the northern cities, to obtain jobs. The same problem was faced by school-leavers entering the labour market for the first time, especially by high school 'drop-outs'. In employment, as elsewhere, negroes came off worse than whites. In nine large cities surveyed in 1966 by the US Department of Labour, 7·3 per cent of negroes were unemployed (the figure was 9·3 per cent in the poorest negro districts) compared with only 3·3 per cent of whites.

Moreover, despite the long-term improvement in educational opportunities for negroes, wide discrepancies between the races continued to exist. White males continue, on average, to receive considerably longer schooling than do non-white males although the difference is less than it was. Much the same pattern is apparent in income distribution. In spite of a decline in the proportion of negro families with incomes of less than $3,000 per annum and an increase in the proportion of negro families in the higher income groups, substantial income differences between the racial groups are evident. The median income of gainfully employed negro males increased threefold (in real terms) between 1939 and 1962. In spite of this increase, however, the median income of negro families in 1966 was only 58 per cent of that of white families. In the same year, 28 per cent of negro families and 55 per cent of white families had an income in excess of $7,000. At the other end of the income scale, 32 per cent of negro families and 13 per cent of white families had an income of less than $3,000.

With the exception of the numerically small (but expanding) black bourgeoisie, the lot of negro Americans, however much it had improved in absolute terms, had not been improving *relative to whites*—at least not in the fields of employment, income and education. This continued deprivation among the mass of negroes led to a growing despair in the inability of the non-violent civil rights movement to effect any significant short-term gains for them. The race riots in the ghettos of most major American cities, starting in the summer of 1963, grew out of negro resentment against this continued inequality and the hopelessness of the situation. Most of these riots have been violent. In the Los Angeles suburb of Watts in August 1965, for example, the rioting lasted for more than two days and nights. Both police and rioters made heavy use of firearms. Thirty-four persons were killed and hundreds severely wounded. The number of arrests totalled almost 4,000 and the damage done by arson and bomb throwing was estimated at $35 million.

These riots marked the end of unqualified support for moderate leaders committed to a strategy of non-violent demonstrations. Younger negro leaders began to reject integration into white society as a possible or desirable goal. 'We feel that integration is irrelevant; it is just a substitute for white supremacy', argued Stokeley Carmichael in 1966. Yet militant 'black power' leaders, such as Carmichael, the late Malcolm X and Eldridge Cleaver, appear—so far at least—not to have gained widespread support among negroes (in spite of the lavish reporting—and misreporting—of their speeches and activities in the press). They have, nevertheless, had an important effect upon patterns of negro protest in that they have acted as a 'ginger group', helping to sustain and even to increase the militancy of more moderate civil rights leaders. They have drawn attention to the plight of the mass of urban negroes and away from the outward trappings of white supremacy such as segregated theatres and bowling alleys. There is now a greater awareness among moderate leaders in the protest movement that they are engaged in a struggle for power, a struggle for a share in the control of the political and economic institutions of American society. Take, for example, the following passage from the last book written by Martin Luther King. In it he argues against the separatism urged by many black power groups:[10]

Just as the Negro cannot achieve political power in isolation, neither can he gain economic power through separatism. While there must be a continued emphasis on the need for blacks to pool their economic resources and withdraw consumer support from discriminating firms, we must not be oblivious to the fact that the larger economic problems confronting the Negro community will only be solved by federal programmes involving billions of dollars. One unfortunate thing about Black Power is that it gives priority to race precisely at a time when the impact of automation and other forces have made the economic question fundamental for blacks and whites alike. In this context a slogan Power for Poor People would be much more appropriate than the slogan Black Power.

However much we pool our resources and 'buy black', this cannot create the multiplicity of new jobs and provide the number of low-cost houses that will lift the Negro out of the economic depression caused by centuries of deprivation. Neither can our resources supply quality integrated education. All of this requires billions of dollars which only an alliance of liberal – labour – civil rights forces can stimulate. In short, the Negro's problem cannot be solved unless the whole of American society takes a new turn toward greater economic justice.

Clearly, King was coming to see the struggle for civil rights as a class struggle shared by poor whites, even though they tend to be the most intransigently prejudiced of all white groups.

From its inception, the negro protest movement in the USA produced a counter-movement on the part of whites anxious to maintain the *status quo*. Poor whites, in particular, have not moved beyond their dependence on negro subordination as a source of self-esteem. Newly affluent whites, insecure in their new-found affluence, feel threatened by the increasingly urgent negro demands for *their* share of the cake. It is here that the 'white backlash' has erupted with its greatest fury. The open advocacy of armed insurrection by some 'black power' sects has only served to increase the scope and intensity of the reaction, and armed 'vigilante' groups have been formed by whites in many cities. In this manner, the violence of the confrontation has tended to escalate. There has also been a tendency towards racial polarization. Negroes have come increasingly to distrust and reject the help of sympathetic whites, and whites who formerly supported the negro cause have become alienated by the increasing advocacy and use of violence.

The escalation since 1954 of negro protest towards greater militancy, the trend since 1963 towards greater organized and unorganized violence, and the corresponding escalation of the white reaction, have presented a serious shock to the American social fabric. It remains to be seen whether rapid advance can be made towards the solution of the 'American dilemma' without significant changes in American society, or whether frustration at the slowness of advance towards their goals will lead more negroes to support the advocates of armed insurrection. If the advocacy and use of violence increases, the white response is likely to be massive. White control over industry, government, the armed forces and the police would enable any such insurrection to be crushed. In the process, power in the white community would probably shift even further towards anti-negro groups, and the emergence nationally of a virulently racist regime would be a distinct possibility.

Brazil: development towards racial integration?

A comparison of negro–white relations in the USA with their counterpart in Brazil provides another indication of how a society's course of development affects its patterns of race relations. While the degree of racial integration and equality in Brazil has often been exaggerated, there is little doubt that the barriers there against negroes are less clearly defined than those in the USA. Most Brazilian negroes are poor and ill-educated. Most of them work in less prestigious, less well-paid, mainly manual occupations. But those who manage to acquire wealth and education, particularly if they are light-skinned, are not consistently rejected by whites of comparable social standing (except with regard to marriage). There is, thus, some basis to the popular Brazilian sayings that 'money bleaches' and 'a rich negro is a white man'. (Of course, the emphasis on 'whiteness' in these sayings is also indicative of the general dominance of whites.) In Brazil, moreover, black and white members of the working classes are not so segregated residentially as they are in the United States. Trades unions are more racially integrated and negroes sometimes hold positions of authority over whites (though not as frequently as their proportion in the population as a whole would lead one to expect). In short, in Brazil,

distinctions between the races are not so sharply drawn and the different social classes are more integrated racially than is the case in the USA.

The emergence in Brazil of this specific pattern of negro–white relations forms one strand in the overall social development of that country. It can only be understood in relation to this wider social process. In many ways, the peculiar pattern of Brazilian social development stems from the level of development of Portugal, the colonizing power, at the time of colonization. Although nationally unified at an early stage (which helps to explain why they were the first European societies to embark on colonization), Portugal and Spain were, in other respects, characterized by a 'medieval' social order. Church, king, and the landed, military aristocracy remained the principal social 'powers'. There was a small commercial bourgeoisie, but it was weak and was accorded low social status. By and large, this social configuration was transferred to the Brazilian colony. A consequence was that most colonists strove to recreate on their plantations the patriarchal form of social relations that had characterized their estates at home. Production for the market in order to make a profit was not their primary orientation. Most of them held to the chivalric concept of *hidalgo*, an ethic which celebrated the man who did no work with his hands and to whom business was contemptible. By contrast, the planter aristocracy in the Southern USA modelled itself more on the English concept of the 'gentleman' and this did not impose such a strong taboo on engaging in trade and making a profit.

In the course of the nineteenth century, market-oriented plantations did spring up in parts of Brazil. These were comparable in many respects to the type which arose in the USA, but their sugar and coffee were produced mainly for the Brazilian and Portuguese markets. Unlike the plantations in the American South, production never became geared, during the period of slavery, to an expanding industrial market. Within the Brazilian colony, moreover, transport and communications remained poor. This imposed further restrictions on production for a wider market. The growth of 'capitalist' plantations was, therefore, limited. They did not become the dominant institutional setting of slavery in Brazil.

In such a social situation, the laws and customs relating to domestic slavery which had grown up in Portugal and Spain—they were codified as early as 1263–5 in *Las Siete Partidas del Roy Alfonso*—could be transferred, more or less effectively, to the colony. The colonists did not have to create a slave code *de novo*. A student has summarized *Las Siete Partidas* as follows:[11]

> The slave might marry a free person if the slave status was known to the other party. Slaves could marry against the will of their master if they continued serving him as before. Once married, they could not be sold apart, except under conditions permitting them to live as man and wife. If the slave married a free person with the knowledge of his master, and the master did not announce the fact of the existing slave status, then the slave by that mere fact became free. If married slaves owned by separate masters could not live together because of distance, the church should persuade one or the other to sell his slave. If neither of the masters could be persuaded, the church was to buy one of them so that the married slaves could live together. The children followed the status of their mother, and the child of a free mother remained free even if she later became a slave. In spite of his full powers over his slave, the master might neither kill him nor injure him unless authorized by the judge, nor abuse him against reason or nature, nor starve him to death. But if the master did any of these things, the slave could complain to the judge, and if the complaint were verified, the judge must sell him, giving the price to the owner, and the slave might never be returned to the original owner.

In practice there may have been divergence from this code. Nevertheless, it reflects a general type of slavery which could only have grown up in a non-capitalist context. In Brazil, as in Portugal and Spain, slave marriages and slave families enjoyed some protection in law, and the laws relating to slavery were, to some extent upheld by the church. Slaves had access to the courts and their legal status was that of unfree *persons*, not that of a commodity that could be treated arbitrarily by the owner in order to maximize his short-term advantage. *Las Siete Partidas*, moreover, defined the conditions under which slaves could be manumitted—and manumission was a not infrequent occurrence. Since slaves were allowed to earn money and own property, it was possible for some to buy their freedom. The children of slave women and white fathers were often freed. Sometimes they were fully acknowledged and brought up as part of the white family, a fact which helps to explain the comparative tolerance shown towards light-skinned negroes in Brazil. Slaves who were not needed on the master's estate could go to the towns where, although they usually had to remit a fixed monthly sum to their owners, they were often able to earn enough to buy their freedom as well. The whites, therefore, became accustomed to the existence of free negroes as a social category long before the final abolition of slavery in 1888. A corollary was the fact that substantial numbers of negroes became accustomed to a degree of independence prior to this date. Even those who remained slaves were better able to maintain—at least to some degree—a sense of self-esteem and personal autonomy. This maintenance of a separate identity was aided by the fact that African tribal and linguistic groups were not systematically dispersed as they were in the USA. Some slave groups even maintained their religious identity as Moslems. Given such conditions, the Brazilian slave was better able to conceive of himself as a rebel than his northern counterpart. During the seventeenth century, for example, escaped slaves established the Palmares Republic and successfully defended it for more than fifty years. In general, slave uprisings were more frequent and more successful than they were in the USA.

In Brazil, emancipation came peacefully over a period of several years. The final decree was issued in 1888 in a situation where continued pressure by the British navy on the slave trade had led to a shortage of slaves and rising costs. Further, economic developments in the late nineteenth century—particularly the beginnings of Brazil's emergence as a major producer of coffee for the world market—made it increasingly apparent that it was cheaper and more efficient to run plantations using wage labourers who were formally free.

Large numbers of negroes moved into the towns immediately after emancipation. Their lack of familiarity with urban life and a free status led many to lapse into vagabondage and drunkenness. At first, they formed a kind of sub-proletariat within the towns. As a result, the economic position of the established white manual workers was not seriously threatened—a factor which may go some way towards explaining the relative lack of anti-negro prejudice. When, in the early 1900s, large-scale immigration from Europe began, many negroes were already second-generation town dwellers. Although, for the most part, they were uneducated and unskilled, they were able to compete, more or less effectively, with the newcomers (many of whom were also uneducated and unskilled). Rather than developing a view of themselves as an underprivileged *racial* group, negroes who had established themselves in the towns began to see themselves as part of an emerging *working class*. Their acceptance into the trades union movement at all levels has enhanced this tendency.

Race relations in Britain

Britain has been centrally involved in the development of white dominance all over the world through her slave trading activities, her colonialism and her industrialization. Yet until the immigration of coloured people began to assume significant proportions in the 1950s, the comparative absence of a coloured population meant that there were no *domestic* problems of race relations in this country. Of course, there had been previous foreign immigration. The arrival of linguistically and culturally distinct groups, such as Jews, Italians or Poles, frequently aroused hostility and prejudice. But the fact that they were not racially distinct (although the British often *viewed* them as being so) made it relatively easy for them to integrate with the host society. The more recent coloured immigrants, because of their racial distinctiveness, find such assimilation much more difficult. There is therefore a greater possibility that, if it is in the interests of powerful groups (in the working class as well as in the upper and middle classes) and if the immigrants themselves remain powerless and unable to resist, they may become a more or less permanent and easily exploitable 'sub-proletariat'.

Commonwealth immigration into Britain in the 1950s and 1960s was part of a more general movement. Between 1945 and 1957, for example, there was a net migration of more than 350,000 Europeans into the United Kingdom. This, and immigration from the Commonwealth until the Commonwealth Immigration Act of 1962, corresponded to the chronic labour shortage of the post-war period. At first, the majority of Commonwealth immigrants came to Britain from the West Indies. Since 1961 the numbers of Indians and Pakistanis have also been growing. Thus, of the estimated 1,113,000 coloured people in England and Wales in 1968, 49 per cent were from the West Indies and 39 per cent were from India and Pakistan. Table 11.2 gives a more detailed breakdown of Britain's coloured population.

Table 11.2 Total estimated coloured population resident in England and Wales, 1966 census, by area of origin

Area of Origin	Born overseas	Born in the United Kingdom	Total
India[1]	180,400	43,200	223,600
Pakistan[2]	109,600	10,100	119,700
Ceylon	12,900	3,200	16,100
Jamaica	188,100	85,700	273,800
Other Caribbean	129,800	50,500	180,300
West Africa	43,100	7,600	50,700
Far East	47,000	13,000	60,000
Total	710,900	213,300	924,200

[1]Excluding white Indians
[2]Excluding white Pakistanis

Source: E. J. B. Rose *et al.*, *Colour and Citizenship*, London: Oxford University Press, 1969.

Whatever their country of origin coloured immigrants to Britain have tended to be employed in jobs that are losing ground in terms of pay and status (such as those in public transport) or in jobs that are generally considered unpleasant (such as refuse collection or foundry work). With the relatively full employment of the post-war years and the increasing demand for skilled and/or highly paid labour, the locally born labour force has tended to move out of the less desirable (but nevertheless essential) jobs, thereby creating vacancies which coloured immigrants have been willing and able to fill. Such jobs require few skills and even the lowest British wage rates have allowed a higher standard of living than is normally possible in the Indian sub-continent and the West Indies. The nature of economic change in post-war Britain, then, has encouraged and facilitated immigration, and has concentrated the immigrants in the lowest paid and lowest status jobs in the country.

In addition to these economic forces, coloured immigrants also had to contend with colour prejudice. This is nothing new in Britain (despite the small numbers of coloured inhabitants before 1950). As long ago as 1602 an order was issued commanding certain 'blackamoors' to be transported from the country; in the late eighteenth and early nineteenth centuries the St Giles 'blackbirds' were concentrated in a kind of ghetto; and in 1919 the sudden increase in the numbers of negro immigrants following the first world war sparked off serious disturbances in a number of towns. Such incidents, however, since they were infrequent and relatively minor, did little to disturb the complacent view that racial disturbances were foreign to British society. The myth of a racially tolerant Britain remained unchallenged until the racial disturbances of 1958. Thereafter the 'problem' of race relations grew. In riots in the Notting Hill district of London in 1958 126 white and 51 coloured people were arrested, mainly on charges of causing grievous bodily harm, possessing offensive weapons, or using threatening words and behaviour. In Nottingham, also in that year, a 'pub brawl' in which four Englishmen were stabbed by West Indians led large crowds to gather and fight every evening for a week. By 1962, fear of coloured immigration, especially among certain sectors of the working classes who saw immigrants as a threat to their employment and their housing, prompted the government to pass an act restricting immigration from the Commonwealth. In 1964, race became, for the first time, a major issue in a British election when a Conservative candidate, standing on an anti-immigrant platform, was returned in Smethwick—generally reckoned to be a 'safe' Labour seat.

The anti-immigration movement found a leader in Enoch Powell, a former Minister of Health who, in a speech in Birmingham in April 1968, argued that the 'flood' of coloured immigrants was likely, in the near future, to dislodge native-born Englishmen from several British towns. He therefore proposed that, in order to prevent the repetition in Great Britain of what he later called 'the haunting tragedy of the United States', immigration be stopped totally and that measures be adopted to 'promote the maximum outflow'. Mr Powell's speeches became the focus for the immigration issue. Condemned by the majority of leading politicians, clergymen, television and radio commentators, and by most national newspapers, his views nevertheless commanded considerable popular support. More than a thousand dockers marched from the West India docks to Westminster to demonstrate in his favour. Later, the leader of a group of Smithfield meat porters proclaimed:[12]

At last the Englishman has had some guts. This is as important as Dunkirk. We are becoming second class citizens in our own country. Immigrants have been brought here to undercut our wages in times of crisis. When there is vast unemployment in this country, immigrants will compete with you for your jobs.

It is clear from this comment that, in periods of crisis, 'national' and 'racial' sentiments can easily outweigh any identification with the coloured population as fellow workers who share certain interests with members of the white working class. It is significant that the main expressions of support for 'Powellism' come from men employed in work which is unskilled and notoriously insecure. Such men tend to be poorly educated. They are likely, in consequence, to come into *direct* competition with immigrants for jobs, especially in periods of high unemployment.

However, antagonism towards coloured immigrants does not always stem from factors so apparently rational as competition in the labour and housing markets. Such evidence as is available suggests that approximately 10 per cent of the total population is generally prejudiced against them. In a study (carried out in 1966–7) of five English boroughs with relatively high proportions of coloured residents, one-third of all the white adults interviewed expressed views with virtually no trace of hostility towards coloured people. A further two-fifths were strongly disposed in the direction of tolerance whilst the remainder, although strongly inclined towards prejudice, were not unconditionally hostile and were prepared to make exceptions. The highest incidence of extreme prejudice was found among skilled manual workers and their wives and among the lower-middle classes. Such prejudice may stem in part from their status marginality and their consequent insecurity. That is, they may perceive immigrant competition as a threat to their relative affluence—recently gained and all too uncertainly held.

But prejudice is not the only factor of significance—nor perhaps the most important one. Unprejudiced people can (and do) also engage in racial discrimination if they perceive it to be in their interests. Thus, in spite of some evidence suggesting a relative lack of prejudice, there is also considerable evidence of racial discrimination in the fields of employment and housing and in the provision of goods, facilities and services. The seriousness of the situation and the prevalence of discrimination were recognized by Parliament in the passing, in 1968, of a Race Relations Act whereby racial discrimination in these fields was made illegal. If, in spite of the Race Relations Act, such discrimination continues, the coloured immigrants—and more importantly their children—will probably develop into a more or less permanent and easily exploitable 'sub-proletariat'. The outcome will depend partly on whether they can organize themselves successfully to protect their own interests and here they face several problems. Most coloured immigrants are strangers both to the English way of life and to the urban-industrial environment in which it takes place. Many of them are consequently too fully occupied in finding and keeping jobs and houses to devote time and energy to the development of organizations with the long-term aim of securing integration into British society (or even to raising the standard of living of immigrants as a group). In addition, the linguistic and cultural differences between West Indians, Pakistanis and Indians form a formidable barrier to a comprehensive immigrants' organization. Even the West Indians come from a variety of different islands many of which have long-standing traditions of hostility towards each other. West Indian society is, moreover, based upon a form of social stratification in which dark brown skins tend to be associated with low status and light brown skins tend to be associated with high status. The tensions and conflicts arising from these differences are often transferred to the British context where they undermine the common experiences of immigrant status.

Pakistani immigrants are also divided among themselves—principally between those from East Pakistan (or Bangladesh as it is now called) and those from West Pakistan. In spite of their capacity to organize successful commercial enterprises, they have so far failed to create effective political organizations. A striking exception is their activity in local elections, most notably in Bradford where a Pakistani councillor was elected as early as 1964. A more recent form of 'political' organization has taken the form of defensive vigilante groups against the 'Paki-bashing' activities of 'skinheads'.

By far the most successful of immigrant groups in terms of political organization have been the Indians. Their relative success has its origins in the India League and the Indian Workers' Association. These were formed before the second world war by Indians in this country in order to help the Indian struggle for independence. The Indian Workers' Association was revived in 1953 when large-scale migration from the Punjab began. The Punjabi origin of the majority gives the Indian migrants a homogeneity in experience, beliefs and values which helps to explain their organizational success relative to other immigrant groups. In addition, the nature of their communities, with their strong emphasis on mutual obligations between groups of kinsmen, has helped to draw individuals into the activities of the IWA. The organization was strong enough in 1966 to engage in a six-week strike in a Southall rubber factory over the dismissal of one of its members. Such organization is perhaps a precondition of achieving a measure of equality with the host population in key areas of social life. Yet successful organization, too, has its problems in that it may produce a counter-reaction—a 'white backlash'. Indeed, Mr Powell has already identified the halting development of immigrant organizations as a move towards 'black domination' (domination, that is by 2 per cent of the population over the 98 per cent who include the incumbents of all the major and minor power positions in the land)! Such are the dangers of political organization. Without it, however, immigrant groups are likely to remain outsiders. With hard work and sacrifice some of them may become comparatively affluent, but affluence, as the experience of the Jews shows so clearly, is no guarantee that they will not become a target of hostility, especially in times of national stress.

Notes

1 Eric Williams, *Capitalism and Slavery*, London: Deutsch, 1964, p. 19.
2 Quoted in Kenneth M. Stampp, *The Peculiar Institution. Slavery in the Ante-Bellum South*, New York: Knopf, 1956, p. 171.
3 George M. Stroud, *A Sketch of the Laws relating to Slavery in the several States of the United States of America*, Philadelphia, 1856, quoted in Michael Banton, *Race Relations*, London: Tavistock, 1967, p. 121.
4 Quoted in Stampp, op. cit., p. 172.
5 John Pendleton Kennedy, *Swallow Barn*, quoted in S. M. Elkins, *Slavery: A Problem in American Institutional and Intellectual Life*, University of Chicago Press, 1959, p. 132.
6 Edward A. Pollard, *Black Diamonds Gathered in the Darkey Homes of the South*, quoted in Elkins, op. cit., p. 132.
7 Alexis de Tocqueville, *Democracy in America*, Vol. I, New York: Vintage, 1945, p. 373.
8 Quoted in C. Vann Woodward, *The Strange Career of Jim Crow*, New York: Oxford University Press, 1960, pp. 44–5.

9 Martin Luther King, *Chaos or Community*, Harmondsworth: Penguin, 1969, p. 50.
10 Ibid., pp. 53–4.
11 Frank Tannenbaum, *Slave and Citizen*, New York: Vintage, 1946, p. 49.

12 Speech by Dennis Herbert Harmston, quoted in Bill Smithers and Peter Fiddick, *Enoch Powell on Immigration*, London: Sphere, 1969, pp. 12–13.

Reading

Banton, M., *Race Relations*, London: Tavistock, 1967. A useful introduction to the study of race and race relations.

Franklin-Frazier, E., *Black Bourgeoisie*, New York: Collier, 1962. This study by a negro sociologist remains the best so far carried out on middle-class negroes in the United States.

Killian, L., *The Impossible Revolution*, New York: Random House, 1968. A thorough, thought-provoking study of negro protest in the USA.

Mason, P., *Race Relations*, London: Oxford University Press, 1970. A short introduction which reviews biological, psychological and anthropological approaches to the subject and sets current racial problems in the perspective of world history.

Rex, J. and Moore, R., *Race, Community and Conflict*, London: Oxford University Press, 1967. By far the best sociological study so far carried out of race relations in Britain.

Rose, E. J. B. *et al.*, *Colour and Citizenship*, London: Oxford University Press, 1969. Not sociological but none the less a useful and instructive compendium of information on race and immigration in the United Kingdom.

Further reading

Genovese, Eugene D., *The Political Economy of Slavery*, New York: Pantheon, 1965. A stimulating study by a Marxist historian of the consequences of slavery for the social structure of the American South.

Genovese, Eugene D., *The World the Slaveholders Made*, London: Allen Lane, 1970. Contains two important essays: a comparative study of colonialism, slavery, and social structure in various parts of the 'New World', and an essay on the ideology of slaveholders in the Southern USA.

Hunter, G. (ed.), *Industrialization and Race Relations*, London: Oxford University Press, 1965. A useful symposium on industrialization and race relations in world perspective.

Mason, P., *Patterns of Dominance*, London: Oxford University Press, 1970. A useful, highly readable comparative and historical analysis of patterns of racial dominance.

Schermerhorn, R. A., *Comparative Ethnic Relations*, New York: Random House, 1970. Compares the usefulness of different approaches to the comparative study of ethnic and race relations. Lucid, readable and brings together a wealth of information in a systematic way.

12 Industrial relations

In industrial societies almost everyone is, has been or will be an employee at some time during their life. Indeed, for most of us this particular status will dominate much of our adult life. This situation is in marked contrast to that in non-industrial societies where three-quarters or more of the occupied population are employers, self-employed or family workers. Thus, the focus of this chapter—the social relations of employers and employees—is one which directly concerns all of us who live in industrial societies. This state of affairs is relatively recent and has been associated with the emergence of the factory system of production, a system which only became dominant during the nineteenth century, first in Britain and then elsewhere.

The factory system

The factory system of production developed in Britain alongside the craftsman and the domestic system and only over a period of several decades did it come to predominate. Even now self-employed craftsmen remain important in several occupations, such as shoe repairing and picture framing, where the demand for capital is not great; and 'putting out' is also still to be found, for instance in the hosiery industry in the East Midlands. In industrial societies today, however, factories are dominant in manufacturing industry and, even in other spheres, work is characterized by a similar pattern of social relations.

The organization of production in factories was the outcome of several distinct changes from earlier modes of production. It resulted, moreover, in marked changes in the social situation of the worker. In the first place, it meant the concentration of labour in one workshop or factory, and the consequent separation of home and work. Second, it involved the discipline and control of the workers by the manufacturer, and this made possible a much more elaborate and far-reaching division of labour than had existed among craftsmen or under the domestic system. Third, it was associated with the use of power machinery and the mechanization of tasks wherever possible and thus with the employment of very much greater amounts of fixed capital than even the merchant employer had required. Whilst isolated examples of the concentration of workers into workshops, and even of their working under the discipline of the employer, can be found much earlier than the eighteenth century, the use of water- or steam-powered machinery, which developed from the middle of that century onwards, was only possible within a factory system.

In contrast to the situation of the factory worker, the independent craftsman owned his tools and place of work, purchased his raw materials and sold the finished product direct to the consumer. The worker under the domestic system was more dependent on the merchant employer, but might still own his own tools and place of work. Within the limits set by the need to do enough work to support themselves and their dependants these workers could work in their own way and at their own pace. It was common experience in the domestic system for work to be concentrated into the latter half of the week. For example, the Children's Employment Commission provided the following description of the West Midland's lock and key industry in 1843:[1]

> The majority of the working classes do no work at all on Monday. Half of them do not work much on Tuesday. Wednesday is the market day, and this is an excuse for many of them to do only half a day's work; and in consequence of attending the market they are often very unfit for work on Thursday morning. Lights are seen in the shops of many of the small masters as late as ten and eleven o'clock at night on Thursday. During the whole of Friday the town is silent in all the main streets and thoroughfares, and seems to have been depopulated of all its manufacturers. Lights appear in the workshops to a late hour in the night— sometimes till morning. All Saturday morning the streets present the same comparatively barren and silent appearance. Everybody is working for his life. Among the small masters, their wives, children and apprentices are being almost worked to death. Kicks, cuffs, curses and blows are abundantly administered to the children at this crisis of the work . . . .
> About two o'clock . . . some of those who did some work on Tuesday begin to appear in the streets; and large masses issue forth between 4 and 5 o'clock. The wives and elder girls go to market; the husbands and other adults to the beer shops. By 7 or 8 o'clock the market is full; the streets are all alive; the beer-shops and gin-shops are full; and all the other shops are full. The manufacturers are stretching their limbs, expanding their souls to the utmost, and spending their money as fast as they possibly can. No one ever thinks of saving a shilling.

By contrast, although he was legally free, the factory worker was subordinate and dependent, economically and socially. He was subject to the discipline of the employer, who demanded that he started and stopped work at fixed times and that he worked with regular intensity. The factory system also made possible much greater division of labour and specialization developed further as machine power was introduced. Thus much factory work (though not all) involved, and indeed still involves, performing semi-skilled or unskilled tasks which are only a fragment of the total process. The intrinsic satisfactions which might be derived from the task itself and from the completion of a finished product were diminished.

Work life involving inherent deprivations became sharply separated from home life and leisure in which satisfactions might be hoped for.

These marked differences in the formal social relations of production between the craftsman, domestic and factory systems represent changes in the individual's socially defined rights of access to means of making a living. However much the autonomy and independence of the craftsman depended on guild regulation of an occupation, it stands in marked contrast to the economic dependence of the factory worker who has no rights over materials, tools or product, and is related to his employer by impersonal market forces and subject to factory discipline. Social relations at work under the factory system vary considerably depending on a variety of other factors, but they must be considered within this initial framework.

Some of the contrasts and changes outlined above may be made more meaningful by considering a detailed account of such changes and resistance to them. Two American social scientists, Lloyd Warner and J. O. Low, have outlined the changes which took place in the organization of the shoe industry in 'Yankee City' (Newburyport) in New England.[2] In the seventeenth century, shoe production was carried out in the family using a few simple hand tools and producing primarily for domestic needs. Gradually certain people specialized in shoe-making and made shoes to order for local customers. This system was changed with the emergence of entrepreneurs who got workers at home to make shoes for them to sell in a wider market. On the basis of this domestic system it was also possible to introduce a measure of specialization; materials were sorted in a central shop and each workman performed only some of the operations necessary for making a complete boot or shoe. The market was local and only when it began to expand with improved transport facilities did the 'merchant-master' come to dominate the journeyman and their interests begin to conflict seriously.

The introduction of machinery from the middle of the nineteenth century onwards was associated with the growth of a factory system; the process of manufacture was transformed from a single skilled trade carried on by craftsmen from start to finish, to one of several thousand operations carried out by semi-skilled operatives on specialized machines. A trade union, the Knights of St Crispin, was unable to prevent this process of increasing mechanization and the consequent substitution of 'green hands' for old-time crafts-men, and was short lived (1868–72). The workers remained subordinate to the factory owners (mostly local men) and subject to the effects of cyclical and seasonal trade fluctuations and to the pressure for lower costs and greater productivity. However, because the owners were prominent members of the local community, the conflict of interests between them and their employees was mitigated somewhat by the fact that they were thought to be guided in their actions by com-munity as well as commercial considerations and by the personal relationships between the two groups.

The final stage came with the transfer of owner-ship and control from local families to businessmen in distant New York for whom the 'Yankee City' factories were only one unimportant producing unit among many others. With this change were associated further mechanization and the use of assembly-line methods so that nearly all jobs were low skilled and many were highly routinized. The market became even wider but retail outlets were controlled by the big manufacturers. A large industrial union organized the workers (who took part in a successful strike) and it made possible some protection of workers' interests in the face of a large, impersonal, bureaucratic management organization.

Attempts to resist the spread of the factory system were not confined to the New England shoe industry, but were widespread in Europe and North America. Some of this resistance can be attributed to the harsh and unpleasant conditions of work in many establishments during the early stages of industrialization, but often another important factor was the loss of autonomy and the imposition of disciplined work habits which factory employment involved. Thus employers can be found complaining that because they valued their independence workmen would not 'walk across the street' to work in a factory even though their earnings under the domestic system were markedly less. One of the most interesting examples of an attempt to preserve this independ-ence and yet to gain the advantages of steam power was the building of 'cottage factories' for the Coventry ribbon weavers during the 1850s. In these cases rows of weavers' houses, each with a workshop on the second floor, were built with a steam engine at one end and shafting running along the row to supply power for the looms in each cottage. Each weaver could thus work in his own home for whatever time he chose and could employ members of his family as ancillary workers, but could also use a power loom.

Employer–employee relations are often con-cerned with this 'frontier of control' in the workplace, with the employee attempting—partly through collective action and partly by less formal and less organized means—to gain a measure of control over his work situation.

The development of the factory system

Industrialization in Britain and North America took place entirely within a capitalist framework. The initiative in establishing factories, employing workers and exploiting new markets came from the entrepreneur who, using his own or borrowed capital, was oriented to the rational pursuit of economic gain, and attempted to achieve this through the rational organization of free labour. The growth of the factory system and the conse-quent changes in the social relations of production were significantly affected by this; there was an emphasis on free markets, and on the primacy of commercial considerations. In other societies, however, the process of industrialization has taken different forms. In some parts of Western Europe (such as Germany) and in Tsarist Russia the central government played a more active part, though within a basically capitalist framework. In Soviet Russia, Eastern Europe and some of the modernizing societies of the present time the initiative has come from the government and ownership of the means of production has been in the hands of the state. In other modernizing societies colonial administrations or overseas companies have been the prime initiators of such changes and in others a mixed economy has been developed. Thus, whilst relations between employ-ers and employees may have certain elements in common in all industrial societies, there are also important differences and the full significance of these has still to be explored. There are certain common technological and organizational features of large-scale industrial organizations which set limits to the form social relations may take but they do not determine them in all respects.

In order to understand contemporary relations between employers and employees in the industrial West it is necessary to examine the specific developments in these societies. The most important of these are the growth of industrial bureaucracy, the divorce of ownership and control, the changing role of the government and the rise of trade unions.

(1) The early factories had no very elaborate management organization. Managerial tasks were performed by members of the owning family or by the partners in the business, assisted by relatively few foremen and clerks. One common procedure was the use of sub-contractors to perform many of the necessary tasks. These men were autonomous and they recruited, trained, instructed, disciplined, paid and dismissed the workers they needed. In such cases the worker often had a personal relationship with his employer, though this did not eliminate harshness and exploitation. As firms and plants grew in size and as technical methods became increasingly complex, such administrative methods were inadequate; management became increasingly bureaucratic with the adoption of rational formal procedures in place of traditional practices. These changes were reflected in the increased proportion of administrative personnel of all kinds in industry; so that, for example, administrative personnel increased as a percentage of production workers. In Britain in 1907 administrative personnel were 8·6 per cent of production workers; in 1948 they were 20 per cent; in 1966 they were 24·3 per cent. In the USA they were 7·7 per cent in 1899 and 21·6 per cent in 1947. These trends have continued. The employer–employee relationship was affected by the change from relatively small family firms to large corporations and it inevitably became more impersonal. It was increasingly governed by rules and procedures which were intended to apply to all employees without favouritism or malice.

(2) Parallel with the development of industrial bureaucracy there occurred marked changes in the patterns of ownership so that the predominant form of enterprise became the limited liability joint stock company. In smaller companies a small group of important shareholders, sometimes members of the same family, have often continued to exercise control, and this is occasionally the case even in larger companies. In the majority of large firms, however, the dispersal of share-holding means that effective control rests in the hands of full-time directors and top executives who are themselves employees and have no share, or only a nominal one, in the ownership of the company.

The interests of these executives may diverge from that of their subordinates but are nevertheless not always identical with that of the shareholders. They may, for example, place greater emphasis on the long-term growth of their businesses than on the maximizing of profits. Furthermore, in Britain and some Western European societies a substantial part of industry is publicly owned. Top management's responsibility is to the relevant Minister and to Parliament rather than to shareholders and considerations of social policy have influenced industrial relations at least at certain times. In many other respects, however, there appears to be little difference between nationalized concerns and large privately owned companies.

(3) Although the influence of the government on industry and industrial relations is most obvious in societies where the means of production are publicly controlled, nevertheless governments play an important part in industry in all highly industrialized societies. This is in marked contrast to the position in Britain during the early stages of industrialization when *laissez-faire* prevailed very much in fact as well as in theory. Increasingly, however, the government intervened to regulate conditions in factories and mines, to prohibit or regulate the employment of women and children, and to influence industrial relations. This increasing intervention, which can be observed in many industrial societies, is not due primarily to changing ideas about the role of government, though the ideas and interests of various parties and pressure groups have materially influenced the form of the intervention at different times. Rather it is a necessary course of action for any industrial society that is to avoid the widespread social disorganization which would result from an unregulated power struggle between employers and employees.

(4) Employer–employee relations have been even more significantly affected by the growth of trade unions. Collective action by workers in the same trade can be traced back to well before the Industrial Revolution but the development of trade unions in their modern form is very much a phenomenon of industrial societies. Though by no means all employees, even in highly industrialized societies like Britain, are members of trade unions (or for that matter employees' associations of any sort) the terms and conditions of employment for the great majority are influenced directly or indirectly by trade-union action. The growth of trade unions appears to be a universal feature of industrial societies. Their independence, the extent of union organization and the nature of union activities, however, vary widely depending largely on the particular course of development and the political structure in each society. In the

industrial West trade unions now play such an important part in industrial relations that we must look at them in more detail.

Trade unions

Trade unions are primarily interest groups formed to protect and further the interests of a particular occupational group against the interests of their employers, or sometimes those of other occupational groups. In any industrial society where there is in any sense a free labour market the individual employee is in a very weak bargaining position; the employer normally acts from a position of much greater strength. Only if the employee combines with others in his negotiations with employers and takes collective action to improve the terms of the employment contract is some sort of parity possible. Thus trade unionism can be seen as a product of what is sometimes called the *market situation* of the worker in a society in which his livelihood depends on the bargain he can make in selling his labour to an employer. Not all workers share precisely the same market situation, though they may have common interests in some general issues (and this is reflected in the existence of organizations, such as the Trades Union Congress in Great Britain, which aim to represent the interests of all trade unionists). The distinctive interests of workers with particular skills, or associated with particular industries or occupations, are reflected in the existence of different trade unions or other employees' associations to protect their interests.

In addition, however, the individual employee usually shares a common *work situation* with his fellow employees. The extent to which this is so may be important in determining the extent to which employees become aware of their common position in the labour market. In addition the employee is in a relationship of subordination to his employer and has to accept the discipline and loss of autonomy that this entails. Particularly in large bureaucratic organizations manual workers and routine clerical workers are physically and socially separated from management. By taking collective action employees can affect, sometimes very considerably, the way in which the authority of the employer is exercised. Trade unionism can thus also be seen as a defence against arbitrary action by the employer and as an expression of the solidarity which is brought about by the work situation.

The growth of trade unions can therefore be seen as a result of the divisions and conflicts which are a feature of modern economic organization. The activities of the different groups which arise from this division of labour, however, are differentially evaluated by others; people who do similar jobs are usually accorded a common social status. In terms of the dominant value system in most industrial societies this means that manual workers have an inferior social status; non-manual workers, even though also employees, may claim and be accorded higher social status. (There are, of course, important differences within each broad grouping.) Trade unionism may be partly a reaction to just such a shared and inferior status situation. It may be seen as offering hope of an improvement in social status by asserting the value of the activities in question, by securing improved economic circumstances which make possible a more desirable style of life, and by increasing the power of such groups *vis-à-vis* other status groups in the society.

This way of looking at trade unions provides a coherent explanation of the patterns of unionism —perhaps best exemplified by David Lockwood's study of clerical workers.[3] Clerical trade unionism presents two problems. First, why clerical workers, who like manual workers are property-less and dependent on their labour for their livelihood, do not form trade unions to the same extent as manual workers. Second, why in more recent years trade unionism has developed among clerical workers but has become much stronger among some categories of clerical workers than among others.

Although both manual and clerical workers are property-less their market situations are by no means identical. Traditionally, clerks had significantly higher incomes, especially if these are calculated on the basis of a lifetime's earnings. In addition, they had greater job security because of the value of their services to the organization, their superior chances of promotion, and very often the possession of a number of fringe benefits and non-pecuniary advantages not received by manual workers. Their work situation was characterized by personal relations with the employer and not by uniformity of work or conditions, so that the basis for consciousness of common interests with other clerks, or of collective action with them, did not exist. Furthermore, black-coated workers claimed and were granted distinctively higher social status than even skilled manual workers. Thus traditionally neither the market, work nor status situations of clerical workers were really similar to those of manual workers, and the individual clerk could probably best hope to improve his situation by being loyal to his employer and thus maximizing the possibility of promotion within the enterprise.

Increasingly, however, this situation has changed, and with the change has come a growth of 'white collar' trade unionism. In particular, with increasing literacy and with the routinization of many clerical tasks the market situation of clerical workers has worsened relative to other groups, a change which has been reflected in decreased pay differentials and in the spread of fringe benefits of various sorts to manual workers. More or less full employment and certain statutory measures have increased the security of employment of all workers, but especially of manual workers. Even more important, the growth of large-scale bureaucratic organizations of all sorts, employing large numbers of clerks, has radically altered the black-coated worker's work situation. Large numbers of clerks now perform similar tasks under standardized conditions of employment so that personal relationships with employers are no longer possible. Furthermore, the increased number of clerks desiring promotion and the increased demand for formal qualifications, rather than just experience, for entry to higher-level positions in the bureaucratic hierarchy means that chances of promotion are much reduced or even blocked altogether. Finally, the status situation of clerical workers has become ambiguous as they have become a more numerous and more diverse group less clearly distinguished from manual workers in social origins, education and style of life.

Within the general category of clerical worker, however, there are important differences which are reflected both in membership statistics and in the nature of the unions—for example in their militancy. In the 1960s a very high proportion of clerks in national and local government and in the railways were members of their respective unions. A considerably smaller proportion of bank clerks were members of the National Union of Bank Employees, although many others were members of the less militant staff associations. An extremely small but increasing proportion of clerical workers in most other industrial and commercial establishments were members of the Clerical and Administrative Workers' Union or of any other union. Differences in pay, conditions and social status are less helpful in explaining these differences than are the differences in the degree of bureaucratization of the work situation. Uniformity of conditions and blocked chances for upward mobility characterized those industries with strong and militant white collar unions. The banks by contrast did not act together as employers in the provision of uniform conditions and they provided rather better chances of promotion. Under these conditions membership of the less militant staff associations was higher than that of the NUBE. The low membership rates of clerical unions in industry generally reflect the diversity of employment conditions for these clerks.

Differences in the market situation and social status of different groups of clerical workers do not correlate with union membership; thus the high status Civil Service Clerical Association and the low status Transport Salaried Staff Association both have a high level of membership. Such differences do, however, help explain the differences in militancy of different unions and the varying extent to which white collar unions have been prepared to associate with the Labour movement as a whole. The Civil Service Clerical Association is not affiliated to the Labour Party; the Transport Salaried Staff Association is affiliated but has, nevertheless, maintained its separateness from other railway workers' unions. Similarly the increased militancy which has been observable in recent years among bank clerks and teachers stems in part from changes in their economic and social position relative to other groups.

Industrial conflict

Conflict between employers and employees is a normal and permanent feature of industrial society. In most industrial societies, however, there are organizations and procedures for dealing with industrial disputes. Relations between employers and employees are conducted within a framework of rules and for the most part their conflicting interests do not disrupt the industrial enterprise. In other words, industrial conflict has been institutionalized.

The conflict between employers and employees may remain submerged; there are potentially conflicting interests, but for lack of awareness or lack of opportunity they do not break out openly. Conflict may, however, be open, visible and yet unorganized; employees may act individually in ways which are contrary to the employer's interests, for example by going absent without permission, leaving employment or withholding effort. On the other hand, it may be organized, involving collective action whether or not this be through a formal organization. Such action might take the form of a strike, a collective go-slow, or grievances presented by representatives of a group of employees.

The organization of the parties to the conflict is a necessary step in the institutionalization of industrial conflict. It is perhaps obvious that one cannot hope to establish negotiating procedures with an aggregate of individual employees who don't act collectively; it is, however, equally important that employers be permanent and organized parties to agreements, thus obviating any possibility of disowning agreements reached by representatives or escaping their obligations by legal technicalities.

By no means all employees are trade-union members but trade unions dominate the employees' side of industrial relations procedures in Britain and in most other Western industrial societies. At least partly in reaction to this, employers in different industries have organized themselves in federations so as to present a united front. The organization of the parties to the conflict in this way gives rise to further problems in that in such large organizations maintaining adequate communications between union or federation officials and the rank-and-file members becomes difficult. Yet if unorganized manifestations of conflict are to be minimized, the interests of members must somehow be adequately represented. It is also necessary for the parties to the conflict to recognize each others' interests as legitimate. If employers refuse to recognize unions or attempt to eliminate them, or if unions act to produce changes in property ownership by revolutionary means, the institutionalization of industrial conflict cannot take place.

A further necessary stage in the institutionalization of industrial conflict is the establishment of negotiating procedures through which substantive agreements can be arrived at. These are rules governing the relations of the parties to each other at various levels—'rules of the game' as it were. In Britain there is a wide variety of such procedures in different industries and this reflects the relative autonomy of the system of industrial relations in this country; an autonomy which has, however, been restricted by recent attempts to secure an incomes policy and by changes in the law. In some other societies, such as Sweden, collective bargaining procedures are more highly centralized; in others, for example the United

States, they are decentralized but much more uniform because of statutory regulation. All, however, have the same function of making it possible for conflicts of interest to be worked out within a framework of rules and, except in a minority of cases, without resort to force (for example, strikes and lock-outs).

In many societies the institutionalization of industrial conflict has included a further stage, the establishment of procedures for conciliation and arbitration; and in some cases, such as in Australia for over half a century, compulsory arbitration has been statutorily enforced. This means that disputes not previously resolved must be submitted to arbitration and the decision of the arbitrator must be accepted by both parties. In Britain until very recently this has only been the case exceptionally (for example, during and immediately after the two world wars), partly because of the difficulty of enforcing such decisions. However, largely because of government initiative, machinery for conciliation and voluntary arbitration has existed for many years and is of considerable importance.

The institutionalization of industrial conflict does not necessarily mean that there is less conflict (though this may be so), but it does mean that conflict tends to change its outward manifestations. In particular, the strike, which can be regarded as the most important sanction in the hands of employees, may be used less often. The changing pattern of industrial conflict between 1900 and 1956 in fifteen selected countries is summarized in Table 12.1.[4] The figures suggest that strikes are less significant than they were at the beginning of the century. The table also shows that in the most recent period (up to 1956) there were important differences between the fifteen societies. In Britain, Denmark, West Germany, the Netherlands, Norway and Sweden very few union members went on strike in any one year (Britain had the highest rate, averaging 5·9 per cent per year); strikes tended to be short, except in Norway and Sweden; and relatively few working days were lost per union member (Britain was again highest with an average of 22·5 days per 100 union members). In comparison with this group, the USA and Canada exhibited a rather higher propensity to strike; they had somewhat longer strikes, and ten times as many working days lost per union member. In France, Italy, Japan and India an even higher percentage of union members struck each year, but strikes were of short duration, so that the average

Table 12.1   Changing patterns of industrial conflict

Country	Membership involvement ratio			Duration of strikes			Membership loss ratio		
	Workers involved in strikes as a % of union membership (per year)			Working days lost per striker (per year)			Working days lost per 100 union members (per year)		
	1900–29	1930–47	1948–56	1900–29	1930–47	1948–56	1900–29	1930–47	1948–56
Denmark	6·3	2·4	1·4	28·7	24·3	4·3	203·7	64·9	17·1
Netherlands	7·0	2·6	1·3	32·7	21·3	7·5	212·6	51·7	10·4
United Kingdom	16·1	6·4	5·9	23·0	6·6	4·3	434·4	45·2	22·5
Germany	14·2	3·7	2·6	15·6	12·5	9·9	221·3	—	15·1
Norway	27·0	6·8	1·2	33·6	43·0	15·2	941·8	542·2	16·2
Sweden	22·7	3·0	0·3	37·1	51·0	22·6	893·9	183·0	13·3
France	27·1	29·0	62·4	14·4	14·9	2·9	415·7	175·5	171·2
Italy	—	—	35·2	—	—	2·7	—	—	85·5
Japan	30·3	39·0	21·5	—	9·1	4·9	—	170·8	110·1
India	—	102·2	37·2	26·6	11·8	8·8	—	1,192·8	315·2
United States	33·2	20·3	15·4	—	14·6	14·6	—	296·4	235·6
Canada	14·7	13·3	6·3	27·1	11·0	19·3	445·4	138·9	129·7
Australia	18·2	14·8	25·2	14·2	7·0	3·2	261·9	86·7	86·4
Finland	24·5	9·0	13·9	36·0	14·5	15·8	810·4	125·7	579·8
South Africa	24·4	3·9	1·4	15·8	9·4	2·6	315·2	38·1	5·0

Source: A. M. Ross and P. T. Hartman, *Changing Patterns of Industrial Conflict*, New York: Wiley, 1960.

number of working days lost per union member was much the same as in the USA and Canada. Australia, Finland, and South Africa did not fit neatly into any of these patterns. That considerable differences between countries have continued to exist is illustrated by the figures in Table 12.2.

These trends and differences have been explained by two sets of factors: by changes in the social structure of industrial and industrializing societies —changes which include a decline in class antagonism and the growth of more heterogeneous communities; and by the growth of effective industrial relations procedures—so that strikes decline and become means of protest rather than an inevitable stage in long drawn out disputes. The fifteen societies differed in the extent to which these changes in social structure had taken place, and perhaps more obviously, in the degree of 'success' with which conflict had been institutionalized. In the first group of societies there were firm and stable trade-union movements, stable and relatively centralized collective bargaining machinery, and apparently realistic political alternatives to industrial action (in the form of powerful Labour or Social Democratic parties). Moreover, except in Norway and Sweden, the government had intervened to settle industrial disputes and done so largely successfully. In France, Italy, India and Japan, which presented

Table 12.2   Working days lost due to industrial disputes: selected countries 1964–6

Country	Average number of working days lost per 1,000 employees, 1964–6
Republic of Ireland	1,620
Italy	1,170
Canada	970
USA	870
Australia	400
Japan	240
France	200
United Kingdom	190
Denmark	160
Finland	80
Sweden	40
Netherlands	20
Federal Republic of Germany } Norway	less than 10

Source: H. A. Turner, *Is Britain Really Strike-Prone?*, Cambridge University Press, 1969, p. 7.

the most marked contrast, unions were unstable, negotiating machinery was not strongly established, left-wing political parties did not offer a realistic alternative to industrial action, and government intervention, when it occurred, was resented.

The tendency for strikes to decline in frequency and severity, however, has not continued. In many, though not all, of the societies listed in Table 12.1 there was an increase in strike activity in the 1960s, so that the thesis that we have been observing, 'the withering away of the strike' would, at best, appear premature. In Britain, for example, there were more working days lost through strikes (though not more strikes) in 1971 than at any time since 1926, the year of the General Strike.

Explanations of this change in the strike pattern vary. It may appear to be a temporary break in the long-term decline in strike activity in highly industrial countries. Alternatively, it may be seen as an indication that there are limits in the extent to which industrial conflict can be institutionalized. The organization of workers in trade unions gives rise to problems of intra-union conflict between its officials and rank-and-file members, and so to the likelihood of more unofficial strikes which are contrary to the official union policy as well as to the employers' interests. Moreover, the pursuit of the goal of 'industrial peace' may only be possible at the cost of apparently inflationary wage settlements, and government policies to secure wage restraint may be resisted through strike action. Third, an increase in the rate of technical change, or rising expectations on the part of employees, may lead to new demands and new forms of conflict (for example, the 'work-in') which cannot be contained within existing institutions. More radically, the change in the strike pattern may be seen as a reflection of the inherent instabilities of capitalist societies, characterized as they are by marked inequalities of income and wealth, and of their persistent economic problems. From such a perspective, overt industrial conflict is normal, and the problem is to explain the absence, rather than the presence, of strike activity. Thus, even a brief examination of international strike patterns involves a consideration of some of the central problems in the analysis of the structure of industrial societies as a whole.

Conflict in particular industries

Within industrial societies there are differences in the level and intensity of conflict from industry to industry and from firm to firm; differences in the degree to which there is awareness of conflicting interests; and differences in the way in which conflict manifests itself. Thus, while in some enterprises stoppages of work appear to be endemic, in others they are unknown and employees identify with the firm and regard its interests as their interests. The explanation of these differences is complex. Some firms, for example, emphasize a traditional, paternalist relationship with their employees, which plays down the market transaction of buying and selling labour and stresses the employer's responsibility for his 'family' and his 'fatherly' authority over them. Yet such an alternative is not really open to large enterprises or to those with fluctuating demands for labour, and in any case it involves disadvantages as well as advantages.

Nor is this type of explanation, concentrating as it does on managerial policies, entirely adequate to explain the regularities in strike rates in different industries. For differences in propensity to strike are not only to be found between firms but also between industries. Working days lost as a proportion of those employed are consistently high for some industries and consistently low for others (see Table 12.3).[5] Any adequate explanation of such differences must be applicable very

Table 12.3 General pattern of strike propensities

Propensity to strike	Industry
High	Mining
	Maritime and longshore
Medium high	Lumber
	Textile
Medium	Chemical
	Printing
	Leather
	Manufacturing (general)
	Construction
	Food and kindred products
Medium low	Clothing
	Gas, water, and electricity
	Services (hotels, restaurants, etc.)
Low	Railroad
	Agriculture
	Trade

Note: This table is based on data from eleven countries for varying periods between 1915 and 1949. Strike propensity is in terms of man days lost related to the employment size of the industry. The countries are Australia, Czechoslovakia, Germany, Italy, the Netherlands, New Zealand, Norway, Sweden, Switzerland, the United Kingdom, and the United States.

Source: C. Kerr and A. Siegal, 'The inter-industry propensity to strike—an international comparison', in A. Kornhauser, R. Dubin and A. M. Ross (eds), *Industrial Conflict*, New York: McGraw-Hill, 1954.

generally and therefore some popular explanations of high strike rates, such as militant union leadership or bad human relations practices, are unlikely to be true of all cases. Rather, one must look for characteristics which are common to industries with a high propensity to strike but which at the same time distinguish them from industries with low strike rates. The most conspicuous of these is the location of the worker in society.

Industrial workers like miners and dockers tend to be members of relatively homogeneous communities which are socially and/or geographically isolated from the rest of the society. Whilst all workers have grievances, these workers have the same grievances against the same employers, at the same time and in the same place. Because of the absence of other forms of employment in the area they cannot respond to a conflict situation by changing jobs; and because there is little differentiation within the occupation such workers cannot improve their situation by gaining promotion to a more highly paid job. In such circumstances conflict tends to be intensified and it tends more often to take the form of strike action. In contrast workers in industries with low strike rates are typically members of occupationally heterogeneous communities. This means that they have the possibility of occupational choice, of changes in employment, and in addition very frequently the possibility of improving their situation by upward mobility within an occupation or industry. They belong to associations with heterogeneous membership and mix with others who have different grievances against different employers. In cases of industrial conflict there are strong pressures on both sides from neutrals to settle quickly and peaceably.

It is also noticeable that the industries with a high propensity to strike tend to be characterized by jobs which are physically difficult and unpleasant, relatively unskilled, and casual or seasonal. In contrast, the 'peaceful' industries tend to be characterized by jobs which are physically easier, skilled, responsible and steady. Strikes can therefore be expected to occur most frequently where there are large numbers of workers who are socially segregated and doing relatively unpleasant jobs.

These explanations cannot be regarded as accounting for all variations in inter-industry strike patterns. Some industries, steel for example, are much more strike prone in some countries than in others. They can, however, be related to the earlier discussion of trade unionism. It is especially in industries such as mining and dock work that the market and work situations of the employee, and indeed his status situation, lead to awareness of common interests over and against those of the employer. In addition, the structure of the industry and the community provide few, if any, alternatives to direct conflict with the employer if the worker is to improve his situation.

Industrial conflict, then, can and must be explained in terms of social structures. It is latent in all relations between employers and employees because they have conflicting interests in the price of labour and in the exercise of power in the enterprise, if for no other reasons. Differences in the degree and incidence of industrial conflict are to be explained in terms of the social situations of the parties (in particular in the market, work and status situations of the employee), and in terms of the nature and effectiveness of the institutionalized means for resolving such conflicts.

Social relations at the workplace

The pattern of relations between workers and managers at the workplace can to some extent be explained in the same terms as the pattern of industrial relations in a whole industry. The nature of the relevant industrial relations procedures, for example, is obviously reflected in social relations at this level but in order to explain differences between firms or between groups of workers within a firm a more detailed examination is necessary. In addition to such factors as the pattern of industrial relations in an industry or society as a whole one must consider factors which are characteristic of *particular* situations.

One of the most important of these differences between industries or firms is the type of production system. This may vary even within an industry, and can change quite radically over time. In industries without a standardized product, such as shipbuilding or printing, there is less possibility of extreme rationalization and production depends on the skills of the craftsman, who has considerable autonomy and can derive considerable intrinsic satisfaction from his work. On the motor car assembly line, in contrast, there is extreme fragmentation of tasks and the worker's job is characterized by a mechanically controlled work pace, extreme repetitiveness, a minimum of skill, predetermination of tools and techniques, and only surface demands on the worker's mental attention. In a process production industry, for example certain chemical plants, production is entirely mechanized but the worker may again have the possibility of deriving satisfaction from the responsibility of controlling the largely automated system.

'Craft' industries, mass production and process production differ not only in the extent to which the work offers intrinsic satisfaction, but also in the nature of social relations between workers. In craft industries workers of necessity interact on the job and share a common identity as high-status, skilled craftsmen. Process production operatives tend to be organized in work groups which are hierarchically structured internally and which make for a highly cohesive work organization. In marked contrast, workers on the assembly line tend to be tied to one place on the line and lack membership of a clearly defined work group.

Within a single plant the position of a group of workers in the production process is often relevant to its relations with other groups of workers and with management. In general, highly paid high-status groups tend to be 'conservative' in terms of industrial relations behaviour, only rarely using restrained pressure to redress a specific grievance. Those groups which are in the middle ranges of a factory status hierarchy tend to be more active in attempts to improve their relative status position. If such work groups are internally united their attempts are likely to be pursued as part of a consistent and well-organized 'strategy'; if the work groups are less cohesive their attempts to improve their position are likely to be more 'erratic' and less rational. Low-status groups, which generally lack cohesion or have a transient membership tend to be 'apathetic' in their relations with management.[6]

Among British coalminers it has also been shown that the high-status face workers were likely to take concerted action to secure their aims *vis-à-vis* management, while the lower-status haulage and surface workers expressed their dissatisfaction in high levels of absence.[7] The hierarchically structured work groups in the steel industry provide a further example of the importance of the occupational structure of the plant. Production workers in this industry can work up to more responsible and highly paid positions on the basis of seniority, and this is often considered to be an important reason for the relative stability of management–worker relations in the industry.

Thus the nature of the division of labour within a plant has important consequences for relations within and between groups of workers and between workers and management. It is closely related to technology but can vary independently of it. Indeed, several studies have shown how a different allocation of tasks within the same production system can lead to important differences in social relations and behaviour.

In any particular situation other factors may be more decisive than the technology and division of labour at the workplace. One such factor is the economic situation of the firm or industry. The stability of the demand for labour, the extent to which wages are a high proportion of total costs, and the degree to which competition makes for pressure to reduce labour costs are also important considerations for management–worker relations. Certain industries, for example shipbuilding, have been characterized by considerable instability of employment. The relatively high levels of conflict between different occupational groups (demarcation disputes) and between workers and management in this 'craft' industry must be seen in the light of this instability and the continuing preoccupation with the supply of work. By contrast, in an oil refinery, where labour costs are a relatively small proportion of total costs and employment is very stable, there is a good basis for 'productivity bargaining'. In such cases the already relatively peaceful management–worker relations can be improved by an offer of considerably higher rates of pay in exchange for alterations in working practices.

Equally important are the expectations of the workers themselves. These expectations are partly a result of socialization into the workplace (most notably in apprenticeship) and of membership in work groups. To a significant extent, however, they are also a consequence of the situation of the worker outside the workplace and the roles he plays in the family, the community and the class structure. The traditional working-class communities of coalminers, dockworkers and others have been characterized by norms of solidarity with fellow workers and by antagonism towards 'them'—employers, managers and others in authority. This orientation, as well as being a part of the explanation of higher strike rates in these industries, was reflected in workplace relationships.

A rather different example of the importance of the workers' expectations and orientation to work comes from a study of assembly-line workers in a motor car factory in Luton.[8] It might have been expected that these workers would be dissatisfied with their situation and hostile to management because of the nature of their tasks and the difficulty of establishing any stable personal relations with others at work. Such findings have been reported in American studies of assembly-line workers. In the Luton case, however, although there was dissatisfaction with the actual *tasks* to be done, the workers were satisfied with their *jobs* and relatively favourably disposed towards management. Because of their desire to maintain a particular style of life, and in the absence of any contrary pressures in the relatively recently established communities in which they lived, these workers had sought the highest paid jobs available to anyone with their particular abilities and qualifications. Their demands from their work were financial and they did not seek either intrinsically interesting tasks or the satisfactions of having close personal relations with fellow workers. Because their employment by and large met the demands they made of it, they felt no particular antagonism towards management (nor any particular loyalty to the firm). In a situation of full employment they were, to a marked extent, a self-selected labour force. This selection had been made, to their general satisfaction, in terms of a prior orientation to work, and only in terms of this could their attitudes and behaviour at work be understood.

Any study of management–worker relations, even at the face-to-face level in a particular factory or workshop, has to take into account not only the characteristics of the situation itself, but also the 'external' influences upon it. More generally, the pattern of industrial relations at any level—plant, industry or society—can only be understood and explained if it is related to the structure of the wider society.

Industrial relations in modernizing societies

This chapter has so far been confined to industrial societies since it is in these societies that relationships between employers and employees become significant. With the increasing importance of employment in modernizing societies, however, relations of production bearing some similarity to those we have been discussing begin to emerge. In many modernizing societies—most of Africa for example—industrial employment is still relatively rare and employer–employee relations are to be found principally in mining, on the railways and in plantation agriculture. Large-scale mining and plantation agriculture have invariably been developed in the first instance by white settlers or overseas companies; in other words the entrepreneurial activity came from persons and companies with a background of an industrial society. Skilled manual labour, too, has in the past been mainly immigrant labour, especially in South and Central Africa where skilled occupations were, and in South Africa still are, open only to whites. Much of the semi-skilled and unskilled labour of African mines and plantations has been provided by African migrants of varying degrees of permanence. Sometimes they travel annually to spend part of the year in the towns; sometimes they stay for several years, returning to their rural home and their families only when they have earned enough money to pay required taxes or to buy desired consumer goods. Such migrant labour is cheaper and easier for the employer to control than a more stable labour force; its lack of permanence and, in colonial and southern Africa its political subordination, provide no basis for the emergence of powerful trade unions. The relative inefficiency of migrant labour, however, has encouraged some mining companies to introduce elaborate selection and training schemes in an attempt to raise levels of productivity.

Throughout Africa, the northern half of Latin America and, with few exceptions, Asia the proportion of the population engaged in industrial activities is very small. To the extent that industrialization spreads, an increasing number of workers will become permanently dependent upon employment for their livelihood. There is no reason to suppose, however, that the particular course of development which we have surveyed in the industrial West will necessarily be followed elsewhere. Indeed, in the most important example to date of industrialization in a non-Western society—Japan—the growth of the factory system of production has led to a very different pattern of social relations.[9] In spite of a general expectation of permanent employer–employee relations, traditional norms and values have a continuing influence. Employees are recruited at the end of their full-time education. Many employers recruit from a limited number of sources and look especially for workers who have the 'right' personal qualities, who will be 'stable', and who will fit easily into the traditional employer–employee relationship. *Personal* contacts between firms and the schools, colleges and universities are important in this process. The level of education attained determines the level at which the employee enters the firm and the range of positions open to him. Subsequent promotion to such positions depends partly on ability but also on age and length of service (which are closely related). The pattern of payment is similar and a considerable proportion of the total pay packet is determined by factors like age, status and family responsibilities. In addition, larger employers customarily provide a wide range of non-pecuniary benefits, such as subsidized housing, company medical services, and so on. Thus paternalism, kinship and hierarchy, all of which were very important in traditional Japanese society, are reflected in the social relations even of modern Japanese factories. Even large firms, where face-to-face contact between the employer and all employees is impossible, are in many respects 'family-like'.

Important aspects of traditional social relations have survived Japan's rapid industrialization; the factory system of production has been moulded to conform with them. In some respects such a system may appear 'inefficient'. It is not possible for a firm to dismiss employees (with the exception of the small proportion of temporaries) just because they are incompetent or because trade is slack; the payment system too, emphasizes loyalty and commitment to the firm rather than rewarding individual effort and efficiency. The expectations of employers and employees, however, are very different from those common in a society like Britain and, because of the mutual obligation to maintain their relationship for the whole of the employee's working life, some of the grounds for conflict which we have discussed may be less strongly felt. Certainly Japan's comparative industrial performance during the last two decades does not suggest that such a pattern is necessarily less effective in terms of production than that of the West. In Japanese industry trade unions have rather different functions from those described for Britain. With such a close family-like relationship between employer and employee there is little room for a third party. So, although unions are formally quite strong, they tend to be unimportant at the plant and shop-floor level, having as their main function bargaining with the employer about the level of the twice yearly bonus.

The example of Japan should make us aware of the possibility of alternative paths of industrial development from that followed by the Western world. The Soviet Union, with its heavy involvement of the state in the industrialization process is a clear example of yet another course. So even if the contemporary modernizing societies undergo a process of industrialization—and in the short run at least this is by no means inevitable—there is no reason to expect the actual course of events to approximate to earlier industrialization experiences.

Such developments in industrial relations as have taken place already show some very clear differences. The way in which trade unionism has developed in Africa, for example, can only be understood in the light of the total structure and development of African societies. Under colonial administrations any form of union activity tended to be seen by the government as subversive, especially if it was action by government employees. Inevitably, therefore, unions became involved to a greater or lesser extent in opposition to the government and so in the struggle for independence. In some colonies, such as Kenya, the trade-union movement acted as a substitute for the banned nationalist party although it had to pursue non-militant industrial policies in order to avoid being banned itself. In others, like the Gold Coast and Tanganyika, the nationalist party secured dominance over the union movement (though not without some resistance from established union leaders) and the two were seen as part of the same campaign for independence. In either case the wider problems of colonialism provided a context for union growth which encouraged direct political action on the part of the unions. Very often the unions of the newly independent countries were more political bodies than economic.

In Latin America, too, despite the absence of widespread formal colonialism this century, developments have been far from identical with those of the West. Here many of the 'feudal' personal relationships which had been developed between patron and peasant in the rural areas were carried over into the urban industrial situation. The employer was often seen as the provider of protection and services in return for which the employee gave his political loyalty. These personal loyalties cut across class lines so that the unions were more mechanisms for the mobilization of political support and for the provision of medical, legal and other services for their members than agencies of conflict. (Perhaps one should point out that there has also been a group of unions, made up mostly of immigrants from Europe, which has not had this personalist orientation and which has functioned more as an agency of conflict between classes.)

In both Africa and Latin America the contemporary economic situation is one of very considerable unemployment and/or under-employment. One of the consequences of this is that the bargaining power of the industrial workers is very weak (except where their skills are scarce or where they are protected by discriminatory legislation). This, combined with the usually slow growth of industrial occupations, has two correlates. First, the employed workers who form the trade unions are among the economically privileged, and the unions are concerned with protecting their members against new migrants to the towns rather than with protecting them against the employers (and often the state is the main employer anyway). Second, there is a widespread recognition that economic action by the unions is unlikely to prove an effective way of improving their position; political action may be a much quicker road to success. So there are contemporary reasons as well as historical ones why many union movements—especially but not only those in Latin America—are deeply and *directly* involved in the political process. They may even provide the main source of support for the government and in Latin America some unions have even been formed by politicians seeking to create a basis for power.

Enough has been said to show that the nature and development of industrial relations can vary widely. The differences in the development of industrial relations so far are at least as significant as the similarities, and future developments are likely to be different again. Any further industrialization of the modernizing world will add to the already vast variety of human social situations. For the sociologist, this variety provides an opportunity to use comparative methods to increase our understanding of the nature and causes of the different social relations between employers and employees.

Notes

1　Children's Employment Commission, quoted in H. D. Fong, *The Triumph of the Factory System in England*, Tientsin: Chihli Press, 1930.
2　See Lloyd Warner and J. O. Low, *Yankee City*, New Haven: Yale University Press, 1963.
3　D. Lockwood, *The Blackcoated Worker*, London: Allen & Unwin, 1958. The following discussion summarizes Lockwood's argument on trade unionism.
4　The figures in this table and the discussion of them are based on A. M. Ross and P. T. Hartman, *Changing Patterns of Industrial Conflict*, New York: Wiley, 1960.
5　C. Kerr and A. J. Siegel, 'The inter-industry propensity to strike—an international comparison',
in A. Kornhauser, R. Dubin and A. M. Ross (eds), *Industrial Conflict*, New York: McGraw-Hill, 1954. The following discussion is based largely on this source.
6　L. R. Sayles, *Behaviour of Industrial Work Groups*, New York: Wiley, 1958.
7　W. H. Scott *et al.*, *Coal and Conflict*, Liverpool University Press, 1963.
8　F. Bechoffer, J. H. Goldthorpe, D. Lockwood and Jennifer Platt, *The Affluent Worker: Industrial Attitudes and Behaviour*, Cambridge University Press, 1968.
9　J. C. Abegglen, *The Japanese Factory*, Chicago: Free Press, 1960.

Reading

Bendix, R., *Work and Authority in Industry*, New York: Harper, 1963. A study of industrialization in eighteenth- and nineteenth-century Britain and Russia and twentieth-century America and East Germany which contrasts the ideologies through which managers have sought to justify their authority over their employees.

Davies, I., *African Trade Unions*, Harmondsworth: Penguin, 1966. A survey of the development and functions of trade unions in Africa.

Flanders, A. (ed.), *Collective Bargaining*, Harmondsworth: Penguin, 1969. This wide-ranging collection of papers on industrial relations covers a number of societies and gives a good idea of current approaches to the subject.

Gouldner, A. W., *Patterns of Industrial Bureaucracy*, London: Routledge & Kegan Paul, 1955, and *Wild Cat Strike*, London: Routledge & Kegan Paul, 1955. Gouldner studied a gypsum plant during a period in which the management attempted to introduce more bureaucratic means of control and traced the consequences for manager-worker relations. Each book is self-contained, though they describe different aspects of the same situation.

Hyman, R., *Strikes*, London: Fontana/Collins, 1972. An account of industrial conflict in Britain and an incisive critique of explanations of it.

Lockwood, D., *The Blackcoated Worker*, London: Allen & Unwin, 1958. A study of class consciousness which includes an important chapter on trade unionism among clerical workers. Already a 'classic'.

Parker, S. R. *et al.*, *The Sociology of Industry*, London: Allen & Unwin, 1972. An introduction to the whole field of industrial sociology which indicates the scope of the subject and includes suggestions for more detailed reading.

Further reading

Baldamus, W., *Efficiency and Effort*, London: Tavistock, 1961. An important theoretical analysis of the nature and consequences of industrial conflict.

Blauner, R., *Alienation and Freedom*, Chicago University Press, 1964. The author compares the worker's situation in four industries (printing, textiles, motor car assembly, chemicals) which have contrasting technologies.

Burns, T. (ed.), *Industrial Man*, Harmondsworth: Penguin, 1969. This excellent collection of articles and extracts is designed to indicate the range of influences of industrialization on societies.

Eldridge, J. E. T., *Industrial Disputes*, London: Routledge & Kegan Paul, 1968. This volume contains some general essays on industrial conflict and detailed studies of disputes in shipbuilding, the steel industry and the constructional engineering industry.

Goldthorpe, J. H. *et al.*, *The Affluent Worker: Industrial Attitudes and Behaviour*, Cambridge University Press, 1968. A study of workers in three different industries which is of interest in itself and for its critical comments on previous analyses of workers' attitudes and behaviour.

Lupton, T., *On the Shop Floor*, London: Pergamon, 1963. A detailed comparison of two workshop situations. Lupton suggests a range of internal and external factors which need to be taken into account to explain the workers' different responses to incentive payment systems.

Sayles, L. R., *Behaviour of Industrial Work Groups*, New York: Wiley, 1958. An extensive comparison of 'work groups' in which grievance behaviour is related to the workers' varied positions in the production process.

13 Religion

In all societies there are rules of behaviour, ideals of perfection, explanations of disasters and illnesses, and theories concerning the origin of man and the world. Frequently these rules and explanations are related to what we would call supernatural forces. Religion consists of belief in such forces and of the activities which result, directly or indirectly, from this belief. In some societies the belief is the most important thing; in others ritualistic actions are dominant. But different societies have different rules and explanations; phenomena explained by religion in one society may have a non-religious explanation in another; activities which have profound religious implications in one society may have none in another. Whilst this has always been the case, the very rapid social change which has occurred in the world in the last three hundred or so years shows the differences particularly clearly.

The history of mankind may be viewed as the gradual extension of human control over the physical environment. This process has become less and less gradual and the extensions of this control which have occurred even within our own lifetime are enormous. Through the activities of science we can, for example, understand (and therefore prevent or cure) many diseases which in the past were (and in some societies are still) explained in supernatural terms. One of the results of this is that in many spheres scientific explanations have superseded religious ones and, in many ways, modern industrial societies are less religious than were pre-industrial societies. One should however, beware of presenting scientific or 'natural' explanations and religious explanations as alternatives since they have existed side by side in all known societies.

We are chiefly interested, however, in the social conditions under which different types of religious organization flourish and for this purpose we must look at religion in different types of societies and, in complex societies, among different sections of the population. And we must expect to find considerable differences; for although religious activities and beliefs are to be found in, say, industrial societies, they are rarely of the kind that suggest that one's wife will be barren unless an ox is sacrificed at the wedding.

Religion in simple societies

In simple societies people as a rule believe that all activities are under the control of 'supernatural' forces which may intervene to alter the course of events. These forces may take the form of supreme gods, fetishes (material objects, for example statues, believed to have inherent powers), personal spirits, or totems (usually a species of animal with which the members of a clan or descent group are linked). But in addition to such beliefs all simple societies exhibit religious rituals which may be much more important than the beliefs, although the two are usually related. Rituals and beliefs involve the whole community and permeate the whole of life so that, in a very real sense, one can describe these societies as religious societies.

In simple societies a good deal of time and energy is taken up with attempting to influence the gods, spirits or whatever, and there are invariably prescribed ways of doing this. It is convenient to distinguish two main aspects of religious ritual. The first is in the nature of ceremonial which marks important occasions in the life of an individual or a group. Such occasions often mark changes in legal or social position and can best be summed up by the French term *rites de passage* which has been adopted untranslated into English usage to refer to just such occasions. The second aspect of religious ritual is concerned primarily with the well-being of individual members of the society but may also be related to the well-being of society as a whole.

A good example of the first aspect of ritual can be found in the description by the anthropologist Peter Farb of the ceremonies surrounding the initiation into manhood of boys among the Indian bands of southern California.[1]

> Several youths of puberty age were gathered at night into a special enclosure where they drank a concoction prepared from the roots of Jimsonweed. The effects of the drug lasted from two to four days. During that time the initiates experienced visions of spirits, which they believed gave them supernatural powers. Later the initiates had to descend into a pit dug in the ground, symbolic of death, and then climb out again, supposedly indicating rebirth. Inside the pit they had to jump from one flat stone to another, and if a boy stumbled, that clearly indicated a short life for him. They were put through several physical ordeals; the severest one was to lie motionless while being bitten repeatedly by hordes of angry ants. As ordeal passed to new ordeal throughout the ceremony, the candidate received long lectures on proper conduct, on how to become a man of value, and on the religious practices of his band.

In addition to initiation rites, the ceremonies surrounding marriage, childbirth, and death are invariably marked in simple societies (as in modern societies) by solemn ritual. Similarly with the great occasions of the whole community. In agricultural societies the most important events are those connected with the crops and one finds seedtime, the coming of the rains, and especially harvest are usually times of great religious festivals. Thus among the Akan people of Ghana and the Trobriand islanders of the Pacific the yam festival is the great annual gathering.

But these rites and ceremonies not only mark the passing from one period of the farming year to the next, or from one status in an individual's life to the next (for example, childhood to adulthood). They are also believed to be necessary in ensuring success in the next stage. Thus agricultural rites ensure the fertility of the soil; marriage rites ensure the fertility of the women. One can see here the second aspect of rites—that of securing the assistance of supernatural forces in the ordinary events of daily life. We find ritual behaviour particularly intense, however, in situations of danger, at times of illness, or when the normally benevolent gods turn nasty—for example in time of famine: in short, when the well-being of an individual or a community is threatened. In societies with a high level of belief in the supernatural, illness or a great calamity such as famine or defeat in battle is often thought to be brought about by some fault in the individual or community concerned. The gods or spirits have been wronged and matters cannot be set right until the wrong has in some way been atoned. This may involve the performance of a specific ritual or it may involve the whole society in the adoption of a more moral way of life. The story of the people of Israel as told in the Old Testament is full of such incidents. For example:[2]

> And the Lord sent fiery serpents among the people and they bit the people; and much people of Israel died. Therefore the people came to Moses and said, We have sinned for we have spoken against the Lord and against thee; pray unto the Lord that he take away the serpents from us. And Moses prayed for the people. And the Lord said unto Moses, Make thee a fiery serpent and set it upon a pole: and it shall come to pass that every one that is bitten, when he looketh upon it, shall live. And Moses made a serpent of brass, and put it upon a pole, and it came to pass, that if a serpent had bitten any man, when he beheld the serpent of brass, he lived.

Indeed, the reader of the Old Testament is struck by the way in which the whole history of Israel seems to be a cycle of disobedience to God; a crisis of some sort, interpreted as a punishment; atonement either by sacrifice or by the reinstitution of a moral way of life; followed by success in battle or in some other material field.

It is at such times of crisis that the power of the religious specialist is at its height. His knowledge of what it is the gods require—moral behaviour, sacrifices, performance of ritual, etc.—gives him power to command obedience. Once again the Old Testament provides us with many illustrations of the efficacy of religion in obtaining adherence to the rule of law. An example of a threatening God will perhaps suffice:[3]

> Behold I set before you this day a blessing and a curse; A blessing if ye obey the commandments of the Lord your God, which I command you this day: And a curse, if ye will not obey the commandments of the Lord your God.

In a society where there is belief in divine retribution the religious specialist therefore has considerable power and is often, as was the case with Moses, the political leader as well.

This second aspect of ritual is not, in essentials, different for a community in trouble through famine or war than for a sick individual. The problem is to find out in what way one's behaviour has been lacking and to correct the fault. Such is the propensity of man not to live up to his ideals that the resultant searchings of conscience invariably reveal such inadequacies. Nevertheless, it is not always possible to locate personal or communal behaviour which has angered the gods or spirits. An alternative supernatural explanation is that evil influences are seeking to do the sick man or the community harm. Frequently these evil influences are conceived of in human terms or as spirits who take possession of human beings thus giving rise to the phenomena of witches and witchcraft.

If it is not recognized that misfortune can occur by chance, witchcraft provides an acceptable explanation for undeserved misfortune. One of the earliest and best studies of witchcraft—that of witchcraft among the Azande (a tribe of the Sudan-Congo border) carried out by the anthropologist Evans-Pritchard—also showed that belief in witchcraft is by no means incompatible with what we should call natural explanations. There are obvious 'natural' explanations of death caused when a charging elephant treads upon a human being. What is not so obvious is why the paths of the elephant and that particular man should have coincided. Once chance is eliminated as an explanation the man might well ask, 'what have I done to deserve this?' If the answer is 'nothing' the only other explanation provided by the belief system of societies such as the Azande is that the man concerned was the victim of witchcraft. In cases of death of this kind or in cases of illness, attempts may be made to identify the witch through whom

the evil was passed and those who had recently quarrelled with the victim were the first to be accused. So along with witchcraft one invariably finds counter-witchcraft which may take the form of trials followed by the execution of the guilty.

Witchcraft beliefs and activities, then, relate to a personification of forces of evil (and/or good) in human beings. But in some societies such forces are also believed to inhere in inanimate substances and can therefore be used to force confession by the guilty or to judge the innocence or guilt of a suspect. This is another of the ways in which the supernatural is invoked in support of the rule of law in simpler societies. An eye-witness account of such a trial may help to convey something of the nature of such societies. The description is of a trial by ordeal (of boiling oil) of a young man in Liberia accused of theft.[4]

> Keke (the diviner) would allow no one to assist him in the smallest detail of preparing for the trial. He had a skin pouch slung over his shoulder, his *baka* which contained his medicine and magic. This was the tangible source of his power, his link with the supernatural, and it must not be contaminated by anyone's touch.
>
> Finally, he had everything just the way he wanted it, the fire properly hot, a three legged iron ring over it to support an enormous clay pot, the supply of rich red palm oil to be heated, the polished brass belled anklet which Comma was to pluck from the bottom of the pot, and a kettle full of leaves which he had bruised in a mortar until they were an arsenic green paste.
>
> Keke now placed the ordeal pot in the iron stand over the fire and poured the palm oil into it. [He] made a long oration while the oil was heating. Keke then talked to the pot, and told it that, if Comma had not stolen, it must not hurt him in the least, but that if he had spoiled the Loma name along with his own, it must bite him deep. Keke next addressed Comma, telling him that he could refuse the trial, confess without the ordeal if he wished and take the punishment the Old Ones would decide. Comma shook his head, indicated that the trial should go on. Keke next took the paste of leaves and smeared it in a thick coating over Comma's right hand and arm, being careful to get it between all the fingers. Then he held up

the three-knobbed brass ring and spoke at length about it. The paste of leaves was meanwhile drying into a crust over Comma's hand. It had turned a shade of sage-green where it was thinnest. There was less smoke coming off the oil now and it was less blue in colour. After another coating of the paste was rubbed on Comma, the brass anklet was dropped into the pot. Quick as a flash, Comma dived his hand in after it and brought it up, dripping oil as red as blood. A great collective sigh swept like a wind through the crowd and then the roar of approval and triumph. They carried him off to the waterside on their shoulders.

The main context for the discussion so far has been tribal societies, but there is much that has been said that is equally relevant to a consideration of religion in more complex societies. Trial by ordeal, for example, was a common feature of medieval Europe and beliefs in witchcraft and the persecution of those suspected of being witches persisted well into the eighteenth century. In Scotland the last known burning for witchcraft took place in 1722 and the widespread belief in witches certainly lasted until much later. Similarly it is not difficult to find examples from contemporary Europe of a belief in the efficacy of ritual and magical actions to avert calamities or to influence deities in the distribution of their favours. The following newspaper report is of an incident which took place in May 1967.[5]

Several thousand Neapolitans prayed throughout the day in the Church of St. Clare that the blood of St. Janarius should liquefy and thus save Naples from what the praying crowds think will be a great disaster. By sunset the small flask of the saint's congealed blood had failed to bubble. St. Janarius was a bishop who was beheaded in 305, somewhere near Naples. In the fifteenth century it was observed that a four inch glass flask, said to contain his blood, would liquefy if there were fervent prayers said to it and, at the same time, its failure to liquefy could only mean disaster. When the dark substance failed to liquefy in 1527 Naples was ravaged by plague; in 1569 there was famine; in 1835 the miracle did not occur and there was cholera. In 1941, the blood remained solid and Allied war planes bombed Naples. In 1943 the blood liquefied ahead of programme—also a bad omen

—and Vesuvius erupted the following year.

When the miracle had not taken place late last night, Archbishop Corrado Ursi ordered the reliquary containing the blood to be carried through the streets so that motorists and other Neapolitans could add their prayers to the city's patron saint that Naples be spared the threatened and still unknown calamity.

Despite such evidence of belief and ritual concerning supernatural intervention in daily life which shows a marked similarity with the religious life of simple societies, there have been numerous and important changes in the religion of European societies especially over the last four hundred years. One of these changes has been the marked decline of such beliefs and rituals both in the society as a whole and within the churches. But in order to understand such changes we must first look briefly at the changes which have occurred in the organization of religion, and we shall draw our illustrations from the Christian religion.

The social sources of religious differences

The most striking change in the organization of religion in Western Europe in the last four hundred years has been the break-up of the monolithic Christian Church into a diversity of sects and denominations. This proliferation of Christian groups can be better understood by looking at differences in the relations between religious institutions and the wider society and also at certain differences in the internal organization of religion. It is convenient and helpful to distinguish between three main types of religious organization: sect, denomination and church. These distinctions allow us to see more clearly the different functions performed by religious institutions in different social situations. The basic distinction, made more than fifty years ago by the German theologian Ernst Troeltsch between church-type institutions and sect-type institutions has subsequently proved to be one of the most useful tools with which to analyse the forms which Western Christianity has taken. The difference between the two, says Troeltsch, is quite clear:[6]

The church is that type of organization which is overwhelmingly conservative, which to a certain extent accepts the secular order and dominates the masses; in principle, therefore, it is universal, that is it desires to cover the whole life of humanity. The sects, on the other hand, are comparatively small groups; they aspire after inward personal perfection and they aim at a direct personal fellowship between the members of each group. From the very beginning, therefore, they are forced to organize themselves in small groups, and to renounce the idea of dominating the world. Their attitude towards the world, the State, and society may be indifferent, tolerant, or hostile, since they have no desire to control and incorporate these forms of social life; on the contrary they tend to avoid them.

Because of these different relationships with the wider society the two types tend to attract different types of people. The fully developed church utilizes, or even dominates, the state and becomes an integral and supportive part of the social order. Because of this the church tends to become identified with the upper classes (although its membership is made up of all classes). The sects, on the other hand, are connected with those elements in society which are opposed to the state or at least indifferent to it, in most cases the lower classes or peasantry.

To this basic distinction between sect and church

it is useful to add a third type of religious organization—the denomination. The denomination combines some of the characteristics of the sect with others of the church and also has characteristics possessed by neither of the other two. Thus the denomination compromises with the secular world (for example with regard to ethical standards) but does not seek to dominate it; it seeks neither the domination of the world nor the domination of its members; it has voluntary membership but at the same time it is an educative institution, laying less stress on particular (usually experiential) characteristics of its members than does the sect. Finally, the denomination differs from both sect and church in its tolerance of other beliefs, even to the extent of allowing that they may possess some part of the truth. The major characteristics of these three types of religious institution are summarized in Figure 13.1.

A scheme such as this allows us not only to observe differences between religious organizations but also provides a framework whereby we can observe the changes and/or schisms which particular institutions can undergo. It helps us to describe such differences and changes. Christianity itself, for example, began in a sectarian form, evolving a church-type organization only with its

Figure 13.1   The sect; the church; the denomination

	SECT	DENOMINATION	CHURCH
Attitude to wider society	Rejects values and way of life	Compromise: no attempt to dominate society	Compromise: seeks to dominate the whole society
Attitude of wider society	Ostracized	Either fashionable or neglected	Fashionable
Attitude to other religious groups	Intolerant	Tolerant	Intolerant
Attitude to members	Ideological and social domination of members	Ideological and social influence over members	Concentrates on domination of world not of members
Type of membership	Voluntary	Voluntary	Obligatory therefore large
Basis of membership	Experiential (exclusive)	Loose formal membership requirements	No membership requirements other than ritualistic
Social background of members	Typically the deprived	Middle classes	All inclusive; but leaders are wealthy and powerful
Scope	Local	National (or international)	National (or international)
Internal organization	Often charismatic	Bureaucratic	Bureaucratic

adoption as the official religion of the Roman Empire. But the church-sect-denomination typology does not in itself explain why such differences exist between one Christian body and another; still less why an organization should change from, say, a sect-type institution to a denomination. The typology merely draws our attention to certain characteristics which may be important in explanation.

The changes within Christianity in the last four hundred years provide rich material for investigating these phenomena. The Reformation and subsequent changes reflect the religious expression of newly emerging power groups and the religious protest of economically and politically deprived sections of the population. By and large the former, for example the nationalistic rulers of the German states, adopted a churchly form of organization and doctrine (such as Lutheranism), whereas the deprived adopted a sectarian form (such as the Anabaptist movement). Thus the emergence of Lutheranism or Calvinism is best understood from the sociological point of view as being the religious expression respectively of the German princes and the rising middle classes of Geneva. The German princes had a political need to be independent of the religious (and political) influence of the Pope. Consequently they championed Luther and made his cause their own. In doing so they entrenched Lutheranism as an established church predominantly serving the aristocracy and wealthy members of society. Not that Luther himself was especially notable for his love of the poor, particularly if they showed signs of attempting to alter their position. 'Remember', he wrote in his pamphlet *Against the Thieving and Murderous Hordes of Peasants*, 'that nothing can be more poisonous, harmful and devilish than a revolutionary.' Thus the peasants of Germany soon made the discovery that the new Protestantism was a protest not against their masters but against their masters' enemies.

With this disillusionment there arose the first sect of Protestantism—the Anabaptists. It was a movement made up from the peasants and poorer craftsmen; from those who were both economically and politically powerless. As has so often been the case when a depressed group has no chance of political or economic protest open to them, their activities were turned into religious channels. The Anabaptists were poorly organized and lacking in adequate leadership and they failed to survive the extreme persecution to which they were subjected. But the pattern of open

religious rebellion of the poor and powerless was to be repeated again and again throughout the next two hundred years in Europe and North America. In seventeenth-century England the Quakers emerged as a form of religious expression of the radical poor; in the eighteenth century the Methodists drew their support largely from the new urban working classes (although their leaders were from a very different social background). Both groups had in common a rapid accommodation to the wider society, swift compromise with some of their original principles and a rapid retreat into respectability. A revolutionary fervour is difficult to maintain for long, and the Quakers soon abandoned their revolutionary ideals of a new social order and instead attempted to ameliorate the effects of the old order by providing mutual aid to their members and later by engaging in social reform. The Methodists, in common with many other new religious formations of the poor (a good later example is the Salvation Army), found that the religious discipline they imposed upon their members resulted, over decades, in a betterment in the social position of those members so that the social composition of Methodism became increasingly middle-class and the nature of their religious requirements changed accordingly. In short, the tendency of many sectarian institutions like early Methodism is to become more and more denominational. Less emphasis is laid upon the peculiar characteristics of members whether in the sphere of doctrine (such as the demand for a conversion experience) or in the field of morality (such as the requirement of total abstinence). They become increasingly respectable, middle-class and tolerant, a tolerance which in the case of Methodism has led to a serious consideration of the prospects of union with other denominations, particularly with the Church of England. Indeed, in all of the features referred to in Figure 13.1, many (but not all) sects lose their original characteristics and become denominations.

The fervour, spontaneity and political violence of the earlier European sects are sometimes repeated when Christianity is exported to modernizing societies. Once again one can see the relationship between the deprivation of sections of the population and the emergence of millennial movements of a sectarian nature. In these societies, however, there are usually additional factors in that those in positions of secular power have often been aliens, and the societies have been undergoing very rapid social change.

In southern Africa many of the 'Ethiopian'

churches broke away from their parent bodies in more or less open protest against the colour bar in the existing churches. Moreover, in most of the modernizing world in the first half of the twentieth century, colonialism resulted in a distribution of power which effectively excluded the possibility of political action by the mass of the population. In this situation, as in Europe earlier, protest frequently took a religious form; the religious breakaway was often symptomatic of a more deep-seated desire for political freedom. A millennial remedy was offered for the political and economic evils under which the Africans were suffering and, depending upon the situation, this could function either to divert attention from material problems on to transcendental ends or to bring these same material problems into sharper focus.

The Messianic movements of Africa have, by and large, functioned in the latter manner. They have been closely bound up with ideas of independent rule and are often inseparable from the early nationalist movements. The Zulu uprising of 1906 found the Ethiopian preachers a ready channel of communication and their pulpits were used to incite the people to rebellion; the Shire Highlands uprising against British rule in Nyasaland in 1915 derived directly from the religious ferment of the Watchtower movement; and it was a Messianic movement among the Kikuyu which sparked off the Mau Mau uprisings in Kenya in the 1950s.

One of the most interesting, and certainly one of the best documented, of these movements that broke away from the orthodox Christianity of the the missions was that founded in the region of the lower Congo by Simon Kimbangu. It serves well as an illustration.[7] Kimbangu hád been brought up in a Protestant mission and worked for some time as a catechist. He first became widely known as a prophet with gifts of healing in the year 1921. He upheld many of the principles of the Christian missions by requiring the destruction of fetishes and by forbidding polygamy and 'obscene' dancing. His fame and following spread rapidly, to the initial delight of the Protestant missions who regarded him as an ally. The interpretation put upon the Biblical (usually Old Testament) passages which were so central to his teaching, however, was primarily anti-European and especially anti-colonial, so that his followers were soon proclaiming him to be the God of the Black Man in contrast to the Christ of the Missionaries. In keeping with the Biblical imagery, the village he

came from was renamed Jerusalem; Kimbangu himself was referred to as a 'saviour'; and he appointed twelve apostles to follow him.

The anti-European element in his preaching soon led him into trouble with the government authorities. He encouraged his followers to defy the government and to refuse to work for Europeans, telling them that this would force the Belgians to leave the country which in turn would bring the millennium. In the end he was arrested and deported by a government which saw no political implications in their actions and he died behind bars in 1950. But, as is often the case, the martyrdom of the leader merely added to the success of the movement. Kimbangu's identification of himself with the sufferings of Moses and Jesus became more real and his successors were able to continue his call for emancipation from white domination.

After his initial deportation the movement was driven underground under the leadership of André Matswa, a Congolese who had fought in France in the first world war and had also been involved in French trade union politics. Like Kimbangu, Matswa was arrested and deported and his death in 1942 raised expectations among his followers of a triumphant, liberating return. The persons of Kimbangu and Matswa thus provided a focus which made the messages of Christianity relevant to the situation of the Congolese. Kimbanguism drew on the Judaeo-Christian tradition of an oppressed people liberated by a Messiah who, in spite of martyrdom, triumphed over his enemies and promised a kingdom in which the injustices of this world would be set right. At the same time, however, it provided its own martyrs with their message of special relevance to the African colonial situation. Orthodox Christianity was seen as a religion which served to keep wealth and power in the hands of the white man and was thus in direct contrast to the message of Kimbangu.

The vitality of the Kimbangu movement and its offshoots can be seen by the reaction to two very different events. The first of them was the arrival in the Congo in 1935 of the Salvation Army. With its interest in humanitarian matters and its lack of connection with the government, the Salvation Army quickly became popular at the expense of the older missions. Moreover, the similarity of some of its emphases to the teaching of Kimbangu —especially the opposition to 'magic' and fetishism —and the appeal of uniforms, flags, drums and bands attracted many Kimbanguists to the Army. Among some of them there formed the belief that these European men and women were the reincarnation of the spirit of Simon Kimbangu and that the letter S worn on the uniform was the insignia of their prophet. Later the Kimbanguist element separated under a new leader, Simon Pierre Mpadi, to form the *Mission des Noirs*, organized on Salvation Army lines and often known as the 'khaki movement' from their khaki uniforms. Here the Kimbangu element became explicit: 'God gave us Simon Kimbangu who is for us what Moses is to the Jews, Christ to white men, and Mahommed to Arabs.'

The second wave of reaction that is of particular interest was to the German invasion and occupation of Belgium in the second world war. Pro-German factions resulted in a new sect proclaiming that the defeat of Belgium heralded the final withdrawal of the Belgian colonial government and the arrival of the millennium preached by Kimbangu. More recently the movement has become more respectable and the local groups have gathered together in a single organization, the *Église de Jésus Christ sur la Terre par le Prophète Simon Kimbangu*. The *Église* now claims to be a non-political religious sect although the favourite texts remained those which denounce the oppressive practices of the white man. During the nationalistic uprisings which preceded independence the *Église* was active in organizing boycotts of the missions, illustrating once again the close relationship between religion and politics in colonial Africa.

The story of Kimbanguism illustrates the two possible functions of religious movements with regard to anti-European, anti-colonial feeling. One possibility is that they may act as a safety valve, diverting protest into religious rather than political channels. As such they provide an alternative to total submission to the ruling (and in this case alien) power. The other is that the protest against the government may be expressed directly through the religious organizations in which case the sects themselves become the organizing agents of political protest.

Some of the most spectacular religious reactions to a situation combining economic and political deprivation with sweeping social changes are to be found in the island regions of the Southern Pacific. Cargo cults (the name derives from the importance placed upon the acquisition by the indigenous people of the 'cargo' or material goods of the white man) have sprung up all over Melanesia and Polynesia with remarkable regularity, at least since the 1870s. With the arrival of the white

man and his cargo boats, the coastal inhabitants of New Guinea and the smaller islands were faced with a totally new situation: large numbers of white men accompanied by crates of extraordinary objects. The cargo cults were the immediate reaction of the coastal peoples, but further inland change was much longer delayed and only with the coming of aeroplanes in the 1930s did the arrival of European goods create the conditions for this type of religious reaction. The details differ from cult to cult but they have in common a belief in a millennium which will occur with the return of the ancestors who will bring with them European goods and plentiful supplies of food so that there will be no need for further work. The consequent abandoning of the fields by the workers was one among several factors which made the cults unpopular with the colonial governments and particularly with the European employers. The only thing holding up the return of the ancestors is believed to be the presence of Europeans, so the first necessity is that the Europeans should be driven out.

The origins of these movements lie in a complex of factors. The establishment of alien rule through colonization; the introduction of a new religion through Christian proselytizing; the destruction of many of the indigenous institutions by the missionaries and administrators; the adoption of a cash crop economy invariably based upon a single product which was highly vulnerable to changes in the world market; and in addition to all this, a failure to provide either an understanding of these changes or the possibility of fully participating in them.

Although the cults have occurred throughout the twentieth century there have been some times when social conditions have been especially suitable to them. Thus the second world war and the years following it provided changes in the domination and administration of many of these societies from English or Australian to Japanese; from Japanese to American; and from American back to Australian. Such changes, especially if the ruling group was driven out by violence, were seen as clear indications of the ending of an era and as heralding the millennium.

As an example of one of these cargo cults let us look at the John Frum movement in the New Hebridean island of Tanna.[8] Tanna was an island which came under formal British administration in 1912. The greater part of European influence, however, had come from Christian missionaries of whom the Presbyterians were the first to arrive.

In 1921 80 per cent 'of |the inhabitants were Presbyterian but their monopoly was broken by the arrival of Seventh Day Adventist missionaries in 1931 and Roman Catholics in 1933. In spite of formal adherence to the missions there was apparently considerable dissatisfaction with mission teaching. In particular, there was widespread disappointment that embracing the new religion did not appear to lead immediately to material gain. It did not enable the islanders to live, as did the white missionaries, without 'working'. To this situation was added, at the beginning of the second world war, a severe economic depression brought by the world slump in copra prices. The first signs of disturbance appeared in early 1940 with the emergence of a prophet by the name of John Frum. John Frum prophesied a volcanic cataclysm after which the reign of bliss would commence when all the material benefits of the Europeans would be rightfully diverted to the local people.

The immediate attainment of utopia was prevented by the presence of white men on the island so the expulsion of all white men was necessary. The use of European money was also to cease and a return to selected traditional customs (polygamy, dancing etc. which had been banned by the missionaries) was encouraged. Any money required in the future paradise would be supplied by John Frum himself. The result was a huge spending spree, a 'bluing' of the soon-to-be-useless European money—a factor which gave the cult a temporary popularity with the white trading community. Huge feasts were also held to use up food. The followers of John Frum deserted the missions and joined the pagan groups in the interior of the island.

A further, and more significant, outbreak occurred a year later and the leaders were arrested. John Frum himself—a young man named Manehivi—was imprisoned and later exiled; other leaders were imprisoned and chiefs who had followed them were heavily fined. But the movement flourished in spite of this repression. Myths built up about John Frum in his absence that would have been difficult to sustain had he been present. One such myth was that he was king of America and that he and the ancestors would return from America. The arrival of American troops in response to the threat of Japanese invasion, therefore, was a clear indication of the imminence of the millennium, particularly as many of the American soldiers were black. The movement consequently prospered all the more; the missions remained deserted; and more and

more arrests and deportations were made.

From time to time during the next five years new leaders arose calling themselves John Frum. One organized Tannese labour to build an airstrip for the arrival, by American Liberator planes, of the 'cargo'. Another instructed his followers to raid the stores and tear price labels off the goods. Both were arrested and imprisoned along with their leading followers. Such continued suppression had a weakening effect on the movement, but probably more important was the revival of the price of copra in 1948 with its attendant general improvement in the economic well-being of the island. Indeed, when the price again fell four years later it became apparent that there was still considerable unrest in Tanna and that the movement still had considerable popular appeal in times of economic and political stress.

The John Frum movement shows how alien rule, the activities of missionaries, a single crop economy highly vulnerable to shifts in world prices and the highly visible but not accessible material goods of the Europeans are all bound up in the cargo cults. It shows quite clearly that in order to *understand* such movements one must look not only at the religious setting but also at the total social situation.

Religion in industrial societies

Even the most casual comparison between life in the non-industrial societies we have been considering until now and life in industrial societies reveals a considerable difference in the place of religion. A comparison of contemporary England with medieval England highlights these differences. Then, the Church was one of the main foundations of the society on both the national and the community level; now it is an organization which deals largely with one small area of men's affairs. Then, leading Churchmen, by virtue of their religious office, exercised great power in the governing of the nation; now they are one among many claimants for the ear of professional politicians. Then, the Church directly influenced the lives of everyone and the overwhelming majority owed allegiance to it; now its active members are a small minority of the total population. The term secularization has come into use as a shorthand term for these processes, but secularization is far from being a simple process. Indeed, the term is widely used to describe two processes which are better distinguished. First there is the way in which the *society* has become more secular; secondly there is the way in which *religion* itself has become more secular.

The secularization of society

It is commonplace nowadays for discussions about religion, from Lambeth conferences to televised discussions, to centre upon the decline in religiosity in England over the last hundred years. Basically there are three main ways in which religion in England may be said to have declined. First, there has been a change in the pattern of thinking common to Englishmen so that everyday patterns of thought are now less 'religious' than once they were. Secondly, religious institutions have declined in the power and influence they wield in the society as a whole. Thirdly, a declining proportion of the population either attend or claim membership of religious bodies.

The first of these will be dealt with very briefly, partly because it is so often exaggerated. There is considerable evidence to suggest that although sociologists and (some) theologians may exhibit a scientific view of the world, this is demonstrably not so of the majority of the population. One would be surprised if this were the case. As a British sociologist has pointed out, 'it would be absurd to suppose that a population widely nurtured on the *Daily Express* and *Old Moore's Almanack* finds the New Testament an intellectual insult or Thomism not compatible with modern logic.'[9] Most people still think in terms of the supernatural (even if not in terms of a traditional Christian God) but such considerations no longer have any influence on the daily life of the majority. The secularization of thought has taken place among ordinary laymen more in the decreased significance of religious questions than in any decline in belief in the supernatural. Similarly, although it might be possible to trace a decline in belief among those who hold powerful or influential positions in the society, there are still religious men to be found in politics, industrial management, journalism and so on. But again the significance of their religion for their day-to-day activities is not always evident.

This brings us to the second aspect of the decline in religion, one which is much more important. Just as religion today plays a smaller part in the lives even of some of those who engage in it, so religious institutions play a smaller part in the life of the nation as a whole. Medieval Europe was dominated by the Church. Throughout the nineteenth century, religious bodies in England were highly instrumental both in promoting and in hindering social reform. In England, of course, one must be careful not to overstate the loss of position of religious institutions—a process which has gone much further in most other European countries. There are still formal ties of establishment between the Church of England and the state; one still finds, as part of that establishment, bishops with *ex officio* seats in the House of Lords (a very different thing from life peerages conferred upon prominent churchmen in that it represents the influence of an institution—the Church of England—rather than the influence of an individual); the major denominations still have the ear of the press on all sorts of issues, both religious in the narrow sense and secular. The difference, however, is that nowadays they have no real power. They no longer make major political, economic and social decisions. They are one interest group, albeit an influential one, among many.

Some examples may serve to make this trend clear. The field of education has been especially noticeable for the decline of religious control. In the early nineteenth century primary education was dominated by religious bodies. Such secondary schools as existed were equally under religious patronage. Now, the last vestiges of institutional control of education by the churches are to be found in the Roman Catholic schools, a few Anglican state schools and in church control of some important public schools. By and large the influence of religion is confined to 'religious instruction' and to the influence of individual teachers. Indeed, the very concept of religious instruction is interesting evidence of one aspect of secularization, separating as it does religious education from education as a whole. In the past all education was considered to be religious education; now religion is allocated a named place on the timetable and usually confined to it.

Equally in the field of politics the place of institutional religion has declined considerably. Until the sixteenth century the highest offices of church and state were often combined and even in the nineteenth century denominational differences were often the very stuff of politics. But religion is no longer a political issue. It is indicative of the decline of religious institutions, in relation to other institutions, that politics is now an issue for the churches rather than the reverse. This decline in the general position of religious organizations in our society is part of the more general process of specialization which can be observed in societies. The process of development consists of precisely

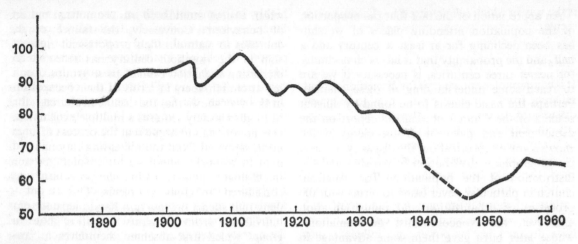

Figure 13.2 Easter communicants in the Church of England per 1,000 persons aged 15 and over, 1885–1962

Source: *Facts and Figures About the Church of England,* Numbers 2 & 3, London: Church Information Office, 1959, 1965.

this sort of change; functions previously performed by a single agency come to be performed by a variety of different ones. In this case there has been a separation of educational, political and religious activities into different institutions.

The third aspect of the decline in religion concerns the question of the size of church attendance and membership. Whatever criteria one takes into account, such a decline is apparent. Membership of the Free Churches has decreased; numbers of Easter communicants in the Church of England have declined; and attendance at Roman Catholic mass, while showing some small absolute increase has declined in proportion to the total population. Figure 13.2 shows the trend in one index of church-going, namely attendance at Easter Communion in the Church of England. Given the importance attached to Easter Communion by Anglicans one may view this as a fair indication of minimum commitment to the Anglican church. For the period concerned, it is generally reckoned that non-Anglicans and Anglicans were about equal in numbers, so we can suggest that between approximately 12 and 14 per cent of the adult population were church-goers in the middle of the twentieth century, compared to 18 or 20 per cent at the beginning of the century. In popular thought the comparison usually made is between the 'religious' Victorians and the 'irreligious' Elizabethans. But if some decline in religious observance since the end of the nineteenth century can be seen from Figure 13.2, a much more striking factor would seem to be the modest proportion of the population involved in church-going *during*

the nineteenth century. The lack of support for religious bodies during this supposedly 'religious' period is confirmed by contemporary comments on the situation. Writing of the City of Sheffield in 1817 the Reverend Mark Docker claimed:[10]

> Sheffield is not the most irreligious town in the Kingdom, and here are great numbers, I trust, who pay a becoming respect to Divine worship, both in the Establishment and out of it . . . yet when compared with the bulk of the population, how small. I believe all the various places of worship in the town will not be found to contain accommodation for above one third of its inhabitants, and are they filled by regular attendants? Not by far. Look at the families surrounding your dwellings, and you perhaps see a solitary instance where a whole household of several persons are regular attendants.

There is no reason to doubt Rev. Docker's statement that Sheffield was not exceptional in its lack of religious observance, and this at the beginning of the nineteenth century. It would appear that church attendance in England as a whole had become a minority phenomenon by the second half of the century. Consequently, rather than the normal view of a religious England that has suddenly turned secular in the twentieth century a more accurate assessment reveals a long-term decline in church attendance, punctuated by shorter periods (such as the second half of the nineteenth century) when the decline was slowed but scarcely ever stopped.

An appreciation of the fact that the proportion of the population attending places of worship has been declining for at least a century and a half, and the probability that it has been declining for nearer three centuries, is necessary if we are to reach some understanding of these changes. Perhaps the basic clue is to be found by diligent readers of the Church of England report on the deployment and payment of the clergy which shows a grave concern about the disparity between the geographical distribution of parishes and the distribution of the population. The Anglican church in particular never came to terms with the processes of urbanization and industrialization and even the Nonconformist denominations, whose later birth gave them some advantage in this respect, had little more success in providing accommodation for the growing urban population of the last two centuries. In particular, the churches failed to attract to themselves a significant number of the urban working classes. From their emergence, the working classes have, as a class, been estranged from organized religion, and indeed many sections of the churches have been totally indifferent to this situation. It was this urban working class which was the first sizeable group among whom *non*-attendance and *non*-membership became the normal pattern. In terms of their institutional attachments they were *from the start* a secular group.

Nor does the relative success of the churches in the second half of the nineteenth century signify any great change in this situation. Archbishop Tait, then Bishop of London, was one of the few churchmen of the day to see the situation at all clearly.[11]

> It is the upper and middle classes who form the churchgoers throughout this country (he wrote), and a vast mass of the population are estranged not only from the Church of England, but from the Gospel itself . . . in our crowded cities and in our remote country districts there is a very numerous body of the poor who cannot, and another who will not enter the churches.

That the religious bodies managed to hold their own in the second half of the century in terms of the proportion of the total population in membership or attending, was not due to any changes in the allegiance of the working classes but rather to changes in the distribution of persons between occupations and classes. The occupational groups which were expanding were the very groups among which church attendance *was* the normal pattern of behaviour. Conversely, the failure of the churches to maintain their proportional membership in the twentieth century has reflected the increasing alienation even of these groups. Looking at church-goers in terms of their occupations in this way shows that the decline in church-going in English society requires a multiple explanation. It is not enough to argue that the process of alienation stemmed from the increasing rationality of man in a world where scientific solutions were increasingly applied to what had previously been considered 'religious' problems. This is not to deny that such a process may have alienated some individuals from religious activities, but the *groups* which first absented themselves in large numbers were the very groups among which such intellectual factors were likely to have the least effect, that is the working classes.

Far more important was the fact that Christianity, born as were the other world religions in a rural (though relatively sophisticated) society, was in England organized to serve the needs of a rural, pre-industrial society. This organization is most clearly shown in the parish system which has survived the many and rapid social changes of the last three hundred years. Whatever the effect of some forms of Christianity upon the transformation of that society into an industrial one, the organization of the religious bodies was not adapted to the ever increasing urbanization process. True enough the emerging middle classes of the new towns embraced religion eagerly—especially the Nonconformist denominations which also served as a rallying point for the political expression of this class—but the mass of the inhabitants of the urban areas, the artisans and the labourers, were, with very few exceptions, estranged from organized religion. Even at the end of the nineteenth century, in a period marked by some revival of religious fortune, the appearance of the Salvation Army and working men's missions is of interest more as a commentary upon the irreligion of the poor than as movements that made any significant statistical difference to the situation. The relative success of Nonconformity in the urban areas of the late nineteenth century can be attributed partly to its political role *vis à vis* the urban middle classes and partly to the nature of its internal organization, especially in the newer branches. Methodism, for example, drew its members into local communities in a way that had more in common with the old rural Anglican parishes than with most of their urban successors.

The twentieth-century decline in religious observance can be traced to a change in the pattern of behaviour of the middle classes. Figures for the period since the first world war suggest a continued drift away from religious membership and worship—a drift that is commonly supposed to be due to changes in fashions. It is now a much smaller group among whom going to church is the 'done thing' and the accepted habit of church attendance has had to contend with new competitors. More fundamentally, however, people have increasingly ceased to support an institution that no longer appears to have relevance to their lives. The churches are no longer political, economic or social units of consequence and are therefore, in general, attended regularly only by those who feel a strong *religious* commitment to them.

The importance of this social setting to religious behaviour can be seen more clearly when we compare this English situation with the strongly contrasting situation in the United States of America. (Other interesting comparisons can be made—for example with Scotland.) In America allegiance to the churches and denominations (and synagogues) as reflected by statistics of membership and attendance has grown since the second world war and, many would argue, throughout the century. And yet America is undeniably largely an urban society and is, by most measures, the most highly industrialized society in the world. In terms of our analysis of English society, then, we are faced with the apparently contradictory position of an urban, industrial society where nearly two-thirds of the population is in membership of a religious body and nearly one half takes part in religious worship every Sunday. In other words, to a very considerable extent, organized religion in America *has* come to terms with the urban situation.

This paradox has been resolved by the theologian-cum-sociologist Will Herberg[12] who has argued that, in post-immigrant America, being religious is one of the most acceptable ways of expressing American-ness. Membership of and attendance at church or synagogue is a national value; commitment to a religion provides evidence of being a complete American. Sufficient religious tolerance has been developed, however, for it to matter little which of the major religious faiths are followed since all reinforce the American way of life. Furthermore, in a society that has moved further than any other towards the pole of bureaucracy and impersonality, religion largely through its establishment of a community, provides one of the few institutions capable of giving

meaning to life. The local churches of America seem to have had considerable success in reinstating religion as an expression of the local community and in this they are singularly different from their counterparts in Europe. More surprisingly this has been the case in spite of the higher incidence of geographical mobility in America.

The secularization of religion

But Herberg and other observers of the American religious scene have also pointed to certain changes in the activities of the churches. They have maintained and increased their membership and attendance, but at the same time some of them have lost their sole emphasis on 'religion' in its narrow sense. In our terms religion itself has become more secular; or in terms of our earlier typology there has been an increasing compromise with worldly values. Perhaps this is most graphically pictured in Peter de Vries's amusing caricature of American liberal Christianity.[13]

Our church is, I believe, the first split-level church in America. It has five rooms and two baths downstairs—dining area, kitchen and three parlours for committee and group meetings—with a crawl space behind the furnace ending in the hillside into which the structure is built. Upstairs is one huge all-purpose interior, divisible into different sized components by means of sliding walls and convertible into an auditorium for putting on plays, a gymnasium for athletics, and a ballroom for dances. There is a small worship area at one end. This has a platform cantilevered on both sides, with a free form pulpit designed by Noguchi. It consists of a slab of marble set on four legs of four delicately differing fruit-woods, to symbolize the four gospels and their failure to harmonize. Behind it dangles a large multi-coloured mobile, its interdenominational parts swaying, as one might fancy, in perpetual reminder of the Pauline stricture against those 'blown by every wind of doctrine'. Its proximity to the pulpit inspires a steady flow of more familiar congregational whim, at which we shall not long demur, going on with our tour to say that in back of this building is a newly erected clinic, with medical and neuropsychiatric wings, both indefinitely expandable. Thus People's

Liberal is a church designed to meet the needs of today, and to serve the whole man. This includes worship of a God free of outmoded theological definitions and palatable to a mind come of age in the era of Relativity. 'It is the final proof of God's omnipotence that he need not exist in order to save us,' Mackerel had preached. . . . This aphorism seemed to his hearers so much better than anything Voltaire had said on the subject that he was given an immediate hike in pay and invited out to more dinners than he could possibly eat.

This is a particularly perceptive piece of satire in that it clearly locates two aspects of the secularization of the religion. First, it points to the secularization of the church's activities—the gymnasium, the ballroom, the clinic; secondly it points to the secularization of theology—the decline in transcendental belief. Clearly we may expect these twin processes (which may, however, occur independently of each other) to be related to the secularization of the wider society but they are far from being a simple reaction to the wider process. In the first place, many of the origins of the secularization of patterns of thought can be traced to the theology and organization of the Reformation—itself ostensibly a religious phenomenon. The decline in ritual, the changing patterns of authority and the relative freedom of thought consequent upon the Reformation broke the monolithic pattern of the Middle Ages and made it more possible for scientists and philosophers to challenge religious statements or beliefs if they so wished. The significance of the name 'Methodists' has often been remarked upon. The methodical approach to life that they advocated exemplifies one aspect of the process of rationalization which the sociologist Max Weber emphasized as the crucial transformation of the Christian ethic under Protestantism in general and Calvinism in particular. Changes within Christianity in the general direction of a more 'secular' theology were thus partly responsible for the development of the wide processes of social change associated with industrialization in Western Europe; and the process of industrialization in turn led to the situation of a largely secular Europe.

The churches, faced with this process of the secularization of the society, have two possible courses of action. Either they can adopt a defensive attitude, that is they can retain their traditional beliefs and practices in an alien milieu. Or alternatively they can accommodate to the new situation; they can re-interpret their message to suit the new age. Thus the 'Rediscovery of the Church'—a theological movement led by the Swiss theologian Karl Barth—may be seen as the ideological reaction of the churches to the perceived need in a modern urban society for more tightly integrated community structures. Or more recently, the 'New Theology' in England and the 'God is Dead' school in America are self-confessed attempts to re-interpret Christianity to a new age—to generations who find the transcendentalism of the past difficult to swallow. Interestingly enough, the choice of alternatives does not seem materially to affect the success of religious bodies in holding their members or gaining new ones. If, once more, we take England and America as our examples, we find that in England fundamentalist and liberal groups both have small memberships. In America, on the the other hand, both are expanding. American life is, however, sufficiently compartmentalized for there to be little or no conflict between fundamentalist denominations such as the Southern Baptists and the basic values of the secular society. It is no longer necessary to construct sectarian barriers to protect members from the wicked world, because the world is not concerned with things religious and fundamentalist Christianity is not concerned with things secular. Their religious focus is upon a transcendental God and an after life. De Vries's fictional Rev. Mackerel provides an extreme case of the adherents of the more liberal beliefs. In real life the Congregationalists provide the best denominational example, but liberal (and radical) beliefs tend to cut across the lines of the major denominations. While expanding in terms of absolute numbers the liberals are, as near as one can judge, merely holding their own in proportion to the total population. This suggests that theological 'compromise' —the re-interpretation of belief and doctrine to suit the new age—does not necessarily produce success in terms of statistical expansion. This may, however, well be because, in America especially, the greatest scope for expansion of membership lies among the lower classes who are not much interested in theological (or any intellectual) speculation.

All strands which we have distinguished in the process of secularization can be related to the earlier typology of Christian groups. The process of the secularization of society corresponds to a movement away from the church-type, characterized by its domination of society, to a society whose religious life is characterized by sects or denominations. As such a secularization of society proceeds, religion retreats into one corner of society where it may become sectarian in its rejection of the values of the world or (more usually in societies which have developed a value of tolerance) denominational in its accommodation to worldly standards and values. In this latter case, the theological position of the denominations may be either traditional or liberal, and in the latter case especially the theological or doctrinal element tends to decline in importance in relation to social beliefs and practices.

This leads us directly to the last section of this chapter, namely to an analysis of the ecumenical movement which has become important in the Christian church during the last half century. The ecumenical movement is closely tied to the process of secularization not so much because it is, in part, an attempted consolidation of their declining position by religious bodies that have become relatively weak, but for two other reasons which may at first seem contradictory. In so far as it is largely (although not entirely) a movement of religious professionals, it reflects the retreat of religion into one part of society by its concentration upon the internal relations of the denominations. But this is to place too much emphasis upon the church unity element of the ecumenical movement which, while it may be the most important and most visible element, is not the only one. Secondly, and paradoxically, it is those denominations who have abandoned (or who never held) a fundamentalist position that are most deeply involved in the ecumenical movement. The aspects of ecumenism not directly related to unity concern the extension of Christian influence into other spheres of society. It is concerned with the influence of the church rather than with its numerical expansion and its evangelism is aimed at the salvation of the world rather than the salvation of individuals *from* the world. Thus the ideology of the movement represents the secularization of religion while its personnel suggest that it is part of the secularization of society. There is consequently much more concern with the secular institutions of society—with politics, race relations, industrial relations and so on. In other words the ecumenical movement is made up largely of the more secular wing of organized Christianity so that its relationship with the whole complex process of secularization is far more complicated than it at first seems to be. It is as

much a part of the secularization of religion as of the secularization of society.

What has the sociological perspective to contribute to an understanding of the narrower question of church unity? One explanation relates the growing unity to the secularization of society by pointing out that movements towards unity tend to take place when religious bodies are weak and becoming weaker.[14] At times when the expansion of the European churches must seem like little more than a pipe-dream, the transference of the focus from the church-world relationship to inter-denominational relationships must be reassuring to clergymen. Nevertheless such an explanation, although contributing fuel to the fire of unity in some circumstances, is far from being a satisfactory explanation. The movement towards unity is also strong in the USA where, as we have seen, the denominations are thriving. Moreover, the movement in England started in earnest at the *beginning* of the twentieth century (the Edinburgh conference of the International Missionary Council in 1912 was particularly important) at a time when the denominations in Britain had enjoyed their most successful half century since the beginning of industrialization.

Much more significant is the fact that the denominational divisions themselves were originally primarily social divisions not theological ones. We need not here repeat the evidence on this point but simply remark that, by the twentieth century, the social divisions that gave rise to denominationalism no longer existed. More accurately perhaps one should say that the social divisions have lost their sharpness, and those which still exist find their expression not in new religious movements but in political activities. While the separate religious institutions have long survived the particular social protest which gave rise to them, these changed social conditions mean that there is much less resistance to union schemes than would otherwise be the case. The major objections that are offered are now theological (partly because of the prominence of theologians in the consultations) and these are less intractable than social differences. The increasing homogeneity of society, or at the very least a softening of the original lines of division, is therefore a basic pre-requisite of any movement towards unity. In any situation where religious organizations still reflect meaningful social divisions which cannot be expressed in political action (for example, the racial division in South Africa) there are no substantial movements towards unity.

Thus, while there are relationships between the three processes—the secularization of society; the secularization of religion; and the movement towards unity—it would appear to be unwise to postulate direct causal relationships between them.

Rather, all three seem to be connected with the broad processes of social change broadly subsumed under the headings industrialization and urbanization.

Notes

1 Peter Farb, *Man's Rise to Civilization*, London: Secker & Warburg, 1969, pp. 71–2.
2 Numbers 21: 6–9.
3 Deuteronomy 11: 26–8.
4 Esther Warner, *Trial by Sasswood*, Harmondsworth: Penguin, 1965, taken from pp. 208–14.
5 *Guardian*, 8 May 1967.
6 E. Troeltsch, *The Social Teaching of the Christian Church*, London: Allen & Unwin, 1931.
7 This account is based chiefly on E. Anderson, *Messianic Popular Movements in the Lower Congo*, Uppsala: Almqvist & Wiksell, 1958.
8 This account is based chiefly on P. Worsley, *The Trumpet Shall Sound*, London: MacGibbon & Kee, 1957.
9 D. A. Martin, *The Sociology of English Religion*, London: S.C.M., 1967, p. 114.
10 Quoted in E. R. Wickham, *Church and People in an Industrial City*, London: Lutterworth, 1957, pp. 84–5.
11 Quoted in ibid., p. 113.
12 See W. Herberg, *Protestant, Catholic, Jew*, New York: Doubleday, 1960.
13 P. de Vries, *The Mackerel Plaza*, Harmondsworth: Penguin, 1963, pp. 10–11.
14 See B. R. Wilson, *Religion in a Secular Society*, London: Watts, 1966.

Reading

Howells, W., *The Heathens*, New York: Doubleday, 1962. Despite a somewhat unfortunate title, this is an attractively written and informative introduction to religion in simple societies. It includes a discussion of magic, witchcraft, totemism, and ancestor worship and draws examples from a large number of societies.
Lanternari, V., *Religions of the Oppressed*, New York: Mentor, 1963. A study of millennial movements throughout the world. Excellent in its description: less satisfying in its explanations.
Niebuhr, H. R., *The Social Sources of Denominationalism*, Connecticut: Shoe string, 1954. Highly readable discussion of the social roots of the Reformation, Methodism, and a variety of other religious groups.

Robertson, R. (ed.), *Sociology of Religion*, Harmondsworth: Penguin, 1969. A useful collection of articles and extracts relating to societies at various levels of development.
Scharf, Betty R., *The Sociological Study of Religion*, London: Hutchinson, 1970. A clearly written introduction along textbook lines.
Wilson, B. R., *Religion in a Secular Society*, Harmondsworth: Penguin, 1969. An analysis of the process of secularization in England and America, and of the religious response to this process.
Wilson, B. R., *Religious Sects*, London: Weidenfeld & Nicolson, 1970. A brief but comprehensive study of different types of Christian sects. Full of excellent descriptions.

Further Reading

Glock, G. Y. and Stark, R., *Religion and Society in Tension*, Chicago: Rand MacNally, 1965. One of the most perceptive and sophisticated discussions of religion in modern America.
Lessa, W. A. and Vogt, E. Z., *Reader in Comparative Religion*, New York: Harper & Row, 1965. A collection of anthropological writings which is impressive in its quality and its breadth. Contains sections on myth, totemism, Shamans, ancestor worship, and magic, as well as on theoretical and methodological problems.
Troeltsch, E., *The Social Teaching of the Christian Churches*, London: Allen & Unwin, 1931. First published in 1911, but still one of the most useful

sources for those interested in the social history of Christianity.
Weber, M., *The Protestant Ethic and the Spirit of Capitalism*, London: Allen & Unwin, 1968. Weber's classic work in which he traces the relationship between Protestant asceticism and the capitalist ethos.
Wilson, B. R. (ed.), *Patterns of English Sectarianism*, London: Heinemann, 1967. Studies of nine English sects prefaced by Wilson's important article 'An analysis of sect development'.
Worsley, P., *The Trumpet Shall Sound*, London: MacGibbon & Kee, 1957 and Paladin, 1970. An analysis of Melanesian cargo cults.

14 Crime

Law and lawbreaking

In all societies there are shared ideas about how people ought to behave. These ideas form the morality and the customs of the society—sometimes called norms. Each generation passes these ideas on to the next; they are preached in pulpits and 'problem pages' of women's magazines and are implicit in most of our everyday conversation, in our literature, in our art and even in the very language we speak. They vary considerably in the extent to which they are held to be important, from the most deeply felt and central ones—like the norms forbidding incest, high treason and the taking of life—to the more trivial customs of the society—ideas about etiquette, proper dress, eating habits and so on. It is often difficult, especially in complex or rapidly changing societies, to assess the importance of any particular norm. How important, for example, is the norm condemning adultery in Britain? In the past those sections of society that condemned adultery (the churches are the most obvious example) dominated the moral scene, whereas today their influence is waning and many people do not think adultery matters very much. There is ambiguity and disagreement about the whole question. To some degree, however, the norms of society are internalized in the course of the socializing process, so that in adulthood they are experienced as conscience—the inner sense of what is right or what is 'done'.

But internalization alone is not enough to make people conform to the norms of their society. Some people fail to internalize them properly and we are all tempted to rebel at one time or another. 'For, after all, there is no need to prohibit some-thing that no one desires to do,' as Freud put it.[1] Furthermore, the norms themselves sometimes conflict and do not give adequate guidance for action in some situations. For instance: 'a man should do all he can to support his wife and family'; 'a man should not steal'. Poor people may often have to choose between these two maxims. Internalization of the customs and moral ideas of the society is supplemented by external methods of social control. These vary from one pound fines, gossip, smiles of encouragement and 'tuts' of disapproval, to imprisonments, a place in the Birthday Honours List and the angry father's 'never darken my doors again'. Some of these sanctions are informal in the sense that they are not applied according to any set of rules, but are a spontaneous reaction of others to a person's conformity to, or deviation from, the norms. The unmarried mother may be 'dropped' by her friends; the long-haired boy finds it hard to get an office job; the honest businessman has the respect of the local community. Other sanctions are formal in that there are rules according to which some kinds of behaviour are positively or negatively sanctioned and these sanctions are administered impersonally. Saving money is rewarded with interest; saving lives with a medal (though in war, taking lives is rewarded with a medal too). But unprofessional behaviour by a doctor is sanctioned by removal from the Register and 'professional' behaviour by a prostitute by a fine or imprisonment.

At the level of society as a whole the criminal law is the most conspicuous formal mechanism of social control. (Civil law, too, is a means of controlling social relations in a wide variety of spheres. It will not be discussed here since the behaviour it deals with is not defined as crime.) In industrial societies, however, the administration of justice and the treatment of offenders is becoming less and less formal. In the case of children, this is true, not simply in the sense that the procedure in juvenile courts is becoming less ritualistic and more intimate and everyday, but also in that the treatment of the delinquent is decided increasingly according to the particular needs of the individual child. Formal justice has traditionally operated without respect to persons, making the punishment fit the crime; the modern juvenile court is moving in the direction of making the treatment fit the delinquent. The police now have juvenile bureaux which deal informally with young first offenders rather than taking them to court at all. There is thus a tendency for the penal system to merge with social work in the control of unwanted behaviour among young people. There is developing a new kind of social control agency, centrally organized yet relatively flexible and informal. The reason for this change is that as people become more sophisticated in their understanding of human behaviour, they become less willing to assign deviants absolute responsibility for their actions. There is an inclination to see them as 'sick' rather than 'sinful' and to give them 'help' rather than 'punishment'. One result is that the distinction between delinquent and disturbed children has become blurred, and in Britain, for example, children who are 'in need of care and control' are on probation and in community homes along with delinquents, and delinquents are in children's homes along with orphans and those from disrupted homes.

The treatment accorded to adult criminals, too, is becoming less formal. There is an increasing use of systems of probation, of psychiatric treatment and other forms of counselling in prison, and of after-care for ex-prisoners. The indeterminate sentence, whose length is not decided by the court but depends in the end on how likely the prisoner is to stay out of trouble, is another example of less formal treatment, and one that was recently introduced for adults in Britain in the form of parole. The distinctive feature of these kinds of treatment is not so much that they lack the harsh, punitive character of much treatment of criminals from the seventeenth century onwards, but that they are adapted to the particular offender and rely on the establishment of a personal relationship between him and the rehabilitative agent.

The criminal law, however, is only one among many mechanisms of social control. It covers only a narrow range of behaviour and would be quite ineffective even there, were it not that norms are internalized and supported by strong informal sanctions. Although the law with its attendant penal sanctions represents the power of the state in the control of behaviour, it is not always the most potent form of social control. In many situations the fear of exposure to informal sanctions is probably more of a deterrent than the fear of actual legal sanctions. This would be true, for instance, of sharp practice by a businessman or perjury by a public figure. Neither does the law necessarily deal with the most important norms of the society. There are no laws against adultery, fornication or, in general, against telling lies, yet there are laws against failing to license a dog and parking a car in the wrong place. In many cases laws have been introduced to regulate behaviour precisely because the relevant norms were not well enough established to ensure conformity without the threat of formal penal sanctions.

In many ways it is misleading to think of laws as the embodiment of norms of the *society* at all. The creation and enforcement of laws are social activities in which some groups play a greater part than others—parties, pressure groups, parliament, civil servants, judges, police and so on; laws are made by some people within society in order to control the behaviour of other people. The laws relating to the hours at which shops may be open, for instance, are made in the interests of the larger shops who employ assistants, to reduce competition from smaller family shops. Even the laws against stealing, while they are clearly in almost everybody's interest to some extent, nevertheless are much more important to the interests of the people who own more property; they are primarily laws which protect the property of rich people.

The actual content of the law varies considerably from society to society and the more complex societies generally have by far the most complex bodies of law, while some simpler societies have no written law at all. The laws of each society are closely related to the structure of that society. Seventeenth-century Puritan Massachusetts[2] provides a good example, though a rather unusual one since the law there did not evolve gradually as in so many countries, but was created in a brief period by the early colonists. The Puritans believed there should be a very close connection between church and state; everyone was a member of the church and subject to its control. Yet those who left England for Massachusetts believed also that the church should have a membership comprising only 'visible saints', men who could be seen to be among the elect of God. The laws of the new colony were therefore closely based on the Bible— so much so that in cases of doubt, ministers of religion were often asked to 'set a rule' which they would justify with Biblical quotations. Everyday life was governed with great severity and in the minutest detail. Court records contain the following revealing examples:[3]

(1) Francis Usselton fined for cursing a swine of Henry Hogget, 'A pox o' God upon her and the Devil take her.'
(2) Joseph Swett's wife fined ten shillings for wearing a silk hood.
(3) It is further ordered, that no person, householder or other, shall spend his time idly or unprofitably, under pain of such punishment as the Court shall think meet to inflict . . . especially . . . common costers, unprofitable fowlers and tobacco takers.

We have seen that law varies from society to society, both in content and in its importance as a means of social control. By and large urbanization and industrialization enhance the importance of legal means of social control as compared with less formal means with the result that 'breaking the law' is more common. There are three aspects of the complexity of urban industrial society which help to explain why this is so.

1. Informal forms of social control, which operate well in the kind of community where everyone knows everyone else's business, are made ineffective by urbanization. In the city it is easier to deviate without others noticing, and even when they do notice it is easier to be unaffected by informal social pressure. So legal mechanisms are more frequently used to govern behaviour that was previously controlled informally. The police are more likely to be called in to deal with street fights and even family quarrels.

2. In industrial societies people engage in many new activities which bring them into new and complicated relationships with others. The co-ordination of these relationships requires formal—often bureaucratic—rules, opening up new opportunities for infringement of the law. The advent of the motor car provides a good example for it has created a whole new class of laws for people to fall foul of and today a large

proportion of 'crime' is against these laws. (Incidentally, *some* of the modifications to laws arising from new activities of this kind are in the direction of more lax rather than more stringent control. As fatal road accidents have become more common, a new offence of 'causing death by dangerous driving' has developed, which is treated more leniently than the general offence of manslaughter.)

3. The greater complexity of society also creates new opportunities for the infringement of old laws. The fact that our city streets are lined with empty cars for much of the day creates endless opportunities for larceny, so we need not be surprised to find that the increase in the number of cars on the roads is accompanied by an increase in the common juvenile offence of larceny from motor cars. The complexity of financial and business life has created an intricate web of paper transactions, record-keeping, delegated authority and trust which is full of new opportunities for embezzlement, tax evasion, false description of goods, as well as for newer offences against monopoly acts and so on.

Some laws, of course have disappeared with industrialization. With the separation of church and state, for instance the church gradually gave up its control over secular behaviour, and the state its control over religious behaviour. The church has no monopoly over marriage in contemporary Britain, while heresy, blasphemy, having commission with the devil, suicide and failing to attend church are no longer civil crimes (though the crime of sacrilege and laws relating to Sunday observance still exist). But on balance we have gained far more laws than we have lost: the law has become more important as a means of social control. Wider ranges of behaviour are defined as criminal than formerly.

Crime and changing social structures

Changes in the organization of crime

On the whole, with urbanization and industrialization people become less, rather than more, law abiding. While this is partly due to the greater number of laws, some of the increase in crime can be attributed to the greater complexity and efficiency of criminal organization. The earliest full-time thieves were crude brigands and robbers living often in the forests or the hills and making a livelihood by waylaying travellers or attacking farms. Medieval outlaws, such as Robin Hood, are typical of this kind of criminal. Their followers were able-bodied men with no particular skills and they relied mainly on violence to gain their ends. Sometimes this kind of brigandage has developed into a more sophisticated form: some of the criminal tribes of India—and in particular the notorious Thugs who were suppressed in the early decades of the nineteenth century—used elaborate techniques of strangling or poisoning to overcome their victims.

The kind of crime that relies mainly on simple violence declines in importance as societies become urban and industrial. Highway robbery and street robbery in towns were the last to survive; they flourished in England as late as the eighteenth century, but disappeared, except as amateur activities, once the country through which the highways passed became more densely populated and the city streets became better lit and better policed. Today, the professional criminal normally eschews violence and in doing so keeps himself relatively safe from the worst sanctions of the law. It is true that violence plays a minor part in the carefully planned bank robbery and the like, but the plan basically relies on timing, co-ordination and expertise for its success. It is also used in some rackets, such as the 'protection racket', where the victim himself is on the wrong side of the law and cannot seek its protection. But otherwise, violent robbery is the province of the amateur and the juvenile.

The kind of crime that dominated the scene from the end of the Middle Ages right through the early industrial period was highly specialized, skilled theft and trickery. The techniques of picking pockets and cutting purses, of 'lifting' goods from stalls, of inveigling out-of-town victims into trying to cheat at cards or at bowls and then cheating them in turn—all these were well worked out in Elizabethan London and have been used with very little variation ever since. Each technique is practised by groups of two or three people, who go through the same routine time and time again with one victim after another. Skilled thieves can make a steady, but not very spectacular, income if they work regularly using these methods. Thieves of this kind form an underworld, a distinctive subculture within urban society, with its own haunts, its own slang, its own standards of behaviour. The underworld probably first emerged in the sanctuaries of fifteenth-century London, the areas where, in medieval times, men had been safe from the execution of justice. By the nineteenth century there was a distinct 'criminal class' living in areas known as 'rookeries' in the larger cities—London, Liverpool, Bristol, Manchester, Birmingham, Leeds. They frequented 'flash houses'—pubs, lodging houses, coffee shops and cook houses—where they could expect to meet other criminals, to gossip and make business arrangements. Children who lived in these areas were early recruited into the ranks of professional crime, often assisted, as Dickens shows in *Oliver Twist*, by a man who made a business of receiving stolen goods, for every thief needed a Fagin if he was to make a living from his operations. The 'criminal class' living in a predominantly criminal neighbourhood has virtually disappeared, but the criminal of the traditional type still exists and still practises his 'craft' developing new tricks to meet new situations.

In the more advanced industrial societies, however, there are more tempting prizes than the contents of a man's wallet or even his bank account, and more attractive booty than can be found even in the fur and jewellery departments of the most elegant shops. For wages and bullion in transit and the contents of bank vaults are now of such value that they offer a worthwhile reward for months of planning by a team of men. So new forms of criminal organization have emerged to exploit these new opportunities. As well as the permanent team of two or three equals doing a series of small repetitive 'jobs' together, there are now also *ad hoc* groups of specialists gathered together by a leader to carry out a particular big 'job'. A typical robbery of this kind will be based on initial information bought for a percentage from one man; another man will get in touch with a team of men, some of them previously unknown to him or known only by reputation, through an underworld runner or 'spiv'; he may need a 'peter' man or safe expert, a lock man, an alarm system specialist, a 'wheel' man or driver, a gun man and a strong-arm man. After careful observation of the target, lasting days or weeks, a detailed plan will be formulated and a date chosen. The plan specifies the timing and allocation of tasks and the arrangements for leaving the scene of the crime in such a way that as few people as possible know that the robbery is taking place until the thieves are well away; thus the need for violence, intimidation and restraint are minimized. The plan also covers the disposal of the booty—even banknotes can be traced—and the division of the proceeds; and the thieves must be careful not to alter their spending habits or make themselves conspicuous in any way.

The greatest examples of this kind of robbery have been the 'Great Brink's Holdup' in Boston, Massachusetts in 1950 when the stronghold of an armoured-car company was robbed of $2¾ million, and the Great Train Robbery in England in 1963, when a train carrying £2¼ million in used bank-notes was waylaid. Each of them took over a year to plan and in each case the *ad hoc* gang carried out other robberies during the planning stage to provide working capital or needed information. The organization of this new kind of crime is more complex than that of routinized 'craft' crime; it is more hierarchical and at the same time more flexible. But the profits are immensely greater and as the participants gain experience they learn to reduce the risks. The two 'Great' robberies were failures, for most of the men got caught; but similar principles are regularly used with success on smaller but none the less lucrative jobs.

Another form of criminal activity that required complex organization is racketeering. The racket does not involve stealing money but getting it from a more or less willing person (with his knowledge) by one of two ways: by extorting it under the threat of force or by providing illegal goods and services to people who are ostensibly law-abiding citizens. Extortion has a long history but only flourishes where state power is weak. The Mafia in Sicily provides a good example of a racket of this kind in a non-industrial society. For centuries Sicily has been governed ineptly but exploitatively from outside. Within the country unofficial organizations, which have become known as Mafias, grew up, taking over many of the functions nominally belonging to the government. One Mafia, for instance, controlled an area including eleven villages from about 1895 to 1924. It had a private police force of over a hundred armed men; it eliminated freelance banditry and thieving; it collected unofficial taxes from all the landowners and supervised all agricultural and economic activities in the area. But the members of such a Mafia benefit at the expense of the rest of the population. Their 'private government' enables them to engage in robbery, blackmail and murder with impunity. The 'protection racket' of the Kray brothers and the American 'labor racket' are versions of this kind of crime which have flourished in an urban-industrial setting.

The scope of the second kind of racket, the evasion of regulations, depends on how much people are willing to pay for things that are illegal in any particular state. In England a black market flourished under wartime rationing and controls, but now there are relatively few controls that full-time criminals can take advantage of. The Prohibition period in the United States opened up an enormous illegal market for liquor, and since then, gambling, drugs and prostitution have provided ample opportunities for racketeers. In America the opportunities have been so great and state control so ineffective that professional criminals have moved into all sorts of activities that can be turned into rackets and have created a vast network that has been described as 'the government of crime'.

Rackets of both kinds—extortion and illegal provision—share three features which distinguish them from other kinds of criminal activity. 1. To be effective both require a permanent organization to keep up the pressure on victims in the one case, to keep the market open in the other. 2. To make a profit the organization tries to maintain a monopoly in its field of activity; extortionists to preserve the credibility of their threat of force; the providers of illegal goods and services to prevent the under-cutting of their prices. 3. Racketeers must try to evade the enforcement of the law but the fact that they get their income from a large number of 'respectable' citizens means that they cannot keep their activities a complete secret. These conditions account for many of the characteristics of rackets: their hierarchical organization with a boss; the constant struggle for dominance between rival groups of racketeers, often resulting in 'gangland murders'; and the fact that the most successful racketeers—those in the United States—influence agencies of law enforcement as well as controlling the racket organization itself. This kind of development, one that occurs as society becomes more complex with industrialization, has led to an enormous increase in the amount of crime committed. It has increased it more than the crime figures reveal, for one aspect of the greater efficiency of organized crime is the greater effectiveness in avoiding detection and conviction.

The effects of rapid social change

The disruption of social relationships produced by rapid industrialization or urbanization typically results in a sharp increase in crime. With urbanization, in particular, the old institutions based on kinship become less effective as agencies of social control. Yet the new institutions and organizations of urban society take some time to form and they have to absorb a constant flood of migrants to the town.

In Ghana, for example, the rural kinship system used to provide for the upbringing of any orphans of the lineage. In the subsistence economy such children were useful extra hands on the farm. Nowadays, however, children are more or less obliged to attend school and are less of an economic asset. One result is that orphaned children are more likely to be neglected by their kinsmen and sometimes even drift to the towns on their own. In this situation they may easily take to crime to support themselves. The kinship group no longer looks after orphans as a matter of course but charity orphanages and local authority children's departments have not yet filled the gap. Furthermore, in modernizing societies towns often grow faster than industry and commerce, with the result that many townsmen are unemployed or under-employed. In addition the provision of housing fails to keep pace with the inflow of migrants, so that people live in grossly over-crowded conditions. In such conditions people are more likely to turn to crime.

Another factor contributing to the upsurge in crime rates is the difference between the norms and laws of industrial societies and those of the traditional societies. In traditional Algeria, for instance, when a woman committed adultery her family of origin was disgraced and her father or her brother was expected to kill her; when French law was introduced, such killing became illegal. Similarly, in Sicily a man whose daughter was seduced was expected to kill the seducer; one Sicilian immigrant to the United States was surprised to find that when he did this in defence of the family honour it was considered illegal. Individuals who find themselves at the confluence of two sets of ideals are placed in a situation of conflict by such variations. In following the dictates of one culture, they must defy those of the other. Such was the tragic case of Siberian women when a new Soviet law forbade the wearing of veils; so important were veils to traditional Siberian society that women who abandoned them were killed by their relatives for obeying the law. Obviously, crimes are likely to be common when the new laws thus contradict traditional customs.

The conflict of cultures also has an indirect effect on the crime rate. For when people move from a traditional rural area into the world of the city, their old codes of conduct and standards suddenly become inappropriate. The things they were trained to strive for—a subsistence living, the respect of the village, the good of the family—are either much easier to achieve or else irrelevant.

Things become possible that had once seemed impossible. When such a change is abrupt, socially approved norms and standards break down and man's conduct is less strictly controlled. This situation was described by the French sociologist Emile Durkheim at the turn of the century as anomie (or normlessness). He used the concept to explain why suicide rates sometimes rise at times of crisis or rapid change, but anomie and the loss of faith in established norms can procure other forms of deviant behaviour, among them crime and delinquency. When people find themselves in an anomic situation, many of the constraints upon their behaviour lose their force.

Culture conflict and anomie, then, typically accompany rapid social change and also arise whenever individuals move between widely divergent societies. Immigrants to Israel provide a typical example.[4] Many of them had a high level of education and a respected status in the countries they came from, but found that these counted for nothing in the new country. Others had unrealistically high hopes of a new and successful life in a new land, and they too were often disappointed. Many of them found that their ideas of patriarchal authority were very different from the ideas of modern Israel, so that their children, accepting the new ideas, appeared defiant and ungovernable. One immigrant from North Africa expressed this feeling when he said:[5]

> I cannot really understand what happens here with parents and children. . . . At home we knew our place with our father, and he would not allow any disobedience. He knew what was right for us. But here the children are becoming wild and unruly. They think they should not obey the parents, that they are much wiser than the father and mother. . . . It is the school, their teachers and their 'groups' that teach them all this. Whoever heard that children should have groups of their own and not obey the elders?

These are words that may well soon be on the lips of Pakistani and Cypriot immigrants in Britain.

When the first generation are at loggerheads with the society to which they have come, their children are torn between two opposing ways of life. They commonly turn away from their parents and find companionship among their own age groups, frequently in groups which are oriented towards delinquency and often, in adulthood, towards crime.

The distribution of crime in industrial societies

Age, sex and social class

Barbara Wootton once wrote, 'the crude criminal statistics suggest (that) crime is the product of youth and masculinity',[6] a statement that is vividly illustrated by the figures for England and Wales published in the annual *Criminal Statistics* (see Table 14.1). They show that the age distribution of offences is similar for both sexes. The frequency of

Table 14.1   Crime rates in England and Wales

| Age or age group | Number of persons found guilty of indictable offences per 100,000 of population of the age group | | | |
| | Males | | Females | |
	1950	1971	1950	1971
10*	1,399	330	90	19
11*	1,667	715	117	53
12*	1,872	1,434	148	139
13	2,101	2,302	173	272
14	2,303	3,606	206	453
15	1,540	4,285	188	538
16	1,415	4,694	184	547
17	1,292	6,027	171	723
18	933	5,705	158	664
19	958	4,987	149	570
20	823	4,181	137	511
21–4	856	2,827	114	376
25–9	699	1,937	95	318
30–9	449	1,280	85	260
40–9	279	634	67	174
50–9	157	318	47	138
60 and over	64	101	19	37
All ages	553	1,414	76	210

*Declining rates in these age groups are largely due to an increased reluctance to prosecute youngsters formally.

Source: Adapted from *Criminal Statistics for England and Wales, 1968*, London: HMSO, 1969, Cmnd 4098, p. lix and *Criminal Statistics for England and Wales, 1971*, London: HMSO, 1972, Cmnd 5020, p. liv.

convictions rises steeply from the age of ten—the age at which criminal responsibility formally begins—to a peak at fourteen to seventeen and declines fairly steadily after that, more rapidly for females than for males.

The figures in Table 14.1 refer to 'indictable' offences, that is offences (often thought of as the most serious ones) which can usually be tried by a jury instead of being dealt with summarily in a Magistrates' Court. About half of the people convicted of indictable offences are under twenty-one, although in the country as a whole only about 20 per cent of people over ten are under twenty-one. So the conviction-rate for young people is about double that for older people. The picture is rather different for non-indictable offences. Here young people are under-represented among those found guilty—largely because motoring offences predominate in this category. In other words the offences that juveniles tend to commit are treated more seriously than those which adults go in for.

The fact that the delinquency-rate declines after the middle teens suggests that youngsters tend to grow out of delinquency. Most of those who appear before a court only appear there once and even among those who appear more than once, most of them are not arrested once they are adult. On the other hand delinquency can sometimes be an apprenticeship for crime; for although most delinquents do not become criminal, they are more likely to do so than non-delinquents. Similarly, although many criminals begin their careers in adulthood, a large number of them begin as juveniles.

This discussion of the age-distribution of crime points to the need to distinguish between two broad categories of criminal. For while it is true to say that adolescence is the peak period for crime, it would be ridiculous to say that adolescents are a prominent group among criminals—if by criminals we mean professional and systematic rather than casual offenders. A large proportion of crimes are committed by people who do not earn all, or even a significant part, of their income by crime. Indeed many crimes—like murder, many sex offences and crimes of violence—are rarely money-making at all. We must separate, therefore, the casual from the professional criminal. Juvenile delinquents are generally casual criminals and account for a large proportion of crime of this type.

The other striking thing shown by the figures in Table 14.1 is that women and girls are brought before the courts far less often than men and boys. Perhaps this is partly due to the fact that there are alternative ways in which girls can protest against conformity and against the adult world; ways that are not usually defined as delinquent. For example, the stronger condemnation of early sexual behaviour for girls means that sex can serve as a protest in a way that it cannot for boys. In any case girls engage less in ordinary delinquent behaviour and the offences they do commit tend to be simple larceny rather than 'breaking and entering' (which accounts for a third of boys' convictions), violence or robbery. Among adults, too, women's crimes are typically less sophisticated in technique and organization and frequently tend to be interpreted as expressions of unhappiness or resentment, rather than as instrumental to financial gain.

The published statistics do not reveal the occupational class background of offenders, but other evidence shows that, both in Britain and in the United States of America, a larger proportion of the lower classes than of the middle classes are convicted of crimes. A number of surveys of London boys in remand homes and in borstal institutions show that very few of them have fathers who are businessmen or professionals, while a large proportion have fathers who are unskilled manual workers. This distribution of delinquents can be compared with that of the total population and it can be calculated that manual workers' boys are four times as likely to be found delinquent as the sons of businessmen and professionals.

The limitations of criminal statistics

Does this really mean that working-class boys are four times as likely to engage in stealing, vandalism and so on? We have already pointed out that crime statistics are not a good measure of actual criminal behaviour, because many criminals do not get caught and never get into the statistics. Roughly 40 per cent of all crimes that are 'known to the police' are cleared up. So 60 per cent of *recorded* crimes never get into the court statistics and we can never know much about the kind of person who committed them. With a large number of property offences the culprit is never caught, whereas some crimes, such as sexual offences and embezzlement, are seldom known to have happened unless the author of the crime is known. In addition, of course, there are many crimes that nobody bothers to record. 'No Parking' areas are often lined with cars, but the police and traffic wardens do not have time even to record most of them. Big department stores suffer enormous losses—some American shops lose as much as 5 per cent of the value of their turnover—which they euphemistically call 'inventory shrinkage' but which are mainly due to shoplifting and thefts by shop employees. There must be a great deal of minor fiddling of records and accounts by shop and office employees that never comes to light.

Probably the most serious source of bias in adult criminal statistics is the fact that those who live by crime, the professional criminals, are extremely skilled at evading detection and conviction. They know the safest times and places to work; they plan each 'job' carefully; they arrange a method of leaving the scene of the crime; they have trustworthy channels for disposing of stolen goods or money; they know when and how to bribe the police and others to act in their interests. The amateur, on the other hand, frequently acts impulsively and does not have the experience and contacts to protect him from detection and conviction. This is not to say that professional criminals never get caught: few go through a career of crime without one or more convictions. But the likelihood of a professional being brought to justice for any one crime is much lower than that for an amateur. So the court's records, the probation officer's case-load and the prison population all have a gross over-representation of amateurs.

In the case of juveniles, the most important reason why the court figures are inaccurate measures of delinquency is probably that the police, when they catch a delinquent, do not always think it wise to take him to court. Particularly if it is the first time a boy has come to their notice, they may think that the best thing to do is to warn him sternly or to talk to his parents or his school teacher rather than give him the stigma of being officially labelled as a delinquent. We have already mentioned the juvenile bureaux in the British police which have institutionalized this practice. They also keep in touch with boys who are potentially delinquent, and try to ensure that they do not get into serious trouble. All police also have power to take the official action of 'cautioning' an offender without taking him to court. Private people, too, when they catch a delinquent, have the option of reporting him to the police or using more informal methods of control.

Both the police and other people are likely to use the most severe methods in the cases they think of as being the most intractable. If they think parental discipline will have the desired effect, they will tell the boy's father rather than use the more formal approach. The result of this is that some delinquents are less likely to come before a court than others. If it is his first offence, if he seems to have been led astray by his friends, if his behaviour can be seen as a 'boyish prank', if his home seems to be a 'good' one, if it is felt that a court record would be damaging to his future life—then the less severe, informal sanctions will be used. On the other hand, if his appearance, clothes and family make him seem a potential delinquent and there are no influences in his neighbourhood or at home that would tend to keep him in check, then the formal legal sanctions will be brought into play. Justice is thus rather unequal in its treatment of different people. It seems to aim at a punishment just sufficient to correct each particular offender, rather than at one proportionate to the heinousness of the offence.

For similar reasons boys are more likely to be dealt with in court than girls. The police 'caution' 46 per cent of the girls they deal with officially for indictable offences but only 28 per cent of the boys (1971 figures): they are more willing to use the less formal sanction for girls. So police decisions are part of the reason why there are fewer girls than boys among the officially recorded delinquents. Similarly, police decisions account in part for the fact that there are more working-class than middle-class boys. It is the working-class (and especially the rougher working-class) boys who will seem to the police to be tougher nuts to crack, to come from rougher neighbour-hoods and broken or undisciplined homes, and to have less to lose by going to court in the sense that they have less hope of growing up to a 'respectable' position where a court record would matter. Also the police tend to see their behaviour as serious and the middle-class boys' as pranks.

All of this makes the criminal statistics rather meaningless as indicators of how much criminal behaviour goes on and who engages in it. Is there any other measure? Some investigators have conducted surveys in which they asked people to report their past illegal actions. It is difficult, of course, to be sure how honest people are even under the cloak of anonymity, but the results are rather surprising in the extent of illegal behaviour revealed. In various countries between 50 per cent and 90 per cent of the people questioned admit to having engaged in some kind of illegal behav-iour. Perhaps even more surprising, some studies found the percentages were much the same in each of the different social classes. The evidence on this important matter is still not very adequate, but it does seem that the self-reported delinquency of working-class boys is more persistent and more often of a serious nature than that of middle-class boys; and in spite of the considerable element of chance in getting caught, the self-confessed delinquency of officially labelled delinquents is more extensive than that of others. While sporadic delinquency and delinquent fads are a part of almost all teenage life, systematic and persistent delinquency and gangs oriented towards delin-quent behaviour are characteristic primarily of lower-working-class neighbourhoods.

Recent trends in delinquency

Since the young feature most prominently in crime statistics it is of some interest to look briefly at some of the trends in juvenile crime. During the years since the second world war the delinquency figures as recorded in the annual *Criminal Statis-tics*, have risen considerably. These increases are due in part to the increase in the number of boys in the juvenile age group. But, even when we take the changes in population into account, the juvenile delinquency *rates* can be seen to have increased as well (see Table 14.2).

The rates for some crimes have increased more than others. In particular, in recent years the rates for crimes of violence have increased more than those for other offences. This sometimes causes considerable concern, but three things should be remembered. First, crimes of violence are a very minor proportion of all crimes and have been ever since the eighteenth century (they now represent about 6 per cent of indictable crimes for the under-21's). Second, the typical form of 'violence against the person' is not the coshing of a defenceless old shopkeeper but a fight among friends, neighbours, or relatives, or a public brawl; weapons are rarely used. Third, the increase in convictions is likely to be due to a greater intoler-ance of violence and a greater willingness to call in the police as well as to an upsurge in the amount of violence actually going on. Vandalism—especially mischievous damage to such things as schools, railway carriages, public telephones and vending machines—has been growing, though not in the under-17 group. Again vandalism is not a very large proportion of crime, representing only about 1 per cent of all crime. Among juveniles the offence of 'taking a motor without consent'—often for a joy-ride—has been increasing in the United States and in other European countries as well as in Britain.

One particularly interesting development is the occurrence in various countries of a new pheno-menon: waves of teenage rioting. West Germany experienced such a wave in 1956–8 when showings of the film *Rock Around the Clock* and appear-

Table 14.2 Recent trends in juvenile delinquency in England and Wales

Year	Number of persons found guilty of indictable offences per 100,000 of the population of the age group			
	Males		Females	
	Age 14–16	Age 17–20	Age 14–16	Age 17–20
1950	1,758	1,022	193	153
1951	2,044	1,192	195	160
1952	1,981	1,229	210	172
1953	1,663	1,066	192	168
1954	1,548	1,021	188	165
1955	1,603	1,099	172	161
1956	1,783	1,285	177	155
1957	2,058	1,555	198	182
1958	2,274	1,974	227	221
1959	2,313	2,033	240	201
1960	2,436	2,189	275	236
1961	2,535	2,275	310	265
1962	2,606	2,457	336	276
1963	2,764	2,525	340	272
1964	2,907	2,459	420	277
1965	3,076	2,667	491	295
1966	3,199	2,944	516	318
1967	3,242	3,024	479	346
1968	3,489	3,496	488	381
1969*	4,252	4,721	516	469
1970*	4,484	5,102	557	544
1971*	4,184	5,231	512	617

*The figures for 1969 and later years are affected by the Theft Act 1968, under which all theft became indictable. Many of these offences (particularly 'taking and driving away a motor vehicle', which is a common juvenile offence) were previously non-indictable.

Source: Adapted from *Criminal Statistics for England and Wales, 1958*, London: HMSO, 1959, Cmnd 803, pp. xlvi–xlvii, *Criminal Statistics for England and Wales, 1968*, London: HMSO, 1969, Cmnd 4098, pp. lvii–lviii and *Criminal Statistics for England and Wales, 1971*, London: HMSO, 1972, Cmnd 5020, p. liii.

ances of 'Rock'n Roll' groups were greeted not only with screams and fainting but with uncontrolled dancing in the aisles and damage to the auditorium. The running battles of 'mods' and 'rockers' in English seaside resorts during 1964 and 1965 were somewhat similar in the sense that for a short while they were a 'craze'. People went to certain places at certain times expecting that there would be trouble because there had been in similar situations previously and police and others expected trouble and were ready with a dramatic reaction. Both were also examples of crowd behaviour in that quite ordinary people found themselves behaving in extraordinary ways because they got involved in the unthinking contagious excitement of the mob. Crazes of this kind are made possible by the rapid transmission of news through the mass media. These occasional waves of rioting are very different from the 'rumbles' of rival fighting gangs in the slum areas of the big cities; for fighting gangs are permanent semi-organized groups and their hostilities are chronic and along clear-cut lines.

The explanation of crime and its distribution

The sociologist is interested in explaining various aspects of crime. Why is there crime at all? Why does it take certain forms? Why is it committed by certain groups of people? The answer to the first two questions is largely implicit in the earlier discussion. There is crime because there is law; there is theft because there is property; there is fraud because there is trust; there is illegal diamond traffic because there is a legalized diamond monopoly. The kinds of crimes that predominate and the way that crime is organized change with other changes in society. So at any given time the individual who turns to professional crime adopts the techniques and operates within forms of organization that are currently in use in the criminal world. Let us examine the third question, in the context of industrial societies. Why is 'amateur' crime so heavily concentrated among working-class teenage boys, rather than among some other groups?

The youth culture

To understand why 13–20 is the peak age for crime we need to look at the situation of the teenager in industrial society. The word teenager is a new one, coined to designate the member of a new social group. In non-industrial societies, the terms child and adult are adequate for referring to two distinct age roles; the transition from a dependent, incompetent and subordinate childhood to full adulthood is usually clear cut and may even be marked by an initiation ceremony. In industrial societies, on the other hand, the transition takes many years; in Britain there is a series of formal stages from the age of criminal responsibility at ten to the age of majority at eighteen. The main reason for this lies in the complexity of the adult roles that have to be learned. There is some compulsory schooling in all industrial societies and for many people formal education continues far beyond the school leaving age. Yet full adult status is still not granted to students—even those in their early twenties. Similarly the unmarried are often not thought of as fully adult; yet, because of the responsibility entailed in marriage and the establishment of a separate household, the age of marriage is much higher than in most non-industrial societies.

Paradoxically although the transition to full adulthood is so long delayed, the period of complete subordination to parental or other adult authority is relatively short. English teenagers, as contrasted with say, young Indians, are very free to manage their own lives. They can spend their evenings out, choose their own friends, spend their pocket money how they will, and go away for holidays on their own. Children in school and students in colleges and universities expect to have some part in the running of the organization. All of this freedom is a preparation for the eventual assumption of adult responsibility in a society where *individual* responsibility is important.

So there has emerged a new, distinct period of life which is neither adulthood nor childhood; and teenagers have little in common with either adults or children. They form a social group whose distinctness is enhanced by the development of a separate 'youth culture', centring round taste in entertainment—particularly music—and in clothes. This in turn has been fostered by the commercial exploitation of the new teenage purchasing power, which changes in the labour market and relatively high wages for young people have made possible. In addition, the wide and changing variety of adult occupations means that very few sons follow in their father's footsteps, and even those who do often find the job has changed greatly since their father's day. Teenagers tend to identify with others of their own age and to feel somewhat isolated from older people. This accounts for the importance of gangs and friendship groups in teenage life. These peer groups often have more control over teenage behaviour than do older people.

The emergence of a youth culture, however, is only half the picture. The teenager is also in an ambiguous position. There are a number of aspects to this. First there is a good deal of disagreement about how teenagers should be treated: How much pocket-money? How late should they come home? Should their parents know where they have been and with whom? Second, some of the demands made of the teenager are contradictory: he is expected to be responsible, yet is not given responsibility; he is sexually mature—indeed at his most potent—yet is apparently expected to be chaste; and so on. Third, the teenager's social status is not always clear: a child has the status of his father; an adult's status is determined mainly by his job, in a society where social mobility is possible and is encouraged; but a teenager's status is still indeterminate—yet he is told that his future depends on what he does now, whether he gets a dead-end job or goes to evening classes. It is during the teenage years, the last years of school and the first years of work, that the optimistic aspirations of childhood must be converted into the realistic plans and resignation of later life. The frustration involved is blamed either on those who encouraged the aspirations, or on the system which makes their fulfilment impossible. This goes far towards explaining the teenager's hostility to the grown-up: but the grown-up is also hostile to the teenager. Because the teenager's situation is ambiguous, parents and other adults often find that he does not come up to expectations. He is neither obedient nor responsible; he has too much money and carries too few burdens; he lives with his parents but refuses to participate in their family life.

Conflict is not the whole story of adult-youth relations but it is an important element of them. Delinquent behaviour among teenagers and the adult reaction to it are one of the forms that this conflict takes. Also, many children who are not themselves in direct conflict with their parents are involved in a youth sub-culture and so come to participate in delinquency and hooliganism.

Social class

It used to be thought that the very poor were so lacking in the necessities of life that they stole in order to supply their needs. While in Victorian times this may have seemed a plausible explanation, it is hardly adequate today when the poor are, in absolute terms, much better off. Real poverty does still exist, but it tends to occur in isolated pockets—among the long-term unemployed, especially in depressed areas, among old people and among families with no father or with no adequate wage-earner. Yet delinquency is not much more frequent among these groups than among other lower-class people.

Why, then, are working-class boys more delinquent than others? At the beginning of this chapter, we saw that conformity to the norms of a society is ensured partly by socialization and partly by the distribution of rewards, which is structured in such a way that people are *motivated* to conform. These two mechanisms reinforce one another. There are, however, many regional and class variations in the beliefs and behaviour patterns considered appropriate. Some of them may differ markedly from those enshrined in the law and there may even be a few parents who encourage directly criminal attitudes in their children. Lower-class culture differs from middle-class culture in the things that it stresses and the goals that it encourages people to pursue. It tends to stress 'staying out of trouble' rather than being 'good' or 'bad'; to encourage a tougher approach to life and to reject dependency and gullibility. This culture helps to account for the orientation towards delinquency of many lower-class groups. If people brought up in this culture become delinquent, it is not because they have been 'inadequately' socialized but because they have been socialized into a different culture from the dominant one.

If we look at the way in which the second mechanism of social control, the reward structure, operates for the lower-class teenager, as compared with the middle-class boy, we see that it is less in his interest to be law-abiding.[7] In a society which has an ideology of equal opportunity for all whatever their class origins, everyone is likely to have aspirations to 'succeed'. Indeed, it is considered weak to be satisfied with a low position in society. Yet in fact, equal opportunity is a myth; many able people cannot achieve upward social mobility and, even if they work hard at school and in their jobs, they see little hope of 'getting on'. The goals that are socially prescribed cannot be achieved by the legal means. In this situation some people continue to pursue the goal of economic success but make use of illegitimate means, such as stealing. Other forms of 'deviant' behaviour, such as becoming a down-and-out or a drug-taker, or the more constructive one of joining a revolutionary party, are alternative ways of dealing with the situation. And many people, of course, just struggle on and end up feeling that they must be failures.

The nature of class in our society, then, explains a number of things about the distribution of crime. It explains why more of the poor than of the rich become criminal: because it is they rather than the rich who have severely limited opportunities for (legitimate) success. It explains why the young in this group are more criminal than the old: for

it is around the time of leaving school and embarking on work that people gain a depressingly realistic picture of how limited legitimate opportunities are. It explains why boys are more delinquent than girls: for class position and economic success or failure are primarily male characteristics, women deriving their status first from their father, and later from their husband. And finally it explains why delinquency is higher in the United States than in European countries, and possibly why it is rising in Britain: for the class system affects crime not through absolute or even relative poverty, but through the disjunction between aspirations and opportunity. Opportunity, as measured by the amount of social mobility, is much the same in all highly industrial societies, but aspirations vary. In the United States there is a deep-dyed egalitarian ideology; in some European countries, where the present class system has only slowly emerged out of a feudal society, there is still strong support for social distinctions based on birth rather than achievement and many people do not expect or hope to 'better themselves'.

Delinquent subcultures

Delinquency is a social activity: not only are more than one half of delinquent acts committed in groups, usually of two or three boys, but even the solitary delinquent is very much affected by his friends and associates. Edwin H. Sutherland, the American criminologist, put the matter succinctly when he said, 'Criminal behaviour is learned in interaction with other persons.'[8] In this respect it differs little from most other kinds of human behaviour. If we think of crime as 'deviant' behaviour, we tend to assume that none of the ordinary rules apply to it, whereas in fact criminal behaviour patterns are acquired in much the same way as other behaviour patterns.

If we trace the career of someone who becomes an amateur golfer we find that other people enter into it in a number of ways. He probably meets a few people who play golf, or comes from a golf-playing family or neighbourhood. The closer and more enduring his contacts with other golfers the more likely he is to take it up and stick to it. Then he needs others, and books written by others, to teach him the skill of golfing; he needs to become a member of a club and he needs merchants who supply golfing equipment and, later, he needs organizations which hold tournaments. Through his contact with other golfers and with friends and family members who favour golfing, he develops an appropriate frame of mind so that, unlike most of us, he comes to see a fine Saturday or Sunday as 'a good day for golf' rather than a good day for the zoo or a nap in the garden. Furthermore, non-golfers think of him as a golfer and expect him to behave like one. All of these forms of learning from other people find their parallels in the career of the criminal. If a boy becomes a delinquent he is likely to be aided in various ways by other people. Because of this some boys—those who are more likely to meet these other people—have a greater chance of becoming delinquent than others. In other words *illegitimate* opportunities are as unevenly distributed as legitimate ones. One boy grows up in the kind of neighbourhood where delinquency is very common, so there is a very high probability that he will pick up delinquent habits. Another grows up where delinquency is rare, so that even if he were suffering from a gross blockage of legitimate opportunities, he finds that the illegitimate opportunities are almost equally unavailable and he is unlikely to get involved in any systematic or regular form of delinquency.

What kind of neighbourhood is likely to provide plentiful opportunities for delinquency? In many cities there are small areas that have exceptionally high delinquency rates. These are often the 'zones in transition' or 'twilight areas', the areas of rented property in poor condition, inhabited by a variety of lower-class people, many of them unmarried, and many newcomers to the city. It is in this sort of population that one finds individuals in the frustrating situation of blocked opportunities. Indeed, the very fact of living in such a 'bad' area tends to close some of the doors of opportunity, for the schools are poor, the accent

and clothing fashions are 'rough', there is little stimulus to ambition and few people around to help. So, to one degree or another, all the boys in such an area are prone to delinquency. Being thrown together in one neighbourhood they develop a 'subculture' of their own, different from the dominant culture of the society and favourable to delinquency. There are neighbourhoods in all our major cities where a boy can say, 'Three quarters of the boys in this school swipe things. Nearly everyone in our class (4B) has except X. He's too posh, him.'[9]

In addition to the influence of other young delinquents, the twilight areas also contain an undue proportion of adult criminals. For these are areas at once heterogeneous and anonymous, where deviations from respectability are too common to be conspicuous. The presence of these adults opens up opportunities for more systematic delinquency. If there are adult criminals in contact with juveniles, they encourage more purposeful thieving and deprecate delinquent activity that is merely spiteful or 'for kicks'. They can also make it easier for the young thieves to sell their booty and can help them when they get into trouble with the law. In the absence of such adult aid, delinquency is more likely to be sporadic and disorganized and to take the form of violence or vandalism, rather than of stealing for profit.

So delinquency, which to the naïve observer may appear to be an individual act against society, turns out on closer inspection, to be very much a social activity, intimately linked with important aspects of the wider social structure and in particular with the age structure, with social class and with the neighbourhood structure of cities.

Notes

1 Sigmund Freud, *Totem and Taboo*, London: Routledge & Kegan Paul, 1960, p. 69.
2 See Kai Erikson, *Wayward Puritans: A Study in the Sociology of Deviance*, New York: Wiley, 1966.
3 Ibid., p. 169.
4 See S. N. Eisenstadt, 'Delinquent group formation among immigrant youth', *British Journal of Delinquency*, II, 1, 1951, pp. 34–45.
5 Ibid., p. 43.
6 Barbara Wootton, *Crime and the Criminal Law*,

London: Stevens, 1963, p. 5.
7 The discussion that follows is based on Robert K. Merton, *Social Theory and Social Structure*, Chicago: Free Press, 1957, chapters 4 and 5.
8 E. H. Sutherland and Donald R. Cressey, *Principles of Criminology* (5th ed.), New York: Lippincott, 1955, p. 75.
9 David H. Hargreaves, *Social Relations in a Secondary School*, London: Routledge & Kegan Paul, 1967, p. 114.

Reading

Chambliss, William J. (ed.), *Crime and the Legal Process*, New York: McGraw-Hill, 1969. A collection of twenty-five articles dealing with the

emergence of legal norms and the way in which they are implemented through systems of policing, justice and punishment. Together with the valuable introductions to each section, the collection provides a good basis for relating the sociology of law to the sociology of crime.

Cloward, R. A. and Ohlin, L., *Delinquency and Opportunity*, New York: Free Press, 1966. A study of the way in which different kinds of urban neighbourhood provide different opportunities for becoming delinquent. Already a classic.

Downes, David, *The Delinquent Solution: A Study in Subcultural Theory*, London: Routledge & Kegan Paul, 1966. A sophisticated analysis of delinquent sub-cultures and the way in which they embody a delinquent solution to typical problems of adjustment experienced by lower-class boys in towns. Backed by a study of delinquency in two East London boroughs, Stepney and Poplar.

Gibbons, Don C., *Society, Crime and Criminal Careers*, Englewood Cliffs: Prentice-Hall, 1968.

An introductory textbook in sociological criminology. Focuses on the nature of the deviant career for various types of crime in contemporary America.

Hibbert, Christopher, *The Root of Evil: A Social History of Crime and Punishment*, Harmondsworth: Penguin, 1966. A lively and balanced history, concentrating mainly on law, detection and punishment.

Hood, Roger and Sparks, Richard, *Key Issues in Criminology*, London: Weidenfeld & Nicolson, 1970. A straightforward introduction to some of the disputes in criminology and presentation of evidence relating to them.

Taylor, Laurie, *Deviance and Society*, London: Michael Joseph, 1972. A valuable introduction to recent thinking and research in the study of deviance.

Further reading

Cressey, Donald R. and Ward, David A. (eds), *Delinquency, Crime and Social Process*, New York: Harper & Row, 1969. A collection of sixty-three 'readings', both theoretical and descriptive. The best selection in the field.

Hobsbawm, E. J., *Bandits*, London: Weidenfeld & Nicolson, 1969. A fascinating analysis of the 'social bandit' (a type of hero-robber like Robin Hood) found in many peasant societies. Illustrates the problem of distinguishing between the social reformer and the criminal.

McIntosh, Mary, 'Changes in the organization of thieving' in Stanley Cohen (ed.), *Deviants and*

Others, Harmondsworth: Penguin, 1971. Discusses the effects of urbanization and industrialization on professional thieving in England since the Middle Ages.

Mannheim, Herman, *Comparative Criminology: a text book*, 2 vols, London: Routledge & Kegan Paul, 1965. A comprehensive and eclectic survey of research and theorizing on 'factors and causes related to crime'.

Tobias, J. J., *Crime and Industrial Society in the Nineteenth Century*, London: Batsford, 1967. A useful historical survey of crime in England at an important stage of development.

Index